WHAT WE KNOW

ABOUT

JEWISH EDUCATION:

A handbook of today's research for
tomorrow's Jewish education

EDITED BY DR. STUART L. KELMAN

Torah Aura Productions
Los Angeles, California

Spring, 1992 5752

Library of Congress Cataloging-in-Publication Data

What we know about Jewish education : a handbook of today's research for tomorrow's
    Jewish education / edited by Stuart L. Kelman.
        p. cm
    Includes bibliographical references.
    ISBN# 0-933873-67-0
    1. Jewish religious education--United States. 2. Judaism--Study and teaching--United
States. I. Kelman, Stuart L.
    BM75.W48 1992
    296.6'8'0973--dc20   92-6656
                                                                                CIP

Published by Torah Aura Productions

Torah Aura Productions
4423 Fruitland Avenue
Los Angeles, California 90058
(800) BE-TORAH (213) 585-7312
MANUFACTURED IN THE UNITED STATES OF AMERICA

Dedication

This volume of essays is dedicated to my favorite child—
to each of them: Navah, Ari, Etan and Elana, who have
taught me far more than I them; who have listened to
countless facts and theories about Jewish education and
who have been involved in this research all along the
way. Directly or indirectly, they have met and touched
the lives of thousands.

WHAT WE KNOW ABOUT JEWISH EDUCATION

TABLE OF CONTENTS

Introduction

Preface
Stuart L. Kelman

Understanding Jewish Educational Research
H.A. Alexander

Jewish Schools
Walter I. Ackerman

Preface

IN 1986, A BOOKLET, *WHAT WORKS: RESEARCH ABOUT TEACHING AND LEARNING*, WAS PUBLISHED BY the United States Department of Education. In the foreword there was a quote attributed to President James Madison from a letter that he wrote on August 4, 1822 to Lieutenant Governor Barry of Kentucky. In this letter Madison said: "Knowledge will forever govern ignorance; and a people who mean to be their own governors must arm themselves with the power which knowledge gives". That booklet was the initial impetus for this current volume; for there, in that small pamphlet, the insights gathered from years of research were put into a format that might be useful to practitioners and policymakers alike. Each chapter in *What Works* contained a primary research finding, comments on that conclusion and references where any interested party might search for additional discussion and information.

What We Know About Jewish Education is modeled on that secular version—that is, what I have attempted to collect are newly written articles, each of which summarizes the research on a single, particular subject area, and draws conclusions and implications which stem from that research. Each chapter is written by a recognized expert in that particular field.

This is a 'handbook'—or possibly a 'reader'. Its intended audience is lay and professional leaders alike. The original focus of this volume was to assist policymakers in congregations, institutions, and communities in making decisions based upon research available; i.e., what we know about a certain subject. The volume came about also as a result of listening to conversation after conversation in which an individual would claim: "Here's what we know about 'x'." While it would have been possible to argue with the conclusions of the research or its implications, in fact, more often than not, the research itself was misquoted and thereby misused. Thus, in reading this volume you may find information that either validates or denies what you thought to be true. Some of the findings do substantiate 'conventional wisdom"; others do not. So be it.

Frequently, research literature tends to be written for the scholar. Indeed, there are those who claim that placing the results of research in the hands of those "unqualified" to use it endangers the whole enterprise of Jewish education. Clearly, the essays in this volume attempt to do exactly the reverse. They were designed to bridge the gap between professional and lay readers as well as the obvious one between research and practice. As a matter of fact, that very gap was the issue addressed by Isa Aron in an article entitled "The Relationship between Research and Practice in Jewish Education: Can We (And Should We) Close the Gap?" in *Jewish Education, 56*(4). Each author received a copy of that article to use as a framework in which to focus his or her work. Each chapter is, nonetheless, written with the passion of the author—fully invested with the notion that his or her specialty frames the article. It is passion which was intended; not polemic.

Thus, this is a book about what came before; what is now; and presents an opportunity to make informed decisions about what will come to be in the future based on general knowledge.

Contents

Joseph Schwab suggested that when one thinks about education, there are four commonplaces to consider: the teacher, the setting, the learner and the curriculum. This volume is organized around these four themes. While today, one might modify that classification, still, it remains a primary way of reflecting about education.

This volume is a selection—it does not pretend to represent ALL of Jewish education—or ALL of Jewish education worldwide. Obviously, its focus is on North America. There are many pieces yet to be written (in particular, about curriculum). Perhaps that is for a second volume. It is also, to my knowledge, the first time so broad a collection of articles has been gathered together in one volume. Indeed, our field suffers from the paucity of publication of research based literature. Furthermore, while holding the principle that the sum is greater than the parts, this editor acknowledges the danger with a volume such as this. Taken together, its parts represent a microscopic view through individual lenses. Missing is the macroscopic view of the whole. Rather than try to compose such an essay, or invite authors to present multiple scenarios, I have deliberately left such synthesis for another occasion.[1]

Almost every essay leaves the reader feeling that not enough research is being conducted in Jewish education. Indeed, most of "what we know about" comes from the pens (or computers) of authors engaged in doctoral studies. And while it is certainly commendable that students choose to work specifically in the arena of Jewish interests, it is lamentable that the research efforts for which they were trained cease upon the granting of their Ph.D or Ed.D. Few are the institutions, agencies or synagogues which pursue research as a general part of their philosophy and encourage professionals to continue to use that which they have learned in graduate school. Sadly, some individuals who were approached to contribute to this volume were unable to to eke out the time from their jobs in order to write a chapter. Yet, truth to tell, almost everyone whom I called agreed to write and took the pains to do so with much grace—and found the time to do so in the midst of other heavy commitments.

The chapters also reveal that there are holes in systematic thinking about a particular subject. Each essay was not meant to present a total picture about a certain subject but rather a starting point. Furthermore, there are few actual program examples in the chapters. Fortunately, there are thousands of programs in existence which document the principles elucidated; their description was not the intent of this volume.

Each chapter typically contains:
> an introduction to the subject and the author
> a statement of the problem
> what we know from the general and Jewish research
> implications and/or policy recommendations
> conclusions
> notes on what's missing in the research or the field
> highlights of the article
> a bibliography
> one paragraph attempting to place the article in a larger context

Two articles by Samuel Heilman and Eugene Borowitz are included in the appendix. While they do not formally follow the pattern of each of the other chapters, each is truly a classic.

My thanks go first and foremost to Joel Grishaver, with whom I have had the pleasure of spending countless years in true engagement—around the issues of Jewish education. Through his wisdom and encouragement and arguing, I have come to understand Jewish education through new lenses. To each of the authors, my profound gratitude for joining me in an effort to make what we know public.

To Elaine Bachrach, Edwin Bernbaum, Carolyn Hessel, Lynn Holmes, Doris Kagan, Barbara Peleg—my appreciation for their assistance. A special word of thanks to the staff and board of directors of the Agency for Jewish Education in the Greater East Bay—for helping, assisting and encouraging me to pursue these efforts. An to Torah Aura—Jane Golub, Carolyn Moore-Mooso, Alan Rowe, Linda McClanahan-Shulkin—for making it happen. Finally, *acharon acharon chaviv*, to Vicky Kelman for sharing thoughts, insights, life—and the computer.

I also wish to acknowledge the influence of my father, Wilson Kelman, *zichrono livracha*, who saw drafts of this book but did not live to *shep nachas* from seeing the final version of this volume in print. May his memory be for a blessing.

We estimate that this volume has a immediate marketable life of probably 5-10 years. By then, each of the authors should be able to say, "There's new research that needs to become public." At that time, this book will move from the realm of sociology and public policy to that of history— reflecting the state of Jewish education in the early 1990's. As a document of its time, it will remain, I believe, a fairly accurate, if microscopic, view of the Jewish educational enterprise in which we are engaged —'lehagdil torah ulehaadira'—'to make Torah great and to enhance it'.

Shavuot 5752
Berkeley, California

Bibliography

Aron, I. (1988, Winter). The Relationship Between Research and Practice in Jewish Education: Can We (And Should We) Close the Gap? *Jewish Education, 56*(4).

Cohen, S.M. (1989). The Quality of American Jewish Life. In S. Bayme (Ed.), *Facing the Future.* New York: Ktav and the American Jewish Committee.

United States Department of Education. (1986). *What Works: Research About Teaching and Learning.* Washington, DC: U.S. Govt. Printing Office.

Footnotes

[1]See as an example of this summative literature, The Quality of American Jewish Life by S. M. Cohen (1989) in S. Bayme (Ed.), *Facing the Future.* New York: Ktav and the American Jewish Committee.

What We Know About...
Understanding Jewish Educational Research:
A Guide for Decision Makers

H. A. Alexander

It is fitting that the opening chapter of this volume be devoted to a discussion about research. In effect, this introductory essay presents us with a handy guide to what might very well be a rather complex issue. Dr. Alexander, who is Dean of Academic Affairs and Associate Professor of Philosophy and Education at the University of Judaism in Los Angeles, provides us with a framework, a perspective from which to view the research and the articles contained in this book.

WHY SHOULD POLICYMAKERS AND PRACTITIONERS BE INTERESTED IN EDUCATIONAL RESEARCH? DOES it tell us anything we do not already know? Research tells us that supplemental schools are under financed (Aaron and Philips, 1990), that camping and Israel experiences affect Jewish identity (Alexander, 1990a). But we knew all of this. The policy maker's problem is to decide how to improve the situation and the practitioner's problem is to implement what policymakers decide. What can research tell us about these tasks—without taking too long or costing too much? Those who talk this way tend to assume that the task of research is to collect data about what 'works' upon which to 'base' decisions. Once we know what works, decisions about how to improve education are simple. In a sense, the research does the decision-making. Most decision-makers including lay policymakers and professional practitioners believe they know what works. Research is very often seen as merely confirming these beliefs. So why do research to make decisions? They can be made more quickly and cheaply without it.

This view misconceives both the tasks of educational research and its role in decision-making. The purpose of this chapter is to offer a broader picture of what educational researchers do and how educational policy and practice can benefit from their work.

The Tasks of Educational Research

To say that the task of educational research is to find out what works assumes that it is concerned primarily with program evaluation, and with one particular approach to evaluation at that. In fact, educational researchers not only use a variety of approaches to evaluation, but address a host of other empirical, conceptual, and normative questions as well (Alexander, 1990b). Evaluation is concerned with what works, but in comparison to what? Asking what works without qualification suggests that programs be compared to predetermined standards of success (Weiss,1972). For example, if the goal of a summer camp is to inspire synagogue participation among campers, we should determine what percentage of alumni need to participate in which aspects of synagogue life to what degree in order for the program to be considered successful. Another approach requires that we compare programs with one another (Scriven, 1963). In this view, to evaluate a specific Hebrew textbook means comparing it with the alternatives on the market (see Walker and Schaffarzick, 1974). According to a third viewpoint programs should be examined without preconceived standards or comparison groups (Cronbach, 1963). When we look at program objectives we tend to see only what the objectives lead us to expect. Free from such biases we can see whether the actual outcomes are desirable (Scriven, 1972). Evaluation research, then, is concerned not only with what works according to a predetermined standard, but with what works in comparison to alternatives and with actual as opposed to expected outcomes of programs as well (Alexander, 1981).

Educational research is not restricted to evaluation; it also encompasses empirical, conceptual, and normative inquiry. Empirical research is concerned with facts (Hume, 1748). For example, how many students attend Jewish schools in North America? How many attend Jewish summer camps? What does it cost to educate a student in each of these settings? How many teachers teach in our schools? How are they prepared to teach? What is the average teaching salary? (See Himmelfarb and DellaPergola, 1989.) The task of empirical research is not only to find out what works, it is also to gather the other information needed to make it possible for educational programs and institutions to work.

Conceptual questions have to do not with facts but with the meaning of things (Winch, 1959). What, for example, does it mean for a Jewish educational program to work? Traditionally, a program is considered successful if its graduates accept certain canons of religious belief and practice, though there is by no means agreement over which beliefs and practices ought to be accepted. Communal conceptions of Jewish life, on the other hand, approach what it means for Jewish education to work in terms of Jewish identity, though there is also no agreement as to the precise meaning of this term (Chazan, 1972). The task of conceptual research is not to tell us which programs work but rather to clarify ways of understanding what it would mean for a program to work.

While empirical and conceptual research describe facts and meanings as they are, normative questions address how things ought to be (Frankena, 1963). What, for example, should be the goals of Jewish education? Should an educated Jew have studied specific subject matters such as Hebrew, Bible, history or rabbinics? What should they know in these fields? Should they have acquired special beliefs or behavior patterns as a result (Rosenak, 1987)? The task of normative inquiry is to tell us neither what works nor the possible meanings of 'working', it is rather to help us decide which of those meanings we should accept as our own.

Educational research, then, is concerned not only with what works in Jewish education, but also with the varieties of information needed to make it work, with ways of understanding what it means for it to work, and with those meanings we ought reasonably to embrace.

What Research Cannot Do For Decision-Making

Not only is the field of educational research much broader than is captured by the "what works" mentality, decision-making is more complex as well. Decisions do not follow automatically from research like conclusions in a logical argument, they require the considered judgment of decision-makers at important junctures along the way.

Strategic Decisions

First, in order to reach an evaluative or empirical conclusion, strategic decisions must be made about the methods of inquiry to be employed. For example, in program evaluation we will need to decide whether to look for predetermined or comparative standards of success, or whether we want to look for any preconceived expectations at all (Cronbach, 1982). Similarly, if we are concerned with the empirical question of how teachers feel about their social status, we will need to choose among a variety of alternatives. We could select survey methods that pack into a questionnaire our preconceptions about how teachers might feel (Borg and Gall, 1983). We might also choose participant observation that would allow the researcher to observe teachers while attempting to set his or her own biases aside (Bogdan and Biklen, 1982). Each of these options has advantages and disadvantages that affect the conclusions that we are able to draw. There are many other options as well.

If we choose one approach, it can always be claimed that we would have found different, more reliable, or more relevant results had we taken the alternative strategy. There is, in other words, always another way to look at a research question. Consequently, any application of research to policy or practice is a product of strategic judgments about how to collect the information needed, and the findings always represent one of a variety of ways of approaching a problem.

Fallibility

Second, research is fallible. One of the reasons for formalizing research methods is to standardize checks on the mistakes in our everyday observations and opinions. Statistics is the science of measuring the chances that a statement is wrong. Research designs that use statistical methods are intended to rule out possible mistaken conclusions in various ways. Even research methods that do not use statistics have alternative strategies for avoiding error. Philosopher Karl Popper (1963) went so far as to say that the whole point of science is to prove hypotheses wrong, and that the most we can conclude from any scientific inquiry, including social science and educational research, is that our conjectures have yet to be refuted. If the evidence upon which we base a policy or practice is never completely decisive, then the decision to rely on that evidence remains the responsibility of those who choose to do so. This responsibility can be transferred neither to the research nor to the researcher who is obliged to point out the limitations of the work to those who would rely upon it (Cronbach and Associates, 1980). It would be wise, moreover, to build into educational decisions opportunities to check the directions that have been chosen so that changes of course can be negotiated midstream if the need arises.

Ambiguity

Third, research findings are not unambiguous. For example, a study of good Jewish youth programming (Alexander, 1990a) found that participants, staff, and lay supporters of 15 representative programs complained of the lack of assistance they received from their sponsoring agencies. Should we conclude that good programs do not require organizational support or that they would be even better if they had it? Either option is supported by the data. Not only are there alternative strategies for conducting research, there are alternative ways of interpreting the conclusions as well. Application to policy and practice can only be based, therefore, on one of several possible interpretations of fallible data.

Normative Decisions

Fourth, all educational decisions—from the broadest policies to the most minute practical details—are normative (Bode, 1927). They always prescribe what someone should do. Principals should allocate funds according to specified guidelines. Teachers should teach in special ways. Students should learn certain subjects. But prescriptions do not follow from descriptions without normative assumptions. For example, if the shortage of qualified Judaica teachers in a particular community can be traced to the fact that they are paid less than their counterparts in the public sector, it does not follow that Judaica teachers should be better paid. This depends entirely on the sort of Judaica teachers the community wishes to have. Educational decisions, therefore, can never be derived directly from the findings of evaluative, empirical, or conceptual research without the presence of either explicit or implicit normative judgments.

Educational decisions, then, cannot be based on unambiguous research findings in the sense that once the findings are in no judgments need to be made. Research does not make decisions, people do, and they do so based on strategic, interpretive, and normative judgments drawn from fallible data.

What Research Can Do For Decision-Making

It does not follow, however, that policymakers and practitioners are better off without research, even if their own hunches occasionally turn out to be more on target than research findings. The reason for this revolves around what it takes to make good judgments.

When I plan to buy a new car, for example, I will usually read up on what's available in my price range. I want to find out about the features of different models, about repair records and replacement part costs. I may not read all that has been written, and some of what I do read may be inaccurate. I may also ask friends about their experiences and, if pleased with a particular make that I've owned, rely on my own experience as well. In the end, I will make a decision based on my best guess as to what will suit my needs most effectively. The decision may turn out to be right or it may not. Often, each of the alternatives is equally good and it would have made no difference how I decided. Equally often, I will be satisfied with my choice even though another would have been better, and never know the difference. Occasionally, I will be unhappy with my choice, wishing I had made another. But would I have been better off having not done any research prior to making my decision? Hardly!

Why not? Because research provides concepts and information that can help prevent me from making mistakes. It can also help me decide what I really want. Suppose the newest models have computerized equipment that was not in existence when I bought my last car. Unless I am given some conceptual guidelines about what this equipment is supposed to do and what to look for in purchasing it, I could end up spending money on something I don't need or not purchasing a feature that would have been very desirable. Research, then, offers decision-makers concepts that can be used in evaluating alternatives, without which they may not see what the alternatives are.

Research also provides information. What kind of gas mileage do the alternatives get, for example, and how often do they need to be serviced? Without this information, I could end up spending much more on fuel and servicing than necessary. Finally, research helps to clarify alternatives, forcing me to take a closer look at what I am actually looking for. Do I really need or do I really want, the expensive stereo, the power windows, the plush seat coverings? Because I have both concepts and information, I can define more clearly what my values are.

Although educational decisions may be more complex than this, the same principles apply. Educational research cannot tell policymakers and practitioners what to do. But it can provide concepts and information so that the decisions they make will be better informed. As a result, they will make fewer mistakes. A school board, for example, wants to make a change in its Hebrew language curriculum. A good conceptual analysis of the various types of Hebrew curricula could be enormously important to this group in evaluating the alternatives available. A synagogue is considering opening a suburban branch. Where should it be located? Here, empirical demographic data can tell where the Jewish population is located today and where it is likely to be in ten years.

Research can also help to clarify educational values. For instance, a new principal is looking to improve the quality of classroom instruction. Is he better off investing in new curricula or in higher salaries for teachers? The principal would be aided by clarifying what is meant by improvement in classroom instruction, a task for conceptual research, and by a study of the teachers available, an empirical task. If it turns out that higher pay would produce the same teachers, improvement may come from investment either in curriculum or in other alternatives such as in-service training of the current staff. On the other hand, higher pay for teachers may produce one kind of improvement and curriculum reform another. In this case, the principal will have to make some hard choices based on the sort of improvement that would benefit the school the most. And this depends on the educational values of the principal and the community.

Summary

Research, then, does not make decisions. It helps to clarify the alternatives by providing conceptual tools and valuable information. In so doing it can prevent needless mistakes. It can also aid in making value judgments by placing in clear relief the probable consequences of different alternatives. Though it may be expensive and time-consuming, it need not be. Given the breadth of questions and techniques that it embraces, practitioners and policymakers can engage in their own analyses to address questions facing their organizations. They can also turn to the data available in the professional literature and from local and national agencies. Networking with scholars and other professionals in the field is especially important in this connection. The judicious decision-maker would be wise to keep up with the *Newsletter of the Network for Jewish Educational Research* which publishes abstracts of the ongoing research in the field.

When especially complex problems or large sums of money are involved, it may be worthwhile to invest in professional consultation. This may be expensive and time-consuming, but in the long run, the errors prevented and the time saved may more than pay for the cost of the research.

Bibliography

Alexander, H. A. (1981, Spring). Evaluating Jewish Educational Programs. *The Melton Newsletter,12.*

Alexander, H. A. (1990a). *Good Jewish Youth Programming: Nonformal Education and American Jewish Identity.* Los Angeles: Commission on the Jewish Future of Los Angeles Taskforce on Alternative Frameworks.

Alexander, H. A. (1990b). *Jewish Educational Research: A Conceptual Analysis.* Unpublished paper prepared for the Stanford University School of Education and the Wexner Foundation.

Aron I.(1989, May-June). The Malaise of Jewish Education. *Tikkun, 4*(3), pp. 32-34.

Aron, I. & Phillips, B. (1990). *The Los Angeles Jewish Teachers Census.* Unpublished paper presented at the Fourth Annual Conference of the Jewish Educational Research Network.

Bode, B. (1927). *Modern Educational Theories.* New York: Macmillan.

Bogdan, R. & Biklen, S. (1982). *Qualitative Research for Education: An Introduction To Theory and Methods.* Boston: Allyn and Bacon.

Borg, W. & Gall, M. (1983). *Educational Research: An Introduction* (4th Ed.). New York: Longman.

Chazan, B. (1972). *The Language of Jewish Education.* New York: Hartmore House.

Cronbach, L. (1963, May). Course Improvement Through Evaluation. *Teachers College Record, 64*(8), 672-83.

Cronbach, L. & Associates. (1980). *Toward Reform of Program Evaluation.* San Francisco: Jossey-Bass.

Cronbach, L. (1982). *Designing Evaluation of Educational and Social Programs.* San Francisco: Jossey-Bass.

Himmelfarb, H. & DellaPergola, S. (1989). *Jewish Education Worldwide: Cross Cultural Perspectives.* New York: University Press of America.

Hume, D. (1748). *An Inquiry Concerning Human Understanding.* C. W. Hendel (ed.). Indianapolis: Bobbs-Merrill (1955).

Frankena, W.(1963). *Ethics.* Englewood Cliffs, New Jersey: Prentice-Hall.

Popper, K.(1963). *Conjectures and Refutations.* New York: Harper and Row.

Rosenak, M.(1987). *Commandments and Concerns.* Philadelphia: The Jewish Publication Society.

Schiff, A. (1988). *Jewish Supplementary Schooling: An Educational System in Need of a Change.* New York: The Board of Jewish Education of Greater New York.

Scriven, M. (1967). The Methodology of Evaluation. In R. M. Gange & M. Scriven (Eds.), *Perspectives of Curriculum Evaluation.* AERA Monograph Series on Curriculum No. 1. Chicago: Rand McNally, 39-83.

Scriven, M.(1972). Pros and cons about goal free evaluation. *Evaluation Comment. 3*, pp. 1-4.

Walker, D. & Schaffarzick, J. (1974, Winter). Comparing curricula. *Review of Educational Research, 44*, pp. 83-111.

Weiss, C. (1972). *Evaluation Research.* Englewood Cliffs, New Jersey: Prentice-Hall.

Winch, P. (1959). *The Idea of Social Science and its Relation to Philosophy.* London: Routledge and Kegan Paul.

What We Know About.... Schools

Walter I. Ackerman

*One other perspective is needed by way of introduction: the historical per-
spective of "school", the primary educational institution for Jewish learning in
North America. This institution once stood as the cornerstone of the educational enterprise. While its place in the overall picture of Jewish education
may be changing, Dr. Ackerman, who is Shane Family Professor of Education
at Ben Gurion University of the Negev in Beer Sheva, focuses on the school—
which is still regarded as the quintessential agency of Jewish education, its
changed role not withstanding.*

FACILITIES FOR THE FIRST JEWISH SCHOOL OF RECORD IN THE UNITED STATES, YESHIBAT MINHAT
Arab, were "made codez" (consecrated) by the members of Congregation Shearith Israel
in New York "on the 21st day of Nissan, the seventh day of Pesach, 5491 (1731)" (Dushkin, 1918,
p.449). For lack of a teacher, however, instruction did not begin until some six years later. At that
time Mr. David Mendes Machado was elected *Hazan* of the congregation. Among other things Mr.
Machado committed himself "...to keep a public school in due form for teaching the Hebrew language either the whole morning or the afternoon as he shall think most proper." He also agreed
"that any poor that shall be thought unable to pay for their children's learning, they shall be taught
gratis." Another teacher, engaged by the congregation some thirty years later, was required "to keep
a public school in the Hebra, to teach the Hebrew language and translate the same into English,
also to teach English, Reading, Writing and Cyphering" (Dushkin, 1918, p.450).

Yeshibat Minhat Arab, actually an elementary school, was the forerunner of an astonishing array
of institutions dedicated to engaging the loyalties of successive generations of Jews and guaran-
teeing the maintenance of Jewish life in this country. The development of Jewish education in all its
forms and varieties reflects the different conceptions of Judaism which have won a place in the
American Jewish community. It also tells us something about the ways American Jews understand
themselves and their relationship to a society in which they have moved from the stigma of for-
eignness attached to immigrant communities everywhere to a sense of feeling "truly at home in
America" (Liebman & Cohen, 1980, p.49).

The efforts of individual Jews and groups, similar to those of like-minded people committed to
maintaining the language and traditions of their own ethnic groups (Seller, 1987; Fishman, 1966),

combined over time to create an educational configuration which includes schools of all levels, tal-mudical academies, institutions for training rabbis and other religious and communal functionar-ies, Jewish studies programs in universities, centers for continuing education, summer camps, youth groups, sojourns in Israel and other frameworks. Despite this proliferation of settings, the school is still regarded as the quintessential agency of Jewish education, its changed role not with-standing. This is so, in part, because Judaism is a text-centered tradition; schools with their planned, ordered and sequential programs are the agencies considered best equipped to develop the capa-bilities required for an understanding of the canon (Ackerman, 1989).

The voluntary nature of Jewish education permits anyone who is so inclined to establish and maintain a Jewish school. There is an interesting, if not intended, parallel between the fact that in the eighteenth century all Jewish schools were sponsored by religious congregations, as was the case with non-Jewish schools of the time, and circumstances today when, since the virtual demise of the secular or Yiddish schools, almost all schools are integrally connected to synagogues. The broadening of the base of support for education which took place in the general community in the nineteenth century was matched among Jews. In addition to those established and maintained by synagogues, schools were founded by neighborhood groups organized for that purpose and even by private individuals (Pilch, 1969; Himmelfarb & DellaPergola, 1989).

Schooling

The first Sunday School in this country, an adaptation of the Christian model which had origi-nated in England, was established in Philadelphia in 1838 by Rebecca Gratz. One of the better pri-vate schools in New York around the middle of the century was that conducted by Dr. Max Lilienthal, the founder of a "modern" school in Riga, who had arrived in this country shortly after his trip to Russia and the realization that he had been "used by the Czarist government in its attempt to 'reform' Jewish schools in that country" (Philipson, 1915). The Jewish community of Detroit, at that time sixty people in all, opened a Hebrew Day School in 1850 and maintained it until its closing in 1869. The all day Hebrew Free School was established in 1864 by a group of lay people in order to combat the influence of a missionary school on the East Side of New York. That school subsequently grew to include five afternoon schools in other parts of the city. The Hebrew Education Society of Philadelphia opened a day school in 1851 and taught both Jewish and general subjects, sometimes with Christian teachers, until its closing some twenty years later. A particularly noteworthy exam-ple of private endeavor was the Talmud Torah established by Pesach Rosenthal in 1857 in New York for "free of charge" instruction of poor children after public school hours (Grinstein, 1969).

The influx of German Jews, particularly after the revolution of 1848, gave a new impetus to the still struggling attempts of American Jews to establish a firm basis for Jewish education. The influ-ence of the new immigrants, above and beyond the significant increase in the number of school age children brought about by their arrival, was most evident in the new cities of the midwest. Their relatively large concentration in that part of the country stimulated a spurt of interest in day schools, sometimes more as a response to the absence or poor quality of public schools than as an expression of concern for the Jewishness of their children. In some of the schools established by German Jews the German language received as much attention as English or Hebrew. Indeed their attachment to the culture brought with them from Europe led on occasion to cooperating with liberal Germans in opening "German-English Academies" (Gartner, 1969).

The importance attached to schooling as *the* instrument of Jewish survival became more pronounced once the home, neighborhood and community lost their Jewishly formative character, which lends more than ordinary significance to the statistics of enrollment. It is estimated that there were 40,000 to 50,000 Jewish children of school age in the United States in 1880; of these, 15,000—approximately 33.3%—received some form of Jewish education. The data for New York indicate a somewhat higher rate of participation than in the rest of the country (Grinstein, 1969). A study published in 1918 reports that out of a total of "nearly 300,000 Jewish children of elementary school age (i.e., 5-14 years) in New York City.... The total number of Jewish children receiving some form of Jewish training... is 65,400... less than 24%.... The total number of high school pupils enrolled in a number of Jewish schools in New York in 1917 was 395... hardly one percent of the entire number of Jewish boys and girls in the public high schools of [the] city" (Dushkin, 1918). Current data permit comparisons: It is estimated that at any given time approximately 40% of the Jewish children of elementary school age in the United States are in attendance at a Jewish school of some kind; as many as 80% have been enrolled in some kind of Jewish school at least one time in their lives. Following a high of 540,000 children enrolled in Jewish schools of some kind in the early sixties, a census conducted two decades later counts 370,000, of whom 110,000 are in day schools. The latter figure represents an increase of 80% during that twenty-year period. The overwhelming majority of children, however, leave the Jewish school upon reaching the age of Bar/Bat Mitzvah. Despite the extraordinary growth of Jewish studies programs in colleges and universities, no more than an estimated 25% of Jewish college students avail themselves of these opportunities (Commission on Jewish Education in North America, 1990).

The overwhelming elementary character of Jewish schools—apparently endemic to modern, open societies—was a cause of concern even a hundred years ago. An example is found in the organization of the Jewish Education Society in Chicago and the appeal to the community it issued in 1876: "Where are the schools from which you expect your future rabbis and teachers and the well read laymen to come? The latter can certainly not be imported from the old country for the purpose of upholding our Jewish institutions.... We must have a Jewish high school in every large community where especially gifted young people from the eleventh or twelfth year are to be advantageously taught in Hebrew literature and Jewish history in addition to the various branches of a general high school, the Hebrew forming an organic part of the entire school system; where, moreover, lessons in Jewish religion, history, and literature are given twice or thrice during the week to such young people who are anxious to receive information about Judaism while pursuing their mercantile or scientific course during the day..." (Wirth, 1928).

As is already evident, the "marketplace" of Jewish education has always provided a number of options—one-day-a-week schools, afternoon schools which meet several times a week after public school hours and on Sunday mornings, and all-day schools which provide both general and Jewish education. The dominance of the part-time school, almost always favored by the vast majority of American Jews, was assured once the public school won its place in American life. Jews only nominally interested in traditional Jewish learning or in maintaining more than a minimal pattern of personal observance enthusiastically embraced the opportunities and promise provided by a free, tax-supported school system open to all children.

Unlike the Catholics, who waged a bitter, if futile, battle against the non-sectarian Protestantism of the common school and finally felt compelled to establish their own independent school system, nineteenth century American Jews, like their descendants a century later, were ardent supporters of the public school. Even statements such as that of Horace Mann—"Our system earnestly inculcates all the Christian morals; it founds its morals on the basis of religion" (Tyack, 1967, p.218)—did not stem the stream of Jewish children entering the public school.

Day Schools

The public school as one of the more evocative symbols of American democracy, together with the freedom a republican form of government grants its citizens to establish private, sectarian schools, is the ground upon which American Jews have debated the merits of day schools or part time schools for over a century. The basic elements of contention are clearly evident in an exchange between Isidor Busch and the Rev. Isaac Leeser which appeared in Jewish newspapers in 1854-55. Busch, an immigrant Jew who fled Europe after the revolution of 1848 and soon after his settlement there became a prominent figure in the Jewish and public life of St. Louis, enjoined his fellow Jews to "support as much as you can the public school system and lend no help whatsoever to sectarian institutions." To those Jews, clearly a minority, who favored separate Jewish schools, Busch would say, "Should our children be educated as Jews only or even as foreigners in language and spirit or shall they be educated as Americans, as citizens of the same free country, to be with them a harmonious people...?"Busch's own position was unequivocal: "The common welfare, the interests of the whole people, the safety of our republic demand of us to be in favor of public as opposed to church schools... The most effective setting for the religious instruction of Jewish children was the congregational 'Sabbath or Sunday School' or 'evening schools for the teaching of Hebrew...'"

Among those who favored day schools and the promise of a more intensive form of education than that provided in part-time schools of any kind, none was more persistent than the Rev. Isaac Leeser. From his pulpit at Congregation Mikveh Israel in Philadelphia, in the pages of the *Occident*, a periodical of which he was both publisher and editor, in the textbooks he wrote and published and in sermons and lectures he delivered in the major Jewish centers of the time, Leeser waged a determined and unrelenting struggle for the grounding and improvement of Jewish education in the United States. Leeser's many-leveled justification of Jewish education was sharpest when he argued the merits of a separate Jewish school which offered a combined curriculum of Jewish and general studies. He was convinced that Sunday Schools, afternoon and evening schools, and all other forms of supplementary education were simply inadequate to the task of transmitting any sort of meaningful understanding of Judaism. Leeser's own experience in Philadelphia led him to oppose Busch's plea for the primacy of the public school and the relegation of Jewish education to a secondary role played out on weekends, afternoons, and evenings. The restrained tone of his response— "Mr. Busch… underrates the difficulties of evening religious schools. The mode of instructing children in the Hebrew etc. in the extra hours, has been tried and has signally failed"—does not altogether reflect the force of his feeling.

Leeser's support of the day school, a school in which "it is not to be a secondary matter whether the child learns Hebrew and religion," was rooted in his sense of what was required for intelligent adherence to Judaism as well as in his perception of life in America. His admiration of the United States, repeatedly expressed in editorials and sermons, did not blind him to the fact that, even in the freedom of the new republic, Jewish children were subject to "open or secret attack against the religion of their fathers." Years before Busch's appeal to Jews to forego separate Jewish schools in favor of the public school, Leeser had pointedly warned parents that Jewish children who attend public school "hear prayers recited in which the name of a mediator is involved; they hear a book read as an authority equal if not superior to the received word of God…. We are in great error if we suppose that Christian teachers do not endeavor to influence the sentiments of their Jewish pupils; there are some at least, who take especial pains to warp the mind and to implant the peculiar tenets of Christianity…." A proper Jewish education, possible only in a school responsible for the total education of the child, would not only remove youngsters from the damaging influence of overzealous Christian teachers but would also provide them with a "conscious dignity" and "a becoming pride in the name of Jew." The Jewish school thus conceived was more than a place which taught the information and skills necessary for life as an observant Jew; it was to be the institution which so shaped the character of the child as to place him beyond the "approach of a contrary conviction" and make him "proof against the open and silent attacks of those differing from us… and firm in the profession of the lineage and faith of Israel, though alone in the midst of thousands" (Gartner, 1969, pp.68-76).

The Supplementary School

The proponents of a combination of public school and supplementary Jewish religious schools received vigorous and sustained support from Rabbi Isaac Mayer Wise, the "father" of Reform Judaism in America. Wise's privileged position as a rabbi, first in Albany and then in Cincinnati, together with his considerable gifts as a journalist and teacher, placed him in the forefront of those who insisted on the necessity of Jewish participation in the public schools. His commitment to the common school expressed itself in, among other things, his service as a member of the Board of Examiners of the Cincinnati school system and of the Board of Directors of the municipal institution of higher education, the University of Cincinnati.

Jewish religious education as conceived by Wise was the province of the congregational Sabbath School. The time and place of the school's meeting, obviously borrowed from the model of the Protestant Sunday School, were clearly designed to prevent accusations of Jewish separatism and to insure the possibility of Jewish involvement in the life of the larger community. Wise's position here reflects his clearly held conviction, fundamental to an understanding of his conception of Judaism and its relationship to American life, that "outside of the synagogue we are citizens of the land of our nationality or adoption and need not perceptibly differ from any fellow man. In public life, in business, in culture, in all worldly aspirations, we have lost our identify and very few, if any, wish to restore it" (Ackerman, 1977).

The tide of Jewish immigration which flooded America during the closing years of the nineteenth century and in the two decades immediately following created new opportunities for those concerned with Jewish education. For the first time in the history of Jewish settlement in the United States, there existed that combination of density of population and human resources which is the precondition of a sustained and organized effort in education. The growing centers of Jewish population in the major cities of the eastern seaboard guaranteed a reservoir of pupils in numbers sufficient for the establishment of schools which were effective educational units. Among the immigrants could be found a sizable number of learned and educationally experienced men who were prepared to devote themselves to the work of Jewish schools.

The Yeshivot

The inadequacies of the then existing schools in New York spurred a group of Orthodox Jews to found Yeshivat Eitz Hayyim in 1886.[1] The purpose and program of the yeshivah were "to give free instruction to poor Hebrew children in the Hebrew language and the Jewish religion—Talmud, Bible, and Shulhan 'Arukh—during the whole day from nine in the morning until four in the afternoon." The directors of the yeshivah were sworn to "conduct themselves only according to the customs of Poland and Russia, in accordance with the customs of our fathers and our forefathers" and to prevent "...an admixture or inkling of any change or alteration or deviation even from the smallest of the least of the customs of Poland" (Dushkin, 1918, p. 480).

It is clear that the founders of Eitz Hayyim as well as those responsible for the beginnings of similar institutions of the time and later were guided by the image of the great yeshivot of Eastern Europe. That model of Jewish education had been refined over centuries of continuous practice and had set an uncompromising standard by which to judge those who claimed to be educated Jews. Whatever the variations between the yeshivot of different times and places they were of style and detail rather than of principle and purpose. The scope and range of studies were ordained in a divine command whose authority was no less binding in New York than in Volozhin.

The influence of the European Yeshiva was clearly evident in the attitude of the directors of Eitz Hayyim toward secular studies—"...two hours [each day] shall be devoted to teach the native language, English." The secondary role assigned everything connected with America and its culture led opponents of this form of education to proclaim "...the New York Yeshivah an anachronism for which the United States [has] neither the time nor the place and every dollar spent for its maintenance is that much waste or worse. A legitimate use can be found for every dollar that the Jews of the United States can spare and there is none to waste for transplanting in American soil an institution of the medieval ghetto" (Klapperman, 1969, p.137). Opposition, even hostility, could not, however, dull the determination of the supporters of the Yeshiva.

The Yiddish Schools

At the same time that Orthodox Jews were building the institutions necessary for the maintenance of a traditional form of Jewish life, Jewish socialists undertook the establishment of a network of Yiddish schools whose purpose it was "…to move children with the desire to join the ranks of the fighters of freedom and to give them the appreciation of the movements which contributed to the progress of humanity." The Yiddish schools (Krug, 1954), no less than the schools of the Orthodox and the Zionists in the United States, drew their inspiration from Eastern Europe. The Polish originals, intended as they were for the children of working-class families, built their program on the foundations of secularism, socialism and the Yiddish language and its literature. The choice of Yiddish was both ideological and pragmatic—ideological because it symbolized a break with the Hebrew of the religious tradition of the past; pragmatic because it was the language of the masses. Illegal Yiddish schools had been established in Warsaw as early as 1899; by 1921 there were 182 schools affiliated with the Central Yiddish School Organization.

The first Yiddish school in America was founded in 1908 in Brownsville, a section of New York City noted for the socialist leanings of its largely working class population. Yiddishists in other cities followed suit and in the years immediately after World War I there were Yiddish schools of various kinds in every major center of Jewish settlement. The charges of separatism directed against Yiddishists, not unlike those used against the Orthodox and their schools, and the claim that the experience of Eastern Europe was not applicable to the circumstances of American democracy, led one of the leading theoreticians of *Yiddishkeit* to point out that "…when Americans compel the various ethnic groups in the country to Americanize themselves, that is neither a manifestation of human solidarity nor an example of brotherhood. The drive for Americanization is a veiled form of slavery, but slavery nonetheless."

The more militant socialists among the Jewish workers found the nationalistic proclivities of the National-Radical Yiddish schools sponsored by the American Poale Zion Party—schools which acknowledged that "Hebrew is… a language of substantial national importance"—no less nettling than the teaching of religiously oriented Jewish schools. The parallel strains of secularism and radicalism were the dominant motifs of the network of Yiddish schools established by the Workmen's Circle (Arbeiter Ring), the fraternal organization of Jewish working men whose growth and decline is a mirror of the Jewish immigrant experience in America.

The Workmen's Circle schools were conceived not only as alternatives to other forms of Jewish education but also as an antidote to the bias of the public schools. Yiddish schools rooted in the temper of active radicalism were necessary because "… in a capitalist society the public schools are controlled largely by capitalists, the enemies of the working class…. The teachers are forced to plant in the young innocent hearts reactionary chauvinism. Therefore, every clear minded worker who strives for a more beautiful and better world for humanity cannot permit himself to remain indifferent to the education of his own children.… The foundations of the new order must be carefully prepared.… Without the younger generation,…the future of the ship of life and the workingman's fight will be lost.…"

Among the reasons offered by Yiddishists for the maintenance of a separate school system, none is as poignant as that which addressed itself to the gulf which separated immigrant parents from their American born and educated children. An article by Abraham Liessen, the Yiddish poet, is worth quoting at length:

> …The Jewish students in the schools and colleges everywhere are the brightest and most diligent.…; the lists of prizewinners are proof. The children of homeless… and driven Russian, Galician, and Rumanian Jews win the most prizes. In the old country these children would have had little chance of going to school; in the old country thousands of these children could not even have been sure of remaining among the living…and here in America they win first prize… But there is a question we must ask. What have we gained from these educated youngsters? Why have these admirable college graduates disappeared from the Jewish street? Why do we neither see nor feel them? Where are they?… They are mostly the children of poor people, the children of workers. Why do they not feel their obligation to the poor? Why do they so easily forget the suffering and self-sacrifice of their parents? Why do they become traitors to their class?… Those fathers and mothers who are incapable of thinking deeply about education are happy and feel themselves fortunate with the opportunity provided by the American school. The intelligent ones, however,…soon come to the conclusion that something has gone wrong in the American school… That school rends a terrible tear in the Jewish soul… it touches and destroys the foundations of that which is the holiest and most beautiful in our long-suffering Jewish life; the Jewish family.… In those schools our children have become estranged from us.… It matters little that they live with us under one roof, that they eat together with us at the same table.… We are separated by an abyss, an abyss of the soul.

The inference, of course, is clear: proper Jewish schools in which Jewish children are taught *Yiddishkeit*, the culture of their parents, would stem the tide of disaffection and bridge the gap between the immigrant generation and its American born and educated offspring.

The Yiddish schools, a few of which are still in existence even today, never enrolled more than a small number of children attending Jewish schools. They are important, however, for more than the record. Standing outside the mainstream of both the larger society and of their own immediate reference group, the Yiddish schools, particularly the more radical among them, are an example of education as social critic.

The Talmud Torah

As has already been indicated, neither the Orthodox day school nor the Yiddish school was to become the dominant form of Jewish schooling in the United States. The latter has all but disappeared, like the language-oriented secular schools of other ethnic groups, and the day school, despite impressive growth and adoption by the Conservative and Reform movements, still enrolls only a minority of the children in Jewish schools. The school of choice, now for more than a century, remains the part-time afternoon school, today called the congregational school and once known as the Talmud Torah.

The Talmud Torah of Eastern Europe was a school conducted by the community for the children of families too poor to pay tuition for a private *Heder*. Used at first in this country in a somewhat casual fashion to distinguish a part-time school from a day school, the term became an important part of the lexicon of the Bureau of Jewish Education of New York, established in 1910 for the improvement and promoting of Jewish religious primary education in the city, in its effort to establish the principle of communal responsibility for Jewish education (Dushkin, 1918). The commitment of the Bureau to part-time schooling was born of a conviction, drawn from the teachings of John Dewey, that to separate children in parochial or sectarian schools during their formative years and to deny them the opportunity of shared experience with children of different beliefs and backgrounds was to deny them opportunities critical to the development of that sense of interdependence and cooperative effort without which a democracy cannot function. Schools should not prevent children from associating with "their neighbors with whom they are destined to live together as American citizens;" "Jewish schools should not interfere with America's cherished plan of a system of common schools for all the children of all the people" (Berkson, 1920; Ackerman, 1975).[2]

The program of the Talmud Torah as conceived by the staff of the New York Bureau of Jewish Education and like-minded educators in other parts of the country was heavily influenced by the ideas of Ahad Ha'am, the mentor of spiritual Zionism. It was based on a presumption of ten hours of instruction per week (every afternoon Monday through Thursday and Sunday morning) for six years. The course of study centered on the Hebrew language and its literature and included ".... Sacred literature which is read and taught in Hebrew...the Hebrew Prayer book" as well as history, customs, institutions and holidays. The emphasis on Hebrew, both as a subject of study and as the language of instruction, proclaimed the school's Zionist orientation. In that view language was the instrument which forged the connection between the individual and his people. Like the day schools, the "Hebrew" schools, even during the period of their greatest growth between the two world wars, never engaged more than a minority of the age appropriate children. They did not survive the transition from first to second generation American born Jews and the accompanying move from poor urban, ethnic neighborhoods to middle class suburbs.

The Talmud Torah was the ground which provided pupils for the intensive Hebrew high school which in turn prepared students for the Hebrew colleges. This structure, arguably the most coherent ever developed in American Jewish education, could be compared to that which permitted a youngster who began his school career in an Orthodox elementary school to advance to "learning" in a higher Yeshiva. In addition to their function as both training institutions and settings for higher Jewish learning, the Hebrew Teachers Colleges, through their entrance requirements which influenced the curricula of lower schools, set the standards for Jewish education in the communities where they were found.

These schools—elementary, high school and college alike—were visible expressions of the Hebrew movement in America. Together with books, periodicals, lectures, clubs, conferences and other cultural and social activities—all conducted in Hebrew—they proclaimed the effort of an intellectual elite dedicated to the creation of a mode of Jewish life in the United States which drew its inspiration from the sources of Hebraism which spurred the national renaissance in Palestine. The ultimate failure of that effort, not unlike that of similar groups in other ethnic groups who were equally committed to the language of their national or religious tradition, is testimony to the difficulty of maintaining distinctive forms of group behavior in the face of the enveloping embrace of American culture.

Just as the religious school of the contemporary Reform temple maintains a commitment to the prophetic Judaism and ethical monotheism preached by Wise, the Conservative congregational school still bears traces of the influence of the Talmud Torah. Hebrew, however, has fallen from its place of prominence and is taught, in almost ritualistic obeisance, in order to enable youngsters to follow the synagogue service.

The autonomous nature of Jewish schools—they are now and have always been ultimately responsible only to their own boards; the enterprise of Jewish education in the United States is best understood as a voluntary federation of loosely coupled units—places the center of curricular decisions in each individual school, the efforts of various regional and national educational agencies notwithstanding. Even though the nature of the Jewish tradition creates some commonality, sponsorship, ideology and time available lead to significant differences between schools in what is taught. Bible as presented in the Sabbath Schools championed by Isaac Mayer Wise was hardly the Bible taught either in Yeshibat Eitz Hayyim or in a New York Talmud Torah. The centrality of Hebrew in the latter was unmatched in any other kind of Jewish school, either then or now. The serious study of Talmud was and remains in the province of Orthodox day school. The idea of common elements, however, is evident in public examinations conducted in New York from 1875 until the end of the century by the Young Men's Hebrew Association of that city. In 1876, seventy students for all-day schools, afternoon schools, two, day-a-week schools and Sunday schools were examined in Hebrew Bible and History (Grinstein, 1969).

In Conclusion

The time available for schooling is one of the more powerful determiners of curriculum. The argument for day schools, today as in the past, rests on the assumption, one among several, that only in that setting are the hours of instruction adequate to developing the beginnings of cultural literacy—the ability to decode the signs and symbols of Judaism. Fluency in Hebrew, the key to classical texts, is beyond the reach of the time allotted to that subject in part-time schools. Only the most traditional schools, with their long school days often including Sundays, provide young-sters with the competencies required for "swimming in the sea of the Talmud." As language com-petence and religious and ethnic traditions become less and less important in the lives of children and their parents, as is the case with each remove from the immigrant generation, greater emphasis is placed on discussing "values," rather than on studying text. Schools teach "what the "Bible says about..." rather than Bible itself.

All Jewish schools share a desire to inculcate their students with the desire and ability to conduct their lives in keeping with the teachings of the Jewish tradition. The various components of that tradition—God, Torah and Israel—are differently understood and interpreted. The varieties of Jewish schooling discussed here and the demands they place on children and families are important indices of acculturation and assimilation. A commitment to a form of Jewish education capable of providing the student with the competencies necessary for an understanding of Jewish tradition in all its var-iegated expressions meant a willingness to stand somewhat apart from the larger society. A lesser investment meant, at most, attachment to a belief system—a positive attitude toward Jewish tra-dition, acceptance of one's obligation towards other Jews and acceptance of the obligation to take care of Jewish needs—which did not interfere with life as an American.

Bibliography

Ackerman, W.I. (1975). The Americanization of Jewish Education. *Judaism. 24*(4).

Ackerman, W.I. (1977). Some Uses of Justification in Jewish Education. *AJS Review, 2.*

Ackerman, W.I. (1989).Strangers to the Tradition: Idea and Constraint in American Jewish Education. In H.S. Himmelfarb & S. 4 (Eds.), *Jewish Education World Wide: A Cross Cultural Perspective* (pp. 71-115). Lanham, MD.:University Press of America.

Berkson, I.B. (1920). *Theories of Americanization.* New York: Teachers College Press.

Commission on Jewish Education In North America. (1990). *A Time to Act; The Report of the Commission on Jewish Education in North America.* Lanham:MD.: University Press of America.

Dushkin, A. M. (1918). *Jewish Education in New York City.* New York: Bureau of Jewish Education.

Fishman, J.(Ed.) (1966). *Language Loyalty in the United States.* The Hague: Mouton.

Gartner, L. (Ed.). (1969). *Jewish Education in the United States; A Documentary History.* New York: Teachers College Press.

Grinstein, H.P. (1969). In the Course of the Nineteenth Century. In J. Pilch (Ed.), *A History of Jewish Education in America.* New York: American Association for Jewish Education.

Klaperman, G. (1969). *The Story of Yeshiva University.* New York: MacMillan.

Krug, M. (1954). The Yiddish Schools in Chicago. *YIVO Annual of Social Science. 9.*

Leiman, S.Z. (Winter, 1990). Yeshivat Or Hayyim: The First Talmudical Academy in America? *Tradition. 25*(2).

Liebman, C. S. & Cohen, S. M. (1990). *Two Worlds of Judaism.* New Haven: Yale University Press.

Philipson, D. (1915). *Max Lilienthal: American Rabbi, Life and Writings.* New York: Block.

Pilch, J. (Ed.). (1969). *A History of Jewish Education in America.* New York: American Association for Jewish Education.

Seller, M. S. (1987). *To Seek America: A History of Ethnic Life in the U.S.* Englewood, NJ: S. Ozer.

Tyack, D. (1967). *Turning Points in American Educational History.* Waltham: Blaisdell Press.

Wirth, L. (1928). *The Ghetto.* Chicago: University of Chicago Press.

Footnotes

[1]Eitz Hayyim is generally accounted the first Orthodox Yeshivah in the United States. It was, however, an elementary school and studies there did not lead to rabbinical ordination. There is some evidence which indicates that the first talmudical academy for older students, Yeshivat Or Hayyim, was established in New York in 1895 by Rabbi Moses Weinberger (Leiman, 1990, pp.77-88).

[2] The author of that statement, Alexander Dushkin, one of the architects of Jewish education in the United States, would declare fifty years later:

> ...There has grown up a third generation of American Jewry whose parents are American born and who...feel themselves at peace as citizens of the American democracy...the Jewish community is now larger, better organized, more influential, actually and potentially than it was fifty years ago...In the years ahead it will be increasingly obligatory for Jewish educators to promote the establishment of day schools as the intensive core of the American Jewish school system...to include 25% of our children...

The Teachers

Teachers
Isa Aron

Women
Rela Geffen Monson

Learning to Teach
Sharon Feiman-Nemser

What We Know About...
Jewish Teachers

Isa Aron

Somewhere in our not too distant past, each of us was touched by at least one outstanding teacher who was our "model" of good teaching. We have a mental image of this individual and can often remember the subject matter, the setting and perhaps, even our classmates. In fact, we may recall many "models". Most pre-service and in-service programs in teacher education try to generalize from the behaviors of these individuals and attempt to guide future teachers in replicating them. Dr. Isa Aron, Associate Professor of Jewish Education at Hebrew Union College—Jewish Institute of Religion in Los Angeles, writes from the vantage point of having conducted major research about teachers, particularly in the greater Los Angeles area. She describes what we know about "good teaching" in both the secular and the Jewish fields, and suggests how we might raise the current quality of teaching as well as recruit new people into the field.

QUALITY TEACHERS ARE A CRITICAL INGREDIENT OF QUALITY EDUCATION—WE KNOW THIS MUCH, AT least, with certainty. But how good is our current pool of Jewish teachers? What can the Jewish community do to recruit better teachers, and raise the level of those currently teaching? Had this article been written in the 1970's it might have been entitled "What We Don't Know About Jewish Teachers." In the past decade, however, important research on teachers in both secular and Jewish education has begun to accumulate. Today, while we are still far from having definitive answers to these questions, we do have a framework within which to conduct research, and some starting points to suggest to policymakers wishing to tackle this key issue.

The following discussion of what we know about Jewish teachers is organized around five questions: 1) What constitutes good teaching? 2) How can one judge whether or not a teacher is sufficiently good? 3) What percentage of Jewish teachers meet the criteria of a "good enough" teacher and what percentage are truly excellent teachers? 4) How do we raise the level of teaching in our current teacher population? 5) How do we recruit new teachers who will meet our criteria?

What Constitutes Good Teaching?

Debates on whether teaching is an art or a science, an innate talent or a skill to be developed, are perennial. With the issue of upgrading the quality of public school teachers foremost on the minds of key educational reformers, a consensus on this issue has begun to emerge. To meet the dual challenge of student diversity, on the one hand, and ever-changing subject matters, on the other, a teacher must be more than a technician — he or she must be a professional. That means he or she must have expertise that is based in a body of research and scholarship; it also means that he or she must have a special commitment to students, to the subject matter, and to the educational enterprise as a whole (Aron, 1990).

How Can One Judge Whether or Not a Teacher is Sufficiently Good?

Researchers in teacher education have been grappling with this question for two decades, and have begun to develop some rather sophisticated techniques for teacher evaluation. For example, a team of researchers from Stanford University, working under a grant from the Carnegie Foundation, are developing a series of assessment exercises which will, ultimately, be combined into a National Teacher Examination. Professor Lee Shulman, director of the Teacher Assessment Project, points out that the key to accurate evaluation is the realization that there are at least seven dimensions to a teacher's expertise (Shulman, 1987, p.8):

1. knowledge of the subject matter to be taught
2. generic teaching skills
3. an understanding of various curricular approaches to the subject
4. "pedagogical content knowledge," i.e., knowledge of the best way to teach various aspects of the subject
5. an understanding of students (both psychological and sociological)
6. familiarity with the various contexts (both narrow and broad) of education
7. a philosophical understanding of the goals and purposes of education in general

In order to evaluate a teacher, one must consider all seven dimensions, and not just subject matter knowledge or mastery of generic skills. It goes without saying that the methodology for such an evaluation must go beyond paper and pencil tests. Among the evaluation processes being investigated at Stanford are classroom observation, analysis of cases in a variety of teaching situations, and the accumulation of a "portfolio" of evidence for accomplishment (Millman and Darling-Hammond, 1990).

Some of the techniques developed by teacher assessment projects such as the one at Stanford might be easily adapted to the evaluation of Jewish teachers; but techniques which are specific to a particular subject matter will be more difficult to adapt. Research into the special curricular and pedagogical content knowledge of Jewish teachers is still in its infancy (Chervin, n.d.; Schoenberg, 1987). Clearly, however, this research ought to be a high priority for the Jewish community, for it holds the key to devising a mechanism for teacher evaluation that is both comprehensive and workable.

How Good is our Current Pool of Jewish Teachers?

Lacking the techniques for the sophisticated assessment outlined above, we can only guess at the level of professionalism of our current pool of Jewish teachers. In the past few years, surveys of Jewish teachers have been conducted in a number of cities (Aron and Phillips, 1990; Sheskin, 1988; Federation of Jewish Agencies of Greater Philadelphia, 1989). From these surveys we can deduce something about the qualifications of these teachers, at least on paper. From these studies, a number of broad generalizations emerge:

1. Between a third and a half of the teaching population seems highly qualified, at least on paper. Teachers in this group have completed more than seven college-level courses in Judaica, Hebrew, or education.
2. About a third of the teachers appear to be unqualified, having taken no college-level courses in either Judaica, Hebrew or education.
3. Although a higher percentage of qualified teachers are found in day schools than in supplementary schools, the difference is not as large as one might expect; nor is there a large difference between Orthodox, Conservative, Reform and Community schools. In Los Angeles, for example, at least 30% of day school teachers (in all four types of schools) have taken no college-level Judaica courses.
4. The Los Angeles study used a variety of sophisticated statistical techniques to determine what other factors account for the great variation among teachers in terms of their qualifications; this analysis, however, did not yield any significant results. Teachers who see teaching as their career are somewhat more likely to be more qualified, as are teachers in Orthodox schools; taken together, however, these two factors account for only 9% of the variation among teachers (Aron and Phillips, 1990).
5. One surprising finding from the teacher surveys is that Jewish teachers have considerable experience. Over half the Los Angeles teachers had four or more years of experience in the setting (day or supplementary) in which they were teaching, and fewer than 10% of the teachers were entirely new to the setting. Researchers in secular education have found that teachers accumulate considerable expertise during their first five years of teaching; by this standard, Jewish teachers appear to be relatively experienced.

Before one jumps to conclusions regarding the qualifications of our current teaching population, a number of caveats are in order. First, qualifications on paper are not necessarily indicative of quality. Only a sophisticated assessment along the lines of the Stanford project will yield information about the quality of Jewish teachers. Second, it is likely that the teaching populations of Los Angeles, Miami and Philadelphia, are not typical. Los Angeles, for example, has a larger percentage of Israelis than other areas of the country; it also contains two graduate programs in Jewish education and three rabbinical seminaries.

A third important caveat is that teaching in a Jewish school, even if it is a day school, is very part-time work. Fewer than a quarter of Jewish teachers in Los Angeles teach 20 hours or more per week, and fewer than a third consider themselves to be "full-time" in Jewish education. A teacher who teaches only part-time, and who works in a different field as well (as over half of Los Angeles teachers do), is not likely to bring a fully professional commitment to his or her work.

Finally, we must remember that teaching in a Jewish school, even for only a few hours a week, is very difficult work. Unlike public schools, most Jewish schools do not have fully articulated curricula, with specific goals and objectives (Reynolds, 1988). And unlike public school teaching, Jewish teaching is not generally validated and reinforced by the students' home and community (Heilman, 1984; Schoem, 1989). I would argue that Jewish teachers require a higher level of professionalism to succeed under these conditions. College-level courses and several years of experience in the classroom may not be enough.

Thus, the only fair and balanced answer to the question "How good are Jewish teachers?" is "We don't really know." Without a more precise statement of a school's goals, and without sophisticated assessment techniques, this question cannot be answered satisfactorily.

How Do we Raise the Level of Teaching in Jewish Schools Today?

Fortunately, we don't need to have a complete answer to the previous question in order to begin taking steps to improve the quality of teaching in Jewish schools right away. The first steps in this process, in fact, go far beyond teachers; they require parents, professionals, and lay leaders to work together with teachers to take an honest look at their school and its goals. The following are some things that the stakeholders in a particular educational institution can do to begin the process of creating a quality teaching staff:

1. Articulate a clear vision of the school's goals, and think through, very carefully, whether or not these goals can be accomplished (Johnson, 1990, p.29). One of the fundamental problems of Jewish schools is that they try to be all things to all people, and end up meeting no one's needs. Even day schools have only a limited number of hours available for Judaica, and a significant number of students from homes where Judaism is not practiced regularly. Schools need to make choices as to whether they see their primary function as instruction or enculturation (Aron, 1989); they need to decide on realistic expectations in terms of Hebrew, Bible, and other subjects. Above all, they need to communicate their goals to parents, students, and teachers.

2. Include parents as partners in the process of their children's Jewish education. No school, no matter how perfect, can educate without parental support. For too long, Jewish schools have allowed parents to be passive, ambivalent bystanders. Now things are beginning to change, as the chapter in this book on family education attests. The school must make clear to parents that its teachers are not expected to be the sole motivators and disciplinarians of their children.

3. Provide teachers with clear curricular guidelines, and abundant resources. One of the shocking findings of the Los Angeles teacher census was that nearly half the teach-

ers receive no curriculum at the start of the school year, other than a textbook, and perhaps some advice from the principal. Even the most professional of teachers in a public school setting would be hard-pressed to teach well without a clearly articulated curriculum, and without the abundant learning materials available through commercial publishing houses. But teachers in Jewish schools are routinely expected to do just that. A decade ago the excuse might have been that few curricular resources were available, but today this is no longer the case. Every movement has developed curricular guidelines and resources; a number of commercial publishers offer attractive, books, learning packets, manipulatives, and audiovisual materials. There is no longer an excuse for any Jewish teacher to be left on his or her own to plan lessons.

4. Each school should have at least one person on staff whose primary responsibility is staff development. Theoretically, staff development is the purview of the principal. But principals have wide-ranging responsibilities, and the result is that staff development, in most settings, degenerates into a series of one-shot workshops conducted by guest speakers. This kind of stimulation is certainly important, but it is no substitute for ongoing, intensive consultation with individual teachers, which includes help in planning, observation, feedback, and problem-solving (Flexner, 1989). If this task is beyond the principal's ability to handle (and it is likely that it is) another staff member must be added for this purpose. In fact, as I suggest in the next section, some of the truly excellent teachers in our schools might be given additional responsibilities in this area.

How Can We Recruit New High-Quality Teachers?

Given the part-time nature of most of Jewish teaching, I personally think it unrealistic to expect that all teachers can be fully professional, meeting the criteria outlined at the outset of this paper. On the other hand, each school must have a number of fully professional teachers, who set the tone of the school and serve as mentors for the others.

A number of high-level commissions in secular education (Holmes Group, 1986; Carnegie Forum, 1986) have grappled with this question, of how to balance the need for a high level of professionalism among teachers against economic constraints. They have arrived at the same answer, which is the answer I offer here as well: differentiated staffing.

As teaching is currently configured, the career pattern of most teachers is essentially flat. A teacher with many years of experience and a great deal of expertise does the same job as a novice teacher; the only way to advance in education is to leave the classroom for administration. A differentiated staffing structure, on the other hand, would recognize and reward a number of different levels of expertise, and would set different requirements for teachers at different levels. At one end of the continuum would be avocational teachers, who would be satisfied with part-time teaching, perhaps for a limited number of years, and who would be required to meet only minimal standards. These teachers might be trained, supervised and supported by a small cadre of teachers at the other end of the continuum, who are highly professional. In between the two poles, any number of levels of expertise and commitment might be defined (For a fuller explanation and discussion of differentiated staffing, including hypothetical cases of different staffing structures in Jewish schools, see Aron, 1990).

If one accepts the principle of differentiated staffing, the problem of teacher recruitment changes significantly, and becomes easier to tackle. Teachers at the avocational end of the continuum can be recruited broadly: from the parent body, from within the congregation (Aron, 1988), from camps, youth groups, college campuses and anywhere else that enthusiastic, appealing, but inexperienced teachers might be found. It would be the job of the school, with the assistance of the central agency, to give these teachers some basic training, and a great deal of curricular and supervisory support. Avocational teachers who demonstrated sufficient talent and expressed an interest in becoming career professionals, might be given the opportunity for further training, either at a College of Jewish Education, or at some kind of national training institute. The school and the central agency would work together to assure that these neophyte professionals were offered a reasonably attractive salary for either full-time or part-time work. As professional teachers accumulated experience and expertise, they might require additional training, perhaps an M.A. or even a Ph.D. in Jewish education. Professionals at the upper end of the continuum would earn salaries that were competitive with those in other professions. Though they would still teach part of the time, their responsibilities to the school would be broadened to include curriculum development, staff development, parent education, adult education, community programming, and/or outreach activities.

Conclusion

The shortage of quality Jewish teachers has been an issue of concern for the American Jewish community for over half a century (Shevitz, 1988). But the true nature and dimensions of the shortage cannot be fully understood in the absence of the type of research discussed above. Nor can a completely satisfying solution to the problem be achieved without appropriate techniques for assessment; these too must derive from research. Clearly there is a significant research agenda to be met in the area of Jewish teachers.

In the meantime, stakeholders at every level of Jewish education have many things to accomplish on their own, including goal setting, curriculum articulation, parent involvement, and ongoing staff development. For one of the things we know about teachers is that teachers alone cannot make the difference.

Bibliography

Aron, I. (1988). From Where Will the Next Generation of Jewish Teachers Come? *Journal of Reform Judaism, 35*, 51-66.

Aron, I. (1989). The Malaise of Jewish Education. *Tikkun, 4*, 32-34.

Aron, I. (1990). *Towards the Professionalization of Jewish Teaching.* Cleveland: Commission on Jewish Education in North America.

Aron, I and Phillips, B. (1990). *Findings of the Los Angeles Bureau of Jewish Education's Jewish Teacher Census.* Paper presented at the Fourth Annual Conference on Research in Jewish Education, New York City.

Carnegie Forum on Education and the Economy. (1986). *A Nation Prepared: Teachers for the Twenty First Century.* New York: Carnegie Forum.

Chervin, S. (n.d.). *Knowledge and Beliefs of Torah Teachers in Jewish Religious Schools.* Unpublished dissertation proposal, Stanford University.

Federation of Jewish Agencies of Greater Philadelphia. (1989). *Preliminary Report of the Philadelphia Jewish Teacher Census.* Unpublished manuscript.

Flexner, P. (1989). The Goals of Staff Development: An Overview. *Pedagogic Reporter, 39*, 3-5.

Heilman, S. (1984). *Inside the Jewish School: A Study of the Cultural Setting for Jewish Education.* New York: American Jewish Committee.

Holmes Group.(1986). *Tomorrow's Teachers: A Report of the Holmes Group.* East Lansing, MI: Author.

Johnson, S. M. (1990). *Teachers at Work.* New York: Basic Books.

Millman, J. and Darling-Hammond, L. (1990). *The New Handbook of Teacher Evaluation.* Newbury Park, CA: Sage Publications.

Reynolds, R. (1988). Organizational Goals and Effectiveness: The Function of Goal-Ambiguity in Jewish Schools. In J. Aviad (Ed.), *Studies in Jewish Education, Vol. 3.* Jerusalem: Magnes Press.

Schoem, D. (1989). *Ethnic Survival in America: An Ethnography of a Jewish Afternoon School.* Atlanta: Scholars' Press.

Schoenberg, Z. (1987). *The Practical Knowledge of Day School Teachers.* Paper presented at the First Annual Conference on Research in Jewish Education, Los Angeles.

Sheskin, I. (1988). *The Miami Jewish Educator Study.* Miami: Central Agency for Jewish Education.

Shevitz, S. (1988). The Deterioration of the Profession of Jewish Supplementary School Teaching: An Analysis of the Effects of Communal Myths on Policy and Program. In J. Aviad (Ed.), *Studies in Jewish Education, Vol. 3.* Jerusalem: Magnes Press.

Shulman, L. (1987). Knowledge and Teaching: Foundations of the New Reform. *Harvard Educational Review. 57.* 1-22.

Highlights

*Good teachers possess an expertise based on a body of research and scholarship.

*Good teachers have a special commitment to students, subject matter and the educational enterprise.

*According to at least one researcher (Shulman, 1987), evaluating teachers has to take into account a teacher's:

1. knowledge of the subject matter to be taught
2. generic teaching skills
3. understanding of various curricular approaches
4. knowledge of the best way to teach the subject
5. psychological and sociological assessment of the students
6. familiarity with the narrow and broad contexts of education
7. understanding of goals and purposes of education

*The quality of teaching can be raised by:

1. articulating a clear vision of school goals
2. including parents as partners in the process of education
3. providing teachers with clear curricular guidelines and abundant resources
4. encouraging ongoing staff development

*Institutions ought to recruit teachers using the concept of "differentiated staffing", and provide training opportunities either locally or regionally.

The Larger Context

In the secular literature the current buzzword is"excellence". No less than that which is implied by this rather ambiguous term is acceptable—both in business and in education. Yet, in spite of definitional vagaries, the demand for "quality teaching" remains high. How remarkable then, that both teacher standards and salaries remain so low. Curiously, to most teachers, perks seem to be more important than do actual wages. We still don't really know how a teacher's religiosity, spirituality, personal commitment, and "mentschlichkeit" have an impact upon and bring about "good teaching". We have just begun to consider which traits are needed in order to become a "good teacher", or indeed, whether these can be learned or are somehow, genetically present, or for that matter, are even necessary at all.

What We Know About...
Women and Jewish Education

Rela Geffen Monson

One consequence of consciousness raising here in North America during the last part of this century has been to make us more aware of both the differences and the similarities between men and women. Dr. Monson, who is Professor of Sociology and Dean of Academic Affairs at Gratz College in Philadelphia, analyzes the nature and degree of this new consciousness on both students and teachers.

UNTIL CONTEMPORARY TIMES, AND TO SOME EXTENT EVEN TODAY, JEWISH WOMEN HAVE RECEIVED significantly less formal Jewish education than men. Despite recent trends toward more equal education, the disparity was still remarked upon in recent articles. For instance, in a review article on Jewish education in America, Ackerman (1989) writes:

> In the mid-1950s study of Jewish Education in the United States it was reported that boys and girls were enrolled in equal numbers in one-day-a-week schools, almost twice as many boys as girls were in day schools, and boys outnumbered girls by a ratio of close to three to one in afternoon schools. The NJPS (National Jewish Population Survey) of 1970 reported that "While differences in Jewish education exposure between boys and girls to age nine are small, they become important at age ten and beyond. . .(p. 84).

Neither Ackerman's earlier summary article *(American Jewish Year Book*, 1980), nor the *First Census of Jewish Schools in the Diaspora* (Dubb and DellaPergola,1986) report actual enrollments in each school by gender though they do report on the overall number of coeducational and gender-segregated schools.

Feminization of the Teaching Profession

Dubb and DellaPergola describe the feminization of the Jewish teaching profession, in which 98% of the preschool teachers are women and 61% of the Jewish studies and 78% of the general studies teachers in day schools are women. In New York where there are more Orthodox and gender-segregated schools, there were more male teachers, which means that outside of New York, the proportion of women teachers in Orthodox schools was considerably higher (p. 58). Other than noting the feminization of the teaching profession in the United States, no attempt is made to analyze this gender differential.

With the exception of Orthodox day schools and Yeshivot for boys, most of the teachers are, and have been, women at both the elementary and high school levels. This has historically been due either to the non-professionalization of teachers, the low esteem in which the field was held by the sponsors of Jewish education, and/or the commensurately low salaries available for teachers. Added to this was the perception that Jewish education was a part-time job. Thus, it was appropriate for men to engage in it as a means to put themselves through undergraduate or professional school, but not as an end goal profession in itself. The only recent exception to this in the non-Orthodox community has been the assumption by men of the role of administrative head of an educational system—congregational or communal. This devaluation has been particularly strong in supplementary schools. In general, the more "serious" the perception of the schooling, the higher the age level of the students, the greater the monetary and values commitment of the parents to formal schooling, the more likely it is that there will be male teachers, particularly in classical Jewish studies such as bible and rabbinics. The prevalence of this situation goes unremarked partly because of the parallel paucity of male teachers in the United States public school system through junior high school.

One consequence of the phenomenon described above is that most of the role models in non-Orthodox Jewish education are women, some of whom are also Israelis. Ironically, these same women are often untrained and uncomfortable with leading public religious services and unpracticed in leading home rituals. The long-term impact on personal practice of having role models who are uneasy or unsure is unknown—but within the classroom it may lead to a shift from performance orientation to theoretical study. Moreover, given the lingering values of American society even in this "liberated" generation, religion and culture are often considered the province of women. The fact that women lead small group rituals may eventuate in a subtle devaluation of Jewish ritual practice. As a consequence, institutions led by women become devalued (Elazar,1973).

Alternatively, ritual performance may be shifted from the small group setting to school-wide assembly programs where male leaders often take over. In much the same fashion the synagogue and school have taken on many of the ceremonial rituals previously thought of as being in the province of the home. The larger, more impersonal group replaces the personalized primary group experience.

In general, Americans and especially American Jews value goal-oriented over non-goal-oriented education. However, other than bar and bat mitzvah preparation and amorphous "Jewish identity" injections to immunize against intermarriage and insure some type of Jewish survival, the goals and expectations parents have of formal Jewish education are often unclear or even ambivalent (Wachs,1991). Parents want children to be aware of their heritage, to care about Jewish continuity, to know some Jewish history, to be able to function in the synagogue of the movement of the family's preference and to seek out Jewish social circles and ultimately Jewish mates. They most often do not, however, want them to change their personal way of life to conform to halakhic practice at a level higher than that of the nuclear family (Schoem, 1989). The fear that personal practice may change is often expressed when parents make the decision to send children into experiences which as a matter of ideology promote observance levels higher than those at home. (I have even heard of families who "ritualistically" go to Chinese restaurants the evening of their children's return from camp to make sure that the children will eat there.)

The trend toward devaluation of Jewish education because its goals are not critical ones in the real life of most American Jews is exacerbated by the feminization of the delivery of formal Jewish education, except at the level of the principal.

The Impact of the Exclusion of Women From Classical Jewish Studies

It is impossible to speak or write of what we know about women and Jewish education without a discussion of the impact of the exclusion of women from classical Jewish studies throughout Jewish history—particularly from the world of the Yeshiva. Access to and knowledge of rabbinics has always been an important key to power in the Jewish community. It is impossible, for instance, to argue convincingly about the role of women in ritual life of the home and the synagogue without the ability to study codes of Jewish law and the previous biblical and rabbinic texts upon which they are based. One is reduced to spouting derivative, apologetic arguments pro and con if one cannot handle the primary texts upon which the arguments are based. In a very real sense, knowledge was (and in some communities still is) power in the traditional Jewish community. This historical exclusion is ignored by most scholars who write of Judaism and the Jewish people.

Cynthia Ozick, in her important essay "Notes Toward Finding the Right Question" (1983) makes the following agonizing statements:

> Item: In the world at large I call myself, and am called, a Jew. But when, on the Sabbath, I sit among women in my traditional shul and the rabbi speaks the word "Jew", I can be sure that he is not referring to me. For him, "Jew" means "male Jew". . . .My own synagogue is the only place in the world where I am not named Jew (p. 125).

> Consider the primacy and priority of scholarship: scholarship as a major Jewish value; scholarship as a shortcut-word signifying immersion in Torah, thought, poetry, ethics, history—the complete life of a people's most energetic moral, intellectual, spiritual, lyrical soarings and diggings. Or look for a moment to Adin Steinsaltz's definition of that aspect of Torah called Talmud:

> *From the strictly historical point of view the Talmud was never completed...(The Talmud) is the collective endeavor of the entire Jewish people...*

When Adin Steinsaltz, the eminent contemporary scholar and interpreter of Talmud, writes that the Talmud "is the collective endeavor of the entire Jewish people", he is either telling an active and conscious falsehood, or he has forgotten the truth; or he has failed to notice the truth. The truth is that the Talmud is the collective endeavor not of the entire Jewish people, but only of its male half...A loss numerically greater than a hundred pogroms; yet Jewish literature and history report not one wail, not one tear. A loss culturally and intellectually more debilitating than a century of autos-da-fe; than a thousand evil bonfires of holy books—because books can be duplicated and replaced when there are minds to duplicate and replace them . . . (p. 138-39).

I have quoted at length from this remarkable essay because it states so powerfully the point that I have been trying to make. The exclusion of women from classical Jewish education was much more than it seems. If one considers that the name of the one woman scholar quoted by name in the Talmud—Beruria—has come down to us in corrupted form as "Beria", the ultimate compliment for an outstanding Jewish housewife, one sees the all-pervasive influence of this exclusion.

The traditional role of women in the study of Torah has always been to encourage and enable their husbands and sons to pursue it. There are many stories in the Talmud such as that of Rachel the wife of Rabbi Akiva in which women are glorified for being enablers in difficult circumstances.

Even in the twentieth century, the controversy over the extent to which women should be allowed to study Torah continued in the traditional community. Early in this century in eastern Europe there was a controversy over the establishment of the Bais Yaakov schools for girls—today considered the bastion of stringent orthodoxy. In this century the argument has been less over the establishment of some formal Jewish educational systems for girls, than the extent to which they should be taught rabbinic texts or the primary sources for codes rather than the laws themselves. The reasoning is that women need to know the law in areas that they will be responsible for such as kashrut and family purity, but do not need to be able to understand halakhic reasoning as such, and should not be taught mishna and gemara.

Both in Israel and the United States there has been a trend in the recent past to open up the study of rabbinics to women within the framework of centrist Orthodox schools and on the secular university campus. One of the major impacts of the contemporary Jewish feminist movement on Orthodoxy has been precisely in the area of equal access to Torah study, particularly rabbinics, for women. Thus, in her book on *Women and Jewish Law* (1984), Rachel Biale, an exponent of this trend, writes:

> ...authority in the Jewish tradition comes less from formal titles than from learning. Jewish women of all religious persuasions and commitments must become learned in the Halakhah, even if they do not actually live by it, for it is the framework and vocabulary of Jewish life. The first and most important step in the dialectical revolution of preserving and changing is talmud torah: the serious study of the Halakhah. Only those who explore the historical roots

of the Halakhah and master its logic may become part of its future growth
(p. 266).

It is important to note that it was not only in the Orthodox world that women were denied access
to study—and obviously those who do not study cannot teach. Graduate level Jewish studies, with
a very few exceptions such as at Columbia University in New York, were virtually unavailable before
1960 outside of religious frameworks to any Jewish women in North America.

Graduate level classical Jewish studies, moreover, were not available to women even at those
religious institutions such as the Hebrew Union College and the Jewish Theological Seminary until
the 1970s because they were included in the rabbinical training frameworks. Nearly all of the professors of classical Jewish studies who began to teach at the secular colleges and universities during
the flowering of Jewish studies in the United States in the 1970s and 80s were men who followed
the path of rabbinical school followed by attainment of the Ph.D. Since women had no access to
grounding in rabbinics, and even to some extent in Bible, unless they could afford private tutors
and find men willing to teach them, they had no means to study.

The few women Ph.D.s in Jewish studies who completed their degrees before 1970 in the United
States were in the field of Jewish history. In Israel, they were more often in modern Jewish literature, with a few in philosophy and history. The great Bible scholar Nechama Leibovitz is one of the
rare exceptions to this rule. There were a few women in the fields of language, archeology and
anthropology, but these fields were considered peripheral to the major subjects of Jewish study.

Policy Changes

The curriculum demands of the secular as well as modern Orthodox school frameworks in Israel
together with the proliferation of Orthodox and Conservative Jewish day schools throughout the
diaspora led to a demand for trained women to teach in these schools. University, Seminary and
College of Jewish Studies graduate programs of study of Bible, rabbinics and medieval and modern
responsa literature opened these areas up to women. The establishment of graduate programs of
Jewish studies in these areas at schools such as Brandeis, Yale and Brown as well as at Israeli
Universities finally enabled women to become scholars in formerly forbidden subject matter areas.
Let us not forget, however, that the first woman Ph.D in Talmud finished in the decade of the 80s,
that the current fulltime faculty of the Hebrew Union College in Cincinnati and New York includes
one woman and that it was only in 1989 that the distinguished Professor Urbach of the Hebrew
University gave his first Ph.D in Talmud to a woman—in the year of his own retirement!

Exploring A Paradox

"But how can this be?!", you should be asking by now. How can we square the exclusion of
Jewish women from formal Jewish education with the predominance of women in religious school
teaching? After all, as noted above, those who are excluded from study surely cannot teach! The
combination of a shortage of teachers and the part-time nature of most positions led to the hiring of

Israelis for their language ability, public school teachers who had little Jewish studies training and college students working to put themselves through school. Many women found the part-time work in their own neighborhoods consonant with lifelong interests—if not specialized training—in religious education.

Notes on the Future and Policy Implications

Women will only stay in Jewish education if they perceive it as a career with potential for growth. Even with more role models of women scholars, more practice in personal performance and leadership of synagogue and home rituals and higher salaries, our best and brightest women may decide that the role of Jewish educator is a stereotyped one which they do not wish to enter.

Several current factors have the capacity to effect a change in the personnel situation in Jewish education and may already be doing so:

1. Day school education is growing and providing more full-time jobs in settings where certification is required and professionalism encouraged.

2. The last decade of this century should see the growth of more Conservative and community day high schools in addition to the continued growth of the Orthodox system.

3. Rabbinical schools and graduate programs of Jewish studies will be producing a cadre of women, some of whom will want to work within the formal and informal educational systems.

4. With the tremendous growth of dual career families, careers within Jewish life which make it easy to follow the Jewish calendar will appear attractive to some women who wish to combine family, career and commitment to traditional Judaism with less "overload". These careers will be especially attractive if clear professional steps on the path to upward mobility in the Jewish school system are built and made known.

5. With the downturn of the economy and a movement toward improving the quality of life to give meaning to life, careers in the helping professions should generally become more attractive than in the last few decades, especially to women who wish to balance career, family life and Jewish observance (Dodge, 1990).

6. Federations' interest in and contributions to Jewish education should enable salary enhancement and growth of benefits to educators.

7. Finally, cooperative conceptions of synagogue programming should lead to the hiring of shared full-time personnel to work in education from day care through adult learning and youth work. This cooperation should be possible between synagogues of the same movement even if not between movements (Reimer, 1990).

One of the ironies of Jewish life has been that women, who have not had as much access to formal Jewish education as Jewish men, have consistently shown higher resistance than men to assim-

ilation—particularly to mixed marriage (Kosmin et al., 1989). One possible explanation of this paradox is that, outside the Orthodox community, sons do not have enough male role models who both
teach and show them how important Judaism is in giving meaning to their lives. So, at the same
time as we encourage women to study Torah, we have to enable more Jewish men to become full-time
Jewish educators.

Bibliography

Ackerman, W. (1980). Jewish Education Today. In *American Jewish Yearbook*. Philadelphia: American Jewish
Committee & Jewish Publication Society, 130-149.

Ackerman, W. (1989). Strangers to the Tradition: Idea and Constraint in American Jewish Education. In H.
Himmelfarb and S. DellaPergola (Eds.), *Jewish Education Worldwide*. Maryland: University Press of America,
71-116.

Biale, R. (1984). *Women & Jewish Law*. New York: Schocken Books,Inc.

Dodge, S. (1990). More College Students Choose Academic Majors that Meet Social and Environmental
Concerns. *The Chronicle of Higher Education, 37*(14).

Dubb, A.A. and DellaPergola, S. (1986). *First Census of Jewish Schools in the Diaspora 1981/2-1982/3, United
States of America*. Jerusalem: JESNA and Hebrew University of Jerusalem.

Elazar, D. J. (1973, Nov. 23). Women in American Jewish Life. *Congress Bi-Weekly*.

Kosmin, B. A., Lerer, N. and Mayer, E. (1989, August). *Intermarriage, Divorce and Remarriage Among American
Jews 1982-87*. New York: North American Jewish Data Bank.

Ozick, C. (1983). Notes Toward Finding the Right Question. Reprinted in S. Heschel (Ed.). *On Being A Jewish
Feminist*. New York: Schocken Books, Inc.,120-151.

Reimer, J. (1990). *The Synagogue as a Context for Jewish Education*. Cleveland: Mandel Associated Foundations.

Schneider, S.W. (1984). *Jewish And Female*. New York: Simon & Schuster, Inc.

Schoem, D. (1989). *Ethnic Survival in America: An Ethnography of a Jewish Afternoon School*. Atlanta:
Scholars Press.

Wachs, S. P. (1992). Jewish Education: Erev Shabbat or New Year's Eve? In S. Katz, (Ed.), *Jewish Concepts
in Today's World*. New York: Ktav and B'nai B'rith.

Highlights

*   With the exception of Orthodox day schools and Yeshivot, almost all teachers at
    both elementary and secondary school levels are women.
*   This has been due either to non-professionalization of the profession (low esteem)
    or to the commensurately low salaries.

* The long-term impact of having predominantly women as role models is unknown.
* The fact that women lead small group rituals may eventuate in a subtle devaluation of Jewish ritual practice.
* Until quite recently, women have typically been excluded from classical Jewish studies.

The Larger Context

Squaring the exclusion of Jewish women from formal Jewish higher education with the predominance of women in religious school teaching may be a paradox. Women will only stay in Jewish education if they perceive it as a career with potential for growth, says Dr. Monson. As a consequence, we are unable to predict with any precision what the impact of current employment trends may be. Is the predominantly female teaching profession, at least on the elementary and secondary level, adding to the devaluation of Jewish education in general? Enrollment data aside, possible changes in the tradition of sexism in Jewish educational circles and the continuing rise of dual career families, plus the whole issue of women in the public and private marketplace, will be areas to watch in the future.

What We Know About...Learning to Teach

Sharon Feiman-Nemser

This chapter is unique. Written by an acknowledged expert in the secular field, Dr. Sharon Feiman-Nemser, Professor of Teacher Education at Michigan State University, summarizes from a strongly secular perspective what we know about this new field. Focusing on different aspects of learning to teach, the author provides us with a framework for considering the education of future Jewish teachers.

WHAT DO TEACHERS NEED TO KNOW IN ORDER TO TEACH? HOW DO TEACHERS LEARN THE PRACTICE of teaching? How do they find their own voices within the boundaries of the teacher's role? Each of these questions highlights a different aspect of learning to teach. The first question focuses on the special knowledge that teachers must acquire and develop in order to do their work well. The second reminds us that teaching is a practical art which depends on developing judgement and skill. The third question suggests that taking on the office of teacher involves a personal transformation.

The questions also imply that learning to teach is not a simple, straightforward process. While the phrase "learning to teach" rolls easily off the tongue, we really do not have a good understanding of what goes into the making of a teacher. There are, of course, various lay theories about learning to teach. "Good teachers are born, not made." "If you know your subject well, you will be able to teach it." "Anybody who is warm and caring can teach." "Most of what you need to know about teaching can be learned on the job." These myths, however, do not find strong support in the classroom or the research literature.

Recently, educational researchers have begun to give serious attention to questions about teachers' learning. For example, my colleagues and I at the National Center for Research on Teacher Education, located at Michigan State University, have been studying the impact of liberal arts, professional education and classroom experience on teachers' knowledge, skills and dispositions. From these and other studies of teacher knowledge and teacher learning, we are beginning to understand more about what good teaching entails and how teachers can be helped to learn their craft and improve in their work.

In this chapter, I briefly discuss four propositions about learning to teach that grow out of this literature. The first proposition focuses on teachers as learners. The second deals with the relationship between academic courses and teachers' subject matter preparation. The third proposition concerns the problematic role of experience in learning to teach and the fourth points to forms of support that can help teachers learn new practices. Each of these propositions has some empirical support and each, I believe, has important implications for Jewish teaching and teacher education.

Proposition 1: Teachers as Learners:

From their experiences as students, teachers form strong conceptions of teaching; however, these views may interfere with their ability to consider more powerful ideas and approaches.

Prospective teachers are no strangers to teaching. From twelve or more years of teacher-watching as pupils in elementary and secondary schools, they have built up strong personal beliefs about teaching and learning, students and knowledge. Such beliefs are pervasive, often tacit, and resistant to change (Lortie, 1975).

Researchers have found that education students have a limited view of their role as teachers (Ball, 1988; Feiman-Nemser et al, 1989; Paine, 1989). They see teaching as a matter of telling pupils what they know and measuring their ability to recite it back. Beginning education students view learning as a process of memorization and practice, not as a process of constructing meaning from new ideas. When asked what they would do if their pupils did not understand a particular concept, education students said they would "go over it again." They could not envision an alternative strategy.

Beginning education students also have limited views about learners who are different from themselves (Freeman & Kalaian, 1989; McDiarmid, 1990). They believe that some children cannot master basic skills and they attribute school failure to poor home environments, limited abilities, and poor student attitudes. In short, they tend to blame students for school failure, thus sidestepping the issue of responsible teacher action.

While such beliefs are understandable given the conventional schooling that most prospective teachers have experienced, they represent a limited picture of what schools and classrooms could be like. They may also keep prospective teachers from giving serious attention to richer possibilities for teaching and learning than those derived from their own experiences. Cognitive psychologists tell us that people tend to hang on to familiar ways of thinking, ignoring conflicting ideas or reinterpreting them to fit their current views. Teacher educators have been slow to pick up on this insight.

Growing evidence suggests that conventional teacher education does little to challenge or transform teachers' entering beliefs. Teachers who leave teacher education programs with their initial beliefs intact are more likely to teach as they were taught, perpetuating practices that may not be in the best interests of students. If we want to expand teachers' perspectives on teaching, then we must take into account the images and beliefs teachers already hold.

Proposition 2: Academic Courses and Teacher Subject Matter Preparation:

Liberal arts courses do not necessarily provide teachers with adequate subject matter preparation.

Teachers cannot teach what they do not know. This is true regardless of one's view of teaching. Unfortunately, many teachers' knowledge of the subjects they teach is thin and fragmented. To remedy this situation, reformers have called for prospective teachers to spend more time in arts and science courses (and less in education courses) on the assumption that more academic study will strengthen teachers' subject matter background. Research on what students learn from their arts and science courses should make us skeptical about such reforms (Boyer, 1987; McDiarmid, 1990).

What do teachers need to know about their subjects to teach them effectively? Every field, although continually changing and growing, embodies particular information, ideas, theories and explanations. While this "content" may be subject to differing interpretations, no conception of subject matter knowledge can leave it out.

Substantive knowledge is one important aspect of subject matter knowledge. But subject matter knowledge also includes a host of understandings about the field of inquiry, including the relative importance of different ideas, the major disagreements, the way claims are justified and validated, and what the work entails. What does it mean to "do" history? How does scientific knowledge grow? What counts as a literary "truth" or a mathematical proof? Answering such questions depends on knowing the set of assumptions, rules of evidence, and forms of argument used by people who work in a field. If teachers are going to represent different subjects accurately, they also need this kind of knowledge.

Liberal arts courses represent a potentially rich source of knowledge for teachers, a place to learn content as well to develop ideas about the nature of the field and how it can be taught and learned (McDiarmid, 1989). But evidence is mounting that college level courses do not provide students with opportunities to gain a deep understanding of their subject matter. Various studies show that college level teaching, like elementary and secondary teaching, focuses on discrete facts rather than on "big ideas", their significance and interrelationships, their relevance to everyday life.

Studies of what undergraduates actually learn also suggest that college courses may not be the place to develop conceptual understanding. In one study, for example, students who did well in college calculus and high school geometry could solve simple geometric problems but had a hard time explaining why the solutions worked (Schoenfeld, 1985). In another, math majors planning to teach produced more correct answers than did elementary education majors, but they still had trouble making sense of division with fractions, connecting mathematics to the real world, and coming up with explanations that went beyond restating the rule (Ball, 1988). Though limited, the research should make us cautious about assuming that teachers will develop the kind of subject matter knowledge they need in their liberal arts courses.

Proposition 3: The Role of Experience:

In learning to teach, unexamined experience is not always the best teacher.

If you ask teachers how they learned to teach, they will inevitably say they learned to teach by teaching. Clearly experience is necessary in learning to teach and we are only beginning to understand and value the practical knowledge that teachers create through the experience of teaching. At the same time, research on teacher socialization and the conditions of teaching suggest that experience is not always a good teacher.

Studies of teacher socialization show that teachers become increasingly more bureaucratic and authoritarian over time. The challenges and demands of beginning teaching quickly erode the idealism and energy of new teachers. Conventional practices, prominent in most schools, set the boundaries within which novices learn their craft.

The first year of teaching is generally considered a formative time in learning to teach (Feiman-Nemser, 1983). Facing the same responsibilities as their more experienced colleagues, novices focus on what is necessary to get the job done—manage the class, plan and teach lessons, keep students quiet. Strategies that help them survive in the short run can easily become the basis for a teaching style that endures. Without help in crafting an approach that fits their ideals, novices may abandon their commitment to foster active learning, integrate the curriculum, and connect school learning with the community.

The daily work of teaching shapes teachers' views of how one becomes a good teacher. Many teachers believe that learning to teach is a matter of independent trial and error with occasional assistance from others. This view is built into their working conditions. Accustomed to working alone in their classrooms, teachers are cautious about revealing problems or asking for help. They rarely observe one another teaching or engaging in serious conversation about their work. The isolation of teachers from one another makes it easier to stick to comfortable practices without having to justify them in terms of student learning.

How can we increase the likelihood that teachers not only "have" experience but profit from it? In part, the answer lies in creating schools where continued learning is part of the job of teaching.

Proposition 4: Support

Teachers are more likely to learn to teach well and to continue learning from teaching if they have regular opportunities for thoughtful conversation and observation.

Most people think about good teaching as a function of the teacher's personal resources. But many studies also suggest that good teaching is a reflection of the opportunities and expectations that surround teachers in their work. If this is so, then changing the roles and work environment of teachers can help improve the quality of teaching.

Researchers (e.g. Little, 1982; Rosenholtz, 1985) have identified characteristics of schools where teachers view their own continued learning as part of the job of teaching. In these schools, teachers talk together about their work. They regularly observe one another. They develop and critique curricular materials together. They teach and learn from each other. Some current proposals to "restructure" schools (e.g., Holmes Group, 1991) reflect these commitments.

Implications of Propositions for Jewish Education

If these propositions apply to the field of general education, how much more so in the field of Jewish education, where we often rely on part-time teachers with limited academic and/or professional preparation and where much teacher education, by necessity, takes the form of staff development and in-service education. Below I briefly spell out some of the implications that seem to flow from the propositions discussed above.

1. *Jewish teachers need opportunities to examine critically their taken-for-granted beliefs about teaching.* Jewish teachers will likely teach as they were taught unless they get help in critically examining their taken-for-granted beliefs about teaching, and in considering alternatives. If we want to change the character of Jewish teaching and learning in schools, we have to uncover the images of teaching and learning that Jewish teachers hold. What are those images? Where did they come from? Do they reflect the kinds of practices that we want to foster in our schools? Principals, curriculum specialists, teacher educators must help Jewish teachers recognize how much their thinking and actions are shaped by deeply held, often tacit beliefs that may not reflect their explicit personal and educational philosophy.

2. *Jewish teachers need opportunities to develop conceptual understanding of Judaica content while experiencing exemplary teaching.* Teachers learn not only from the content they encounter, but also from the pedagogy they experience. Scholars interested in problems of Jewish teaching and learning must work together with educators to create opportunities in which teachers encounter serious Judaica content in authentic ways, analyze the experience of being a learner of that content, and then consider the problems of connecting that content to students of different ages in meaningful ways. The simultaneous focus on content and pedagogy can be both efficient and potentially powerful.

3. *Jewish teachers need regular opportunities to study teaching, their own and others.* Jewish teachers cannot learn to teach well on their own. They need to see good teachers in action (live and on videotape). They need to get feedback on their own teaching. They need to learn how others address similar problems. Considerable ingenuity will be needed to create such opportunities for part-time teachers. Effective use of technology combined with on-site mentoring and teacher study groups should be explored.

4. *Research on Jewish teachers' knowledge, skills and beliefs should inform the practice of Jewish teacher education.* There are more people in the business of educating Jewish teach-

ers than in the habit of studying the knowledge and beliefs of Jewish teachers. How do Jewish teachers construe teaching and learning? What do they know about different content areas? How are Jewish teachers' knowledge and beliefs related to their own Jewish education and upbringing? What are the dominant pedagogies in Jewish schools? Answers to such questions can be enormously helpful in planning programs to support and extend teachers' learning and improve their teaching. Educators recognize the importance of knowing about learners' prior knowledge, skills, and interests. The same holds true for Jewish teachers as learners.

Bibliography

Ball, D. & McDiarmid, G.W. (1990). The subject matter preparation of teachers. In W.R. Houston (Ed.), *Handbook of research on teacher education* (437-449). New York: Macmillan.

Boyer, E.L. (1987). *College: The undergraduate experience in America.* New York: Harper and Row.

Feiman-Nemser, S. (1983). Learning to teach. In L. Shulman & G. Sykes (Eds.), *Handbook of teaching and policy.* New York: Longman.

Holmes Group (1986). *Tomorrow's teachers: A report of the Holmes Group.* East Lansing, MI.

Little, J.W. (1982). Teachers as colleagues. In V. Richardson-Koehler (Ed.), *Educator's handbook: A research perspective* (491-518). New York: Longman.

Lortie, D. (1975). *Schoolteacher.* Chicago: University of Chicago Press.

McDiarmid, G.W., Ball, D.L., & Anderson, C.W. (1989). Why staying one chapter ahead doesn't really work: Subject specific pedagogy. In M.C. Reynolds (Ed.), *Knowledge base for the beginning teacher* (pp. 193-205). New York: Pergamon Press.

McDiarmid, G.W. (1990). What do prospective teachers learn in their liberal arts courses? *Theory into Practice, 29*(1), 21-29.

McDiarmid, G.W. & Wilson, S. (in press). "You pick it up later…" The subject matter knowledge of liberal arts graduates. *Journal of Teacher Education.*

Resnick, L. (1987). Learning in school and out. *Educational Researcher, 16*(9), 13-20.

Rosenholtz, S. (1985). Effective schools: Interpreting the evidence. *American Educator, 13*(4), 16-22, 46-88.

Schoenfeld, A. (in press). Reflections on doing and teaching mathematics. In A. Schoenfeld (Ed.), *Mathematical thinking and problem solving.*

Schon, D. (1983). *The reflective practitioner: How professionals think.* New York: Basic Books.

Shulman, L. (1987). Knowledge and teaching: Foundations of a new reform. *Harvard Educational Review, 57,* 1-23.

Highlights

Four propositions from secular education:
* From their experience as students, teachers form strong conceptions of teaching; however, these views may interfere with their ability to consider more powerful ideas and approaches.
* Liberal arts courses do not necessarily provide teachers with adequate subject matter preparation.
* In learning to teach, unexamined experience is not always the best teacher.
* Teachers are more likely to learn to teach well and to continue learning from teaching if they have regular opportunities for thoughtful conversation and observation.

Four implications for Jewish education:
* Jewish teachers need opportunities to examine critically their taken-for-granted beliefs about teaching, learning, students, etc.
* Jewish teachers need opportunities to develop conceptual understanding of Judaic content while experiencing exemplary teaching.
* Jewish teachers need regular opportunities to study teaching, their own and others.
* Research on Jewish teachers' knowledge, skills and beliefs would inform the practice of Jewish teacher education by providing insights about teachers as learners.

The Larger Context

We owe a debt of gratitude to the world of secular education. We have much to learn from a rich and growing body of research. Yet our particularly Jewish circumstances are even more challenging. All too often, our teachers are "one day ahead" of their students. Most are not licensed nor have they been trained academically. Our challenge is to successfully apply the findings of secular education and their implications for Jewish teachers to the settings where Jewish teachers do indeed learn to teach.

The Learners

Enrollment
Leora W. Isaacs

Demography
Gary Tobin

Early Childhood
Ruth Pinkenson Feldman

Youth Programming/Non-formal Education
H.A. Alexander and Ian Russ

Adult Education
Betsy Katz

Jewish Identification
Arnold Dashefsky

The Marginally Affiliated
Steven M. Cohen

Faith Development
Roberta Louis Goodman

New Americans
Misha Galperin and Patricia Cipora Harte

What We Know About...Enrollment

Leora W. Isaacs

Numbers are important to us. Each day we rely on data presented to us by the media and in our work—a for good reason: numbers help us ground our thoughts and opinions. Dr. Isaacs, Director of Research at the Jewish Education Service of North America, documents well the current figures related to student enrollment in North America. This article provides the background for assessment of needs and development of programs and initiatives that we must undertake.

Why Do We Need to Know About the Demography of Jewish Schools?

TIME WAS THAT JEWISH ENCULTURATION AND IDENTITY DEVELOPMENT WAS A MORE SPONTANEOUS, organic absorption process. The Jewish calendar determined the rhythm of Jewish life. Home celebration and observance of Shabbat, holidays, and Jewish life milestone events were the contexts in which Jewish children first became familiar with Jewish customs and tradition, as well as law, language, literature and lore. Formal education was a complement and extension to the Jewish identity forged in the home and neighborhood. As generations of Jews became more acculturated into American society, the relative balance between home and school shifted. For most American Jews, the school has become the primary, rather than complementary, venue for Jewish education.[1]

Providing institutionalized Jewish education is an expensive venture. It is estimated that more than $1 billion is spent annually on Jewish education, with funds coming mainly from tuition fees, congregational budgets, fundraising, and federation allocations (Liebman, 1984, 1990). Federation allocations to Jewish education rose from $32 million in 1979 to nearly $72 million in 1989, representing over 25% of all local federation allocations. Although many would argue that providing effective Jewish education requires even greater sums of money, and more importantly, the re-involvement of home and family in the education/enculturation process, the amounts spent do reflect the organized community's recognition of its reliance on institutionalized Jewish education to promote and ensure Jewish continuity. It is not at all surprising that with increased investment in Jewish education have come increased demands for accountability.

Just as in the broader society, where there is growing awareness that the educational system has not adapted quickly enough to the needs of a rapidly changing world and where increased resources are being provided for educational improvement, lay and professional leaders in many Jewish communities have begun to ask questions about their schools and other educational institutions, and how they might be modified to meet societal needs of the present and future. Comprehensive and reliable information about current conditions and short-term effects provide the background for assessment of needs and development of programs and initiatives to meet them.

How Do We Know What We Know?

The American Jewish community has not yet invested in a systematic, coordinated research plan for Jewish education. In the meantime, descriptive information about Jewish schools in the United States comes from a variety of sources. For example, censuses of Jewish schools have been conducted by The Hebrew University's Institute of Contemporary Jewry and Jewish Education Service of North American (JESNA). These surveys have collected information from the perspective of Jewish education "providers" on their enrollment and faculty, their nature and ideological orientation (Himmelfarb and DellaPergola, 1982; DellaPergola and Genuth, 1983; Dubb and DellaPergola, 1986; DellaPergola and Rebhun, n.d.). Many central agencies for Jewish education conduct annual or biennial local censuses of Jewish education in their local communities. Community studies and needs assessments of Jewish education conducted by JESNA in many communities have included descriptive components. The National Jewish Population Study and demographic studies of Jewish communities across the country have collected data directly from representative samples of American Jews. These studies not only provide estimates of the total Jewish population in various areas and age groups, but also report current, past and projected enrollment from the perspective of Jewish education "consumers" (Kosmin, et al., 1991). Dr. Sylvia Barack Fishman of Brandeis University published a secondary analysis of Jewish education data from a number of the community demographic studies, drawing implications and insights from their findings (Fishman, 1987).

The fact that these studies were conducted from different perspectives, using different methodologies and achieving varying degrees of coverage, is a blessing and a curse. On the one hand, there is the benefit of comparing findings from two or more independent sources. On the other hand, caution must be advised in making inferences and drawing comparisons. Understanding of how, when and from whom the data was collected is critical. Furthermore, in the absence of a systematic, coordinated research program, we are left with a series of snapshots from which we must try to piece together "the big picture."

What Do We Know About Student Enrollment?

A. *What percentage of Jewish children are enrolled in Jewish schools in the United States?*

Enrollment in some type of formal Jewish education is a normative experience for Jewish children in North America. Although there is some variation from community to community (with higher rates in some Eastern and Midwestern cities and lower in some Southwestern cities), between 70-80% of America's Jews receive some kind of Jewish education during their lifetimes (Fishman, 1987, p. 17). However, the intensity and duration of these experiences vary greatly.

At any point in time, only about 35-40% of the potential student population (ages 5-18) is enrolled in Jewish schools[2]. The pre-bar/bat mitzvah years continue to be the most intense period of enrollment, with approximately 57% of all Jewish children in the United States between the ages of 10 and 13 enrolled in Jewish schools. Enrollment rates decline to approximately 27% in grades 8-10, and further to approximately 6% in grades 11-12 (Dubb and DellaPergola, 1986). Again, communities do vary. In some communities, as many as 25% of students ages 13-17 are retained (Fishman, 1987, p. 18). Thus, low enrollment rates for any point in time are a result of the exceedingly short duration of Jewish education experiences for most American children.

Contrary to conventional wisdom, the percentage of children enrolled at any particular point in time has not varied significantly within the last 40 years or more (Pilch, 1969). Formal Jewish education in America has never been universal. In fact, based on results of a number of recent Jewish community population studies, it has been suggested that a child born in the United States during the last quarter of this century is far more likely to have received some formal Jewish education than one born in the first quarter (Fishman, 1987, p. 25). One of the most dramatic changes during the past forty years has been the increased enrollment of girls in formal Jewish education programs. In fact, the apparent rise in rates of formal education from the oldest to youngest cohorts can be explained almost entirely by increased Jewish educational opportunities for girls and women.

B. *What is the total enrollment of children in Jewish schools in the United States?*

There have been significant fluctuations in the absolute numbers of children enrolled in Jewish schools over the past three decades. Between 1957 (the peak enrollment period) and 1982, enrollment in Jewish schools decreased by over 35% from nearly 589,000 to 372,000 students.[3] This reduction can be attributed primarily to an overall population decline resulting from low birthrates as well as rising intermarriage rates. Although enrollment rates for children born from conversionary marriages are comparable to those in which both parents were born Jewish, only 20% of children from mixed marriages are enrolled (Mayer, 1983).

The recent "echo" occasioned by "baby boomers'" children reaching school age has been reflected in Jewish school enrollments. Results of the most recent census of Jewish schools in North America conducted during the school years 1986-1988 (DellaPergola and Rebhun, in press), indicate that over 470,000 children are enrolled in formal Jewish education programs through secondary school, including between 50-70,000 in early childhood education programs. However, with preliminary analyses of the National Population Study placing the number of Jewish school-age children in the United States at 1,166,000 (Kosmin, et al., 1991), the percentage of market penetration remains constant at 35-40%.

C. *How does enrollment compare for Supplementary Schools and Day Schools?*

Supplementary schools clearly remain the predominant form of Jewish education in the United States today, with nearly two-thirds of the students in Jewish schools in the U.S. enrolled there. Nevertheless, a number of shifts and changes in both total enrollment and enrollment patterns merit attention. The total number of supplementary schools in the U.S., along with their enrollment, has declined dramatically over the past three decades. In 1987, there were 1,879 supplementary schools throughout the U.S. as compared to a peak of 3,153 schools in 1957, and supplementary school enrollment had declined 43% from 511,000 to 287,000.

The decrease in supplementary school enrollment can be accounted for in great part by demographic decline, although the growth of the day school movement has certainly been a contributing factor. During that same period (1957–1987), the number of day schools more than doubled from 248 to nearly 550, and day school enrollment increased fourfold from 42,650 to over 168,000 students. More significantly, in 1957 fewer than 8% of those enrolled in Jewish schools were in day schools, compared to nearly 36% in 1987.

How enrollment varies:
A. By time-intensity of instruction

Over the past quarter century there have also been major shifts in the time-intensity of Jewish education. On the supplementary school front, the effect has been "homogenizing." There have been significant decreases in the numbers of both one-day-a-week and five-day-a-week supplementary schools, accompanied by an increase in the two/three-day-a-week form. In 1946, 62.7% of students enrolled in supplementary schools attended five days per week; in 1958, 66% of the students attended three days and only 6% attended five days. By 1970 there were almost no five-day-a-week supplementary schools left. Some argue that the day school has filled the niche for those desiring the more intensive Jewish education formerly provided by the more time-intensive talmud torah programs.

Meanwhile, there has been a growing tendency away from one-day-a-week only supplementary programs. Such programs have become most common for younger (ages three to nine years) and post bar/bat mitzvah students, and under Reform congregational sponsorship. In 1982, 24% of those enrolled in Jewish schools attended one day a week, and of these, 72% were enrolled in Reform schools. (That is not to say that most students in Reform schools attend one day a week. In fact, nearly three-quarters of those enrolled in Reform schools attend classes two or more days per week.)

How enrollment varies:
B. By grade level

Jewish education in the United States has been, and continues to be, primarily a pediatric enterprise. Results from community studies as well as the National Jewish Population Study indicate that fewer than 10% of adult American Jews are currently enrolled in adult Jewish education in most cities. Secondary analyses of community studies' results indicate that single young adults (ages 25 -34) are least likely to engage in continuing Jewish education, but current enrollment in all types of Jewish schools and courses falls off at age 18, despite the proliferation of Jewish studies programs on college campuses (Fishman, 1987, p. 19).

Even among the school-age population, Jewish education is largely restricted to the elementary level. As noted earlier, enrollment declines precipitously in the post bar/bat mitzvah grades. This is as true for day school as for supplementary school students. As accepted as day schooling has become, it remains mainly on the elementary level, except within Orthodox circles. The 1987 schools census found 67% of all day school students were enrolled in the elementary grades, 17% were in grades 7-9, and 16% were in grades 10-12. However, 80-90% of those enrolled in grades 7 and up were enrolled in Orthodox schools. Indeed, there are fewer than a dozen non-Orthodox day high schools throughout North America. There is, however, an emerging positive trend worth watching. Compared to earlier census reports, it appears that greater numbers of students are beginning to be retained in Jewish schools slightly longer than in previous years. Whereas bar/bat mitzvah continues to be the predominant exit point, greater percentages of students, particularly in supplementary schools, are continuing through tenth grade, presumably through some form of confirmation program (DellaPergola and Rebhun, in press).

While it may be that children are staying in Jewish schools longer, there are definite indications that they are starting earlier. Within the past decade a new trend has emerged — Jewish education for newborns through kindergartners. Jewish preschool and day care programs are proliferating nationwide. Between 50 and 70,000 children are enrolled in all types of Jewish early childhood programs, including independent preschools, Jewish Community Centers, and those associated with day schools and synagogues (Kosmin, personal communication).

How enrollment varies:
C. By denominational affiliation

Although communal heders and talmud torahs flourished at the beginning of the century in North America, congregational or denominational sponsorship of supplementary education has predominated for the past forty years or more, particularly in the United States. Over 80% of all supplementary schools in the United States are under denominational auspices, despite some sporadic movement in recent years toward pooling resources to form communal or inter-congregational schools. Most commonly, such initiatives have been limited to the post bar/bat mitzvah level or where declining enrollment or the shortage of teachers have made mergers necessary. However, a number of communities have begun to develop innovative communal and cooperative supplementary school programs to promote the concept of *Klal Yisrael* and Jewish religious pluralism, encourage participation in Jewish community life, improve instructional effectiveness and enrich supplementary school experiences. Of the 1,879 supplementary schools enumerated in the 1987 schools census, 42.7% are under Conservative auspices, 10.9% Orthodox, 33.2% Reform, 12.1% Communal, and 1.1% "Other." In terms of enrollment, 41% of all supplementary school students are enrolled in Conservative sponsored schools, 6.1% in Orthodox, 42% in Reform, 10% in Communal, and .5% in "Other."

Throughout the past century day school education in the United States has been a predominantly Orthodox enterprise. However, in the past two decades, non-Orthodox day schooling has expanded dramatically. Of the approximately 550 day schools currently in existence, 14.5% describe themselves as Communal, 14.7% as Conservative, 28.3% as Orthodox, and 2.5% as Reform. With regard to enrollment, 5.9% of the nearly 168,000 day school students are enrolled in schools under Communal sponsorship, 9.8% in Conservative schools, 83.1% in Orthodox schools, and 1.2% in Reform schools. The two "branches" of the day school movement which have experienced especially noteworthy development most recently are the nascent Council for Reform Jewish Day Schools and RAVSAK (the Hebrew acronym for the Jewish Community Day School Network). In only 18 years, Reform day schools have overcome substantial initial rejection from their sponsoring movement, and now enroll more than 2,000 students in over a dozen schools (with several new school openings planned for the near future). Founded in 1987, RAVSAK was organized to improve the effectiveness of independent and communally sponsored day schools that embrace a pluralistic approach to transmitting Jewish heritage and values in their educational programs. The Network now numbers nearly 40 schools.

What Should We Know?

The need for research into all aspects of Jewish education has been recognized and documented. For better or worse, the American Jewish community has come to rely intensely on Jewish educational institutions to help ensure Jewish continuity and identity. Substantial amounts of financial and other resources have been expended on a variety of Jewish educational ventures, and the vast majority of American Jewish youth participate in such ventures, to greater or lesser extents. Decisions about how to maximize the effectiveness of the Jewish educational system should be based on knowledge of what works — and what doesn't; who is being reached — and who isn't; which needs are being met — and which aren't. However, because sufficient resources have not been available for appropriate research, this is very often not possible.[4]

Regular monitoring of enrollment trends is one of the most basic information needs, and some progress has been made in that area. However, it is important to remember that such general statistics, in and of themselves, are not sufficient. Knowing how many children are enrolled in any particular type of program, or even comparisons of enrollment figures over time will do nothing to improve the quality of Jewish education. Collecting descriptive enrollment statistics is no more worthwhile than counting beans if we do not go beyond the compilation of esoteric trivia to analyses of the underlying factors accounting for them. Statistical data can only be a valuable resource if they are utilized as background for an assessment of Jewish educational needs, and if they lead to other questions about the quality and outcomes of educational programs.

On the national level, our current knowledge of enrollment rates might lead us into inquiries about:

A. *General factors influencing enrollment and retention in Jewish school programs.*

What are the characteristics of programs that most successfully attract and retain students?

Why do certain communities and programs experience greater success, for example, in retaining students in post-bar/bat mitzvah programs?

If there have been changes in rates of enrollment over time, what factors might account for them?

What are the characteristics of the 20–30% of the school-age population who don't enroll in Jewish education programs? Are there alternate types of programs that might attract them?

What is the relationship between parental Jewish education and children's enrollment?

How do various programs affect their participants?

B. *More detailed information about various subpopulations.*

Why has there been such growth in the area of Jewish early childhood education? What are the characteristics of such programs? Why do parents choose them? Would even more parents choose them if they were more available and affordable? What is their impact on future Jewish education of children? What is their impact on the family?

What happens to students after they leave day schools? Do they enroll in supplementary school programs? If so, in what types?

What percentage of students belong to populations that may require special programming and services, such as children of intermarriage, children of divorce and single-parent families, special needs and learning disabled students? How are their needs being accommodated?

C. *Other forms of Jewish education.*

What types of programs, aside from schools for children, currently exist?

How extensive is participation in such programs? What are the characteristics of participants?

What is the relationship between school enrollment and such other forms of Jewish education, including informal education, youth groups, camps, Israel experiences, adult education or family education?

How do various programs affect their participants?

Jewish education has come to be seen as the key to our collective survival. Its effectiveness depends on the ability of the Jewish community to identify its actual and potential clientele, and to devise effective programs that meet the needs of all segments of the population. The task is great. It is not incumbent upon us to complete it—but we must begin.

Bibliography

DellaPergola, S. and Genuth, N. (1983). *Research Report 2: Jewish Education Attained in Diaspora Communities, Data for 1970's*. Jerusalem: The Hebrew University of Jerusalem, The Institute of Contemporary Jewry, Project for Jewish Educational Statistics.

DellaPergola, S. and Rebhun, U. (Preliminary unpublished returns). *The Second International Census of Jewish Schools 1986/7-1987/8, United States*.

Dubb, A.A. and DellaPergola S. (1986). *Research Report 3: First Census of Jewish Schools in the Diaspora 1981/2-1982/3, United States of America* . Jerusalem: The Hebrew University of America, The Institute of Contemporary Jewry Project for Jewish Educational Statistics and JESNA.

Fishman, S.B. (1987). *Learning About Learning: Insights On Contemporary Jewish Education from Jewish Population Studies*. Waltham, MA: Maurice and Marilyn Cohen Center for Modern Jewish Studies, Brandeis University.

Himmelfarb, H.S. and DellaPergola, S. (1982). *Research Report 1: Enrollment in Jewish Schools in the Diaspora, Late 1970's*. Jerusalem: The Hebrew University of Jerusalem, The Institute of Contemporary Jewry, Project for Jewish Education Statistics.

Kosmin, B.A., Goldstein, S., Waksberg, J., Lerer, N., Keysar, A., and Scheckner, J. (1991). *Highlights of the CJF 1990 National Jewish Population Survey*. New York: Council of Jewish Federations.

Liebman, N. (1984). *Federation Allocations to Jewish Education, 1979-1983*. New York: Council of Jewish Federations Statistics Unit.

Liebman, N. (1983). *Federation Allocations to Jewish Education, 1985-1989*. New York: Council of Jewish Federations Statistics Unit.

Mayer, E. (1983). *Children of Intermarriage: A Study in Patterns of Identification and Family Life*. New York: The American Jewish Committee, Institute of Human Relations.

Pilch, J. (1969). *A History of Jewish Education in the United States*. New York: American Association for Jewish Education.

Database of Jewish Schools in North America. (1990). New York: The Jewish Education Service of North America.

Footnotes

[1] The influence of informal education, including camping, youth groups, Israel programs, etc., cannot be ignored. However, such programs fall beyond the purview of this paper.

[2] The difficulty of defining the total Jewish school age population must be acknowledged. Definitions range from highly inclusive (children of a single Jewish parent irrespective of identification as a Jew) to highly restrictive (children having minimally a Jewish mother and identifying as Jews).

[3] Statistical comparisons in this paper are based on comparative analyses of data from: Himmelfarb and DellaPergola, 1982; DellaPergola and Genuth, 1983; Dubb and DellaPergola, 1986; DellaPergola and Rebhun, n.d.; Fishman, 1987; Kosmin et al., 1991; and Pilch, 1969. Certain comparisons from DellaPergola and Rebhun were not possible since data analysis is continuing at the time of preparation of this manuscript. However, it should be noted that any inferences about changes over time should be made with great caution. Improvements in methodology and coverage were introduced with each successive census, making direct comparisons problematic.

[4] Similar statistics on informal programs would also be valuable, particularly for post bar/bat mitzvah age students. Such programs may be the primary vehicle for Jewish education and enculturation of that age group, but we know even less about those statistics than we do about formal education.

Highlights:

* More than $1 billion is spent annually on Jewish education.
* Federation allocations to Jewish education rose from $32 million in 1979 to nearly $72 million in 1989, representing over 25% of all local federation allocations.
* Between 70 and 80% of America's Jews receive some kind of Jewish education during their lifetimes.
* At any point in time, 35-40% of the potential student population (ages 5-18) is enrolled in Jewish schools.
* Enrollment rates decline to approximately 27% in grades 8-10, and further to approximately 6% in grades 11-12. These percentages have not varied during the last 40 years or more.
* A child born during the last quarter of this century is far more likely to have received some formal Jewish education than one born in the first quarter.
* Between 1957 and 1982, enrollment in Jewish schools decreased by over 35% from nearly 589,000 to 372,000 students.
* Although enrollment rates for children born from conversionary marriages are comparable to those in which both parents were born Jewish, only 20% of children from mixed marriages are enrolled.
* Nearly two-thirds of students in Jewish schools are enrolled in supplementary schools; but the total number of supplementary schools has slipped from 3,153 in 1957 to 1,883 in 1987. Enrollment has also declined 43% from 511,000 to 286,000.
* During that same period, the number of day schools more than doubled from 248 to 550 and day school enrollment increased fourfold from 42,650 to 182,000 students.
* There have been significant decreases in the numbers of both one-day-a-week and five-day-a-week supplementary schools, accompanied by an increase in the two/three day-a-week form.

* Jewish education in the United States has been, and continues to be, primarily a pediatric enterprise. Fewer than 10% of adult American Jews are currently enrolled in adult Jewish education.
* While it may be that children are staying in Jewish schools longer, there are indications that they are definitely starting earlier.
* Of the 1,879 supplementary schools in the 1987 schools census, 43% are under Conservative auspices, 11% Orthodox, 33% Reform, 12% Communal and 1% "Other".
* Of the approximately 550 day schools, 15% describe themselves as Communal, 15% as Conservative, 68% as Orthodox, and 3% as Reform.

The Larger Context

Figures are descriptive averages; they do not in any way presume to describe the richness of the total picture. Despite this averaging, Dr. Isaacs' portrayal of the data suggests that while we have much to learn from these numbers that can guide future decisions locally and nationally, our retention rate particularly with teens and adults needs serious attention. Perhaps this suggests programmatic changes, shifting from a concentration on outreach to one on inreach.

What We Know About...Demography

Gary A. Tobin

Demography is defined as the "science of vital and social statistics of a population". It is one way that we have of looking at communities. Gary A. Tobin, Director of the Maurice and Marilyn Cohen Center for Modern Jewish Studies at Brandeis University, is one of North America's leading community planners and demographers. The composite picture he draws is based on a number of North American Jewish communities, with data taken from studies Tobin has conducted largely under the auspices of local Jewish federations. His findings reflect the mainly urban character of our North American Jewish communities.

D EMOGRAPHIC STUDIES CONDUCTED IN JEWISH COMMUNITIES THROUGHOUT THE UNITED STATES IN the past few years have explored a wide variety of issues relating to Jewish education. Among the areas that have been explored are profiles of who receives a Jewish education and who does not, how much Jewish education is received and what kinds, evaluations of Jewish education, expected goals and purposes of Jewish education, and why individuals participate or do not participate in Jewish education programs. This essay examines the recent demographic research that has been conducted in a variety of Jewish communities. It summarizes the most important findings from these studies and outlines the need for further research.

The Cities

Although a number of studies about Jewish education have been completed by Bureaus of Jewish Education, individual synagogues, or other communal organizations, this essay draws upon studies conducted under the auspices of the local Jewish federations. These studies are carefully constructed to include both affiliated and unaffiliated Jewish populations. The communities that have been studied vary by size, region, and institutional structure. They include northeastern communities such as Rochester, New York, Boston, and Providence, RI. They also include midwestern communities such as Cleveland and Milwaukee. Southern communities include New Orleans and Palm Beach, while western and southwestern communities include Denver, Phoenix and San Francisco.

Communities also vary by size, from small Jewish communities of under 50,000, such as Worcester, Massachusetts; medium-sized Jewish communities of 20-50,000 such as Pittsburgh; or large Jewish communities of 100,000 or more such as Essex-Morris Counties, New Jersey. A complete list of the communities that are included in this analysis is presented in the bibliography. These community studies provide the best data for analyzing trends in Jewish education prior to the release of the national Jewish population study in 1991. This essay provides a broad-stroke picture of what is known about Jewish education rather than providing detailed data analysis from a large number of communities. General themes and conclusions are drawn so that a future research agenda can be provided.

Who Receives a Jewish Education?

A majority of Jewish children between the ages of 6 and 12 receive some formal Jewish education. This includes Sunday School, afternoon Hebrew School, private tutors, or other formal training programs. Depending on the community, anywhere from 60% to over 90% of the children in the pre-bar/bat mitzvah age group are currently enrolled in formal Jewish education. However, this does not indicate that each individual child spends all of his/her primary school years receiving Jewish education. Some children may receive no more than pre-bar/bat mitzvah training, or others may be enrolled for a number of years. But prior to bar/bat mitzvah, a majority of Jewish children are enrolled in formal Jewish education.

The number of years of Jewish education varies a great deal. In some communities, a majority of the children receive five years or less of formal Jewish education. In others, a majority receive seven years or more. Differences also appear in the number of hours per week attended. Many children attend one hour per week or less, while in some communities a majority spend three to five hours per week in formal Jewish education.

As might be expected, the proportion of children receiving a formal Jewish education after bar mitzvah age drops precipitously in all communities. In many, the proportion of Jewish children receiving formal Jewish education drops by at least half. This decline continues into young adult and adult years. In most communities, no more than a few percent of adults age 18 and over are currently receiving any kind of formal Jewish education. This includes study groups, private tutors, or any other classroom training. Formal Jewish education, therefore, is primarily a child-centered activity focusing on children ages 6-13, and even more specifically on those who are ages 10-13.

The data also reveal some interesting patterns about which subgroups of Jews are either currently enrolled in Jewish education or have ever received any Jewish education. The "gender gap" in Jewish education has almost disappeared. Currently, Jewish girls are as likely to receive some formal Jewish education or to be currently enrolled in Jewish education as boys. This pattern has changed substantially over the past generation. In prior generations, boys were far more likely to receive formal Jewish education than girls. This is especially true when examining Jewish education patterns by age. Jewish women over the age of 65 are much less likely to have received formal Jewish education than their male counterparts. With each successive age group, the "gender gap" tends to lessen. The growth of female involvement in formal Jewish education is one of the most important trends revealed in the demographic research.

Denomination

Denomination has a key influence in many areas of Jewish education. Those who identify themselves as Orthodox and Conservative are far more likely to have received a Jewish education than those who identify themselves as Reform or "Just Jewish." Furthermore, those who identify themselves as Orthodox are much more likely to have their children currently enrolled in Jewish education. Denomination also influences the intensity of Jewish education. Those who are Orthodox or Conservative are more likely to have more years of Jewish education and to have more hours per week than those who identify themselves as Reform and "Just Jewish." Orthodox Jews are also more likely to have their children enrolled in Jewish day schools than other denominations. Gender differences appear in who receives and who does not receive a Jewish education. These are seen primarily for Jews over the age of 65, where Jewish men were far more likely to have received a formal Jewish education than Jewish women. Currently, Jewish girls are about as likely as Jewish boys to receive some formal Jewish education.

Geography

Region also plays a role in both whether Jewish education is received at all and if so, how intensive it is. Jews in the West and Southwest are far less likely to have received a Jewish education or to have children currently enrolled than households in the Northeast and Midwest. In communities like San Francisco, Los Angeles and Phoenix, Jewish children are less likely to be receiving a Jewish education than those in other regions. This trend is of particular importance since increasing proportions of Jews now reside in the West and Southwest, and these trends are projected to continue. City size seems to play a smaller role. Jews in some large communities such as Baltimore have relatively high levels of children enrolling in formal Jewish education, while enrollment levels in Los Angeles tend to be lower. Again, these trends reveal regional influences more than urban size. It is difficult to assess the effect in very small Jewish communities because data for communities of under 10,000 are relatively scarce. Therefore, most of the comparisons are between Jewish populations of 10,000 and more, where the effects of urban size vary greatly.

Location within an urban area also has some influence. Those who live on the geographic periphery of dense Jewish neighborhoods are less likely to have their children enrolled in formal Jewish education than those who live in densely Jewish areas. Geographic location is, of course, linked with other factors such as membership in Jewish organizations, belonging to a synagogue, and levels of Jewish identity. Nevertheless, the further a Jewish household is from a Jewish neighborhood, the less likely it is that children will receive a Jewish education.

Synagogue Membership

Synagogue membership is also a key determinant of whether or not children receive a formal Jewish education. Those who belong to a synagogue are far more likely to have their children enrolled in formal Jewish education than those who do not belong to a synagogue. Synagogue membership is also closely linked to contributions to Jewish philanthropy, support for Israel, ritual observance, and other elements of Jewish identity and participation. It therefore follows that the proclivity to enroll one's children in Jewish education is also connected to synagogue membership. Furthermore, the desire to have a formal Jewish education for one's children is often listed as the primary reason for people choosing to belong or not to belong to a synagogue. Therefore, it would logically follow that Jewish education enrollment is higher among synagogue members. It should also be pointed out that this phenomenon works in reverse. One of the chief reasons that individuals give for not belonging to a synagogue is that formal Jewish education for their children has ended. Thus, when looking at Jewish education patterns, synagogue membership is closely interrelated with enrollment patterns.

Intermarriage

Intermarriage is also closely linked to Jewish education patterns. Children in households with two born Jewish parents, or with a Jewish spouse and a converted Jew, are far more likely to have their children enrolled in formal Jewish education than mixed marrieds. Indeed, no other factor seems to affect enrollment levels in Jewish education as much as intermarriage. In some communities, those with converted spouses are even more likely than those with two in-married spouses to have their children receive a formal Jewish education. Perhaps no trend in Jewish life has more import for the Jewish community than this finding. Rates of intermarriage have been climbing in the United States for the past forty years. In many Jewish communities rates of intermarriage exceed 50%. They are highest in the West and Southwest. As larger proportions of the Jewish population consist of intermarried couples, the likelihood that growing proportions of Jewish children will not receive a formal Jewish education increases.

Many of the factors discussed above are interrelated. For example, those who identify themselves as "Just Jewish" are more likely to be intermarried. Those who live on the geographic periphery are more likely to identify themselves as Reform or "Just Jewish." Formal Jewish education, then, is one of many factors tied to others that define a stronger Jewish identity as opposed to those factors which tend to weaken Jewish identity and communal participation.

Day Schools

Recent studies have gathered more information about Jewish day schools. The studies indicate that there has been a growing demand for day schools as measured by levels of enrollment and the proportion of children receiving a day school education. A number of studies have also asked whether or not parents who do not currently have their children enrolled in a Jewish day school would consider doing so. Relatively high proportions, anywhere between 15-30%, said that they would consider doing so. However, the vast majority of those who answered this question affirmatively indicated that they were far more interested in a Conservative or Reform day school than an Orthodox day school. However, translating this interest into actual enrollment would be quite difficult.

Costs

In some communities the respondents were asked how much they would be willing to pay for a Jewish day school education. High proportions of those who answered were willing to pay either nothing or less than $1000 per year. Interest versus actual likelihood that they would send their children to a day school, given the cost consideration, are quite different.

Cost factors show up in other dimensions of these studies of Jewish education. A number of surveys have asked why children are not currently enrolled in formal Jewish education. Some individuals indicate that they are not religious, or that they cannot find religious education that they like, but cost factors are also mentioned. Some Jews do not send their children to receive a Jewish education because they either cannot afford it or feel that they cannot afford it. For those who genuinely cannot afford a formal Jewish education for their children, it is often noted by synagogues, Jewish Community Centers, and other Jewish institutions that subsidies are available to those who are in need. The surveys also reveal that a significant proportion of Jews are unwilling to ask for those subsidies because they are embarrassing or humiliating. Therefore, some individuals choose not to belong to a synagogue or have their children receive a Jewish education because they are too embarrassed by the screening procedures to determine need.

Most Jews, however, can afford a Jewish education for their children, including some people who say that it is too expensive. Given their consumer choices, some believe that expenditures for Jewish education are not warranted. Among all the choices that they make about how they will spend or not spend their resources, Jewish education is perceived to be of less value than other expenditures.

Adults

As indicated before, very low proportions of adults age 18 and over are enrolled in any form of formal Jewish education. This includes programs at synagogues, Jewish Community Centers, and other continuing education classes. Yet a number of studies indicate that adult Jews say that they are interested in attending Jewish education classes some time in the future. Translating this potential interest into actual enrollment, as in the case of day schools, is one of the key challenges for the Jewish community. The proclivity to enroll in adult Jewish education is revealed in the studies, yet most individuals do not act upon it. Other studies have shown that lack of knowledge of programs that are available, location, and cost are key deterrents to participation in a wide variety of programs in the Jewish community. Extrapolating from these data, we can conclude that many Jews are unaware of what adult education programs are available. Convenience is an issue, as well as cost. Those who belong to synagogues are more likely to be aware of Jewish education programs for adults than those who do not belong to synagogues as are those who belong to other Jewish organizations. Given the high proportions of Jews who do not have current affiliations with synagogues or Jewish organizations, and an even smaller proportion who are active in these organizations, it is not surprising that many Jews are likely to be unaware of the Jewish education programs that are available to them.

Informal Jewish Education

The demographic research has also asked about whether or not children and adults have been enrolled or are currently enrolled in informal Jewish education. Informal Jewish education includes camping experiences, youth groups, trips to Israel, and other programs as well. Lower proportions of Jewish children have been involved in informal Jewish education experiences and, as with formal Jewish education, the proportion decreases precipitously after bar/bat mitzvah age. Those who tend to enroll in formal Jewish education also have informal Jewish education experiences and vice-versa. There are relatively small proportions of Jews who receive only informal Jewish education experiences and not formal Jewish education experiences also. It may be, with the growing proportion of intermarried couples, that those who receive only informal Jewish education will increase. However, currently these types of Jewish education are mutually reinforcing, with children who receive one likely to receive both, and those who do not receive one unlikely to receive the other. There is no information about whether one receives a formal Jewish education leading to an informal Jewish education, or vice-versa. It is likely that participation works in both directions.

Quality and Curriculum

A number of studies have explored how parents and members of the community in general view the quality of their children's Jewish education and their own Jewish education, and how they would compare the quality of their children's Jewish education with that of their own Jewish education. In most communities, a large majority of those who are asked say that the quality of their children's education is either excellent or good, with a higher proportion saying that the quality is good. Relatively small proportions say that the quality is fair or poor, with very small proportions saying that the quality is poor. It is difficult to assess exactly what these evaluations mean. Some measures indicate that the ranking of good is more likely to signify average or acceptable than high quality. It may also be that levels of expectation are relatively low and therefore the rankings are relatively high. It may also be that the quality of Jewish education is actually quite high in the view of both parents and community members in general. When asked to compare the quality of their own Jewish education to that of their children's Jewish education, most individuals are likely to say that the quality of their children's education is either the same as or better than their own. Relatively low proportions will say that the quality of their children's Jewish education is worse than their own. Therefore, it may be concluded that many Jews believe that the quality of Jewish education has been improving since they were enrolled.

The issue of curriculum has been explored in a number of studies. Respondents are asked what they would like to see taught in their children's Jewish education and what are the most important elements of their children's Jewish education. A wide range of subjects is desired. These include teaching about Jewish holidays, ritual practice, Jewish values and ethics, the Holocaust, and Israel. Teaching about God is also very important. Teaching Hebrew, while considered important by a majority of those who respond, is considerably less important than other subjects. Denomination plays a role in curriculum requirements as well. Those who identify themselves as Reform and "Just Jewish" are far less likely to think that teaching Hebrew is very important than those who identify themselves as Orthodox or Conservative. Teaching a strong Jewish identity is considered very important by the vast majority of Jews and by all denominations and other subgroups as well. Indeed, some studies have shown that many believe that the primary purpose of Jewish education is to build a strong Jewish identity. It is unclear, however, whether or not the majority of parents actually believe that this goal is being accomplished. Evaluation of Jewish education may rest more on opinions of the quality of the teaching staff or the kinds of curricula that are being used as opposed to the achievement of what is considered to be the most important goal, the preservation of Jewish identity. Thus, while many rate the quality of their children's education as excellent or good, and many indicate that the primary purpose of Jewish education is to preserve Jewish identity, it is unclear whether or not Jews are satisfied with the outcome of Jewish education in this regard.

Recap

In sum, the recent studies indicate that most Jews receive some Jewish education in their lifetimes. The levels of intensity vary a great deal. Boys are still slightly more likely to receive some Jewish education than girls, although the gender gap has closed almost completely in the last generation. The proportion of Jews who receive Jewish education drops precipitously after bar/bat mitzvah age and few young adults or older adults are enrolled in any form of formal Jewish education. Individuals indicate that they are interested in formal Jewish education, but for a variety of reasons this interest is not translated into actual attendance.

The amount of Jewish education that individuals receive varies a great deal by denomination, with those who are Orthodox and Conservative much more likely to get both more years and more hours of Jewish education than those who identify themselves as Reform or "Just Jewish." Orthodox and Conservative Jews are more likely to attend a Jewish day school. Geography also has some influence, with Jews in the West and Southwest less likely to be enrolled in formal Jewish education. Synagogue attendance and intermarriage are also factors that affect who receives a Jewish education and how much.

Jews desire a wide range of subjects in the Jewish education curricula that are available, but are least likely to be concerned with teaching Hebrew, although a majority consider it important. The quality of Jewish education is generally ranked as good or excellent, while the purpose, Jewish education, is seen largely as a vehicle to insure Jewish continuity.

The Future From a Demographer's Perspective

These are some of the issues that are known to exist in contemporary Jewish education. Yet other areas remain largely unexplored, and other questions need to be raised. There has been little study that shows the systematic linkages between Jewish identity and Jewish education. The best combination of formal and informal Jewish education to strengthen Jewish identity is also relatively unstudied. The kinds of programs that are required to increase interest in Jewish education, how to promote Jewish education, and how individuals find out about Jewish education are just some of the issues that require further study.

The Jewish education system costs hundreds of millions of dollars each year in the United States. Providing Jewish education is a key function of synagogues, federations, Jewish community centers, and a wide variety of other Jewish organizations. Given the central role that Jewish education is seen to play in the preservation of Jewish identity and the vital elements of Jewish education as a preventative of assimilation in the Jewish community, the necessity to develop a comprehensive research and evaluation agenda grows. If the Jewish community is to accomplish its goals, group cohesiveness and continuity, then the expenditures in Jewish education must be targeted more carefully. This can be done by utilizing more carefully designed and executed research evaluation. Developing such an agenda can help guide policymakers in the Jewish education field. Knowing that most Jews get some Jewish education leads to other questions about how to foster a strong Jewish identity through these Jewish educational experiences. We can also begin to target those groups that are less likely to receive a Jewish education, including mixed marrieds and older adults. Research may lead to a reexamination of the assumptions upon which the Jewish education system operates. We now know that universal Jewish education in itself cannot be a goal. Content, quality and outcome are most important. If Jewish education is really a primary means to preserve Jewish continuity, then much more serious attention must be paid to understanding the nature of Jewish education and its impact upon Jewish life.

Bibliography

JEWISH COMMUNITY POPULATION STUDIES (available through local federations)

Allied Jewish Federation of Denver.(1981). *The Denver Jewish Population Study.* Denver, CO.

Goldscheider, C. and Goldstein, S. (1988). *The Jewish Community of Rhode Island: A Social and Demographic Study.* Providence, RI.

Israel, S.(1987). *Boston's Jewish Community: The 1985 Demographic Study.* Boston, MA.

Phillips, B.A. and Aron, W.S.(1984). *The Greater Phoenix Jewish Population Study.* Phoenix, AZ.

Phillips, B.A. (1984). *The Milwaukee Jewish Population Study.* Milwaukee, WI.

Population Research Committee. (1981). *Survey of Cleveland's Jewish Population.* Cleveland, OH.

Sheskin, I.M. (1987). *The Jewish Federation of Palm Beach County Demographic Study.* Palm Beach, FL.

Tobin, G.A. and Sassler,S. (1988). *A Population Study of the Greater New Orleans Jewish Community.* New Orleans, LA.

Tobin, G.A. and Fishman, S.B.(1987). *Jewish Population Study of Greater Rochester.* Rochester, NY.

Tobin, G.A. and Sassler, S. (1988). *Bay Area Jewish Community Study.* Bay Area Jewish Federations and Cohen Center for Modern Jewish Study, San Francisco, CA.

Highlights

* Depending on the community, between 60% and 90% of North American Jewish children (pre-bar/bat mitzvah) are currently studying in a formal setting—but there is wide variation in terms of hours and years.
* After bar/bat mitzvah, the numbers of students drop precipitously. By age 18, only a few percent remain enrolled.
* Girls and boys are equally likely to receive a Jewish education. The gender gap has all but disappeared.
* Those who identify as Orthodox or Conservative are far more likely to receive a Jewish education than those who identify as Reform or "Just Jewish". They will also be more likely to study more hours each week and for more years.
* Those living in the West and Southwest are less likely to receive a Jewish education than those who live in other parts of the United States.
* The farther a Jewish household is from a "Jewish neighborhood", the less likely it is that the children will receive a Jewish education.
* Synagogue membership is linked to enrollment of a child in formal Jewish education, contributions to Jewish philanthropy, support for Israel, ritual observance, and other elements of Jewish life and participation.
* Children in households with two born-Jewish parents, or with one spouse who was born Jewish and one who is a converted Jew, are far more likely to be enrolled in formal Jewish education than the children of mixed marrieds.
* Cost remains a primary factor in the choice by parents to pursue formal Jewish education—for both supplementary and day schools.
* Adults are by and large unaware of the existence of Jewish educational programs for themselves.

The Larger Context

Descriptions of the Jewish educational community which are drawn from general population studies are potentially powerful statements. As a matter of fact, we often tend to rely heavily on these descriptions—almost as if they hold a magic power to predict the future. It is all too easy to forget that they are numbers which, while somewhat descriptive of a population, tell only a part of the "truth". Also, it is we who choose to interpret these pieces of information in a number of different ways: sometimes, to bolster our case; at other times, to diminish the case of another. In short, we use these "facts" to confirm or deny our own conventional wisdom—what we really believe. The statements presented by Dr. Tobin represent current descriptions of our populations—not prescriptions. At most, they may tell us where we stand now and only hint at the future. Greater care and understanding of how descriptive statistics work should humble our reliance on the ultimate power of these numbers to predict future behaviors of our planning. We will need to avoid letting descriptive statistics alone guide our policies. It will also be interesting to compare this research with the recently released *1990 National Jewish Population Survey.*

What We Know About...
Early Childhood Education

Ruth Pinkenson Feldman

Jewish Early Childhood Education has experienced unprecedented growth over the last decade. Virtually every type of program under the auspices of the Jewish community—synagogue nursery schools, Jewish Community Centers, day care sponsored by Jewish Federations—has expanded. Not only has the enrollment climbed markedly, but schools have expanded the number of classes, extended the hours of the program, and increased the age span of the children served. Dr. Ruth Pinkenson Feldman, who is the Early Childhood Consultant at the Auerbach Central Agency for Jewish Education in Greater Philadelphia, charts the history of early childhood education efforts, examines the current crisis and posits strategies for moving into the 21st century.

The Early Days

PRIOR TO 1980, MOST JEWISH EARLY CHILDHOOD EDUCATION OCCURRED IN THE SYNAGOGUE NURSERY schools—usually a few classes serving mostly 3- and 4-year-old children from 9 a.m. until noon. Most such schools were staffed by teachers who were certified in Early Childhood Education with Bacherlor's and Master's degrees, and others without degrees who may have enjoyed being parents in the program and later joined the staff. Many of these programs had "teacher-directors;" that is, one teacher who had the designated responsibility of registering new families and ordering supplies and materials. These nursery schools often retained the same teachers for many years.

The goals of these early programs were the socialization of young children coupled with meeting their intellectual needs and developing a positive Jewish identity.

The 1990's

As we begin the decade of the 90's, the status and scope of Jewish early childhood education has changed radically. Would that we could claim that the enormous boom in enrollment is due to our success as Jewish educators. However, as we know well, the increased numbers reflect the "baby boomlet" in the general and Jewish population. It is essentially the effect of the baby boom generation having children of its own, combined with the impact of the women's movement. Jewish women are among the most highly educated in the U.S. and are likely to postpone childbearing. When they do have children, they tend to continue their careers (Monson, 1987). According to surveys across the country, when given the option, Jewish parents prefer programs for their young children which are under Jewish auspices (Fishman, 1987). However, where these programs do not exist or where waiting lists are long, parents will enroll their children in nonsectarian or even church-related programs.

Programs which used to serve 3- and 4-year-old children now offer an array of educational programs for children from 18 months through six years, offering everything from part-time "Mommy and Me" programs of two hours a week to extended programs open from 8:00 a.m. until 3:00 p.m., with some open until 6:00 p.m. In fact, the greatest demand is for programs for infants and toddlers.

It is now not uncommon to hear of synagogue nursery schools or Jewish Community Centers boasting early childhood programs averaging 250 children (Livingston, 1989). Many schools have well over ten classrooms and almost fifty people on the staff made up of professional teachers with master's degrees, assistants with BA's and aides without certification. It is also not uncommon (outside of New York) to find many programs with few if any teachers whose backgrounds reflect the same ethno-religious tradition we are trying to teach. Not only are we finding it increasingly difficult to find teachers, but we are forced to admit that the rise in enrollment has not been matched by a rise in the development of appropriate Jewish curriculum materials (Feinberg, 1987).

Jewish Identity and Practice of Parents

In my own experience as a director of a synagogue-based day care program, parents were enthused and involved along with their children. I explored the impact of the (Jewish) day care experience on parental Jewish identity in a study for my doctoral dissertation. The study compared Jewish parents who enrolled their children in child care programs under Jewish auspices with those who enrolled their children in nonsectarian programs. The findings were significant for several important measures of Jewish identity. The study showed that the parents of the children enrolled in the programs sponsored by the Jewish community increased the number of holidays they celebrated, increased rituals observed, reported lighting Shabbat candles and reciting Kiddush, increased the number of new Jewish friendships, became more aware of the Jewish calendar and told of a desire to learn more about Judaism. Conversely, the Jewish families involved with nonsectarian child care reported a decrease in the number of holidays observed and felt less involved Jewishly.

It is important to note that the only measure of Jewish identity of the parents involved with Jewish child care which was not increased was that of synagogue membership. Statistical analysis showed that the majority of people who said they would join a synagogue if they could afford it, indeed had low incomes or had middle incomes which were reduced to low incomes after their child care costs were deducted (Pinkenson, 1987).

A similar study by Ruth Ravid and Marvell Ginsburg, "The Relationship Between Jewish Early Childhood Education and Family Jewish Practice," indicated that there was significant change as measured on scales of Holiday Celebration and Home Content, particularly the celebration of Shabbat as observed in the nursery school itself. The study concluded that "an early childhood Jewish program which emphasized parent involvement, is associated with a significant positive change in the families' Jewish Practice" (Ravid and Ginsburg, 1989).

While the findings from these studies should encourage us, major obstacles are impeding our chances to dramatically affect the Jewish identity level of families with young children. While we have shown the potential for programs impacting positively on the parents, we are seeing more and more cases where people other than the parent (e.g., au pairs, housekeepers) are transporting children to and from early childhood programs. Who will the "adult" be who participates as the "parent" in the program? More important, just as we have been able to demonstrate a positive impact on Jewish identification of families of children in Jewish day care settings, nursery schools, and kindergartens, we are finding it more difficult than ever to attract competent (Jewish) teachers and to develop and disseminate age-appropriate Jewish content curriculum (Ginsburg, 1989).

Sources of the Crisis

The current crisis in Jewish early childhood education is the product of the deteriorating economy, the national shortage of and demand for child care services, and the shortage of professional early childhood educators who also share a commitment to the Jewish traditions and values we want to teach in our schools. The current increase in the growth of programs in early childhood Jewish education has created a gross imbalance between the demand for Jewish education for young children (and their families) and our ability to adequately staff these programs. In many communities throughout the U.S., it is not uncommon for the director of a program to be the only person, or one of a very few, on the staff of a (Jewish) early childhood program who is Jewish!

Trying to balance the size and scope of programs in early childhood Jewish education with our inability to adequately staff these programs forces us to focus on what we are really trying to achieve. We must ask ourselves how seriously we think about the Jewish part of our educational mandate. We must ask ourselves what we are trying to accomplish with young children and their families. Are we trying to increase synagogue or Jewish Community Center memberships at the expense of quality programming? Are we increasing the profit margin in early childhood programs by registering more children than can legitimately be cared for? Are some of our schools making a profit from the early childhood program because the salaries of the nursery school teachers are at times only a fifth of the salary of the Hebrew school teachers within the same synagogue?

If the answer to any of the above questions is even a "qualified maybe," we need to act immediately to provide a legitimate response to the parents' expressed interest in a Jewish education program for their children. Finally, when early childhood programs are administered under Jewish auspices and have no one on the staff with a Jewish background, to whom are they accountable?

A Four-Part Strategy

Developing a solution will require the cooperative efforts of leaders of both the lay and professional communities, as well as recognition of the ways in which the general economy is affecting the need for increased services to families with young children. Competing forces from the public and private sector which are siphoning off many of our most capable teachers must also be faced.

The following four-part strategy can become a means to realize the tremendous potential for success with the large numbers of families who are drawn to the Jewish community for the education of very young children.

1. *Conceptually, Jewish early childhood programs should be changed to Jewish Family Resource Centers where the entire family is viewed as an integral part of the educational environment.* In this ecological approach, teachers, parents, children, rabbis, Jewish communal professionals and lay leaders are all viewed as participants and are equally committed to the education of all the members of the Jewish community.

   Parents, for example, need to be more than "visitors" to early childhood programs. They need to learn on their own level as well as vicariously through their children. They need to socialize with other parents, to celebrate Jewish holidays as a family, to take a leadership role in family religious celebrations, and to be given opportunities to learn at their own pace. The enrollment of a child in a Jewish early childhood education program may be a family's first opportunity to enter the organized Jewish community.

2. *Fiscal responsibility must shift to include a third party (federations, synagogues, Jewish Community Centers) in order to supplement the tuition base.* Improving the quality of Jewish education for our youngest children must be tied to a structural change in the way we view financial allocations. Tuition must, of course, rest primarily on the parents. But, if we share a commitment to the Jewish education of all our children, the provision of scholarships should be shared by the community at large and not only by the other parents in the programs. The financial needs of families in relation to their combined costs of participation in the Jewish community ought to be examined. For instance, does a family's need for full-time child care preclude their membership in a synagogue? If so, which institutions, or departments within an institution, should be subsidized? In families with two or more children, if choices have to be made between Jewish child care, day school and synagogue membership, where should the subsidy come from? Ideally, a community mechanism should be established to support families involved in a variety of programs in the Jewish community.

3. *A mechanism must be developed for the training of teachers, directors, consultants and family educators capable of creating an optimal Jewish learning environment.* The greatest obstacle we have in reaching the very real potential for success is our current inability to attract and retain a cadre of professional educators who hold not only professional early childhood certification but who share a knowledge and commitment to Judaism, its values and traditions.

In areas around the country where early childhood professionals without a Jewish background are employed, the support of other local Jewish educators, rabbis, and lay people should be enlisted. This calls for a training model which takes the teacher's own spiritual development as one of the goals of the teacher training program. A training model must include understanding of child development and age-appropriate curriculum, and must also build on a teacher's commitment and openness to exploring an understanding of Judaism as an adult.

4. *The curriculum must do justice to actualizing the potential of each child, while conveying a Judaism which is vibrant and real.* To date, no formal established criteria have been promoted as standard for the Jewish content of early childhood programs. However, a recent doctoral dissertation took a comprehensive and intensive look into the areas of curriculum in Jewish early childhood programs (Feinberg, 1987). Feinberg's study attempted to determine the importance to teachers in Orthodox, Reform and Conservative Jewish schools of seven curriculum areas: Bible, Jewish way of life, Hebrew language, Israel, Jewish peoplehood, faith in God and Jewish values and attitudes. Her study clearly indicated that each of the seven curriculum areas was consistently rated highest by Orthodox teachers, lowest by Reform teachers and midway between by the Conservative teachers. Orthodox teachers showed the least difference in age-related ratings and felt that each area was important regardless of the age of the child. Finally, the curriculum area "Jewish way of life" and "Jewish values and attitudes" were rated highest by most teachers and Hebrew language rated the lowest across all religious denominations (Feinberg, 1987).

The Secular World

The secular world abounds with recent research in the fields of both child development and early childhood education (Seefeldt, 1987). The National Association for the Education of Young Children has published guidelines for appropriate early childhood education (NAEYC, 1984). There are definite theoretical approaches reflective of philosophies of education and development. To name but a few, the works of Piaget have inspired schools based on his theory of intellectual development (Lavatelli, 1970); the Montessori approach is based on the writings of Maria Montessori on self-directed, sensory-based learning (Montessori, 1964); the Bank Street approach, representing what is frequently referred to as the "developmental-interractive approach," based on the combined theories of John Dewey, Erik Erikson and others. Yet in the world of Jewish early education we have seen few systematic attempts to combine theoretical approaches to early education and child development with the goals of Jewish education. There ought to be funding for educational research into approaches to educating the "whole child" in environments which see Jewish identity and the religious/spiritual aspects of development as but one of the many dimensions of development (e.g., intellectual, personal-social, emotional, and physical) which all must be supported for each child to actualize his/her potential.

The Future

The worst case caricature of early childhood Jewish education as "arts and crafts Judaism" is definitely changing, in part through the efforts of the members of the newly formed National Association of Jewish Early Childhood Specialists. Programs in colleges should be expanded to offer specialization in Early Childhood Jewish Education which meet state requirements for educational certification. Subsidies in the form of scholarships, fellowships, and salary incentives should be made available to allow maximum participation in the programs being offered. In addition, opportunities must be provided for teachers outside of large cities to learn and train in this burgeoning field.

Research is urgently needed to identify the most appropriate methodology and the developmental abilities necessary for young children to grasp the content of Bible study, values, attitudes, and other Jewish identity variables. I strongly recommend research on the broader issue of teaching a Judaic curriculum to children from homes which reflect the full spectrum of religious practice, affiliation, and commitment.

Future research might include the effect of teachers' secular background in early childhood education, as well as the influence of their Jewish knowledge and background on a) their choice of curriculum content; and b) the quality and style of their teaching.

The Jewish people have repeatedly been referred to as the "people of the book". The book is the Torah, and it is not made of construction paper. The goal is to teach a Judaism which young children can understand and participate in, but which is not only for children. To offer but one brief example, both children and their parents should grasp the idea that the holiday of Purim is not only an opportunity for a costume party, but an occasion on which to perform the mitzvot of hearing the Megillah and giving gifts to friends and to the poor.

Our challenge is to touch the Jewish 'neshama' in each child and to teach in such a way that the Judaism a child encounters is not one you grow out of when you reach first grade, but a Judaism you grow into for the rest of your life!

Bibliography

Feinberg, M.P. (1987). *Placement of Sectarian Content for Jewish Nursery Schools and Kindergartens in the United States.* Unpublished doctoral dissertation, University of Maryland, Baltimore.

Feldman, R. P. (1988). The Impact of Jewish Day Care on Parent Jewish Identity. Keynote Address, *Conference on Jewish Day Care.* New York: American Jewish Committee, Institute of Human Relations.

Fishman, S. B. (1987). *Learning About Learning: Insights on Contemporary Jewish Education From Jewish Population Studies.* Waltham, MA.: Brandeis University.

Ginsburg, M. (1989, October). Whither Early Childhood Jewish Education? *Pedagogic Reporter, 40*(2).

Kahn, A. J. and Kammerman, S. (1987). *Child Care: Facing The Hard Choices.* Dover, MA.: Auburn House Publishing Company.

Lavatelli, C.S. (1970). *Piaget's Theory Applied to an Early Childhood Curriculum.* Boston: Center for Media Development.

Livingston, N. (1989, Fall). How is the Preschool Doing in the JEWISH COMMUNITY CENTER? A Ten Year Update. *Journal of Jewish Communal Services, 66*(1).

Monson, R. G. (1987). *Jewish Women on the Way Up.* New York: American Jewish Committee.

Monson, R. G. and Feldman, R.P. (forthcoming). The Cost of Living Jewishly. *Journal of Jewish Communal Service.*

Montessori, M. (1964). *The Montessori Method.* New York:Schocken Books.

Neitlich, C. (1986). ECE Directors' Salary Profile. *The Annual Meeting of the Conference of Jewish Communal Service.* Baltimore, MD.

Pinkenson, R. (1987). *The Impact of the Jewish Day Care Experience on Parental Jewish Identity.* Unpublished doctoral dissertation, Temple University, Philadelphia.

Ravid, R. and Ginsburg, M. (1988). *The Relationship Between Jewish Early Childhood Education and Family Jewish Practices: Phase II.* Chicago: Board of Jewish Education.

Seefeldt, C. (1987). *The Early Childhood Curriculum, A Review of Current Research.* New York: Teachers College Press.

Highlights

* Goals of early early childhood programs have been the socialization of young children coupled with meeting their intellectual needs and developing a positive Jewish identity.
* Jewish parents prefer programs for their young children which are under Jewish auspices.
* Outside New York, it is not uncommon to find many programs where few if any teachers have backgrounds reflecting the same ethno-religious tradition we are trying to teach.
* A Jewish early childhood program, which emphasizes parent involvement, is associated with a significant positive change in the families' Jewish practice.
* It is more difficult than ever to attract competent Jewish teachers and to develop and disseminate age-appropriate Jewish content curriculum.
* There are few systematic attempts to combine theoretic approaches to early education and child development with the goals of Jewish education.

The Larger Context

While the four-point strategy suggested by Dr. Feldman is predicated on the assumption of the centrality of the educational influence on the lives of these young students, the focus is on adults (parents) rather than children. This wholistic approach to education rather than one based on age segmentation may be a more productive way to view the larger enterprise of Jewish education.

What We Know About...Youth Programming

H.A. Alexander and Ian Russ[1]

It is commonly assumed that Jewish Youth Programs such as summer camps, youth groups, and Israel experiences can influence the extent to which participants will eventually identify with the Jewish community by affiliating with its religious or communal institutions. This chapter, written by Dr. Hanan A. Alexander, Dean of Academic Affairs and Associate Professor of Philosophy and Education at the University of Judaism, and Dr. Ian Russ, Saul E. White Visiting Professor in the Department of Psychology, also at the University of Judaism, examines psychological, educational, and evaluation research to discern those characteristics of programs that can accomplish this end. The terms youth programming, nonformal, and informal education are used interchangeably.

The Psychology of Adolescent Development

MOST YOUTH PROGRAMS ADDRESS EIGHT- TO TWENTY-ONE-YEAR-OLDS—ADOLESCENCE AND THE YEARS that precede and follow it. Adolescence is an in-between time of life. Not yet having attained the obligations and responsibilities of adulthood, the adolescent often attempts to distance himself/herself from the perceived stigmas of childhood and dependence. Theories about emotional, social, and cognitive aspects of this process influenced our thinking about why some programs contribute successfully to the development of Jewish identity.

1. Emotional Development

There are two popular models for understanding the emotional dynamics of adolescence. Stanley Hall (1904) described the adolescent's dilemma and consequent inconsistent behavior as "Sturm und Drang" (storm and stress), a period of extreme crisis and turmoil. Offer and Offer (1975) report, however, that most people experience adolescence as a part of the continuity of growth from childhood to adulthood.

Erikson (1980) offers a second model of adolescence which is more appealing because it captures the dynamics of the adolescent experience. He sees each stage of development as a crisis between two polarities. Healthy resolution is defined by a person's ability to balance the issues of both poles. Adolescent development is viewed according to this model in terms of a tension between identity and role confusion. Identity includes a conscious effort to distinguish oneself from others, while role confusion (Erikson, 1963) or diffusion (Erikson, 1980) tugs at the adolescent to mold into surroundings and abandon a sense of distinction. This tension can result in uneven industriousness where some interests are pursued to excess, while other activities are abandoned totally. In some extreme situations, negativism develops (Erikson, 1980). When identity and role confusion are balanced, however, the individual develops a healthy sense of fidelity, "the ability to sustain loyalty freely" (Erikson, 1964). Fidelity is the backbone of identity because only one who is loyal can bind himself to social commitments.

According to this view, fostering identity involves providing an environment in which the youngster can express both independence and conformity. We can conclude, therefore, that the youth program that is successful at fostering Jewish identity will provide participants with opportunities to balance independence from parental authority with conformity to some Jewish society. This requires careful attention to the development of a semi-autonomous youth culture on the one hand and to behavior management and limit setting on the other.

2. Social Development

At times youth requires an extended moratorium from adult responsibilities to attain proper balance between these two Eriksonian poles. During this moratorium the adolescent becomes involved in accomplishing important tasks such as loosening ties with parents (Blos, 1979) or accepting adult sexuality. Conflicts arise resulting from increased expectations on the adolescent (Elder, 1968) and new roles that he or she may be asked to play (Thomas, 1968; Coleman, 1980). This can lead to dependence upon peers for emotional support and stability. Sociologists such as Coleman (1963) and Eisenstadt (1956) argue that adolescence is a culture unto itself with its own childhood. This, they claim, is a natural by-product of the individualistic orientation of modern industrial societies in which the family is replaced as the primary source of economic and social identity. More recent research has suggested, however, that for most youth there is little rebellion against society. In fact, on major issues of morality, political opinions, religious beliefs, and sexual attitudes, the divergence between adolescents and their parents is minimal (Douvan and Adelson, 1966; Fogelman, 1976).

The conflicts of adolescence may not produce a completely independent youth culture of the sort described by Coleman and Eisenstadt, but they do provide adolescents with common experiences that can lead to the development of less discrete peer cultures such as street gangs, clubs, youth groups, and school societies. These groups may vary with regard to their values and norms, but they do serve as aids in responding to the common experiences of adolescence. Like the adolescents who comprise them, these groups will sometimes rebel against adult authority and at other times welcome it. They can play a pivotal role, however, in the development of adult identity among participants.

It is likely, therefore, that successful informal educational programs attempt to influence the values of the peer cultures within their midst. One way of accomplishing this is through peer leadership. When the proclivities of peer leaders are developed and appropriate values among them are reinforced, the peer culture will tend to reflect the values of adult Jewish society more readily than when such leadership is not encouraged. Youngsters involved in such Judaically oriented peer cultures will become more likely to identify with the Jewish community as adults.

3. Cognitive Development

The development of cognitive skills plays an important role in the development of individual and social identity. At the beginning of the adolescent years, young people become able to think abstractly, hypothetically, and logically (Inhelder and Piaget, 1958). Suddenly, idealism is possible and fantasy takes on a new role. The adolescent is not yet burdened with the internalization of what society says is possible and impossible. This new-found ability allows many teenagers to discover creative solutions to social problems. It can also contribute to a new form of egocentrism (Elkind 1967; 1976; 1978). The teenager is not only preoccupied with his or her own expanding thoughts, but is also absorbed in the fantasy that others are preoccupied with his or her behavior as well.

To positively channel these tendencies, it is important for the successful youth program to espouse an ideology that expresses a certain amount of idealism. Such idealism calls upon the young person to give up some of his or her needs to serve some nobler cause. For this idealism to be placed in the service of the Jewish identity, commitments to the Jewish people or religion are in order.

Lessons of Educational Research

Historical, philosophical, and pedagogic sorts of educational inquiry can be instructive in understanding successful youth programming.

1. Historical Lessons

In 1896 a university student from Berlin began to organize hikes for high school pupils who were happy to leave the city streets to enjoy the open countryside. There they found freedom from the adult world of strict conventions, a chance to commune with nature, and the opportunity to experience a deep sense of camaraderie with their peers. From this nucleus developed the first youth movement—the Wandervogel or Rambling Folk. Its aim: to enable its members to wander the hillsides of the fatherland in order to gain a deeper appreciation of the German spirit. The movement spread rapidly and by 1913 gathered three thousand strong to declare that "the free German youth want to shape their own lives according to their own decisions, taking responsibility for themselves, and guided by their own inner truth" (Laquer, 1962; Becker, 1946; Schatzker, 1965). The German youth movement grew not only in strength but also in influence. It very quickly became the model for many of the programs that have come to characterize nonformal education such as scouting and religiously oriented youth groups (Alexander and Dorph, 1987).

Four aspects of the Wandervogel model continue to play a significant role in informal Jewish education: intensity, emotional impact, extensivity, and environment. A program is intensive to the extent that it packs a lot of activity into the time available. The activities involved can be as varied as hikes in the woods or discussions of ideology. They can involve physical as well as intellectual energies. However, they will generally provide the participants with many opportunities to get to know one another in different settings. From these acquaintances close friendships can emerge based on common experience.

Second, the emotional impact of programming is especially significant. Schatzker (1965) has pointed out that the Jewish youth movements that were influenced by the Wandervogel in the early decades of this century strove "to move the inner being of Jewish youth, to create internal exhilaration," through the use of powerful symbols that influenced attitudes. This sort of programming has the potential of creating what Maslow (1968) has called "peak experiences" which constitute both the end and the beginning of learning. These experiences involve momentary states that have far-reaching impact on the directions and meanings of our lives.

Third, extentsivity means that the successful Jewish youth program will not see itself merely as supplementary educational framework. Rather, it will strive to involve substantial portions of its participants' time. This may transpire through encampments of several days to several weeks during summers and other vacation periods; it may involve regular periodic activities during the school year; it may even encompass yearlong programs for intensive study.

Fourth, the environment in which programming takes place is likely to be significant. The Wandervogel "took to the hills" in order to escape the authoritarian environment in which its members lived. Through hiking and scouting activities, they were able to experience a sense of freedom and self-determination. It is this sense of ownership and control that we are expecting to find in the settings of successful youth programming. This may be found in a special classroom, in a summer camp, or in a clubhouse. Israel trips involve the quality in especially powerful ways because the state itself is a symbol of Jewish autonomy and self-determination.

2. Philosophical Lessons

It was John Dewey (1916) who observed that, although it is necessary for a culture to train youngsters to follow certain prescribed canons of behavior, it is also necessary that they be taught how to criticize the very values and traditions in which they are being instructed. Without this potential for criticism, informal education can become routinized and cultish. Successful programs for Jewish youth are likely, therefore, to provide opportunities for and instruction in criticism.

3. Pedagogic Lessons

In the epic study *The Dynamics of Groups at Work*, Herbert Thelen (1954) argued that "the needs of individuals cause them to participate in groups; and…that through experiences in the groups of the community, the individual develops and changes his patterns of needs."

In order to influence such patterns of needs, Thelen proposed several techniques to bring about change. These include developing opportunities for individuals within the group to become leaders, setting clear expectations of participants, seeing that the group members insist that their colleagues follow through on their commitments to the group, and communicating the purpose of the group clearly to others. The end result is a sense of common ownership of group activities. This sense of ownership can give adolescents a feeling of control over the Jewish society with which they affiliate. To promote identity, therefore, it can be useful for Jewish youth programs to employ techniques of group process such as these.

Evaluation Studies

There has been little research on informal Jewish educational programs. Two groups of studies, however, confirm our own intuitions. A recent study of educational programs in Israel (Hochstein, 1988) identified seven characteristics of "good programs;" that is, programs in which participants tended to be inspired by the Israel experience and to be willing to recommend the program to friends. Of these, four had to do with staffing. In short, the professional staffs of these programs were critical to their success. The staffs, the study contends, need to have knowledge of both the subjects they are to communicate and the populations with which they are to work. They need to be committed to the educational goals of the program, properly selected and trained, and have roles that are clearly defined. Though not surprising, this study confirms our inclinations that staffing is critical to the success of informal educational programs.

A second group of studies which focused on the Ramah camping movement (Lukinsky, 1969; Lerner, 1971; Farago, 1972; Dorph, 1976; Alexander, 1985) has been summarized by Alexander (1987). Among the findings of this summary is the suggestion that successful informal programs need to be embedded in a strong organizational structure that effectively coordinates a variety of activities in which participants are engaged. The organizational context of a program provides political support within the adult community, linking it both to funding sources and to the adult world into which the youngster is eventually to be integrated. It is reasonable to suppose therefore, that for Jewish youth programs to achieve their maximum impact they should be supported by strong lay organizational structures.

Summary

In sum, on the basis of psychological, educational, and evaluation research, the following qualities are likely to be characteristic of successful informal Jewish educational programs:

1. Youth programs that are successful at fostering Jewish identity will probably provide participants with opportunities to balance independence from parental authority with conformity to some Jewish society. This requires careful attention to the development of semi-autonomous youth cultures on one hand and to behavior management and limit setting on the other.

2. In all likelihood such programs will also attempt to influence the values of the peer culture by co-opting some of its most dynamic leaders.

3. It is important for successful youth programs to espouse an ideology that expresses a certain amount of idealism. Such idealism calls upon the young person to give up some of his or her own needs to serve some nobler cause. For this idealism to be placed in the service of Jewish identify, it should relate to the Jewish people or religion.

4. Successful programs are likely to pack a lot of activity into the time available.

5. They also attempt to have an emotional impact. These efforts should lead to close friendships among participants.

6. Successful programs probably demand substantial portions of participants' time. This may transpire through encampments of several days to several weeks during summers and other vacation periods; it may entail regular periodic activities during the school year; it may also encompass year long programs for intensive study.

7. The environment in which programming takes place is likely to be significant in successful youth programming, especially to the extent that participants come to feel a sense of attachment to or ownership of the setting in which it transpires.

8. Without the potential for criticism, informal education can become routinized and cultish. Successful programs, therefore, probably provide opportunities for and even informal instruction in criticism.

9. Good Jewish youth programs are likely to employ techniques of group process that foster a sense of ownership of the groups' activities on the part of participants.

10. Staffing is critical to the success of informal educational programs. The staff needs to be trained, knowledgeable, and committed to the goals of the program. In this sense, the staff needs to serve as effective role models of the values the program seeks to promote.

11. Good Jewish youth programs are supported by strong lay organizational structures.

Bibliography

Alexander, H. (1985). *The Qualitative Turn in Evaluation.* Unpublished doctoral dissertation, Stanford University, Palo Alto, CA.

Alexander, H. (1988). Ramah At Forty: Aspirations, Achievements, Challenges. In N. Cardin & D. Silverman, (Eds.), *The Seminary at 100.* New York: Jewish Theological Seminary.

Alexander, H., & Dorph, S. (1978). From Organization to Exhilaration. In S. Dorph (Ed.), *Issues at Irvine: A Sampler of Jewish Educational Thought and Practice.* Los Angeles: Coalition for Alternatives in Jewish Education.

Bandura, A. (1972). The Stormy Decade: Fact or Fiction: In Rogers, D. (Ed.), *Issues in Adolescent Psychology,* (2nd ed.), New York: Appelton-Century-Crofts.

Becker, H. (1946). *German Youth: Bond or Free.* London: Kegan, Paul, Trench, Traubner, & Co.

Blos, P. (1979). *The Adolescent Passage.* New York: International University Press.

Coleman, J.S. (1980). *The Nature of Adolescence.* New York: Metheune.

Coleman, J.S. (1963). *The Adolescent Society.* New York: Free Press.

Dewey, J. (1916). *Democracy and Education.* New York: Macmillian.

Dorph, S. (1976). *A Model For Jewish Education in America.* Unpublished doctoral dissertation. Teachers College, Columbia University, New York.

Douvan, E. & Adelson, J. (1966). *The Adolescent Experience.* New York: John Wiley.

Eisenstadt, S. (1956). *From Generation to Generation.* Glencoe, IL: The Free Press.

Elkind, D. (1976). *Child Development and Education.* New York: Oxford University Press.

Elkind, D. (1978). *A Sympathetic Understanding of the Child, (*2nd Ed.). Boston: Allyn and Bacon.

Erikson, E. (1963). *Childhood and Society,* 2nd Edition. New York: W. W. Norton.

Erikson, E. (1964). *Insight and Responsibility.* New York: W. W. Norton.

Erikson, E. (1980). *Identity and the Life Cycle.* New York: W. W. Norton.

Farago, U. (1972). *The Influence of a Jewish Summer Camp's Social Climate on the Campers' Identity.* Unpublished doctoral dissertation, Brandeis University, Waltham, MA.

Fogelman, K. (1976). *Britain's Sixteen-Year-Olds.* London: National Children's Bureau.

Hall, S. (1904). *Adolescence.* Englewood Cliffs, NJ: Prentice-Hall.

Hochstein, A. et al. (1988). *Educational Programs in Israel.* Jerusalem: Native Policy and Planning Consultants.

Inhelder, B. & Piaget, J. (1958). *The Growth of Logical Thinking; From Childhood to Adolescence.* New York: Basic Books.

Laquer, W. (1962). *Young Germany.* New York: Basic Books.

Lerner, S. (1970). Ramah and its Critics. *Conservative Judaism, 24*(5).

Lukinsky, J. (1969). *Teaching Responsibility: A Case Study In Curriculum Development.* Unpublished doctoral dissertation, Harvard University, Cambridge, MA.

Offer, D., & Offer, J.B. (1975). *From Teenage to Young Manhood: A Psychological Study.* New York: Basic Books.

Schatzker, C. (1965). *Jewish Youth Movements in Germany Between the Years 1913 and 1933.* Unpublished doctoral dissertation, The Hebrew University, Jerusalem.

Thelan, H. (1954). *The Dynamics of Groups at Work.* Chicago: University of Chicago Press.

Thomas, E. J. (1968). Role, theory, personality, and the individual. In Borgatta, E.F. and Lambert, W. (Eds.). *Handbook of Personality Theory and Research.* Chicago: Rand McNally.

Footnotes

[1]This study was funded by a grant from the Commission on the Jewish Future of Los Angeles of the Jewish Federation Council of Greater Los Angeles.

Highlights

Youth programs that are successful at fostering Jewish identity will:
*   provide participants with the opportunity to balance independence from parental authority with conformity to Jewish society
*   co-opt dynamic peer leaders
*   express idealism
*   pack a lot of activity into the time available
*   have emotional impact
*   demand substantial time of their participants
*   require attachment and ownership of the physical setting and program
*   employ techniques of group process
*   provide opportunities for criticism
*   select staff who are trained, knowledgeable and committed to the goals of the program
*   be supported by strong lay structures

The Larger Context

We usually believe that camps, youth groups and Israel experiences are among the most powerful tools in the formulation of positive Jewish identities. It is really surprising how little research there is which supports this assumption. If we really knew the degree to which this type of educational activity affected future identity, we would reconsider the separation of formal and non-formal education (as well as our well-established funding priorities) and turn to programs which integrated the two.

What We Know About...Adult Education

Betsy Dolgin Katz

All too often, Jewish education has been equated with learning by and for children. Dr. Katz, the Director of the Department of Reform Jewish Education for the Board of Jewish Education of Metropolitan Chicago and the North American Director of the Florence Melton Adult Mini-School, provides us with a view of adult Jewish learning. She shows how the new science of the teaching of adults (androgogy) is finding an increasingly important place in the Jewish community.

Growing Importance

ONE HUNDRED YEARS AGO AND MORE, A MAN WOULD APPROACH HIS REBBE AND SAY, "REBBE, DON'T YOU worry about my children. I'll take care of them. I can teach them. I want you to teach me." For decades of this century, the man and woman approaching their rabbi would say, "Rabbi, don't worry about me. Just take care of my children. Teach them." More recently there is a new type of exchange taking place. "Rabbi," the man and the woman say. "Teach my children and teach me too. I want to learn, and I want to help you teach my children and grandchildren."

The frequency of these dialogues is increasing. Even amidst the conflicting demands of modern society or, perhaps, because of these demands, Jewish learning remains a personal ideal. Studies of students enrolled in the Florence Melton Adult Mini-School, for example, have shown that on-going study can be rewarding and fulfilling and lead to increased involvement in Jewish life. For many adults, Jewish learning has ceased to be merely a leisure time activity. The existence of almost 1500 mini-school students who make a minimum of a two-year, 30 weeks per year commitment to study speaks to the seriousness with which some adults approach Jewish learning (Horenczyk, 1990).

Adult education is rising higher on the agenda of Jewish institutions. Programs of national meetings of organizations such as Union of American Hebrew Congregations, The Coalition for Advancement of Jewish Education, and The Association of Jewish Community Centers contain growing numbers of sessions on adult education. Jewish Educational Services of North America

(JESNA) convened a conference in Chicago in 1989 devoted to the subject, as was the Spring 1990 issue of the *Pedagogic Reporter*.

Organizations are offering opportunities for their members to study. Effective community leadership, lay and professional, comes from the ranks of well-educated Jews. An educated Jewish adult is best able to make decisions based on Jewish values that will shape the nature of our community, strengthen it, and insure our survival.

Diversity

The field of adult Jewish education can be characterized by the word "diversity." In an effort to meet the great variety of needs of individuals and groups, numerous educational models have emerged. Successful adult learning is frequently defined and shaped by the learners; consequently, goals, settings, design, content and strategies are as varied as those who learn. There are programs sponsored by community colleges, congregations, community centers, central agencies of Jewish education, and independent organizations. They are directed toward a variety of groups including leaders, parents, the elderly, professionals and entry-level Jewish learners. There are lectures, classes, retreats, workshops, support groups, and havurot. The variety is endless (Katz, 1990).

Unity

In spite of the diversity, there are unifying factors which characterize adult Jewish education. Adult Jewish education is nondegree, nonprofessional, lifelong learning that incorporates Jewish content. It should result in increased knowledge, involvement and/or effectiveness in Jewish life. Like all good adult education it must be educationally sound, consider social needs of the learner, and recognize and build upon the learner's experience and prior learning. The more closely what is learned is tied to the learners' life, the more effective the experience (Knowles, 1980). Good adult education takes place in a supportive environment that enhances individual confidence and self-esteem and is sensitive to difficulties experienced by some adult learners entering the adult education setting (Frankel, 1989).

In the adult education setting, the quality of the teacher is crucial. An excellent teacher will greatly increase the possibility of a positive learning experience; a poor teacher can destroy it. Adult learners are voluntary learners. It is unlikely that an adult confronted by a poor teacher will return to a formal class. Because adult education is rarely a full-time profession, there is a shortage of knowledgeable, highly qualified teachers, particularly in smaller communities. As the demand for adult learning increases, the shortage is becoming more pronounced. It should be noted, however, that much adult learning takes place without a teacher. Self-directed learning by intrinsically motivated adults is among the most common forms of adult education (Tough, 1978).

Because of the multi-faceted nature of our community, a unified philosophy of adult Jewish education cannot be content oriented. A general statement cannot be made as to what an educated Jew must know (Lipstadt, 1980). What is more useful to our broad field is a philosophy that addresses the continuity of the learning process, the continuing growth of knowledge and learning skills. The goal of Jewish learning should be conceived not so much as a product, but as a process of nurturing continuous growth and development.

A philosophy such as this encourages adult educational planners to approach their task with an eye to what would be systematic, comprehensive adult learning within their own community. One of the valid criticisms of many of our adult education programs is the lack of opportunity for a unified developmental learning experience. A philosophy that stresses the continuous nature of Jewish learning will lead to a curriculum plan that incorporates increasing depth of knowledge and self understanding, growth in intellectual sophistication through learning experiences that build upon one another.

The Needs

Adult learning is among the most rapidly developing fields in Jewish education. There is a resurgence of participation in adult Jewish learning. Opportunities for individuals to study are proliferating. Community leadership is not only becoming more involved in learning itself, but is choosing to invest dollars in expanding the old and developing new options on a community and national level. Professionals are developing structures and tools for meeting the growing community needs. As the paucity of research indicates, there is a serious need for planned, systematic development of the field.

Whether concerned with a local congregational program or a national educational project, planners need a philosophical framework for adult education as well as objective research on which to base their efforts. If there is to be a profession called "adult Jewish educator," we must begin to accumulate accurate information based on questions specific to adult Jewish education.

Suggestions for Further Research and Development

A. Dissemination

Means for disseminating information must be improved and expanded. We must publish more about adult Jewish education practice; not only the research, but the simple sharing of insights, solutions to problems and successful models. Theoreticians and practitioners should be encouraged to analyze and write about what they do. Although there have recently been local and national seminars and conferences on adult education, Jewish agencies should offer opportunities to exchange information and learn from each other. More conferences such as the 1989 conference on adult education sponsored by JESNA and more groups such as the CAJE Adult Education Network need to be organized. National and local consultants need to make themselves available to those who want to learn about adult education. More central agencies of Jewish education should include adult education on their agenda.

B. Personnel

Studies should be conducted to determine the need for and nature of the training of adult education personnel. Communities must be encouraged to produce trained adult education teachers. Institutions of higher learning must include courses to this end. Rabbis, family educators, and classroom teachers should all be trained as adult educators. Agencies must provide in-service courses and workshops to enhance the knowledge and skills of adult educators working in the field, and those institutions that provide summer teacher education programs should include the teaching of adults on their agenda. The responsibility must also include defining more clearly the qualities of the successful adult educator, and with this in mind, designing a curriculum for the training of adult Jewish educators. This could eventually lead to the accreditation or certification of these professionals.

C. Motivation

Research must be directed toward what motivates specific groups of adult Jewish learners to participate in adult education programs. Attention should be given to individual segments of our potential learning community. Programs such as the Wexner program for educating Federation leadership, Jewish Elderhostel, and the Florence Melton Adult Mini-school indicate that targeted efforts work. Although not advocating the elimination of the broad-based education offerings that presently exist, specific programs can attract new learners and meet specific needs of Jewish adults. Curriculum created for educating Russian immigrants, the intermarried, parents of bar/bat mitzvah age children, or the elderly can be helpful to the most skilled adult educator. Studies in adult education have shown that an adult's active involvement in learning is essential. New curriculum must incorporate modern technology and those teaching strategies that make the learner an active participant in the learning process.

D. Formats

Studies must be conducted to learn the impact of various forms of adult Jewish education on the learners. Do adults change as a result of learning experiences? How do they change? What factors determine how they change and the extent of the changes that take place? How are factors such as motivation, peer pressure, age, or background linked to what happens as a consequence of a learning experience?

E. Recruitment

Refinement and enrichment of adult education practice must be accompanied by new recruitment efforts. Program improvement is only one part of the growth of adult Jewish education. Attracting new students is an important part of the work of all practitioners involved in the field. Creating specific curriculum to meet individual needs can be one direction, but recruitment efforts might also include taking education to potential students. Jewish organizations should include a period of study at all meetings. Jewish professionals should be Jewish learners and should make demands on lay leaders and general membership alike to pursue Jewish study. Thought should be given to exploring other contexts for Jewish learning, such as adding Jewish components to special interest and support groups (Jewish LaMaze and Overeaters Anonymous), health clubs (Squash and Drash), or organizing cultural groups that perform Jewish music, read Jewish books, or present Jewish plays. Travel agents should add Jewish learning components to their tours.

Another means of enhancing participation in adult education would be a system for helping potential learners find the best opportunities among the confusing variety of offerings in a community. It could take the form of a counselor, a phone hotline, or a publication.

We should apply the best of marketing techniques to conduct needs assessments, create new markets, and produce the most attractive publicity pieces possible. Above and beyond all this, each individual must advocate for adult Jewish education and its importance and must take it upon him/herself to be a model of a learning Jew for others in the community.

F. Finances

If progress is to be made, we must provide the financial resources to insure that adult learning is conducted in the best way possible. Many of the efforts described above cost money. Researchers need to be supported; the organization of training programs can be costly; curriculum development is a time-consuming task that requires knowledge and skill; publications and conferences need financial support. There are individuals who have the insight, knowledge, and skills to do all that needs to be done. Our community, however, must decide that adult Jewish learning is a priority and demonstrate its conviction by providing the needed resources. Adult Jewish education is worth it. It can change lives and affect the future of our Jewish community.

Bibliography

American Jewish Committee. (1981, December). *A Consultation on Factors for Success in Adult Jewish Education.* New York.

Campbell, K. J. (1978). *Determinants of Participation in Jewish Adult Education.* Unpublished doctoral dissertation, University of Maryland.

Fishman, S. B. (1987). *Learning about Learning: Insights in Contemporary Jewish Education from Population Studies.* Waltham, MA: Cohen Center for Modern Jewish Studies.

Frankel, P. (1989, Winter). Building Self-Esteem Through New Approaches to Adult Jewish Education. *Journal of Jewish Communal Service, 66*(2).

Horenczyk, G. (1990, August). Research on Adult Jewish Education. *Beineinu, 2*(1).

Katz, B. D. (1990, Spring). Diversity in Adult Jewish Education. *Pedagogic Reporter, 41*(2).

Knowles, M. S. (1980). *The Modern Practice of Adult Education.* Chicago: Follett Publishing Co.

Knox, A. B. (1978). *Adult Development and Learning.* San Francisco: Jossey-Bass Publishers.

Lipstadt, D. (1988, February). *The Debate on Quality of American Jewish Life: Policy Implications for Adult Jewish Learning.* New York: American Jewish Committee.

Matz, M. S. (1985, Spring). Impact of an Adult Education Program. *Jewish Education, 53*(1).

Robbins, E. (1979). *An Approach to Planning and Development of Adult Education Programs in Jewish Community Centers.* Unpublished doctoral dissertation. Washington University, St. Louis.

Stokes, K. (Ed.) (1981). *Faith Development in the Adult Life Cycle.* New York: W.H. Sadlier.

Tough, A. (1978). *Major Learning Efforts: Recent Research and Future Directions.* American Association for Higher Education, 1978 National Conference Series.

Highlights

* Jewish learning for many adults has ceased to be merely a leisure time activity.
* Diversity of learners, settings, goals, design, content and strategies characterizes adult learning.
* Common to adult learning is that students are nondegree, nonprofessional and life-long learners.
* The more closely what is learned is tied to the learner's life, the more effective the experience.
* A unified philosophy of adult Jewish education cannot be content oriented; i.e., one cannot make a statement as to what an educated Jew must know.
* A philosophy that stresses the continuous nature of Jewish learning will lead to a curriculum plan that incorporates increasing depth of knowledge and self-understanding as well as growth in intellectual sophistication through learning experiences that build upon one another.
* The goal of adult learning is not only the content but also the process of continued learning.
* Good adult education takes place in a supportive environment that enhances individual confidence and self-esteem and is sensitive to difficulties experienced by some adult learners.
* Once again, the teacher is crucial to the outcome.

The Larger Context

The assumption that adults learn differently from children is confirmed by the available research, yet many of the meager forays into adult Jewish education duplicate the methodologies that we use with children. Motivating adults to learn is the first problem; teaching them differently is the second. How to teach "process" i.e., that being a Jew means a life of study (not necessarily how much one knows) may be a real challenge in our world of immediacy and relevance.

What We Know About...
The Effects of Jewish Education
on Jewish Identification

Arnold Dashefsky

*Does a child's continued involvement in Jewish study produce an adult com-
mitment to Jewish behavior and identity? Stated differently, how does the
Jewish education of a child contribute to the creating of an self-identifying
adult Jew? This core question is the focus of Dr. Dashefsky's article. He currently serves as Professor of Sociology at the University of Connecticut in Storrs,
where he is also the Director of the Center for Judaic Studies and Contemporary
Jewish Life.*

A WELL-RESPECTED BUSINESSMAN, ACCORDING TO AN APOCRYPHAL STORY, REGISTERED HIS SON IN A well-known western university. As the father examined the bulletin of courses describing the requirements, he began to shake his head dubiously. He turned to the dean and asked her, "Does my son have to take all of these classes? Can't you make it shorter? He wants to get through quickly."

"Certainly he can take a shorter course," replied the dean, "but it depends on what he wants to make of himself. To grow a redwood takes hundreds of years, but it takes much less than one hundred days to grow a cucumber!"

The lesson of the dean's remark is that the more energy invested in one's education, the stronger and more powerful will be the outcome. In general, redwoods are more durable than cucumbers and, I suppose, most people would like to think of themselves as redwoods rather than cucumbers. Does this analogy, however, apply to Jewish education? Does a child's continued involvement in Jewish study produce an adult commitment to Jewish behavior and identity?

Shaping Jewish Identification

In order to assess the effects of Jewish education on Jewish identification, I conducted a systematic search of the recent social science literature.[1] A few early studies based on research carried out in the 1960's did not attribute much independent effect to Jewish education in shaping Jewish identification (Sanua, 1964; Rosen. 1965 and Goldlust, 1970). Only Lazerwitz (1973) found some independent effect of Jewish education on Jewish identification as part of a larger analysis of religious identification, but it was not as powerful as the family factors.

The Home and the School (Cohen, 1974)

Among more recent studies, one of the first to examine the impact of Jewish education on religious identification and practice was conducted by Cohen (1974), who sought to examine the relative contribution of the home and religious school in the development of Jewish identification. A sample of 626 Jewish undergraduates studying at Columbia and Barnard in 1969 returned questionnaires, which covered a variety of dimensions including parental religiosity as well as respondent Jewish education, ritual orientation, and other attitudes toward Jewish life. Four conclusions emerged from cross-tabular analysis:

1. When we control for parental religiousness, there is little difference in the frequency of strong Jewish identification between those who attended some form of part-time religious school and those who reported only Sunday school or no formal religious training.

2. Those who have attended a yeshiva or a day school consistently score higher on Jewish identification measures than those who have not. This relationship is maintained even when we control for parental religiousness.

3. The effect of full-time religious education is most pronounced among those respondents whose parents are the most observant.

4. Though the effect of yeshivas and day schools is substantial for all identification variables, the greatest increment over the part-time respondents is in knowledge of Hebrew — the one cognitive variable measured in this study (Cohen, 1974, p. 325).

As Cohen noted, the first three findings were consistent with those in an earlier widely cited 1966 study of the education of Catholic Americans by Greeley and Rossi. Cohen concluded that religious schools can be as successful (or unsuccessful) as their secular counterparts in imparting knowledge but are less effective in shaping beliefs, which seem to be formed at home.

Jewish Education and Identification (Shapiro and Dashefsky, 1974)

Just about the same time Cohen was conducting his study among college students in New York, Howard M. Shapiro and Arnold Dashefsky (1974) were examining the relative effects of Jewish education on identification among a sample of young adult Jewish men living in metropolitan St. Paul, Minnesota, in 1969. In this study, 183 respondents returned questionnaires which included items on Jewish education, in addition to measures of religious attitudes and behaviors of both the respondents and their parents. Shapiro and Dashefsky started with a premise similar to Cohen's. This premise was based on the suggestion of B.C. Rosen (1965), that Jewish education might have no independent effect on Jewish identification. Nevertheless, Shapiro and Dashefsky, on the basis of correlational analysis, found a significant relationship between Jewish education and Jewish identification.

Four other variables relating to the respondents' childhood and adolescence also were examined: Jewish activities with parents, Jewish activities at home, father's religiosity and Jewish familial expectations for participation in Jewish activities. None of these variables revealed a significant relationship with Jewish education although each was correlated with Jewish identification. The authors concluded: "In sum, our data indicate that Jewish education is one childhood and adolescent experience that is a significant factor in Jewish identification independent of other socialization variables" (Shapiro and Dashefsky, 1974, p. 97). In a lengthier study, they further stated:

> Thus, it seems that the importance of Jewish education does not rest in the fact that it is an extension of parental power or peer pressure, but that, through intellectual content and interpersonal relationships, it influences what a Jew should know, feel, and do. This would be particularly true when Jewish education extends well into adolescence, a key stage in the formation of the attitudes which constitute Jewish identification (Dashefsky and Shapiro, 1974, p.62).[2]

Given the fact that there is an observed relationship between Jewish education and identification, are there any factors that significantly affect this relationship? In probing this area, one finding by Shapiro and Dashefsky (1974) appears particularly interesting. They found some dramatic differences when examining this relationship for three different levels of secular education. Most notable was the finding that for those individuals with advanced degrees, a characteristic which is more common among Jews than the general population, the overall correlation for all cases doubled (from .23 to .49). They argued:

> The further a person has pursued a formal academic career, the stronger the relationship between the principal variables under investigation. Perhaps, differences in secular education specify varying weights to the intellectual basis of ethnic identification. Subjects who have gone on to higher academic attainment may rely more on formal learning (in this case Jewish education) for the formation of their attitudes (i.e., toward the Jewish community). Despite the higher mean amount of Jewish education and the stronger correlation with Jewish identification, those with advanced degrees scored lowest on our scale measuring identification. Thus, formal secular education may erode other sources of Jewish identification even while raising the salience of Jewish education (Shapiro and Dashefsky, 1974, p. 98).[3]

This finding was similar to that which Goldstein and Goldscheider reported in their demographic study of the Providence Jewish community. They stated:

Two factors may thus be operating: (1) religious and secular education go together in terms of proportion and length of exposure, and (2) Jewish education may be one of the major forces preventing the post-college and college trained from rejecting their Judaism and Jewish identification (Goldstein and Goldscheider, 1968, p. 224).

Finally, Dashefsky and Shapiro, in comparing the generation of younger men[4] to the generation of their fathers, found that Jewish education and identification were significantly correlated but could not find support for those effects being independent of the home among the older men:

This is probably because in the older generation a formalized system of Jewish education was not extensive...(but) the decline in the pervasiveness of the Jewish subculture as part of the pattern of acculturation in the generation of younger men has led to Jewish education having a significant independent effect on Jewish identification (Dashefsky and Shapiro, 1974, pp. 85-86).

Adolescence and Identification (Sigal, August and Beltempo, 1981)

While the research by Dashefsky and Shapiro found a significant relationship between Jewish education and identification, they could say nothing about the type of education received. Several years later in a study of 73 Jewish high-school students in Montreal, Sigal, August, and Beltempo (1981) sought support for the hypothesis "that full-time Jewish education, extending into adolescence, may have an impact on Jewish identification, which has not been noted for elementary school Jewish education" (1981, p. 230). Indeed, the authors, in comparing two groups of eleventh grade students and controlling for parental level of Jewish identification, found that full-time day school education can positively affect Jewish identification. For students not in the day school, the home is the predominant influence.

Time (Himmelfarb, 1974)

While the previous study confirmed a positive effect of Jewish education on identification for day school students, the question remained whether this effect could be extended to supplemental schools. During the 1970's at least two Jewish community agencies commissioned reports on Jewish education based on research carried out by social scientists on the effects of Jewish education on Jewish identification. One study, originally conducted by Himmelfarb (1974) and based on a sample of 1009 Jewish adults in Chicago, was published by the Institute for Jewish Policy Planning and Research of the Synagogue Council of America. He reported that "at least 3000 hours of religious instruction are needed before Jewish schooling has any lasting impact" (1975, p. 3). Since very few students actually receive that much schooling, Himmelfarb concluded "in terms of the long range consequences for Jewish identity, these data indicate that the type of Jewish education received by over 80% of these American Jews who have received any Jewish education has been a waste of time" (1975, p. 3).

In other words, Jewish education can effectively influence Jewish identification even in the supplemental school, if children are exposed to it for a sufficient period of time, which of necessity would be well into their adolescence or approximately twelve years of schooling. Since most children do not study for such a lengthy period of time, they are "culturally deprived" according to Himmelfarb.

In a more technical paper, Himmelfarb demonstrated that Jewish education accentuated parental influences. But in two areas of Jewish identification, "devotional and intellectual aesthetic religious involvement, Jewish schools seem to have a conversion effect on a small, but not negligible, number of respondents" (Himmelfarb, 1977, p. 472). Thus, Jewish education, under certain conditions, can have a positive effect on Jewish identification in the devotional area of ritual observance or in the intellectual-aesthetic domain of reading, studying, and accumulating Jewish books, art, and music.

Thus far, the four studies described have demonstrated that Jewish education, under certain conditions, can have a positive effect on identification. Each study had a limited sample of respondents: 1) college students in New York City, 2) young adult males in their twenties in St. Paul, 3) high school students in Montreal, and 4) a sample of Jewish adults in Chicago. It remained to be seen whether a national sample of American Jews might yield similar findings.

Time (Bock, 1976)

Geoffrey Bock (1977) prepared a report for the American Jewish Committee Colloquium on Jewish Education and Jewish Identity based on his earlier research (1976) using data from the National Jewish Population Survey. In the study Bock found that the independent effect of Jewish education on identification was first observed at the threshold of 1000 hours and peaked at 4000 hours. Like Himmelfarb, the maximal effects of Jewish education were observed at three to four times the typical level of Jewish education attained by the typical students who drop out of school at the time of their Bar or Bat Mitzvah after attending four or five years. As Bock stated:

> Generally, 'hours of Jewish instruction' is the best predicting measure of most conceptions of Jewish identification; All other factors being equal, those people who have spent 'more hours' in Jewish classrooms are more religious, more involved in informal social networks with other Jews, feel more knowledgeable about Jewish culture and are stronger supporters of Israel. They have either 'learned more' or have been 'better socialized' by their classroom experiences (Bock, 1977, p. 4).

The author further noted a distinction in the effects of Jewish education on personal and public Jewishness:

> Personal Jewishness (such as personal religious observances, Jewish self-esteem, participation in informal social networks and cultural perceptions) is

mainly influenced by Jewishness of home background. To the extent that Jewish schooling is important, home background is 1.3 to 2.4 times more important....Public Jewishness (such behaviors and activities as attendance at services, participation in secular synagogue affairs, participation in secular organizational activities, support for Israel and attitudes about American political issues) are a different matter. Jewish schooling is often as important as Jewish home background (Bock 1977, p. 5).

In Sum

A small number of studies published largely during the 1970's did not support the claim made in the 1960's that Jewish education did not influence Jewish identification independent of the family effect at home. Nevertheless, these studies suggested that to reach the fullest effect the number of hours of Jewish education had to be substantial and continue through the high school years. Furthermore, Jewish education was generally not as powerful as family influences, but neither was it simply an extension of the home. Finally, Jewish education was relatively more independent of the home environment in certain areas of influence. Thus, for example, in one study the public dimensions of Jewish identification, such as attendance at religious services, participation in secular synagogue affairs, participation in secular organization activities, support for Israel, and attitudes about American political issues, were about as important as home backgrounds (Bock 1977). In another study, Jewish education had a positive independent effect on ritual observance and the intellectual-aesthetic domain relating to books, art, and music (Himmelfarb, 1975).[5]

This substantial body of research cited above is in agreement that for Jewish education to be effective it has to be substantial in duration, thereby tending to minimize the contribution of part-time education. This is where the debate rested in the 1970's until recently when Steven M. Cohen (1988) added a new dimension to this discussion.[6] Based on a large representative sample of 4505 respondents in the metropolitan New York Jewish community, Cohen analyzed separately male and female Jewish school attendance. The dimension of gender has largely been ignored by other researchers despite the differential exposure that boys and girls traditionally received with the former more likely to gain a Jewish education that the latter. Cohen (1988, pp. 94) reported:

> When men and women were grouped and analyzed together—as they were in previous studies—afternoon school students hardly differed on measures of Jewish identification from those with no schooling. However, when men and women were statistically separated, afternoon school alumni generally outscored those with no schooling from comparable parental backgrounds.

Thus, Cohen argued that contrary to many earlier analyses which tended to minimize the role of part-time education, it may be modestly effective. It is necessary, therefore, to seek to replicate this finding in other communities and studies to assess its implications.

For Further Investigation

There is an assumption implicit in much of social scientific research that is useful in two ways: First, it is helpful in its own right in expanding the map of knowledge by explaining phenomena hitherto not fully understood. Second, such research may be helpful in formulating policy that may liberate people from the bondage of past practices which are hurtful to them personally or harmful to the goals they seek to achieve as a community. Nevertheless, as Aron has noted "research is important in its own right" (1988, p. 39). Towards that end, the following directions for additional research are suggested:

1. *Develop one or more theoretical frameworks within which an examination of the relationship between Jewish education and identification can be more fruitfully explored.* In the research Howard M. Shapiro and I conducted, we adopted the symbolic interactionist approach, which views the shaping of religioethnic (or Jewish) identification as part of a process of interpersonal relationships and social interaction in the family, peer group, school, synagogue, etc. Alternatively, Aron (1988) alluded to the possibility of adopting a theoretical frame of reference associated with the "critical school" (intellectual disciples of Karl Marx in the Frankfurt School), in which educational institutions are viewed as a conservative force maintaining the status quo rather than liberating students from the narrow confines of their existence. Of course, other contemporary social scientific theoretical approaches may also be valuable paradigms by which the relationship between Jewish education and identification might better be understood.

2. *Apply "triangulation" to the problem of the relationship between Jewish education and identification.* Triangulation, in navigation and surveying, refers to the taking of different measurements of the same objects by constructing triangles in which lines of known length aid in estimating those of unknown length. Likewise in research, a variety of methods applied to the same problem may provide a more coherent explanation of the phenomenon being studied than does any one approach. If the decade corresponding approximately to the 1970's produced several quantitative analyses of Jewish education, then the subsequent decade was dominated by a small number of qualitative studies, such as those by Heilman (1984), Press (1982) and Schoem (1979). Perhaps the 1990's will give rise to research focusing on the relationship between Jewish education and identification applying the principle of triangulation. These aforementioned latter studies did not analyze the effect of Jewish education on identification, but rather provided a rich description of the Hebrew school context of that education.

3. *Clarify the most effective and efficient ways to deliver the positive effect of Jewish schooling on identification.* For example, is it more effective to deliver hours of instruction in one subject area or another? Is it more efficient to expose teens to study several hours a week for two or three sessions or a large number of hours, equivalent to several weeks of typical study, crammed into one weekend? As a corollary question, is there an optimal mix

of formal classroom and informal experiential learning that can be blended together to provide a more powerful synergistic effect than each approach pursued separately?

Three Recommendations

The type of social science research I have reviewed provides a way to understand and explain social reality and, on that basis, to plan policies for implementation, in this case, presumably to strengthen the existing relationship. Indeed, the findings of social scientists have provided the basis of a variety of social policy formulations (Bock, 1977; Dashefsky, 1970; 1985; and Himmelfarb, 1975).

As a starting point, the three consensus recommendations that emerged from the Colloquium on Jewish Education and Jewish Identity (1976, pp. 23-31) must be highlighted. This panel was sponsored by the American Jewish Committee and involved over thirty academicians, educators and community professionals who met over a period of several years. While these suggestions were published more than a decade ago, the need to broaden their reach still remains:

1. *Expand the opportunities for Jewish education for high school age students with an emphasis on diversity and excellence.* Strategies might include: integration of formal classroom study with informal experiential activities; provision of college credit to high school juniors and seniors for formal Jewish study; inclusion of a study trip to Israel; consolidation of high schools into one or more regional centers.

2. *Enhance educational opportunities for college-age students at both the informal and formal levels.* At the formal level, such collegiate opportunities require communal support for Jewish studies, which serve an academic need for a balanced curriculum, and at the informal level, these opportunities might include the reinstitution of successful ideologically oriented youth movements.

3. *Embark on a variety of family education programs.* These, too, are worthy of community support.

Conclusion

We may ask what effect Jewish education has on Jewish identification.

> There are those who claim that Jewish education in the United States provides no demonstrable influence in the development of Jewish identification. There is no doubt that it is possible to introduce improvements in the Jewish educational system in the United States, in methods and curriculum as well as in the administrative structure and the teaching faculty, but to conclude that there is no relationship between Jewish education and Jewish identification is untenable (Dashefsky and Shapiro, 1978, p. 90).

The above was written more than a decade ago and, in general, these words still ring true. Even the primary consumers of Jewish education, elementary-age school children, agree. As a more recent study noted, quoting the words of one student: "If there wasn't Hebrew School, then what would be the point of being Jewish? Your religion wouldn't be the same. You wouldn't even believe in your religion" (Press, 1984). Most agree today that, under certain conditions, Jewish education can be a positive and independent influence on Jewish identification. Indeed, one approach that could highlight a communal commitment to the importance of Jewish education in shaping identification would be to establish the requirement of some credentials of prior Jewish education or current continued study for leadership positions in the Jewish community. As one expert has suggested, if the community cannot find sufficient "learned leaders," then at least it should seek out "learning leaders" as exemplars of achievement for the younger generation. The task remains to further develop strategies that would most likely maximize the effect of Jewish education on Jewish identification and to continue to monitor the possible outcomes.[7]

Bibliography

Aron, I. (1988). The Relationship Between Research and Practice in Jewish Education. *Jewish Education, 56*, 34-41.

Bock, G. (1976). The Jewish Schooling of American Jews: A Study of Non-cognitive Educational Effects. Unpublished doctoral dissertation. Harvard University, Cambridge, MA.

Bock, G. (1977). *Does Jewish Schooling Matter?* New York: American Jewish Committee.

Cohen, S.M. (1974). The Impact of Jewish Education on Religious Identification and Practice. *Jewish Social Studies, 36*, 316-326.

Cohen, S.M. (1988). *American Assimilation or Jewish Revival?* Bloomington IN: Indiana University Press.

Colloquium on Jewish Education and Jewish Identity. (1976). *Summary Report and Recommendations.* New York: American Jewish Committee.

Dashefsky, A. (1970). A Sociological Perspective on Jewish Identity. In A.L. Peller (Ed.), *Jewish Identity in the 70's.* Philadelphia: Board of Jewish Education.

Dashefsky, A. (1985). Jewish Education—For What and For Whom? *Jewish Education, 53*, 44-47.

Dashefsky, A., DeAmicis, B., Lazerwitz, B., & Tabory, E. (1992). *Americans Abroad: A Comparative Study of Emigrants from the United States.* New York: Plenum.

Dashefsky, A. & Shapiro, H.M. (1974). *Ethnic Identification Among American Jews.* Lexington, MA.: Lexington Books.

Dashefsky, A. & Shapiro, H.M. (1978). *"Hinukh Yehudi V'hizdahut Yehudit B'artzot Habrit" ("Jewish Education and Jewish Identification in the United States. ").* B'tfutzot Hagolah, *19* (Summer), 90-94.

Goldlust, J. (1970). Jewish Education and Ethnic Identification:A Study of Jewish Adolescents in Australia. *Jewish Education, 40*, 49-59.

Goldstein, S. and Goldscheider, C. (1968). *Jewish Americans.* Englewood Cliffs, NJ: Prentice Hall.

Greeley, A.M. and Rossi, P. (1966). *The Education of Catholic Americans*. Chicago: Aldine.

Heilman, S. (1984). *Inside the Jewish School: A Study of the Cultural Setting for Jewish Education*. New York: American Jewish Committee.

Himmelfarb, H. (1974). The Impact of Religious Schooling: The Effects of Jewish Education upon Adult Religious Involvement. Unpublished doctoral dissertation. University of Chicago, Chicago.

Himmelfarb, H. (1975). Jewish Education for Naught: Educating the Culturally Deprived Child. *Analysis, 51,* 1-12.

Himmelfarb, H. (1977). The Interaction Effects of Parents, Spouse, and Schooling: Comparing the Impact of Jewish and Catholic Schools. *The Sociological Quarterly, 18,* 464-477.

Lazerwitz, B. (1973). Religious Identification and its Ethnic Correlates: A Multivariate Model. *Social Forces, 52,* 204-220.

Press, J. (1982). *An Ethnographic and Phenomenological Study of Students' Perceptions About Hebrew School*. Unpublished doctoral dissertation. University of Connecticut, Storrs.

Press, J. (1984). Hebrew School. *Jewish Spectator, 49,* 25-28.

Rosen, B.C. (1965). *Adolescence and Religion*. Cambridge, MA: Schenkman.

Sanua, V. (1964). The Relationship Between Jewish Education and Jewish Identification. *Jewish Education, 35,* 37-50.

Schoem, D. (1979). *Ethnic Survival In America: An Ethnography of a Jewish Afternoon School*. Unpublished doctoral dissertation. University of California, Berkeley.

Shapiro, H.M. and Dashefsky, A. (1984). Religious Education and Ethnic Identification: Implications for Ethnic Pluralism. *Review of Religious Research, 15,* 93-102.

Sigal, J., August, D., and Beltempo, J. (1981). Impact of Jewish Education on Jewish Identification in a Group of Adolescents. *Jewish Social Studies, 44,* 283-290.

Footnotes

[1] To carry out this search, I used SOCIOFILE, a computer assisted reference file covering the period 1974-1988, which yielded only three relevant articles with which to begin this analysis.

[2] Of six significant socialization factors which explained 28% of the variance (out of a maximum of 100%) in Jewish identification, Jewish education ranked third after father's religiosity and friends' expectations. The remaining three factors were Jewish activities with parents, presence of an older brother, and family expectations for Jewish activities. In sum, family factors were 4.5 times as powerful and peer influence only 1.5 times as great as the influence of Jewish education, a fact revealed by regression analysis.

[3] In St. Paul, at the time of the study, the community supported one central school system, the Talmud Torah.

[4] In their analysis of the younger generation, Dashevsky and Shapiro (1974) also introduced measures of contermeraneous social characteristics, in addition to the prior socialization experiences, into their regression analysis. Still, Jewish education ranked fourth in importance out of eight factors. These eight variables explained only 40% of the total (100%) variance. In fact, a comparison of three socialization factors shows the family to be only three times as powerful as Jewish education and the latter actually is 1.5 times more important than peers in explaining Jewish identification when contemporaneous contextual effects, e.g., religious organizational involvement and socio-economic status are included.

[5]A study currently in press also shows for Americans that Jewish education is associated with aliyah, or emigration to Israel (Dashefsky, DeAmicis, Lazerwitz and Tabory, 1992 forthcoming).

[6]Throughout much of the 1980's little research has appeared in the journals on this topic. Cohen's book length study (1988) is all the more exceptional.

[7]I wish to thank the academics and educators, practitioners and policymakers, family and friends, with whom I have debated and discussed this topic for two decades. In addition; I am very grateful to Sandy Waldman Dashefsky and J. Alan Winter and, of course, Stuart Kelman for their careful reading of earlier versions of this paper and their many helpful comments.

Highlights

* When parent religiousness is controlled, there is little difference in the frequency of strong Jewish identification between those who attended some form of part-time religious school and those who reported only Sunday-school or even no formal religious training.
* Those who attended a yeshiva or day school consistently score higher on Jewish identification measures than those who did not.
* The effect of full-time religious education is most pronounced among those whose parents are most observant.
* Though the effect of yeshivas and day schools is substantial for all identification variables, the greatest increment over part-time respondents is knowledge of Hebrew.
* Jewish education is one childhood and adolescent experience that is a significant factor in Jewish identification independent of other socialization variables
* Through intellectual content and interpersonal relationships, Jewish education influences what a Jew knows, feels, and does. This is particularly true when participation extends into adolescence.
* For students not in day school, the home is the predominant influence on Jewish identity.
* All other factors being equal, those people who have spent more hours in Jewish classrooms are more religious, more involved in informal social networks with other Jews, feel more knowledgeable about Jewish culture and are stronger supporters of Israel.
* A small number of studies published largely during the 1970's contradicted the claim made in the 1960's that Jewish education failed to influence Jewish identification independent of the family effect. To the contrary, these newer studies suggested that to reach the fullest effect, the number of hours of Jewish education had to be substantial and continue through the high school years.
* Jewish education is generally not as powerful as family influences, but neither is it simply an extension of the home. In certain areas of influence, Jewish education has an impact independent of the home environment.

The Larger Context

Jewish identification is complicated. While many variables affect future Jewish identity, time spent in studying seems to be central. Yet it is not true that because of the hours available, the day school is the only solution. The impact of the home and parents and non-formal and Israel experiences suggest that supplementary schools may be an alternate route to strong adult identification—providing the student remains through the high school years.

What We Know About...
The Marginally Affiliated[1]

Steven M. Cohen

The term "affiliation" is used to describe any number of relational conditions between an individual and an institution. It seems, however, that most American Jews fall into the category of "marginally affiliated" and not, as we typically believe, into a group called "the unaffiliated". Dr. Cohen, Professor of Sociology at Queens College in New York, discusses this population suggesting that our outreach efforts ought to target already affiliated Jews and that <u>they</u> are the ones whom the organized Jewish community should focus attention on in order to promote affiliation. Although this article was written in 1985, Dr. Cohen's opinions and conclusions based upon his research have not changed.

IN THE LAST DECADE AND MORE, JEWISH EDUCATORS, CENTER WORKERS, AND RELATED COMMUNAL professionals have begun to talk increasingly of "outreach" to so-called unaffiliated Jews. The unaffiliated include, most prominently, the intermarried, young singles, the divorced, and non-participants in synagogues, centers, and federation campaigns (see, for example, two issues of the *Melton Journal*, Fall 1984 and Summer 1985). But, in focusing on these groups, some policymakers may well have lost sight of the "affiliated," a group which is far larger than the unaffiliated, and arguably even more crucial to American Jewish vitality and continuity. And it is here that the now considerable recent social science research on the Jewish identity of affiliated Jewish adults in the United States suggests some broad policy implications for Jewish educators, be they teachers, principals, rabbis, center workers, or lay leaders making policy in the field of Jewish education, broadly conceived.

Five Current Assumptions

It is probably fair to say that most policymakers and professionals concerned with outreach efforts operate under the following assumptions:

1. that the Jewish world can be divided largely into two broad categories: the affiliated and the unaffiliated;

2. that the number of unaffiliated is large, perhaps half or even a majority of the Jewish population, and

3. that the number of unaffiliated is growing, in large part, because

4. too many Jews lack sufficient commitment to Jewish values, and therefore

5. educational efforts ought both to target the unaffiliated, and focus on elevating their Jewish commitment or motivation.

It turns out that most of these assumptions are inaccurate and, in fact, may be producing flawed policies. If so, then those policies and programs need to be rethought and modified. In fact, it may turn out that to have greatest impact, outreach efforts ought to target already affiliated Jews, and try to enhance their connections with other Jews as much as their commitments to Jewish values. These alternative policy prescriptions stem from a critical examination of the commonly held assumptions enumerated above.

The Numbers

We began with the (mistaken) assumption that the number of unaffiliated is numerically large. From a variety of research studies accumulated over the last decade and more, we can paint a very general portrait of what we may call "the vast majority of American Jews," by which we mean at least two-thirds of adult American Jews.

1. The vast majority of American Jews send their children at one time or another to some form of Jewish schooling. While at any one point less than half of all youngsters are enrolled in Jewish schools, by the end of adolescence almost all (87%) young Jewish men have received some Jewish schooling, as have over two-thirds (70%) of young adult women (DellaPergola and Genuth, 1983). These fairly high cumulative enrollment statistics say very little about the quality of Jewish learning; but they certainly testify to the motivation of the vast majority of Jewish parents to perpetuate some form of positive Jewish commitment. And they demonstrate that the overwhelming majority of parents affiliate with a Jewish institution at some time in their lives.

2. The vast majority of Jews celebrate in some way the three seasonal holidays of Passover, Rosh Hashana/Yom Kippur, and Chanukah. About three-quarters of Jewish adults appear in synagogue during the High Holidays, as many or more light Chanukah candles, and about 5 in 6 attend a Passover Seder (Cohen, 1983; Ritterband and Cohen, 1984; Tobin and Kipsman, 1984).

3. The vast majority of adult Jews say they contribute to Jewish philanthropic campaigns, and most (a simple majority) give $100 or more (Cohen, 1983).

4. The vast majority claim a passionate and broad involvement with Israel; and the enormously successful direct mail campaigns among Jews for pro-Israel Senatorial candidates bear them out (Cohen, 1983).

5. In intermediate size older cities—such as Cleveland, St. Louis, Detroit, and Baltimore—the vast majority of Jews belong to a Jewish organization and read a Jewish newspaper. This is not to deny that in the larger cities—such as New York, Chicago, and Los Angeles—only about a third of adults so affiliate (Tobin and Lipsman, 1984).

6. While only about one-half of all American Jews belong to a synagogue, synagogue membership jumps sharply upward when parents have school-age children (Cohen, 1983). In the New York area, with a synagogue membership rate below the national average, as little as 18% of the never-marrieds have joined as contrasted with 60% of couples with school-age children (Cohen, 1988).

7. And last, while it is true that about one Jew in four marries a gentile, the vast majority, or three-in-four, do not. Of the initial outmarriages, about one-in-six of the gentiles (overwhelmingly, the wives) convert. And of the remainder, most of the mixed-married Jews (many more wives than husbands) say they are raising Jewish children (Silberman, 1985; Cohen, 1988).

Thus, in whatever ways one defines affiliation—be it in terms of children's education, or major holiday celebration, or philanthropic contribution, or Israel involvement, or organizational and synagogue affiliation, or marriage patterns—there are certainly a lot of affiliated Jews out there. But, this does not deny that the quality of their Jewishness, the depth and significance of their affiliation, may leave much to be desired.

The great extent to which the affiliated vary among themselves can be well-illustrated using data from the Greater New York Jewish Population Study. The study questioned over 4,500 Jews living in an 8-county area, a region which comprises 30% of American Jewry, and one with extraordinary diversity. It includes such contrasts as heavily Orthodox Borough Park as well as heavily unaffiliated Greenwich Village; largely lower-income Bronx, as well as affluent Great Neck and Scarsdale; and the established Jewish neighborhoods of Brooklyn and Queens as well as the recently settled areas of Suffolk and the upper reaches of Northern Westchester.

Using several measures of observance, communal affiliation, friendship, and marriage, we found that only 4% lacked any sort of connection to Jewish life, and only another 6% had no such ties except by way of having mostly Jewish friends (Cohen, 1988). At the other extreme, about 17% were "activists"—they were heavily involved in Jewish organizational life and 10% qualified as "observant" by virtue of claiming to handle no money on the Sabbath. Between these two extreme (the 10% with few Jewish activities, and the 27% with many sorts of connections with Jewish life), lay the vast middle, nearly three quarters of the Jews in the New York metropolitan region. All those in the vast middle celebrated Passover, Rosh Hashana, Yom Kippur and Chanukah in some fashion, and most belonged to some Jewish institution (usually a synagogue).

And, among parents age 35-49, with school-age children, the Jewish identity distribution was skewed even further in the direction of greater involvement. Fully 87% (!) were affiliated in some way with the Jewish community, either through keeping some aspect of kashrut and Shabbat, or by belonging to some institution, or by being active in some other significant way. and of the 13%

who were unaffiliated, almost all (10%), observed both Passover and Chanukah in some fashion. This means that only 3% of parents age 35-49 in the Greater New York area belonged to no Jewish institution and failed to observe at least two of the most popular holidays!

Not only is the number of unaffiliated much smaller than most suppose, there is no persuasive evidence that their numbers either are declining significantly or increasing. Overall, some trends in American Jewish identification point down, others up, but there is no clear, overall trend in either direction. Thus, the number of unaffiliated is not only small; it does not seem to be growing very much either. And even if it were, there is still clearly a large majority of Jews arrayed along the middle ranges of Jewish involvement.

From all these data we learn that sooner or later, almost all Jews affiliate with some official Jewish agency. If so, then the central policy problem may be something other than simply promoting affiliation. It may be something closer to the heart and expertise of Jewish educators, namely what to do with Jews once they are in the door or on the mailing list. And here, the accumulated social science research of the last few years has given us some hints (though certainly no rules) as to how to reach, inspire, involve, and educate these people, the many Jews who in some way identify as such, but who nevertheless are neither especially active nor culturally sophisticated in Judaic terms.

Entry Points

One lesson we learn from that research is that there are certain times when Jews are most open to educators' intervention, when they may actually seek, or at least be open to receiving, some sort of advice or assistance from a Jewish expert or institution. These special times—"entry points"— may be linked to the calendar, to the family life cycle, or to historical events.

Examples of calendrical entry points include the three widely observed holidays of Passover, Rosh Hashana/Yom Kippur, and Chanukah. Others may include leisure periods, be they weekends or vacation times. The positive reports of educators and others involved with summer camps, Israel missions, and weekend retreats testify to a greater chance for impact when programs are planned for and during leisure periods.

The entry points connected with the family life cycle include: marriage; the birth of a child; child-rearing transitions such as beginning school, bar/bat mitzvah, and confirmation; death and mourning; illness; and even divorce. These are among those times when people throughout the West typically look to religious communities, institutions and experts for guidance, instruction, and solace. Intervention at these times can leave lasting impressions and make for important life-long shifts in Jewish involvement.

Finally, we have entry points provided by the course of historical events. The most notable examples include the wars in Israel. Each such war—in 1948, 1956, 1967, 1973, and 1982—provided a potent stimulus for American Jewish involvement. All except the last resulted in significantly larger donations to the UJA and Israel Bonds. And all, particularly the last three, provoked considerable soul-searching and reevaluation on the part of large numbers of American Jews. Other examples, perhaps less potent but nevertheless noteworthy, are the quadrennial presidential election seasons when Jews engage in intense debates over Jewish political interests and their responsibilities as Americans. They are also times when Jews are keenly sensitive to seemingly anti-Semitic or anti-Israel statements by public figures.

Fundraisers and community relations specialists have long recognized these periods as times for maximal effort, as fleeting opportunities to be exploited, perhaps for narrow institutional gains, but ultimately for the good of the Jewish people. Their example ought also to be emulated by more educators who ought to make themselves ready to capitalize on both the planned and unanticipated historical events which are almost guaranteed to heighten Jewish consciousness and public debate.

Motive and Opportunity or Commitment and Community

Crime investigators need to demonstrate two elements to connect a suspect with a crime; motive and opportunity. They need to prove that the suspect was motivated to commit the crime, and they need to prove the suspect had the opportunity to do so.

As with criminals and crime, so (*l'havdil*) with Jews and Judaism. At one extreme, a small number of Jews are so deeply committed to Jewish life that they are certain to make their life decisions so as to assure their ability to live a rather full Jewish life. At the other extreme, another small number—and, as I have been arguing, a very small number—are so alienated from Jewish life that they have rather little chance of involving themselves in Jewish communal or ritual affairs. For the vast majority, however, social circumstances have a lot to do with their opportunities for involvement.

In Judaism, as with other group involvements, the nature of the available community—be it conceived as family, friends, neighbors, synagogues, organizations, or residential locale—is the key to understanding opportunity. Whatever their levels of individual commitment, those Jews who are more involved with other Jews, or who are more attractive to or more recruitable by formal Jewish communities, are also more likely to be involved in Jewish life. In other words, we ought not automatically to associate the presence or absence of involvement with the presence or absence of motivation, or what some term commitment. A compelling community often makes up for lack of commitment; and, most often, commitment without community cannot be acted upon.

The powerful impact of social circumstances can be seen in a variety of findings. As noted earlier, family stage is the most potent social predictor of involvement levels. In the New York area study, parents of school-age children and parents of grown children were at least four times more likely to qualify as "observant" or "activist" as were the never marrieds (i.e., 36-39% versus only 9% of the latter). Those who have been residentially stable for three years are more active than newcomers. Residents of veteran, intermediate-sized cities are more involved than those living in recent areas of Jewish settlement, large or small. And the more affluent are clearly more active than those with lower incomes. In other words, the composite portrait of a highly active Jew might be an affluent, middle-aged parent of grown children, who has been living for many years in Cleveland. And the portrait of the inactive Jew is a single parent of limited means who has recently moved to Denver.

Despite equal levels of commitment, one is bound to be active in Jewish life, and the other not. As one single parent in a study of a Conservative Hebrew school's parents remarked:

> I'm tired of hearing that single parents don't care about their kids' Jewish education. It's a whole lot harder for me to pay for the education and then to get there...I'm so limited in my ability to get places that I don't allow myself to get interested. It frustrates me. I'd love to do lots of things but I can't (Wall, 1984).

The importance of sound communities for enabling the expression of Jewish commitment is demonstrated in several of the most notable innovations in American Jewish life of the last two decades. The *Havurah* movement, for example, explicitly emulated the strong sense of cohesion which has characterized many Orthodox communities (Reisman, 1977). For *havurot*, community-building became one of the important ultimate ends, on a par with, if not more important than, serious commitment to a certain style of liturgy or to an intense, personalized grappling with religious texts.

The same lesson also can be learned from the UJA's dozens of Young Leadership groups all around the country. Here, individuals in their young thirties, from the same community, and with similar social class background, have been brought together into groups of families which often study, pray, and travel to Israel together with very positive consequences for philanthropic contributions, campaign activism, and elevated ritual observance in the home (Woocher, 1981a; 1981b; 1982). Yet another illustration of the powerful influence of community-building comes in the form of the nation's 100 recently formed Jewish political action committees which have coalesced to influence the political process in behalf of Jewish interests. As might be expected, these groups recruit Jews with a specific set of characteristics. They are generally young to middle-aged adults, and most are fairly affluent people who are able to make $500 and $1,000 political contributions on top of their already considerable philanthropic support of conventional Jewish charities. Here too, the groups attend to the social relations among their members by holding frequent social functions and by drawing upon commercial and professional connections among their members and new recruits.

If it is indeed the case that active Jewish involvement depends both upon well-functioning communities and upon the commitment of their members to Jewish values of one sort or another, then it seems we have two sorts of crucial tasks before us. One is to improve the social cohesion of Jewish communities; that is, to strengthen the connections among Jews already involved in Jewish communities and to extend networks to relatively isolated Jews, all those who deviate from the composite portrait of the activist drawn earlier. These include the young adults, the not-so-affluent, the singles, the residentially mobile, and the dramatically growing number of well-elderly who generally under-participate in Jewish life. The second broad policy is, of course, to foster commitment to Jewish values among those who are already socially connected.

Historically, the Jewish professional world in the United States has been divided into specialists trained only in one or the other of these two tasks; that is, those trained in community-building (principally the social workers), and those trained in transmitting Jewish values (that is, the educators). Only recently has the Jewish human services field recognized the desirability of supplementing its traditional training with explicit training in Judaica—witness the half dozen or so joint or integrated graduate professional programs in social work or social welfare and Jewish studies (Reisman, 1982).

In ways about which I myself am not at all clear, the Jewish education profession needs to recruit and train people in the arts of community-building, but in ways which are appropriate for educators. It is no accident that the field of education draws heavily upon such disciplines as psychology (with its emphasis on the individual) and philosophy (with its emphasis on values). The truly successful Jewish educator may well need to transcend the conventional boundaries of the profession to learn to draw upon the skills acquired and practiced by lawyers, MBA's, journalists, and politicians. In other words, attention to community-building may not only be helpful for achieving educational goals, it may be an inevitable prerequisite.

For as noted earlier, the performance of Jewish activities, the demonstration of commitment to Jewish values however they are defined, depends not only upon the extent of motivation and commitment of the individual. Motive without opportunity cannot be acted upon; and commitment in the absence of community can be neither applied nor expressed.

Plural Models of Jewish Knowledge

That which we choose to call "knowledge," as much as any other human endeavor, is a social construct. Every culture in effect decides what constitutes knowledge, what knowledge is important or socially useful or prestigious, and, ultimately, which knowledge ought to be transmitted to members of the culture. Accordingly, Jewish educators, by the very nature of their profession, have had to evolve a working definition of Jewish knowledge, to decide what ought to be included in their curricula.

Even though Jewish educators have generally failed to develop a consensus on what constitutes essential Jewish knowledge, most of them (particularly the rabbis, principals, and classroom teachers) have in their practice defined Jewish knowledge largely as that pertaining to participation in religious Judaism. Thus, the skills that are taught are most often synagogue skills or home ritual skills. The concepts taught are most often those derived from rabbinic Judaism. The language taught is most often Hebrew. The simple, unadorned word "text" refers almost exclusively to the Bible, Talmud, Midrash, or later rabbinic commentaries.

As we know, the Jewish lives of American Jews consist of many worlds other than what we may for convenience's sake refer to as the religious world. In fact, the religious world is the one where American Jews are not particularly distinguished by frequent synagogue worship attendance, although they do in fact use their synagogues for many Jewish purposes other than worship. They are not particularly adept at, or for the most part, even acquainted with, text study, although they do read rather prodigiously on Jewish matters in books, newspapers, and magazines. They tend not to devote an extraordinary amount of time or energy to punctilious observance of rituals in the home or elsewhere, yet many do expend considerable time, energy, and money on behalf of Jewish communal causes.

If this analysis is correct, then much of Jewish education as currently conceived fails to speak to the actual Jewish concerns of American Jews, many of whom do possess a sort of Jewish knowledge, though one which many formal educators would fail to recognize as such. For example, most American Jews have a shared understanding of Jewish history, an historical mythos which lends meaning to the events in Jewish history they read about every day in the newspapers. Its elements include a belief in Jewish intellectual and entrepreneurial talents, an assertion of Jews' moral privilege and sensitivity deriving from centuries of persecution, ideas about who are Jews' friends or enemies, a sense of obligation to less fortunate or oppressed Jews, a vague notion of a sacred tradition, and an appreciation of the special place of Jews in American society and of America's special meaning to Jews. For the most part, this knowledge is acquired through the experience of participating in the American Jewish sub-culture. It is not particularly systematic, yet Jewish knowledge it certainly is. Compare, for example, what the average affiliated Jew knows about Jews and Judaism, with his or her equally well educated gentile counterpart.

From an educator's perspective, this sort of Jewish knowledge is far from adequate, and leaves much room for improvement. But, if taken seriously, it can be exploited as a useful starting-point for educational enhancement. The thousands of lay leaders and professionals in Jewish communal life would no doubt enjoy a much richer experience, and they may even make for better leaders, were they systematically schooled in the history, thinking, and values which other Jewish communities in other times and in other places utilized in the conduct of their affairs. Few of them have had much exposure to the sort of Jewish texts which they in their current endeavors might find very meaningful. These "texts" includes such items as dialogues and correspondence between communal leaders and gentile authorities, minutes of board meetings, newspapers, community constitutions, *takanot*, and responsa literature. Few of today's activists in the political sphere of Jewish life can articulate the diverse range of alternative political strategies and techniques employed by Jewish communities in the past. Currently, the unabashed application of Jewish power, as exemplified by Israeli military might or by American Jewish political muscle, seems to be the most favored approach to achieving Jewish political ends. Yet such a one-sided commitment to the application of Jewish power ignores a long tradition of the Jew-as-middleman, of s*htadlanut*, of diplomacy, and of coalition-building.

The point here is not to suggest specific educational or programmatic directions of one sort or another. Such determinations are better made by professional educators than by social analysts. Nevertheless, it is important to highlight the disjunction between the interests of those many American Jews involved in philanthropy, social service, and politics, and the main thrust of much of conventional Jewish education, which is heavily oriented toward synagogue, ritual, and religious life. Planning to reach affiliated Jews ought to address their Jewish interests outside the religious sphere, and, in so doing, it might compel us to reconceptualize our understanding of what constitutes a Jewish text, a Jewish skill, or, most generally, Jewish knowledge.

From Reproach to Resource: Developing a New Language of Discourse

One of the common experiences of affiliated American Jews is the encounter with official Jews speaking the language of reproach, evaluation, and ultimately accusation. Rabbis chastise their congregants for failing to attend services, to observe ritual practices, to send their children to Jewish schools, or to marry within the faith. Fundraisers exhort the real and metaphoric survivors of the holocaust to contribute generously to needy, endangered or embattled Jews in Israel and elsewhere. And Israeli emissaries remind them of their ostensible moral responsibility to support Israel politically, financially, and sometimes through migration.

In short, the language of official Jewish life is overwhelmingly a language of demand and chastisement. Such chastisement makes the listener—who more often than not fails to meet the expectations implicit in the remarks—feel as if he or she is being called a "bad Jew". As one parent in the study mentioned earlier said:

> I have a problem with me and the ideal Jew. A "good Jew" keeps kosher,
> observes Shabbat, etc. I hear it in the school and I hear it from the pulpit.
> That's why we're leaving the synagogue. I cannot feel like a good Jew because
> I couldn't or wouldn't do those things (Wall, 1984).

In point of fact, the vast majority of Jews—even those who intermarry and in other ways fall short of some of the expectations enunciated above—feel they are "good Jews," and resent being labeled otherwise. And presumably they also resent the aura of moral privilege which philanthropically generous, or communally active, or ritually observant, or Jewishly knowledgeable Jews arrogate to themselves.

The language of reproach need not be completely abandoned; such a step may inevitably imply an abdication of normative standards altogether. The articulation of norms—the declaration of what's right and wrong—often conflicts with a policy of welcoming those who fail to meet conventional normative standards. To illustrate, I have no doubt the Reform movement has, in effect, foregone the normative prohibition on intermarriage as an inevitable consequence of its overt appeal to the mixed married.

Any move away from the language of reproach entails certain risks which must be counterbalanced against possible gains in attracting potentially alienated Jews. Nevertheless, some modulation in this language may diminish the alienation of Jews from Jewish institutions and their leaders. For we may well be facing a situation similar to that which "did in" the Democratic Party in 1984. Pollsters found that the voters liked workers, but not unions; they liked women's rights, but not feminists; and they liked civil rights, not Black activists. Similarly, many of today's affiliated Jews may well like Judaism and Jewishness, but not the high pressure, demanding, guilt-inducing institutions which they join out of a sense of responsibility and obligations, but perhaps with deep-seated ambivalence, if not aversion as well.

In place of the language of reproach, Jewish educators and other communal professionals might think about developing a language of resource. The sociologist Peter Berger (1985) contends that the transition from traditional society to secularized, voluntaristic modernity has compelled all religions to compete in the marketplace of ideas. If so, then Judaism could be presented not only as a set of obligations, but also as a collection of resources which can benefit their users. Involvement in Jewish life, like involvement in other forms of group life, provides people with several sorely needed benefits. Among them are a sense of belonging to a community in the midst of a frequently alienating and isolating society, a sense of transcendent meaning and location in history for the many who feel bereft of social meaning and historical significance, and, not least, an opportunity to engage in altruistic activity, to feel and be useful, helpful, and important to others in need.

By linking the practice of the norm to the voluntary consumption of a benefit, the language of resource respects the right of the individual Jew to choose as much or as little Jewish involvement as he or she wants without fear of moral stigma, or claim to moral privilege.

Conclusion

The conventional understandings of the contemporary Jewish situation ought to be replaced with a more sophisticated and accurate set of ideas about the affiliated adult Jew in the United States.

First, rather than dividing the Jewish world into two classes, we ought to see Jews as arrayed on a continuum ranging from high to low levels of involvement. If, for policy purposes, we need to divide that continuum, we may be best off using not less than three categories. Thus, instead of simply the affiliated and the unaffiliated, we should think of the "highly involved," the "marginally affiliated" (or those whom some educators call the "semicommitted"), and the "unaffiliated."

The marginally affiliated, in fact, comprise the vast majority of American Jews, and their numbers have been holding steady. Because they are affiliated, they are already located and rather economical to reach. Because they are underinvolved, they offer considerable opportunities for identity enhancement.

The techniques educators and other practitioners develop to reach this large and numerically stable group of marginally affiliated Jews ought to take into account the great extent to which social factors, primarily the availability of community, determine levels of involvement. That is, motivation and commitment alone do not guarantee involvement; and absence of involvement is in itself no sure sign of lack of commitment. Moreover, the widely varying levels of Jewish activity associated with the calendar, the life cycle, and certain historical moments suggest "entry points," times when educators' interventions may be particularly effective. The excellence with which American Jews perform in certain communal spheres, and their lack of enthusiasm for other areas, should suggest some expansion of how we conceptualize Jewish knowledge and Jewish education. Finally, the individualism and voluntary nature of American Jewish society may mean that presenting Jewish involvement only as a moral imperative, when speaking with the marginally affiliated, may create more alienation than involvement. Presenting Judaism as an option, an opportunity, or a resource may have quite the opposite effect.

For years, Jewish communal life has operated within what may be called the politics of fear. To mobilize communal energies, lay and professional leaders conjure up frightening images of the most awesome outcomes, the worst eventualities. They play on fears of anti-Semitism, on the tragic imagery of Israel's physical destruction, and, most recently, on the possibility of an American Jewish community decimated by the ravages of intermarriage and assimilation.

Practitioners of the politics of fear are well-intentioned. They presume that an otherwise complacent American Jewry needs to be roused from its obliviousness to the most pressing problems of the day. However, they ought to realize that fear can paralyze as well as mobilize, and it can depress as well as excite. For no one, and least of all the extraordinarily successful American Jew, is eager to be associated with losing or impossible causes.

Fortunately, the politics of hope offers a practical alternative to the politics of fear, and, in this case, one which is buttressed by the evidence. In the case of American Jewish identity today, there's plenty of reason to be hopeful; there's plenty of reason for policymakers to see their task as elevating the Jewish identity of American Jews rather than trying to hold back the ostensibly advancing tide of assimilation. For the large middle group of marginally affiliated American Jews comprise an ever-present feature of American Jewish life. For educators, communal workers, and others concerned with creative Jewish survival, these Jews present both risks and opportunities, and offer a challenge as well as a source of hope.

Bibliography

Berger, P. (1969). *The Sacred Canopy: Elements of a Sociological Theory of Religion.* Garden City, NY: Doubleday.

Cohen, S. (1983a). *American Modernity and Jewish Identity.* New York: Tavistock.

Cohen, S. (1983b). *Attitudes of American Jews Towards Israel and Israelis.* New York: American Jewish Committee.

Cohen, S. (1988). *American Assimilation or Jewish Revival?* Bloomington, IN: Indiana University Press.

DellaPergola, S. & Genuth, N. (1983). *Jewish Education Attained in Diaspora Communities: Data for the 1970's.* Jerusalem:The Hebrew University, The Institute of Contemporary Jewry.

Melton Journal, (Fall,1984 and Summer, 1985). New York: Melton Research Center.

Reisman, B. (1977). *The Havurah: A Contemporary Jewish Experience.* New York: Union of American Hebrew Congregations.

Reisman, B. (1982). Managers, Jews, or Social Workers: Conflicting Expectations for Communal Workers. *Response, 42,* 41-49.

Ritterband, P. & Cohen, S. (1984). The Social Characteristics of the Jews of Greater New York. *American Jewish Yearbook, 1985.* 128-61.

Silberman, C. (1985). *A Certain People.* New York: Summit.

Tobin, G. & Kipsman, J. (1984). A Compendium of Jewish Population Studies. In S. Cohen, J. Woocher & B. Phillips (Eds.), *Perspectives in Jewish Population Research*. Boulder, CO: Westview Press.

Wall, S. (1984). *Listening to Parents: A Study of Attitudes Toward the Supplementary Jewish School*. Unpublished manuscript.

Woocher, J. (Winter, 1981). The 1980 United Jewish Appeal Young Leadership Cabinet: A Profile. *Forum, 43*, 57-67.

Woocher, J. (1981). Jewish Survivalism as Communal Ideology: An Empirical Assessment. *Journal of Jewish Communal Service, 57*(4), 291-303.

Woocher, J. (1982). The Civil Judaism of Communal Leaders. *American Jewish Year Book*. Philadelphia: Jewish Publication Society,149-69.

Footnotes

[1]This article originally appeared as "Outreach to the Marginally Affiliated: Evidence and Implications for Policymakers in Jewish Education" in the Winter, 1985 issue of the *Journal of Communal Service, 62*(2) and is reprinted here with permission.

Highlights

* The vast majority of American Jews:
     send their children at one time or another to some form of Jewish schooling
     celebrate in some way the three seasonal holidays
     say they contribute to Jewish philanthropic campaigns
     claim a broad and passionate involvement with Israel
     belong to a synagogue when their children are of school age
* The number of unaffiliated is much smaller than most suppose, and that number seems to remain constant.
* Sooner or later, almost all Jews affiliate with some official Jewish agency.
* Rather than dividing the Jewish world into two classes, we ought to see Jews as arrayed on a continuum ranging from high to low levels of involvement.
* There are certain times when Jews are most open to educators' interventions. These "entry points" may be linked to calendar, family life cycle, or to historical events.
* Family stage is the most potent social predictor of involvement levels.
* There is a disjunction between the interests of those many American Jews involved in philanthropy, social service, and politics, and the main thrust of much of conventional Jewish education, which is heavily oriented toward synagogue, ritual and religious life.
* In place of the language of reproach, Jewish educators and other communal professionals might think about developing a language of resource.

The Larger Context

With the publication of the *Highlights of the CJF 1990 National Population Survey,* we now have information which may modify some of the figures presented in this reprinted article. Yet, Dr. Cohen's challenge to posit and create a politics of hope rather than a politics of fear remains the major challenge to professionals and laity alike. Instead of always "fighting"—trying to persuade and/or convince other Jews to join us in perpetuating the status quo—perhaps these suggestions to reframe our message indicate new avenues of exploration.

What We Know About...Faith Development

Roberta Louis Goodman

Faith development offers a way of thinking about how Jewish education can affect the lives of Jews. It is a tool which offers possibilities for addressing the needs and concerns of Jews and Jewish educators alike. Ms. Goodman, a student of Dr. James Fowler, the pioneer in this work, explores the current research and applies those learnings to the Jewish setting.

FINDING A PLACE FOR GOD AND OUR OWN SPIRITUALITY IS A CHALLENGE THAT JEWISH EDUCATION confronts directly. Some argue that by its very nature, God is implicit within Judaism and Jewish education. For our students of all ages, this makes God and the spiritual appear to be nowhere in Jewish educational offerings, and irrelevant to Judaism, rather than everywhere. This, in turn, helps perpetuate the myth that our daily actions, our participation in the secular society, our life-style choices, and our ethics are unrelated to and separate from our rituals, festivals, Jewish tradition, texts, and God. To counter this myth, the Jewish community needs to offer educational opportunities which nurture the human desire for addressing the sacred, for connecting all aspects of our lives, and for finding meaning in one's life. Jewish texts and tradition explore these very concerns.

Changing demographics, in particular the impact of intermarriage, and the distancing from the European experience by generations (fewer and fewer Jewish grandchildren have European-born grandparents), along with the experiment of living in an open pluralistic society, challenge Judaism's ethnocentricity. Jews look, talk, eat, work and play like most other North Americans. This diminishing of the ethnic, increases the importance of the religious and spiritual dimensions of Jewish life. These factors contribute to the concern for intensifying and strengthening commitment among both the present and future generations.

Theories centering around these theological concerns, religious life and language come from the integrated areas of theology and personality. We will discuss one specific area of that literature: namely, faith development, which offers insights into connecting Jewish education, Jewish tradition, and people's lives. This paper is focused around the four relevant themes emerging from the literature and examines some of the implications for policy and practice for Jewish education while suggesting areas for further research.

Four Themes from the Faith Development Literature

1) Knowing, feeling and doing are interconnected. People need to be viewed holistically, combining the cognitive and the affective, the rational and spiritual, the secular and the religious.

2) Human beings make meaning out of their lives continuously throughout their life spans. The way of being in this world is to make meaning.

3) Becoming a maker of meaning involves the individual as an adult who makes commitments.

4) Experience informs faith development. Experience is a source of knowledge. Experience acts as a conduit for turning knowledge into Jewish living.

1. A Whole-Person Approach to Human Development

There are many ways of looking at human development. Faith development theory offers a lens for viewing human development which is compatible with religious life. The term "faith development" comes from the work of Dr. James Fowler (1981), a theologian. Faith or "faithing" is the process by which a person finds and makes meaning of life's significant questions and issues, adheres to this meaning, and acts it out in his or her life span (Fowler, 1981). This definition steers away from the usage of faith as belief, or as referring to a particular religion. It is more expansive intertwining knowing, feeling and doing.

Faith involves loyalty, commitment and values. This is the substance which guides one's life. In our quest for making life worth living, Fowler writes, "we look for something to love that loves us, something to value that gives us value, something to honor and respect that has the power to sustain our being" (Fowler, 1981, p. 5). Judaism can be the source of a person's loyalties, commitments and values. Post-modern secular culture offers an alternative and often competing source of values, loyalty and power.

Both the Jew and the secular person have faith, but their relationship to God differs. Most Jews, from the most observant to the least observant, are influenced by secular culture. It is the central or core orientation of the individual that makes the difference. One can distinguish between Jews whose lives may be only tangentially centered around Jewish loyalties and values and those who place God, Torah and Israel at the center of their loyalties. Rather than compartmentalizing Jewish identity as separate from one's secular or non-Jewish identity, faith development looks at the individual as a whole. This is in keeping with Judaism which resists the designation of being just a religion, and strives to be a way of life, a way of being which informs a human being's whole self.

2. Experience Informs Faith Development

Experience which consists of living through the cycle of each day, each week, each year and the life cycle, informs faith development. One of the clearest ways of viewing the relationship between experience and faith is in terms of the life cycle. Faith formation happens throughout one's lifetime. Life cycle ceremonies and passages are times of transition that offer teachable moments, windows of opportunity, for intensifying and connecting the participants' faith to their Jewish roots. Regarding Bar and Bat Mitzvah, Zachary and Goodman (1991) point out:

> Families spend great amounts of time preparing for and celebrating the Bar/Bat
> Mitzvah. The preparation for Bar/Bat Mitzvah presents a teachable moment
> and thus a motivating force for learning. It provides an opportunity for doing
> educational programming which focuses on substantive issues and considers sig-
> nificant questions and not simply answers to logistical problems (p. 25).

These life experiences foster a bond between Judaic content and living a Jewish life. Life's transitions and passages present opportunities for connecting people's lives to the sacred in an explicitly Jewish way. In some way, knowledge and content must be linked to experience, the fabric of life.

In a similar fashion, everyday occurrences such as tragedies, accomplishments, relationships, first-time happenings, decision making, and moral dilemmas present fertile material for linking people's lives to Jewish values (especially the sacred) and the community on a daily basis. Capturing the richness of experience in the educational setting remains a challenge.

3. Meaning Making

The way humans organize this meaning-making activity is through the story or stories that we create about ourselves, our lives. As we go through life, each of us constructs a story about: who we are; to whom we owe allegiance; what we like and dislike; what we choose to do and not do; and what are our achievements, failures and longings. Throughout our lives we each continually construct and reconstruct this story. Our stories act as filters and frameworks organizing our lives, informing our choices and views.

Each person constructs this story in relation to others, both individuals and groups (Fowler, 1981, p. 17). My story interacts with the stories of my parents, my family, my school(s), my neighborhood, my community, my country, my God and my people, the Jewish people. Moran (1983) describes the relationship between a community and personal stories: "One of the marks of a community is the story its people hold in common, a story expressed in symbols, codes of behavior, styles of humor, modes of dress and address, ways of sharing sorrow and the like" (p. 101). The story of the Jewish people emerges from a variety of sources including the Bible, Talmud, family tales, folktales, personal histories, and historical accounts. Goldberg (1985) speaks of a master story for Jews in the Biblical narrative which offers to Jews "both a model for understanding the world and a guide for acting in it" (p. 13). Stories present Jewish values and behaviors, conflicts and resolutions, views of human beings and encounters with God. These stories inform Jewish tradition. As quintessentially exemplified within the Pesach seder, symbols and ritual link story with concrete forms of expression (Goldberg, 1985).

The task for Jewish educators is to create time and space for individuals to make connections and links between "my story" and the "big story" (Groome, 1980)—the story of the Jewish people.

Torop (1990) models this process. He suggests that cultivating imagination through the use of stories, in this case Biblical stories, in the educational setting can "create a supportive holding environment in which canopies of meaning may come unravelled and be rewoven" (p. 200). The embedding of one's personal story in the Jewish story places Jewish values and loyalties at the core of one's existence.

4. Fostering Commitment

One's story must stand the test of a pluralistic society, the encounter with relativism, and adulthood. The Jewish upbringing that a child receives does not automatically guarantee that as an adult he or she will carry on or even pass on this Jewish affiliation, much less any intensity of adherence to living a Jewish life. Perry's (1981) study of cognitive and ethical development distinguishes between childhood where one is a holder of meaning, and adulthood, where one becomes a maker of meaning (p. 87). A maker of meaning is able to form commitments in a world of relativism, a world full of competing claims and choices. Committing involves taking responsibility and initiative for making decisions, confronting life's questions and situations, and acting upon those choices which affect one's life.

The capacity for forming commitments, both to a larger cause such as perpetuating the Jewish people and in a specific form by joining a particular synagogue, emerges in adulthood. Only in adulthood does the individual become responsible for his or her actions.

The 1987 Religious Education Association's study of faith development in the adult life cycle highlights two age groupings as crucial and receptive periods for substantive changes in one's faith. This occurs most strongly in young adulthood, in one's twenties: "It is a time of disengagement from one's parental home and the establishment of one's own identity in the adult community. This often includes rejection or modification of previous religious and values orientations and the acceptance, often tentatively, of one's own and sometimes very different philosophical and theological life perspectives" (p. 19).

The other period is midlife, from 36 to 45 which shows "a positive correlation between the dealing with and resolution of psychosocial tensions and faith development" (p. 18). This is another age at which assumptions about one's life, its meaning and purpose, are rethought and restructured.

Implications and Directions for Policy and Practice

Jewish education needs to address the whole person, coalescing how a person acts, feels and perceives his/her life. The curriculum can accomplish this by combining the rational and cognitive with the affective and spiritual. This requires dealing explicitly with spiritual needs and longings. For example, it is equally important to provide moments for praying and times for reflecting on the prayer experience, as it is to teach about the prayers.

Jewish education needs to draw upon people's experiences as a starting point for intervention. Life cycle passages and ceremonies, along with everyday occurrences, provide ample opportunities for learning Jewish content which can affect Jewish living. The linking of a person's experiences with the teaching of Judaic content helps personalize Jewish education, connecting the individual's faith formation to Jewish roots and experiences.

Jewish education needs to nurture meaning making. Fundamental is the incorporation of stories, particularly those found in Jewish texts, for the faith formation of individuals. This helps embed the individual's story and values in the Jewish story and values. The stories of the Jewish people present a way of placing God and the sacred in the curriculum in an imaginative and non-didactic approach.

Jewish education needs to set fostering commitment and living a Jewish life as a goal. The necessity, not nicety or luxury of substantive adult Jewish education, lifelong learning, in fostering commitment is obvious. Jewish education in childhood is a link not a causality of adult Jewish commitment. The responsibility rests on the Jewish community to comprehensively seek to influence adult faith formation through adult Jewish education.

Further Research

The interaction between faith development and Jewish education merits further research. Here are some preliminary suggestions:

1) *Examining people's faith journeys (qualitative research):* This type of research could address such issues as: What common themes are there in the life histories of committed Jews versus non-committed Jews? What experiences seem to impact on people's commitments? How do people make meaning out of their Jewish educational experiences? What role do people attribute to parents, Jewish professionals, spouses, and friends in their faith formation?

2) *Connecting stories:* What are the ways in which we connect the story of the Jewish people with an individual's meaning-making story? How is this done with individuals of all ages?

3) *Developing curriculum and programs:* We need to create new materials which seek to enhance the faith formation of Jews of all ages and to find appropriate ways to evaluate both the new and the old.

4) *College students:* How does the university study of Judaic and Hebraic courses affect the student's faith formation?

This new field of research offers a way of thinking about how Jewish education can affect the lives of Jews and, more importantly, how we think about the future education of our children and ourselves.

Bibliography

Fowler, J. W. (1984). *Becoming Adult, Becoming Christian.* San Francisco: Harper & Row.

Fowler, J. W. (1981). *Stages of Faith.* San Francisco: Harper & Row.

Gillman, N. (1990). *Sacred Fragments: Recovering Theology for the Modern Jew.* Philadelphia: Jewish Publication Society.

Goldberg, M. (1985). *Jews and Christians Getting Our Stories Straight: The Exodus and the Passion-Resurrection.* Nashville, TN: Abingdon Press.

Goodman, R. L. (1991). Prayer and God and Faith Development. In A. Marcus, (Ed.), *The Jewish Preschool Teachers Handbook, (rev. ed.)* Denver: Alternatives in Religious Education.

Groome, T. H. (1980). *Christian Religious Education: Sharing Our Story and Vision.* San Francisco: Harper & Row.

Moran, G. (1983). *Religious Education Development: Images for the Future.* Minneapolis: Winston Press.

Parks, S. (1986). *The Critical Years: The Young Adult Search for a Faith to Live By.* San Francisco: Harper & Row.

Perry, W. G. (1981). Cognitive and Ethical Growth: The Making of Meaning. In A. Chickering, (Ed.), *The Modern American College.* San Francisco: Jossey-Bass Publishers.

Perry, W. G. (1968). *Forms of Intellectual and Ethical Development in the College Years.* Cambridge, MA: President and Fellows of Harvard College.

Religious Education Association. (1987). *Faith Development in the Adult Life Cycle: The Report of a Research Project.* Minneapolis: Author.

Stokes, K. (Ed.). (1982). *Faith Development in the Adult Life Cycle.* New York: W.H. Sadlier.

Torop, M. (!990). *The Power of Story and Imagination in Developing Faith: Teaching the Genesis Narratives from a Faith Development Perspective.* Unpublished rabbinic thesis, Hebrew Union College-Jewish Institute of Religion, Cincinnati.

Zachary, L. J, & Goodman, R. L.. (1991). A Learner-Centered Approach to Family Life Education Programming: The B'nai Mitzvah Experience. *Jewish Education. 59*(1).

Highlights

Four themes emerge from the faith development research

* Knowing, feeling and doing are interconnected. People need to be viewed holistically, combining the cognitive and the affective, the rational and spiritual, the secular and the religious.
* Human beings make meaning out of their lives continuously throughout their life span. The way of being in this world is to make meaning.
* Becoming a maker of meaning involves the individual as an adult who makes commitments.
* Experience informs faith development. Experience is a source of knowledge. Experience acts as a conduit for turning knowledge into Jewish living.

The Larger Context

It may seem that only recently have we begun to examine our own stories. In fact, in our earlier history as a Jewish people in various countries and settings, we did share such stories. Thankfully, modern research may have given us a new impetus to reexamine our own faith development. But more is needed: in particular the possibility of sharing face-to-face with others the dynamics as well as the contents of this process.

What We Know About...
Jewish Education for New Americans

Misha Galperin
Patricia Cipora Harte

Patricia Cipora Harte, an American-born social worker with training in Jewish education, and Misha Galperin, a Soviet-Jewish emigre who is a clinical psychologist involved in Jewish communal service, collaborate to draw on their own evolution of thinking, both professional and personal, about the subject of Jewish education for the new Americans from the Soviet Union. Currently, they are developing programs for Soviet emigres at the New York Association for New Americans. The recent waves of new immigrants have raised new and old issues of resettlement and acculturation for those involved in these tasks. In this article, the authors explore just who these new arrivals are and what we might learn from prior experiences of other immigrants about how to assist these New Americans in becoming part of the American Jewish community.

FOR APPROXIMATELY THE PAST 60 YEARS, THERE HAS BEEN A GROUP OF JEWS LIVING IN THE DIASPORA who since the 1930's, have been very minimally exposed to formal Jewish education. Much of the traditional yeshiva system that developed in Russia and Poland was imported into the United States, but was not maintained in the Soviet Union. Given this lack of maintenance of the yeshiva system, we find that there is a group of people who are identified as Jews while their knowledge base of Judaism and things Jewish was formed with the absence of Jewish congregational and communal organizations.

For many affiliated American-born Jews, the expectation with regard to providing Jewish education/acculturation to their newly found Soviet-born cousins has been nurtured by a belief that Jews from the Soviet Union need to be shown the "way" to be Jewish in the United States and that they are eager to shed the shackles of the Soviet system in exchange for American Jewish freedom. The new Americans, on the other hand, have their own notions of the meaning of their Jewishness and their Jewish needs. For instance, many an American Jew would have expected the "Russians" to be thrilled at an opportunity to join a congregation, while a new American may be ecstatic just at the chance to wear a symbol of Jewishness such as a pendant or a ring with a Star of David.

The divergence in views and expectations is a direct result of the divergence in historical experiences of these two branches of the Jewish family. The blueprint for the reintegration of Soviet and American Jewrys must therefore be derived from the understanding of both the commonalities and differences of each group's path.

Soviet and American Jewish Identity

In all probability, the most significant issue in beginning this process is the concept of the meaning of Jewish identity to the two groups. In other words, when the American-born and the Soviet-born Jew talk of Jewishness/Jewish identity, they have different understandings of this terminology. The American-born Jew in describing his/her Jewishness often sees it in terms of belonging to a common history and a common peoplehood, while the Jew from the Soviet Union may describe Jewishness with an emphasis on being Jewish, feeling Jewish and not necessarily acting Jewish. Growing up in the Soviet Union often did/does not allow for the expression of Jewishness which, for the affiliated American-born Jew, is a given. For the Jews of the Soviet Union, being Jewish is what they are rather than what they do. Much of this is rooted in the sociopolitical development of both the Soviet Union and the United States.

Who are the Jews from the Soviet Union?

We often hear Jews from the Soviet Union being referred to as Russians or Soviets. In the Soviet Union, the ethnic identity is stamped in an internal passport and on other documents. It could say "Uzbek", "Georgian", "Latvian", "Russian", etc. "Jewish" is one of these labels, the reference to which is the infamous *"pyataya grafa"* ("fifth item"). Through Stalin's definition of a "nationality" as belonging to a group with a common language, history, culture and territory, Jewishness in the U.S.S.R. ceased being a religious identity and became a national one. Stalin even went so far as to create the "Jewish Autonomous region" in the Birobidzan region of Siberia to satisfy the "territorial" requirement in his definition of nationality. Thus, the Jews of the Soviet Union were deprived of the opportunity to identify with their religion while maintaining a label that marked them for persecution. The notion of Jewishness as a nationality has become so deeply ingrained that even ten years after arrival in the U.S., 61% of new American Jews from the U.S.S.R. believe that Jewishness is a nationality and only 28% believe it is a religion (Kosmin, 1990, p.vii).

Being referred to as Russian has been perplexing for many of these new Americans. They have been persecuted for being Jews in their country of origin and are leaving for that reason, but no sooner do many of them arrive in the U.S.then they are told they are not Jewish because they do not have the same sense of identification that most American Jews have. Once here, they are called Russian or Soviet which had meant, respectively, "gentile" and "communist" where they come from.

In fact, Jews from the U.S.S.R. are an extraordinarily diverse group. The Soviet Union is a very large country, spanning thousands of miles and many and varied areas. Often the Jewish groups in the USSR are broken down into roughly five geographical and cultural groupings:

1. "Westerners" ("*zapadniki*") who live in areas annexed to the USSR in 1939-40 (the Baltic Republics, West Ukraine and West Belorussia, Moldavia; and Transcarpathian Ukraine, acquired in 1944-45);

2. The Ashkenazi group in the European areas of the USSR which have been under Soviet rule since 1917- 1919;

3. Georgian Jews;

4. Central Asian ("Bukharan") Jews concentrated in the Uzbek and Tadzhik republics;

5. The "Mountain Jews" of the Caucasus, concentrated in the Azerbaidzhani and Georgian republics (Gitelman, 1976, p.64).

Characteristics of New Americans

There is a significant body of literature—descriptive, theoretical and research-based—on the subject of the characteristics of new Americans. Without doing an exhaustive review of this litera- ture, let us only mention the most salient points. Jews from the Soviet Union have characteristics that reflect both their Jewishness and the fact that they were born and raised in the Soviet Union. Hence, much of who they are has been shaped by the forces that were at work in Soviet society at large, as well as in the various geographical regions in particular. There are also significant factors related to their educational backgrounds, social, vocational and economic status (these being not always correlated with each other, as in the U.S.). Cultural differences; e.g., Ashkenazi vs. Oriental, as well as profound individual differences related to family history, past political affiliations and degree of exposure. to Judaic knowledge also need to be taken into account in learning to under- stand who the Jews from the Soviet Union really are. Their individual reasons for leaving the Soviet Union and coming to the U.S. should be explored. There is much in these ideas that can prove valu- able in both the development of Jewish educational programs for Soviet Jews and expanding the horizons of the Americans' Jewish erudition.

In trying to understand and educate the Soviet Jews Jewishly, it is important to keep in mind educational, social and cultural issues that can be exchanged and built upon between the two groups (Soviet-born and American-born Jews).

A Program Example

In a New York project co-sponsored by NYANA and JBFCS, a musical entitled, "Immigranti" which brought together a group of Soviet-born and American-born Jewish teenagers who role-played, acted and trusted each other to talk about their experiences, preconceived notions, fears and expec- tations of emigrating and of welcoming and meeting emigres from the series of activities of these teens. The play, lyrics and music were written and the teens rehearsed in order to perform to a wide audience of American-born Jews and emigres. Through the educational model of the theater, the audiences were able to glimpse the process of leaving one's country of origin and arriving and acculturating to a new home. The process for the teens involved has been very profound and has dispelled certain preconceived notions and developed a better understanding of what it is like *to be* an American-born Jewish teenager and what it is like *to become* an American teenager.

This project illustrates some of the most important principles for planning and implementation of Jewish educational/acculturation activities for this population. The principles involved are: a) continuity of interaction for the group; i.e., the project was not a one-shot deal; b) allowing the participants to get to know each other in a context of a structured, goal-directed activity; and c) having a specific end product that required cooperation and active participation of the participants.

What is the Identity of the Soviet Jew?

The American Jewish community would have difficulty in defining itself in a single venue and this is as true for the Jewish emigre community. We cannot simply define ourselves in terms of a singular connection, but rather in terms of many facets of behavior, involvement, beliefs and practices. Our Jewish identity goes beyond religious identification and this is true for those of us born here as well as for those who came here later on in life.

In the 1985 study of *Jewish Identification and Affiliation of Soviet Jewish Immigrants in New York City* (Lachman, Gribetz, Newman, Mindlin, & Baskin, 1985, p.38), the Soviet Jewish immigrant's identity was described in terms of three aspects: a) *cognition*; i.e., how Soviet Jews think of themselves as Jews; b) *affect*; i.e., how Soviet Jews feel about being Jewish; and c) *behavior*; i.e., what Soviet Jews do to express their Jewishness. With respect to all three aspects cited above, the study found that Soviet Jews strongly identify Jewishly.

Barry Kosmin's study refers to the identity of the Soviet Jew in the following way: "Being Jewish is important to over 90%" (Kosmin, 1990, p.50). This is a much higher percentage then is generally seen in the existing American Jewish community. We often hear that we are "losing" the Soviet Jewish community and that they are being lost to the American Jewish community. Our response is often twofold—maybe it is our (the American Jewish community's) problem that we have not learned enough about the new Americans' background to build on their knowledge, expertise and interests so that they should know what it is that they can choose from. Making choices from an array of alternatives is in and of itself a relatively new experience, given decision-making or the lack of individual opportunities to make decisions in the Soviet Union, and it takes time to learn. We need to incorporate this understanding and explanation into our welcome and programming as well. In order to make informed decisions, one must do so having learned about and understanding the variety of options available. For those of us born in the United States it is difficult to unravel the complexities of the Jewish community, let alone for someone for whom this community is entirely new.

Affiliation

One of the major components of the American's Jewish identity is the issue of Jewish affiliation; i.e., belonging to Jewish institutions, contributing to Jewish causes and active participation in Jewish communal life. It is in this respect that Soviet Jewish emigres differ significantly from the standards and the experience of affiliated American Jewry. It is important to note, however, that the Soviet emigre's patterns of affiliation ten years after arrival in the U.S.are not significantly different from the American Jewish community at large (Kosmin, 1990).

The practice/concept of affiliation in the Soviet Union was negligible given the lack of opportunities (minimal number of synagogues, nonexistence of Jewish communal organizations, etc.) and the dire consequences of attempted Jewish involvement. Instead, the major vehicles for the expression of Jewish identity for Soviet Jews have been the preference for Jewish friends, the acquiring of Jewish symbols, interest in Jewish history and pride in the secular achievements of Jews. Surprisingly to many American Jews, Soviet Jews who have come to America express very positive feelings toward the State of Israel and feel committed to the support of Israel. The studies of both Kosmin and Lachman cite the fact that Soviet Jews do in fact make financial contributions to Jewish causes and that there is an understanding of the need to do this.

Perceptions of the American Jewish Community

The notion of the new American population being lost really may have more to do with the "host" community than with the newcomers. Kosmin (1990) reports that only 43% of the newcomers regularly visit American Jewish households ten years after arrival in the U.S. Given this limited contact, it is hard to expect that many American Jews would develop a good understanding of the newcomers or be able to program for them effectively.

The social work adage that comes to mind is "meet the client where the client is." Service providers, professionals and laypeople need to learn to move beyond our own line of vision in order to see with a different set of lenses—to see from the vantage point of the new Americans rather than the perspective we have always used. What have we done to utilize the expertise, interests and strengths of our new American Jews in planning for their future? How many of the Jewish agencies hire Soviet emigres at high-level decision-making positions or develop programs to enable Soviet Jews to move into Jewish communal service? It seems to us one of our goals is to provide experiences that foster an acceptance of the various parts of oneself that includes the various ethnic components (American, Soviet, Jewish, etc.) and that in this country these aspects can live harmoniously within the individual. It is the issue of developing and maintaining a positive Jewish identity that is the key, not merely the practice of specific behaviors; i.e., eating kosher food, synagogue membership, and lighting Shabbat candles.

In the American Jewish community voices are often heard saying that the Soviet Jews who have arrived in the past waves and who are currently arriving are not Jewish, that they are lost to Jewish life, that they come to the U.S. to assimilate. Let us reframe this in such a way as to tackle the problem as a challenge, to introduce and provide Jewish experiences that are welcoming, supportive, encouraging, experiences that utilize the high level of education most Soviet Jews come with as well as tapping into their sense of history and culture. There are varying statistics on the success of the American Jewish community's effort to encourage identification on the part of the unaffiliated American Jew. Has the American Jewish community been in fact expecting Soviet Jews to solve the age-old American Jewry problem of assimilation rather then looking at the recent emigres as a new group to learn from, to share with and to welcome into the larger Jewish community? How do we build upon the interests and strengths of these new Jewish Americans rather than chastise and alienate them because they are not living up to standards we have not been able to achieve?

Gary Rubin, Director of National Affairs for the American Jewish Committee, states it well: "The services we plan and believe to be in the best interest of the immigrant are often not in their best interest according to the immigrant's own logic. No matter what policy we create for them, in the end they will create their own policy and that's how acculturation will ultimately happen. Our planning has to take the immigrant's own perspective into account" (Rubin, 1989, p.29). In public polls, the results have shown that "Americans hate immigration and they love immigrants...while at the same time immigrants tend to love America, but not Americans" (Rubin, 1989). This shows differing feelings that we need to be aware of and take into account in our planning and programming. We need to be able to see from a variety of perspectives in order to provide meaningful experiences for immigrants and the American-born as well.

What We've Learned

We know that approaching new Americans with a heavy hand religiously is usually a turn-off and that an approach using Jewish history and/or Jewish culture is more in keeping with their background and interest, working with them from where they come. In our programming we are continually searching for bridges between Jewish concepts and values, modern behaviors and the ties to Jewish history, texts and traditions.

At times it feels as if there is an expectation on the part of the American Jewish community that there is a right way for our new Americans to be Jewish—that they should be treated as a monolithic group who should all fit into the same mold and should parrot certain behaviors.

The authors agree that to each of us a major aspect of Jewish identity was the fact of belonging to a common people with a shared history. In that context, our common understanding of the process of Jewish education for Jews from the Soviet Union emerges as an interaction between the two groups whose goal becomes the joint discovery of enlarged and enriched Jewish identity.

We need to find ways to expose Soviet Jews both to their common heritage with Western Jews and to those developments in Jewish life that took place while they were shut off from the world Jewish community. We also need to learn from our fellow Jews about their experiences and how to incorporate their learnings in order to preserve and enhance Jewishness as a positive entity under the conditions they experienced of an atheistic, totalitarian state. No matter what our individual, religious and communal identifications are, the best result we can hope to achieve is to allow Soviet

Jews to make an informed choice about how to maintain, enhance, practice, expand, and modify their Jewishness.

Becoming American and Jewish

It is the authors' belief that all Jews should work towards an enhanced positive sense of Jewish identity, but how that may be expressed is up to each individual to determine as he or she sees fit. But, this should be arrived at through an educational process and it is our responsibility to provide opportunities to educate, explain and expose people to the variety of opportunities for Jewish involvement. Recently, while at a presentation, a colleague replied to the question of the Soviet Jews' lack of Jewishness and what we are doing about it. His response expressed his anticipation that the Soviet Jews who come to America will most likely emulate the current American Jewish community (roughly 50% affiliation).

In general, the American Jewish community sees itself as just that, American and Jewish at the same time. When we consider our identities, we can have many varying components that make up our unique persona. Sometimes these components are in conflict with each other but by and large, they can be harmonious. An aspect of being an American and living in a free, democratic society is that we are free to select and engage in the various aspects of Jewishness which we find meaningful.

Bibliography

Carp, J. M. (1988, 11 November). The Impact of Russians on U.S. *Sh'ma, 19*(361), 3-5.

Carp, J. M. (1990, Summer). Absorbing Jews Jewishly. *Journal of Jewish Communal Service, 66*(4).

Friedman, A. (1988, 11 November). Involving Immigrants in Jewish Life Today. *Sh'ma, 19*(361), 5-6.

Gitelman, Z. (1988). *A Century of Ambivalence—The Jews of Russia and the Soviet Union, 1881 to the Present.* New York: Shocken Books.

Gitelman, Z. (1990, April). *Anti-Semitism in the Age of Perestroika.* HIAS paper.

Gitelman, Z. (1976, December). Demographic, Cultural and Attitudinal Characteristics of Soviet Jews: Implications for the Integration of Soviet Immigrants. *Proceedings of the National Symposium on the Integration of Soviet Jews into the American Jewish Community.* New York.

Goldberg, S. (1989, July). *What We Know About the Last Wave of Jewish Immigration From the U.S.S.R.* New York: Council of Jewish Federations.

Kosmin, B. A. (1990, April). *The Class of 1979: The Acculturation of Jewish Immigrants from the Soviet Union.* (Occasional Papers No. 5). New York: CUNY Graduate Center, North American Jewish Data Bank.

Lachman, S., Gribetz, J.; Newman, S.K., Mindlen, M. & Baskin, F. M. (1985, June). *Jewish Identification and Affiliation of Soviet Jewish Immigrants in New York City—A Needs Assessment and Planning Study.* New York: Federation of Jewish Philanthropies of New York.

Pousner, M. (1990, July 27). Reclaiming Russia's Lost Jews. *Baltimore Jewish Times.*

Rubin, G.E. (1989). *Acculturation Overview,* The Proceedings of Making It in America: The Jewish Refugee Experience. New York: New York Association of New Americans.

Szabad, G.M. & Martinez, H. (Co-chairs). (1989). *Educating the Newest Americans, Report of the Task Force on New Immigrants and American Education,* New York: The American Jewish Committee and the Institute on Urban and Minority Education Teachers College.

Zukerman, K.D. (1988, 11 November). Absorbing Soviet Jews: Meeting Ourselves. *Sh'ma, 19*(361), 1-3.

Highlights

* These new Americans identify as Jews, but their knowledge base of Judaism and things Jewish was formed in the absence of Jewish congregational and communal organizations.
* The American-born Jew in describing his/her Jewishness, often sees it in terms of belonging to a common history and a common peoplehood; the Jew from the Soviet Union may describe Jewishness with an emphasis on personally being Jewish, feeling Jewish and not necessarily acting Jewish.
* Jews from the USSR are an extraordinarily diverse group.
* In trying to understand and educate the Soviet emigre Jewishly, it is important to keep in mind educational, social and cultural issues that can be exchanged and built-upon between the two groups.
* While the major component of the identity of an American Jew is that of affiliation, the same is not initially true for the Jew from the Soviet Union. Yet, the Soviet emigre's pattern of affiliation ten years after arrival in the U.S. is not significantly different from that of the American Jewish community at large.
* The major vehicles for the expression of Jewish identity for the Soviet emigre have been the preference for Jewish friends, the acquiring of Jewish symbols, interest in Jewish history and pride in the secular achievements of Jews. As well, they have very positive feelings toward the State of Israel.
* Approaching new Americans with a heavy hand religiously is usually a turn-off. An approach using Jewish history and/or culture is more in keeping with their background and interest.

The Larger Context

"A blueprint for reintegration of Soviet and American Jewrys must therefore be derived from the understanding of both the commonalities and the differences in each group's path." If this is the authors' conclusion, then bringing the Soviet emigre into OUR culture, which is typically how we in the Jewish community view immigrants, denies the strength and vitality of THEIR culture. Are we prepared, for example, to learn Russian and study their history? Are we prepared to approach their acculturation through culture and history rather than religion? Are we prepared to accept some of their rich tradition and customs and make them ours? We who are now two or three generations distant from our own Eastern European roots may be able to rekindle a more immediate link to our own cultural past. This different perception of an immigrant community may give us the opportunity, as well, to document the process of acculturation. What can we learn about the processes of acculturation from working with this group? We have watched and partly documented their entry into American Jewish society and culture. Is there anything we can learn from this experience which might assist us with the other populations such as the "unaffiliated"?

Note: This article was written just prior to the break-up of the Soviet Union and reflects that political reality.

The Settings and the Community

The Jewish Day School
Alvin I. Schiff

The Supplementary School
David Schoem

The Jewish Community Centers
Barry Chazan and Richard Juran

Family Education
Joseph Reimer

Parent Motivation
Stuart L. Kelman

Communal Planning
Chaim Lauer

Changing Jewish Schools
Susan L. Shevitz

Lay People
Bernard Reisman

Funding
J. Alan Winter

What We Know About ...
The Jewish Day School

Alvin I. Schiff

One of the unique phenomena in Jewish education in North America has been the growth and predominance of all-day schools. Dr. Alvin I. Schiff, Executive Vice President Emeritus of the Board of Jewish Education of Greater New York and distinguished professor of education at Yeshiva University has published widely on this subject. In this article, he summarizes what we have learned about this form of Jewish education.

A T THE BEGINNING OF THE NEXT CENTURY, WHEN HISTORIANS AND SOCIOLOGISTS WILL SCURRY TO analyze fully the development of the American Jewish community in the nineteenth century, one trend will be clearly outstanding—the phenomenal growth and staying power of Jewish all-day education (Schiff, 1966, 1974, 1987; Dubb & DellaPergola, 1986; McMillan and Gerald, 1990). Given its relative costliness, especially when compared to the free public school—even in tandem with the cost of Jewish supplementary schooling—the flourishing of this institution during the mid 1900's and thereafter is nothing less than remarkable. This is particularly so in view of the decline of the Jewish supplementary school (Schiff, 1988, 1983, 1991).

Enrollment

In 1990, there were about 177,250 pupils (K-12) enrolled in 652 Jewish day schools and yeshivot in North America (158,381 pupils in 604 schools in the United States and 18,870 students in 48 schools in Canada), compared to 62,000 pupils (K-12) in 296 schools in North American in 1962, the peak year of enrollment (McMillan & Gerald, 1990). During the same period, enrollment in Jewish supplementary schools declined from 540,000 to 260,000 (Schiff, 1983; JESNA, 1985).

The 1990 Jewish day school population comprised about 40 percent of the total Jewish school enrollment in the United States and Canada, compared to eleven percent in 1962 (Schiff, 1983). The Greater New York experience sharpens the contrast even more. In 1940, the year marking the beginning of the Era of Great Expansion, the Jewish Day School enrollment was about 6% of the total Jewish school enrollment (Schiff, 1966). By 1978, the day school population surpassed supplementary school enrollment; in 1990 it composed sixty percent of the total Jewish school population (Schiff & Kessel, 1991). This development appears even more extraordinary when one considers the reaction of Samuel Dinin to the early spurt of day school growth in the 1940's. In 1945, he wrote, "The Jews may get more than 0.8 percent of their children to attend all-day schools (the Protestant percentage); they are hardly likely to go above 2 or 3 percent (2 percent being the percentage of private school pupils in this country) for the whole Jewish child population of 800,000."

Variety is a characteristic of this growth which involves virtually all of the ideological groupings in American Jewry—Hasidic, sectarian Orthodox, modern/centrist Orthodox, communal/traditional, Conservative, Reform, Yiddish, Zionist and general secular. The only feature common to all schools is the all-day format of Jewish and general studies under one roof.

Developed by Orthodox Jews against a backdrop of opposition and doubt by the rest of the Jewish community (Kramer, 1977; Parsons, 1983; Schiff, 1966), its degree of acceptance and support by the broad Jewish community is underscored by the fact that 14.3% of Jewish Federation dollars for local needs were allocated in 1989 to Jewish all-day education. This represents 56.4% of the total dollar allotment to local Jewish education services and programs (Liebman, 1990).

Eighty-three percent of the day school population is enrolled in Orthodox sponsored schools, equally divided between Hasidic/sectarian and modern/centrist institutions. (The fact that Orthodox Jews comprise less than 10% of the total Jewish population in the United States is powerful evidence of the role of Orthodox Jewry in the development of all-day Jewish schooling.) Ten percent of the enrollment is under Conservative auspices, 6% under communal (interdenominational, non-denominational or "other") sponsorship and 1% in Reform day schools.

Despite the reality that day schools exist in every Jewish community with five thousand or more Jews, the Jewish day school is mainly an urban, large Jewish community phenomenon (Schiff, 1983). For example, of the 80,000 pupils (K-12) in New York area day schools in 1990, only 6,455 were in suburban Long Island and Westchester where approximately 45% of the Jewish population resides (Schiff & Kessel, 1991). Ninety percent of the enrollment in North America is in the ten largest urban centers.

Greater New York alone accounts for well over one half of the total day school population. Ninety-five percent of the New York day school enrollment is in Orthodox schools. With rare exception, Orthodox families choose the all-day school format of Jewish education for their offspring, at least through high school grades.

Continentally, 29% of the day school enrollment is in early childhood programs (N-K); 58% is in the elementary grades; and 13% is in high school classes. The percentage of students in high school grades is significantly higher in New York (25%) where the vast majority of secondary Jewish day schools are found (Schiff & Kessel, 1991).

Growth Factors

The initial spurt in day school growth in the 1940's and early 1950's was due essentially to three factors: 1) the zealous activity of a small selfless group of Orthodox Day School advocates; 2) the effect of the Holocaust and the establishment of the State of Israel on the Jewish consciousness of American Jews; and 3) the influx of Eastern European Jews after World War II, especially between 1956 and 1958 (Schiff, 1966).

The reasons for day school growth since the 1960's are, interestingly, the opposite of the factors leading to the decline of the supplementary school enrollment. Whereas the birth rate among the general Jewish population has decreased in the last several decades, causing a drop in supplementary school enrollment, the high birth rate among the Orthodox, primarily the right-wing Orthodox, has accounted for dramatic pupil increases in yeshivot and day schools.

The mobility of the Jewish population—particularly the out-migration of Jews from areas of second and third settlement—has often been accompanied by nonaffiliation with a synagogue in the new areas of residence, and, hence, fewer children enrolled in synagogue schools. On the other hand, the immigration of Jews from the Soviet Union, Israel, Iran and other Moslem lands has added children to the classroom registers of the day schools. Heightened Jewish consciousness (and the *baal teshuvah* movement) is another reason for the increase in the number of day school pupils.

In some areas, dissatisfaction with the public school has motivated parents to choose a Jewish day school for their children, while others prefer it because it is a private school (Schiff, 1987). Finally, a growing number of working mothers and single parents favor an all-day school environment, especially at the preschool levels.

Will these factors continue to motivate growth in the day school in the decades ahead? The proliferation of day schools has enhanced their viability by creating a positive image in the eyes of the community that the Jewish day school has come of age. The challenge is for day schools to capitalize on this image in their recruitment efforts. Indeed, now may be a good time to convene a continental trans-ideological consultation on day school recruitment and retention.

As for future enrollment, one other question must be posed. Early childhood education is a significant aspect of overall day school growth. How can we ensure that greater numbers of early childhood graduates will continue on to Jewish all-day elementary schools? To achieve this all-important objective, Jewish family education, geared to the young parents of these children, must become a regular part of every early childhood day school program.

Governance and Finances

The overwhelming majority of Jewish day schools are independently sponsored by local communal groups. About 15% were organized by synagogues—for the most part, by Conservative and Reform congregations. Almost all day schools are loosely affiliated with one or more national[1] or local organization. Locally, with the exception of some Orthodox yeshivot, they are associated with and receive services from the communal bureau of Jewish education. In the smaller communities, and even in the intermediate and large communities, the day school often competes with the bureau for Federation funding.

Despite their local and national affiliations, the authority and power for policymaking and program implementation rest solely within each school's board of trustees and its professional administration. Each institution was founded by a local group of interested parents and/or communal leaders (often with professional assistance from Torah Umesorah, United Synagogue or Yeshiva University) who are desirous of controlling the affairs of the school and of insuring the continuation of its ideological/philosophical orientation. Moreover, they are loath to give up their power since they are saddled with the financial responsibility for the conduct of their respective institutions.

The cost of day school operation is considerable—what with the dual curriculum and dual sets of instructional staffs and administration. Tuition fees have not kept pace with the skyrocketing costs of all-day education. Average per-pupil costs rose over ninefold in three decades, from approximately $500 in 1962 to $4,600 in 1990; they ranged from $3,000 to $12,000 depending upon locale and grade level of school (Pollack & Lang, 1984; Schiff & Kessel, 1991). High school costs are about 50% higher than the elementary grades.

The largest portion of the school income derives from tuition fees. About 40% of the pupils do not pay full tuition (Pollack & Lang, 1984). Moreover, the full fee does not usually cover the complete cost of a child's education.

Day school operation in America is big business. The aggregate cost of yeshiva/day school education in 1990 was approximately $800,000,000. School boards raised approximately one third of this sum. Over the years, Federations have increased their support of all-day education via scholarship assistance and subsidies for teacher salaries and special programs. In 1989, Federation allocations to day schools ($40,892,886) represented about 5% of the overall day school expenditure (Liebman, 1990).

The Post High School Yeshiva World

An aspect of Jewish all-day education that deserves mention is the development and remarkable growth in the Orthodox community of a dual-level system of full-time (as much as 18 hours per day) post-high-school undergraduate and graduate Torah and Talmud study. While there are no exact enrollment figures available for each of these levels of study, it is estimated that in 1990 there were about 6,000 Bais Midrash (undergraduate) students and 2,500 Kollel (graduate) students. In 1950, there were less than 100 students enrolled in these programs (Helmreich, 1982). The length of stay in the Bais Midrash is generally two to four years; and in the Kollel, one to twenty years. Most students spend three to five years in the Kollel. Tuition in both of these programs ranges from $3,000 to $6,000 per annum, but really depends solely upon ability to pay. Most students pay little or no tuition. More than that, the Kollel students regularly receive stipends averaging $7,000 per year for room and board so that they can devote full time (morning, afternoon and evening) to study without having to worry about finances. Married students often receive as much as $10,000 a year, supplemented by their wives' income, usually from teaching in a local yeshiva. The expenditures for this intensive post-high-school system of yeshiva education were estimated to be more than $50,000,000 in 1990 (Joel Beritz, personal communication). The Yeshivot Gedolot—the post-high- school institutions—are organized into the Association of Advanced Rabbinical and Talmudic

Schools (AARTS), a group recognized by the Federal government as a national accrediting agency for Pell grants.

Personnel

Two problem areas have consistently concerned the leadership of Jewish day schools—a shortage of qualified Hebrew teachers entering the Hebrew teaching profession and the high rate of turnover of Hebrew teachers. Both problems are rooted in the matter of job satisfaction (Himmelstein, 1975; Ravin, 1981) largely derived from the level of remuneration and fringe benefits (Himmelstein, 1975; Pollack & Lang, 1984). To be sure, teacher salaries are significantly less than those paid to public school teachers (JESNA, 1985; Aron & Phillips, 1990; Well, 1975). Because of this condition, one researcher found that more than half of the teachers in his study sample planned to leave their positions within five years (Lebovitz, 1981).

In 1990, in Greater New York, for example, the average salary of male instructors for twenty hours or more of Jewish studies teaching per week was $22,500 and for female teachers $19,120. Salaries for principals averaged $45,000. While the highest teacher salary was $51,000, several principals and administrators earned in excess of $100,000 (Schiff & Kessel, 1991).

Despite their personnel problems, the day schools seem to manage from year to year, hoping that next year will be an easier one financially. The personnel problems relating to supervision and administration are similar, yet different from those regarding teachers. There is a shortage of qualified personnel on both levels despite the significantly higher salaries (two to five times as much) for principals, driven up by supply and demand, by the feeling of lay leadership that they can attract highly qualified supervisory personnel if they can out-bid other schools. To be sure, the ability to hire high caliber administrators depends solely on the availability of such personnel and not upon the salaries schools are willing to offer. That availability derives largely from a sufficient pool of qualified teachers who have supervisory potential and are willing to obtain the necessary training in supervision and administration.

The problems are different because of the difference in job requirements. Lay-professional relationships play an important role in the life of a day school principal. A study of the views of New York City elementary Orthodox Hebrew day school principals' role expectations as perceived by the principals themselves and their lay board chairs revealed that the principals' views of the scope of their decision-making functions were substantially greater than the board chairs' views of their decision-making power (Feuerstein, 1977). This difference was similar in the four areas of schooling examined—religious orientation, curriculum, finance and personnel. It was greatest in the area of curriculum and least in the area of religious orientation. Interestingly, while the lay board chairmen's views of the decision-making power of the principal in establishing the religious philosophy of the school almost coincided with that of the principals, they differed widely in their views about the principal's authority to implement that philosophy via the curriculum. Generally, the principals and board chairs agreed that the area of finance is a board function and that religious orientation, curriculum and personnel are primarily principal functions (Feuerstein, 1977).

Another study demonstrated that directors who are formally evaluated by their boards of education at least once per year showed a greater desire to stay at their present positions than those who were not evaluated. There was no difference between directors with and without written job descriptions. Overall staying power of non-Orthodox day school principals was much greater at the time of the study (1987) than in earlier years. Average length of tenure is eight years and average number of positions held by present directors is two (Rosenthal, 1987).

Most day schools have two principals, one for Jewish studies and one for general studies. The relationship of these supervisors is critical to the smooth functioning of the school. Flatto (1987) showed that there is no relationship between the role expectations and the job satisfaction of the principals of the religious and secular departments.

Another study demonstrated that the older the principal is, the more experienced and the longer in the job, the greater the likelihood of role conflict perception between principals and between principals and boards of directors (Jordan, 1983).

Curriculum

While the common characteristic of all day schools is the dual program of Jewish and general studies under one roof, the Judaic curricula vary greatly. The general studies curriculum is generally set according to State requirements. In most schools, the morning hours are devoted to Jewish subjects when the students are presumably more alert.

The sectarian Chasidic and non-Chasidic all-boys yeshivot spend well over 60% of their instructional time on Jewish studies and concentrate almost solely on Pentateuch, the prayer service and codes in the early grades (Hebrew reading is taught in the kindergarten and sometimes even earlier) and on Talmud beginning with the fourth grade. These schools devote six days a week—between 30 and 40 hours—to Jewish studies where the language of instruction is often Yiddish. The sectarian girls schools teach bible, Hebrew language, customs and ceremonies, Musar (ethics), Midrash and Shulchan Aruch in a Judaic studies program ranging from 15 to 20 hours per week. About the same amount of time is scheduled for general studies.

The modern/centrist Orthodox schools divide instructional time equally between Jewish and general studies. The Judaic studies curriculum includes: Hebrew language arts, Pentateuch, Prophets, Siddur, Jewish history, holidays and ceremonies, and Shulchan Aruch. Beginning with grade six or seven, the curriculum concentration is on Talmud for boys. During these periods, girls study Midrash, Agaddah, Hebrew literature, Jewish history and current events. Between fifteen and twenty hours are devoted to the Hebrew studies program.

The Solomon Schechter Schools and communal schools generally devote about one third of the instructional time (12 to 15 hours per week) to Judaic subjects including Hebrew language and literature, Bible, Jewish history, customs and ceremonies, current events and introduction to Talmud in the upper grades.

In the Reform day schools, Hebrew language and literature are taught as separate subjects. All other Hebraic studies are introduced as part of an interdisciplinary approach to classroom instruction. In all, between 5 and 15 hours are devoted to the Jewish dimensions of the program.

Curricula integration, by and large, is not practiced. In the first instance, Orthodox schools do not advocate it as a matter of principle. However, it is considered an ideological and practical desideratum for Conservative and Reform schools. Nevertheless, as one study demonstrated, these institutions do not integrate Jewish and general subject matter because of a fundamental philosophical problem—their acceptance of a "structure of discipline's view of knowledge and curriculum planning" (Solomon, 1979).

There is a surprising lack of scientific information regarding academic achievement in both Jewish and general studies. There are no standardized tests for achievement in Jewish studies. Yet, from all available evidence it is clear that Jewish day school graduates acquit themselves admirably in high school and university settings. This is due largely to school standards, stringent requirements regarding homework, the general climate of learning in the schools and parent involvement in their childrens' education. Moreover, the sheer volume of hours and the intensity of exposure of Judaic studies have a notable impact upon students, especially upon those continuing their all-day schooling through high school and beyond. In absolute (and certainly in relative) terms, they accumulate a significant body of Judaic knowledge, not unlike the Torah scholarship of yesteryear in Eastern Europe.

Family and School

The role of family in day schools cannot be disregarded. Research in general education adequately confirms the importance of family influence on achievement (Coleman & Campell, 1966; Cohen, 1971; Jencks, et al., 1972; Greeley & Rossi, 1966). This is so in Jewish schools, particularly with regard to the formation and strengthening of Jewish identity. One study demonstrated that family background "makes a large and significant contribution to total Jewish identification" (Shapiro, 1988). It showed that the most important predictors of total Jewish identification are parents' ritual observance, parents' residence-friendship patterns, the children's group activities and parents' parenting behaviors. Clearly, parents with positive Jewish attitudes and family styles prefer to send their offspring to a day school. The synergism between home and school is the key to the successful performance of the children (Heimowitz, 1979).

For high performance in every area of life, Benjamin Bloom (1985) has underscored the importance of the combination of a supportive "sacrificing home" and quality "time-on-task" in and out of school.

Parental interest, motivation and support differ significantly according to ideological orientation. Sectarian Orthodox parents strongly support school policies. For them, there is no choice but to give their children the most intensive, religious Jewish educational exposure in home and in school. Modern/centrist Orthodox parents generally enroll their children in day schools because of the quality and intensity of the Jewish study program and because of their own Jewish concerns

(Nulman, 1955; Adams, Frankel & Newbauers, 1972/3; Schiff, 1966); yet, in the modern/centrist schools many parents are not themselves Orthodox or as religious as the school would like them to be. Consequently, they do not necessarily associate themselves with the religious philosophy of the schools. They are interested in having their children "feel Jewish" but not really "act Jewish" (Lasker, 1976/7).

In one study of modern Orthodox schools, the teachers and principals attributed greatest importance to goals of religious living. Most parents, on the other hand, indicated that goals of Jewish cultural living are most important and goals of religious living least important. Moreover, parents rated the importance of "a secular American orientation" much higher than the Jewish studies personnel (Gans, 1986).

In the non-Orthodox day school sector, parents enroll their children primarily because of excellence in general studies and not for "Jewish reasons" (Kapel, 1972; Kelman,1979). This fact underscores the relationship between the deterioration of the public school system and greater parental interest in the non-Orthodox Jewish day school (Zeldin, 1990).

Day School Impact

Overall, the impact of day school education is significant, particularly when compared to Jewish supplementary schooling (Schiff, 1988). A follow-up study of graduates of selected Hebrew day and supplementary schools focused attention on the relative contribution of these institutions in maintaining Jewish identity and continuity (Hartman, 1976). The findings of this study demonstrate that: Hebrew day school graduates 1) perceive themselves and their parents as more religiously observant; 2) perceive their Jewish education as being more effective in enhancing both their own and their parents' religious behavior; 3) view interdating and intermarriage as more antithetical to their belief system. Hebrew day school graduates interdate much less and intermarry much less.

Graduates of both systems who express a higher degree of satisfaction with Jewish education also perceive themselves and their parents as more religiously observant. Hebrew day school graduates attend secondary or post-secondary schools of Jewish learning significantly longer and select Jewish education and/or Jewish communal work as future vocational choices to a greater degree (Hartman, 1976).

Long-term studies on the impact of Jewish day schooling indicate that it has significant influence on Jewish identity formation, even when a variety of factors including family background are controlled (Bock, 1976; Cohen, 1974; Himmelfarb, 1977). In the final analysis, one of the major reasons for the impact of day schools on attitudes and identification is the full-day Jewish climate in which students are immersed. This, after all, is one of the reasons for the establishment of day schools.

Summing up the day school phenomenon in Jewish life, it seems most appropriate to quote Ludwig Lewisohn (1950), author, novelist and critic, who in his later years became a strong devotee of the day school movement. He wrote in 1950:

The truest advance in recent Jewish history in the United States, the one altogether hopeful phenomenon, has been the initiation and the slow gradual spread of the day school movement. It arose, necessarily, from classical Jewish sources...

Fundamentals must be side by side with the acquisition of an exacting and elegant grasp of English and its literature. The usual [general] subjects of instruction must be augmented by Jewish history, symbol, ceremony, liturgy, with special attention in the grades to the development of the Yishuv, the community in Eretz Yisrael and the re-established commonwealth. All this can be accomplished in the [elementary] grade where a Jewish (day) high school is not practiced. The public grade schools take from six to seven years to teach so pitifully little that advanced educators see in these half-wasted years the chief symptom of the ills that afflict American education. They point authoritatively to the fact that in Europe boys and girls of seventeen to eighteen are ready for what we call graduate or professional studies.

Coming from such [day] schools Jewish children will be reasonably well educated for their age. The possession of one additional language, Hebrew, will make the acquisition of others in high school and college easier. Above all, these children will be, from the beginning, integrated Jews; that is to say, since they are Jews, integrated human beings. As such, as whole human beings, knowing their place in society and in the world, in the realms of man and God, they will be able to meet the non-Jewish world with ease, assurance, dignity. They will neither defensively overemphasize or fearfully underemphasize their Jewishness and their Judaism. They and they alone will be equals in temper, poise, directness of all social approaches of the Catholics and Protestants with whom they will have to mingle and compete in the daily involvement of American life.

Bibliography

Adams, L.J., Frankel, J. & Newbauers, N. (1972-73, Winter). Parental Attitudes Toward the Jewish All-Day School. *Jewish Education, 42*(1).

Aron, I. and Phillips, B. (1990, June). *Findings of the Los Angeles Teacher Census.* Paper presented at the Fourth Annual Conference of the Network for Research in Jewish Education, New York, NY.

Bloom, B. (1985). *Developing Talent in Young People.* New York: Ballantine Books.

Bock, G.E. (1976). *The Jewish Schooling of American Jews: A Study of Non-Cognitive Effects.* Unpublished doctoral dissertation, Harvard University, Cambridge, MA.

Cohen, D. (1971, November) Why Curriculum Doesn't Matter. *The New Leader.*

Cohen, S.M. (1974, July-October). The Impact of Jewish Education on Religious Identification and Practice. *Jewish Social Studies, 36.*

Coleman, J.S. & Campbell, E.Q. (1966). *Equality of Educational Opportunity.* Washington D.C.: U.S. Department of Health, Education and Welfare.

Dinin, S. (1945, October 5). The All Day School. *The Reconstructionist.*

Dubb, A.E. & DellaPergola, S. (1986). *First Census of Jewish Schools in the Diaspora, 1981/82 1982/83: United States of America.* (Research Report No. 4, Project for Education Statistics). Jerusalem: The Hebrew University, and New York: Jewish Educational Service of North America.

Flatto, Z. (1978). *Role Congruency and Job Satisfaction of Principals in Jewish Day Schools.* Unpublished doctoral dissertation, Yeshiva University, New York.

Feuerman, H. (1977). *A Study of the Views of Principal Role in Elementary Orthodox Hebrew Day Schools in New York City Area: Expectations Held by Principals and their Lay Board Chairmen.* Unpublished doctoral dissertation, St. John's University, New York.

Gans, M.Z. (1986). *Parent and Educator Ratings of Goals of Jewish Day Schools.* Unpublished doctoral dissertation, University of Colorado, Denver.

Greeley, A.M. and Rossi, P.H. (1966). *The Education of Catholic Americans.* Chicago: Aldine Publishing Co.

Hartman, E. (1976). *A Follow-Up Study of Selected Hebrew Elementary Education Institutions.* Unpublished doctoral dissertation, Memphis State University, Memphis, TN.

Heimowitz, J. (1979). *A Study of the Graduates of Flatbush Yeshiva High School.* Unpublished doctoral dissertation, Yeshiva University, New York.

Helmreich, W.B. (1982). *The World of the Yeshiva: An Intimate Portrait of Orthodox Jewry.* New York: Free Press.

Himmelfarb, H.S. (1977, April). The Non-Linear Impact of Schooling: Comparing Different Types and Amounts of Jewish Education. *Sociology of Education, 50.*

Himmelstein, S. (1975). *A Comparative Study of Teacher Satisfactions and Dissatisfactions Between Teachers in Selected Jewish Day Schools and Teachers in New York.* Unpublished doctoral dissertation, Columbia University, New York.

Jencks, C., Smith, M., Acland, H., Bane, M.J., Cohen, D., Gintis, H., Heyns, B., & Michelson, S. (1972). *Inequality: A Reassessment of the Effect of Family and Schooling in America.* New York: Basic Books.

JESNA. (1985, Winter). *Trends* No. 9.

Jordan, C.B. (1983) *Perception of Role Conflict Problems Reported by Heads of Selected Private Schools: The Solomon Schechter Schools in North America.* Unpublished doctoral dissertation, University of Houston, Houston.

Kapel, D. (1972, Spring). Parental Views of a Jewish Day School. *Jewish Education, 41*(3).

Kelman, S.L. (1979, Spring). Motivation and Goals: Why Parents Send Their Children to Non-Orthodox Day Schools. *Jewish Education, 47*(1).

Kramer, D. (1977). *History and Impact of Torah Umesorah and Hebrew Day Schools in America.* Unpublished doctoral dissertation, Yeshiva University, New York.

Lasker, A.A. (1976-77, Winter). Parents as Partners: Report of a Research Project. *Impact,* (35).

Lazar, M. (1969). *Religious Academic Achievement of Boys and Girls of Hebrew Orthodox Day Schools as related to Selected Variables.* Unpublished doctoral dissertation, St. Louis University, St. Louis.

Lebovitz, G. (1981). *Satisfaction and Dissatisfaction Among Judaic Studies Teachers in Midwestern Jewish Day Schools.* Unpublished doctoral dissertation, University of Cincinnati, Cincinnati.

Lewisohn, L. (1950). *The American Jew, Character and Destiny.* New York: Farrar Strauss and Company.

Liebman, N. (1990, December). *Federation Allocations to Jewish Education 1985-1989.* Council of Jewish Federations, Research Department.

McMillan, M.M. & Gerald, E. (1990, April). Characteristics of Private Schools: 1987-88. *E.D. Tabs.* Washington D.C.: National Center for Education Statistics.

Nulman, L. (1955). *The Reaction of Parents to a Jewish All-Day School.* Unpublished doctoral dissertation, University of Pittsburgh, Pittsburgh.

Parsons, S. *The Role of Faivel Mendelovitz in the Founding and Development of Hebrew Day Schools in the United States.* Unpublished doctoral dissertation, New York University, New York.

Pollak, G. & Lang, G. (1984). Budgetary and Financing in Jewish Day Schools—Does it Exist?. *Jewish Education, 52*(2).

Ravin, N. (1981). *The Effect of Individual and Job Characteristics on Job Satisfaction of Supplementary and Hebrew Day Schools' Hebrew Teachers.* Unpublished doctoral dissertation, The American University, Washington D.C.

Rosenthal, S. (1987). *An Analysis of Factors Affecting the Mobility of Private Non-Orthodox Jewish Day School Directors.* Unpublished doctoral dissertation, University of San Francisco, San Francisco.

Schiff, A.I. (1966). *The Jewish Day School in America.* New York: Jewish Educational Committee Press.

Schiff, A.I. (1974). Jewish Day Schools in the United States. *Encyclopedia Judaica Year Book.* Jerusalem: Keter Publishing House.

Schiff, A.I. (1983, March). *Jewish Education at the Crossroads: The State of Jewish Education.* New York and Jerusalem: The Joint Program for Jewish Education, in Conjunction with CJF, JWB, and JESNA.

Schiff, A.I. (1983, Spring). On the Status of Jewish All-Day Education. *Jewish Education, 51.*

Schiff, A.I. (1987). The American Jewish Day School—Retrospect and Prospect. *Pedagogic Reporter, 38*(3).

Schiff, A.I. (1988). *Jewish Supplementary Schooling in Greater New York: An Educational System in Need of Change.* New York: Board of Jewish Education.

Schiff, A.I. and Kessel, B. (1991). *Jewish Education in Greater New York: Comparative Demographic Report 1970-1990.* New York: Board of Jewish Education.

Shapiro, Z. (1988). *From Generation to Generation: Does Jewish Schooling Affect Jewish Identification?.* Unpublished doctoral dissertation, New York University, New York.

Solomon, B. (1979). *Curricula Integration in the Jewish All-Day School in the United States.* Unpublished doctoral dissertation, Harvard University, Cambridge, MA.

Well, H.A. (1975). *Finances and the Jewish Day School: An Analysis of the Relationship of Teachers, Instructional and per Pupil Costs to Scholastic Achievement.* Unpublished doctoral dissertation, Loyola University of Chicago, Chicago.

Zeldin, M. (1990, June). *In Yesterday's Shadow: Case Study of the Development of a Jewish Day School.* presented at the Fourth Annual Conference of the Network for Research in Jewish Education, New York, NY.

Footnotes

[1]Nationally, the majority of Orthodox day schools and yeshivot have a relationship with Torah Umesorah (The National Society for Hebrew Day Schools). Most modern/centrist Orthodox day schools and yeshivot are affiliated with Yeshiva University's Max Stern Division of Communal Service via the Torah Education Network (TEN). Conservative day schools are affiliated with the Solomon Schechter School movement of the United Synagogue of America. The thirteen Reform day schools are organized as PARDES—the Progressive Association of Reform Day Schools—an affiliate of the Union of American Hebrew Congregations. In 1986, the transideological, pluralistic day schools which significantly grew in numbers during the 1960's and 1970's were organized into the Jewish Community Day School Network, RAVSAK.

Highlights

* In 1990, there were about 177,250 pupils (K-12) enrolled in 652 Jewish day schools and yeshivot in North America. This represents 40% of the total Jewish school enrollment in North America, compared to 11% in 1962.
* 14.3%of Jewish Federation dollars for local needs were allocated to Jewish all-day education in 1989. This represents 56.4% of the total dollar allotment to local Jewish education.
* 83% of the day school population is enrolled in Orthodox sponsored schools; 10% under Conservative auspices; 6% under communal sponsorship, and 1% in Reform day schools.
* 29% of the day school enrollment is in early childhood programs (N-K); 58% in elementary grades; and 13% in high school classes.
* Average per-pupil costs rose more than ninefold in three decades; from approximately $500 in 1962 to $4,600 in 1990 (ranging from $3,000 to $12,000).
* In 1989, Federation allocations to day schools ($40,892,886) represented about 5% of the overall day school expenditure.
* There is a shortage of qualified Hebrew teachers entering the Hebrew teaching profession and a high rate of turnover.
* Lay-professional relationships play an important role in the life of a day school principal.
* There is a surprising lack of scientific information regarding academic achievement in both Jewish and general studies.
* The synergism between home and school is the key to successful performance of the children.

* Long-term studies on the impact of Jewish day schooling indicate that it has significant influence in Jewish identity formation, even when a variety of factors including family background are controlled.

The Larger Context

Day school education stands as the one format with the best odds of educating Jewish children so as to produce knowledgeable, literate and committed Jews. But, will the same factors that have led to current parental choices, continue to motivate growth of these schools in the decades ahead? Will the centrist, modern Orthodox day schools be able to sustain their rapid growth? Will the non-Orthodox forms of Jewish day school education be able to grow? Will the state of and commitment to public education continue to influence the choice of Jewish day schools? These are but a few of the questions raised by this article.

What We Know About...
the Jewish Supplementary School

David Schoem

When asked about their formal Jewish education, close to 90% of all adults say that they have had "some"—in one form or another. Of those, the overwhelming majority report that these experiences came by way of the supplementary school. What is the effect or impact of this type of schooling and are there alternative ways to obtain similar or better results? Dr. David Schoem , Assistant Dean for Undergraduate Education at the University of Michigan, turns his attention to these questions, implications of the research and some policy considerations.

THE GREAT MAJORITY OF AMERICAN JEWS RECEIVE THEIR JEWISH EDUCATION IN THE JEWISH supplementary school. Yet thirty years of research on the Jewish supplementary school have documented that these schools are failing. If it is unacceptable for the large majority of Jews to be Jewishly illiterate, highly assimilated, and potentially unidentified as Jews upon reaching adulthood, then dramatic changes are needed in the Jewish supplementary school.

Questions—What do the students of these supplementary schools know after completing such schooling? And what is it that the Jewish community wants children to know from this education? Does this form of schooling make any difference in terms of Jewish identity and commitment? Should or could these schools be changed or reorganized in some way to increase the level of educational achievement? Are there educational alternatives to the supplementary schools that might achieve the same or better educational results using new monies or the same monies that now fund these schools?

Earlier Research: Identification Without Substance

The Jewish supplementary school was introduced in the 1920s in the spirit of cultural pluralism (Kallen,1924) with the intention of providing a balance of Jewish education and culture equal to the dominant American values and culture taught in the public school.

In 1959 the authors (Dushkin and Engelman) of the first serious study of the Jewish supplementary schools complained of poor instruction and little learning, criticisms that were to be frequently repeated in Jewish homes over the next 30+ years. They wrote, "The oft expressed attitude of 'what's the use; after all these years the children *know nothing*, may be an exaggeration, but for many American Jews it is a discouraging truth'. A decade later the next major review of Jewish education (Ackerman,1969) lambasted the supplementary school, charging that students came out knowing virtually no Hebrew, Bible, history or anything else the school purported to be teaching.

In the 1970s two studies (Himmelfarb,1975; Bock,1976) showed that only a tiny fraction of students in supplementary schools met the required minimum of hours of instruction necessary before Jewish schooling could begin to substantially affect Jewish identification or increase one's adult religious involvement beyond the level of those who had no Jewish schooling. In a summary report on Jewish education and Jewish identity (Sidorsky, 1977), a task force of the American Jewish Committee reported that "graduates of most Jewish schools are functionally illiterate in Judaism and not clearly positive in attitudinal identification".

Schoem's in-depth study (1989) of a single supplementary school and its Jewish community vividly illustrated the failings described in previous studies. Schoem bemoaned (1988) the appropriateness of the metaphor of the "supplementary" school in light of the Jewish community's disturbingly "part-time" association with being Jewish. He discovered the self-deceptive assumptions underlying the school which spoke of a vibrant "Jewish Way of Life" and "Jewish Community" in America, when for most Jews, being Jewish simply meant an occasional "stepping out" of their "American" routine to do a defined Jewish act.

On a more positive note, Schoem noted the successful short-term effect of the Jewish school in terms of Jewish pride and Jewish identification, even though students (like their parents) described their identity in nonsubstantive terms such as being anti-anti-semites and non-non-Jews. He also pointed out the unexpected positive secondary effects of Jewish schooling, which included new memberships in the synagogue and increased parental involvement in things Jewish through carpooling and even over arguments about making their children go to Jewish school. What mattered most was attendance at the school; what their children did or did not learn was of little consequence or concern to them.

Heilman (1983) discovered much of the same information as Schoem but framed his analysis differently. He suggested that in terms of the highly assimilated condition of the majority of American Jews, these schools were the exact opposite of unsuccessful—they were providing precisely what these Jews wanted from being Jewish. Supplementary schools reflected very closely the successes and failures of modern American Jewish life, i.e., pride in identification as Jews but no knowledge about being Jewish or substance to Jewish identity.

Recently Aron (1989) suggested that schools mistakenly assume that Jewish children come to them knowing "how" to be Jewish. She argued that, in fact, Jews do not know how to live Jewish lives, thus their lessons in Jewish schools are more akin to study of a foreign culture than learning about themselves.

Finally, Schiff's study (1988) of New York City schools demonstrated on a very broad scale that the supplementary schools are not working. According to Fishman (1987), the report confirms that "the schools do a poor job in increasing Jewish knowledge…no success in guiding children toward increased Jewish involvement…inability to influence positive growth in Jewish attitudes."

The conclusions of the research on the supplementary schools are clear. While there is some success in achieving an immediate sense of identification as a Jew, it is an identification without substance and it is not lasting. The schools categorically fail in all areas of teaching content. That these schools, often meeting much less than seven hours per week, represent the primary and often the only Jewish activity in the lives of children and adults associated with them, is indicative of the broader issues facing American Jewish life. Indeed, the problems of the schools mimic Jewish life and, therefore, are indicative of the difficulty most Jews have incorporating their Jewishness into their more dominant modern American lives.

In the Jewish education world, much attention is given to the wrong issues, i.e. specific educational problems such as curriculum, teacher preparation, funding levels, parental commitment, discipline, instructional methodology, etc. While each of these specific problem areas is very real, they take attention away from the much greater systemic problems which must be addressed first, before taking on the specific problem areas.

Implications

Dramatic changes are needed in the Jewish supplementary school. What must change is the "part-time" attitude toward Jewish life and the "part-time" support of Jewish education. Jewish learning must become an activity of the adult Jewish community, certainly more than the exclusive domain of young children, and certainly more than certification for a Bar/Bat Mitzvah ceremony/party.

The key questions for supplementary Jewish education must be how to develop a vibrant, personal, and meaningful Jewish community, how to effectively provide Jewish education for adults and teenagers as well as children, how to provide enculturating experiences for young Jews and, finally, how to make sense of Judaism for modern American Jews so that people can see themselves as a living part of Jewish history, not merely students of an ancient culture or admirers of "real" Jews who live in Israel.

The wrong questions to ask are whether to teach modern Hebrew or liturgical Hebrew, whether to teach the weekly Torah portion or to focus exclusively on the creation story, whether to require three hours or five hours of school each week. Small changes within a failed system will not make a significant difference. Indeed, such changes have been attempted, and they have failed.

Policy Considerations

1. *Dramatically Increase Support for Bold Structural Change in Supplementary Schools at the National, Local and Individual School Levels; Reduce Support for Agencies and Schools Making Minor Adjustments And Addressing Limited Problem Areas.*

2. *Link Continued Funding of Jewish Supplementary Schools to the Development of Substantial Jewish Studies Programs For Adults and Teenagers.*

The "People of the Book" have become the "Children of the Book" when it comes to Jewish education. Through linked funding or reallocation of supplementary school funds, Jewish learning for adults (including young college graduates who have just entered professional life) and teenagers can be dramatically increased in quantity and quality. Perhaps the most important improvement for the supplementary schools would be for children to know that their parents were participating in Jewish study because Jewish study was important to them. As community policy, it makes far greater sense to offer serious study of traditional texts, history, literature, values, and current issues to those who are at least age thirteen and older.

What risk exists in adopting a policy along these lines? Thirty years of research indicates very clearly that the young are Jewishly illiterate after many years of study in the supplementary schools; it would appear that it has not been the risk of a loss of learning that has prevented systemic change, but rather simple inertia or fear of change.

3. *Give Urgent Attention to the Quality and Meaning of Jewish Life for Modern American Jews.*

Recognize that this is the primary issue facing the Jewish schools. When the meaning and value of Jewish life for contemporary living becomes clearer to the "supplementary" Jewish community, the supplementary schools will automatically improve, whatever the structure. But this is by no means simply the problem of Jewish educators; it is the problem of all Jewish religious and communal leaders.

4. *Fund the Teaching of Hebrew in Public and Private Secular Schools.*

The supplementary schools cannot possibly be successful in teaching Hebrew given the limited meeting times. A serious alternative approach might be to provide designated funding to public and private secular schools for teaching Hebrew on a massive scale in those settings.

5. *Design Non-Formal Family, Peer Group, and Community Development Learning Opportunities into the Supplementary School Structure.*

Incorporate into the schools Sabbath weekend retreats, Friday night dinners, youth groups, etc. around Jewish events and activities. Tie these activities into existing *Havurah* activities and open many of these events to families of students. Bring the success of away-from-home programs such as camp, regional retreats, a trip to Israel, etc. into the at-home experiences of the students. Include pre-Bar/Bat Mitzvah students in community-wide activities. Invite Jewish young people to participate in service projects in the Jewish and non-Jewish community, to think about social justice and intergroup relations. Include post Bar/Bat Mitzvah youth in the activities and on the governing boards of Jewish religious and community organizations. Incorporate all the above into the regular format and schedule of the school calendar. Make these activities a part of Jewish education for all age groups.

6. *Design the Curriculum for Grades K-3 around the Theme of Enculturation.*

Our children's daily experiences have become so like those of their non-Jewish counterparts that they must now be shown and given opportunities to practice being Jewish—behaviorally, attitudinally, and socially. When they personally understand the "rewards" of being Jewish—be it holiday celebrations, new friendships, values, prayer, or songs, they will be increasingly interested in learning the skills and content necessary to fully participate in their Jewish culture.

7. *Re-Design the Pre-Bar/Bat Mitzvah Curriculum Around the Theme of Becoming Participating Jewish Adults.*

Teach students the skills necessary to become participating Jewish adults—lead religious services, read Torah, do tzedakah projects and practice other mitzvot, contribute to building a Jewish community.

8. *Develop the Adult/High School Curriculum in Conjunction with University Judaic Studies Programs.*

Offer skills courses, lecture series, and community service seminars together with accredited college level courses in conjunction with university Judaic Studies programs.

9. *Improve the Status of Jewish Educators Within the Jewish Community.*

If Jewish education is important to the Jewish community, then surely Jewish educators should be paid and given the status that will allow them to buy homes and live in the same neighborhood as the Jewish community they serve. Include and consider Jewish teachers in supplementary schools as members of the Jewish community where they teach.

Future Research

The Jewish community would be well-served by attempting the suggestions above in limited, controlled experiments with careful research and evaluation attached. There is also much to learn from comparative research on supplementary school systems of other communities such as the Jews in other diaspora countries, other ethnic groups in the U.S. and abroad, and other religious groups in the U.S. Research on successful supplementary Jewish schools is also advised. Finally, researchers should explore the failure of the Jewish schools in terms of their relationship to the synagogues and temples that house and control them.

Bibliography

Ackerman, W.I. (1969). Jewish Education—For What? In M. Fine and M. Himmelfarb (Eds.) *The American Jewish Yearbook. 70.* New York: American Jewish Committee.

Aron, I. (1989, May/June). The Malaise of Jewish Education. *Tikkun, 4*(3).

Bock, G. (1977). Does Jewish Schooling Matter? In *Jewish Education and Jewish Identity.* New York: American Jewish Committee.

Dushkin, A. and Engelman, U.Z. (1973). *Jewish Education in the United States.* New York: American Association for Jewish Education.

Fishman, S. B.(1987). *Learning About Learning: Insights on Contemporary Jewish Education From Jewish Population Studies.* Waltham, MA: Cohen Center for Modern Jewish Studies

Heilman, S. (1984). *Inside the Jewish School.* New York: American Jewish Committee.

Himmelfarb, H. (1975). Jewish Education for Naught—Educating the Culturally Deprived Child. *Analysis. 51.*

Kallen, H. (1924). *Culture and Democracy in the United States.* New York: Boni and Liveright.

Schiff, A.I. (1987). *Jewish Supplementary Schooling: An Educational System in Need of Change.* New York: Board of Jewish Education of Greater New York.

Schoem, D. (1989). *Ethnic Survival In America: An Ethnography of a Jewish Afternoon School.* (Brown Studies on Jews and Their Societies). Atlanta: Scholars Press.

Schoem, D. (1988). Learning to be a Part-Time Jew. In W. Zenner (Ed.), *Persistence and Flexibility: Anthropological Perspectives of the American Jewish Experience.* New York: SUNY Press.

Sidorsky, D. (1977). Summary Report and Recommendations: Colloquium on Jewish Education and Jewish Identity. In *Jewish Education and Jewish Identity.* New York: American Jewish Committee.

Highlights

* Most American Jews receive their Jewish education in supplementary schools.
* Graduates of most Jewish schools are functionally illiterate in Judaism and not clearly positive in attitudinal identification.
* There is a successful short-term effect in terms of Jewish pride and Jewish identification but no knowledge about being Jewish or substance to their Jewish identity.

The Larger Context

Despite the overwhelming evidence of the failure of the supplementary school, there is hope! Most children are now receiving and will continue to receive their Jewish education in supplementary settings. This endearing Jewish trait of hopefulness is one we can adopt just be changing our attitudes, not the facts. However, it appears that major changes in facts as well as attitudes will be necessary if Jewish supplementary education is to succeed. To quote Dr. Schoem, "what must change is the "part-time" attitude toward Jewish life and the "part-time" support of Jewish education."

What We Know About...
Jewish Education in the
Jewish Community Centers

Barry Chazan and Richard Juran

These are exciting times in the life of the Jewish community center movement in North America. During the past half-decade, the JCC world has made Jewish education a central concern and preoccupation. The commitment to Jewish education in JCCs expresses itself in all spheres of the center world: staff development; biennials; board meetings and programs; Israel seminars; adult study; Jewish programming; Judaic staff appointments; and executive training. Indeed, according to Barry Chazan, Education Consultant for the Jewish Community Centers Association, and Richard Juran, Director of Educational Programs for JCCA in Israel,we currently seem to be in the midst of a Jewish education revolution in the JCC movement.

THIS NEW DYNAMIC IN THE WORLD OF THE NORTH AMERICAN JEWISH COMMUNITY CENTER MOVEMENT was launched by the Jewish Welfare Board's Commission on Maximizing Jewish Educational Effectiveness of Jewish Community Centers (COMJEE) in 1982, culminating in the publication of *Maximizing Jewish Educational Effectiveness of Jewish Community Centers* and the subsequent Committee on Jewish Educational Effectiveness. The "Maximizing" document served as the *Magna Carta* of the new campaign to develop the Jewishness of centers, and led to a host of practical efforts and programs.

By the early 1990s the significance of this process was reflected in enhanced awareness and recognition of the Jewish center world and its commitment to Jewish education. When it was decided in 1988 to establish a national Commission on Jewish Education in North America, to "enlarge the scope, raise the standards, and improve the quality of Jewish education," the JCC Association was invited to be one of the convening partners. The final report of this commission, entitled *A Time to Act*, says the following:

> Jewish community centers are engaged in a major effort to make Jewish education a central element of their programming; the challenge facing them is

how to convert this institution into a major force for Jewish education within a framework that is primarily recreational, social, and cultural (Commission on Jewish Education in North America, 1991).

In a comprehensive report on the state of informal Jewish education in North America, Bernard Reisman (1990) states that:

First, the JCC is the major informal Jewish education setting in North America in that it reaches the largest number of American Jews. Second, many people in Jewish communities have become skeptical of the Jewishness of the Jewish centers. The maximizing initiative seems to be convincing many of its critics that this is a serious endeavor.

Early History

The current passion of centers for their Jewish educational mission brings us full circle in the life of an institution that began over one hundred years ago. In its early years, the center aided in the Americanization of highly identifying Jewish immigrants from Eastern Europe. It served as settlement house, socializer, and language school. In this period (encompassing the era up to end of the 1940's), the dominant vision was acculturation and the underlying ideology was the practical adjustment (language, manners, customs) of immigrant Jews to the American experience.

In its second period the center movement was transformed into a multipurpose suburban venue for recreation, sport, and culture. The suburban center became a springboard for the second generation Jews' entry into the social and recreational world of America. The second period (1940s-1970s) was shaped by the vision of "making it": the belief in the viability of pursuing "full-fledged" American lives, without denying one's Jewishness.

We are now in the third stage of the center movement's history; this is the era of centers' becoming agencies of Jewish life and education. In this period, clientele and leadership increasingly look to centers as agents of Jewish education, Jewish socialization, and Jewish acculturation.

It would be inaccurate to suggest that the previous decades of center life were totally devoid of the Jewish voice. In the earliest period of its existence, there were those such as Mordecai Kaplan (1957) and Horace Kallen (1932) who saw centers as powerful agencies for Jewish socialization and cultural expression.

The second affirmation of strengthening the Jewish mission of centers was voiced in the 1948 Janowsky Report which unequivocally concluded that the goals of the Jewish center should include concern for Jewish content and Jewish identification. The Jewish mission of JCCs surfaced again in 1967-69 when JWB examined and clarified the meaning of "Jewish content" in JCC programming, emphasizing the centers' dual concerns with influencing individual Jewish self-awareness and fostering collective Jewish survival (JWB, 1969).

However, what we are now witnessing is different in depth and intensity than anything that has preceded it. More resources, effort, support and passion have been injected into the Jewish focus of centers than ever before. The current revolution, in contradistinction to previous periods, is buttressed by grass roots support, the investment of resources, and the ability to attract lay leaders and professionals to the cause.

We turn now to look at this new approach which underlies Jewish educational programs in Jewish community centers.

Three Areas of Jewish Educational Activity

The various Jewish educational initiatives may be understood as a three-pronged campaign to reshape Jewish community center activity in terms of: 1) fostering a consciousness of the center's Jewish educational agenda on the part of the lay leaders, the professional staff, members, and the community at large; 2) an infusion of Jewish educational content into staff and board development and educational programs offered for center membership, and 3) the integration of an enhanced Jewish component into regular Jewish community center activities, via program innovation, investment in Jewish ambience of the facility, and cultivation of the Israel dimension of center activity. Together, these areas of activity have changed the substance and the image of Jewish community centers in our generation.

1. Consciousness and Image

By 1989, more than a dozen Jewish community centers had replicated the national COMJEE effort by embarking on a local process in which central lay leaders and staff examined the agency's mission statement, redefining priorities and objectives to reflect the Jewish educational vision they had acquired. Their involvement, in turn, served to strengthen their own consciousness and commitment, generating discussions and documents which facilitated dissemination of the message throughout the community. Some sixty JCCs established ongoing committees for fostering and monitoring Jewish education as part of the center's activities (JWB, 1989a). JWB eventually commissioned a follow-up study, which generated a further wave of reflection on national and local levels.

One by-product of the process was the addition of a full-time Jewish educational consultant at the national agency, the JCC Association, which was paralleled by the hiring of some forty Jewish educators and programmers as staff members in JCCs across North America (Frank, 1990). The Jewish Educators' Forum is another significant outgrowth of this trend. In March of 1989, fifteen Jewish educators working in centers met with JWB educational consultants and senior staff for a two-day conference devoted to understanding what was then taking place across the country, and to charting the course for the next phase of the process (JWB,1989b).

There have been other diverse attempts to effect a system-wide shift in both the reality and the popular perception of the center's raison d'etre. Early childhood education specialists in particular have invested resources and staff time in developing Jewish educational curriculum at the national and local levels. Jewish education has also found its way into regional and national meetings and Jewish study is now an ongoing part of the annual Executive Seminars for North American JCC directors. In a few short years, these and other innovations in the center world have served to alter the perception of center leaders, staff and members regarding the mission of Jewish community centers.

2. "Formal" Jewish Education in an Informal JCC Setting

In what may be an inescapable if somewhat paradoxical trend, educational programs reminiscent of the world of formal education (in the sense of classroom-style Jewish studies) have emerged as a central component of the maximizing process. Projects include staff and lay leadership development, adult education programs and the development of resource materials for center activities.

The use of the Israel seminar for Jewish educational executive staff development may represent the most striking example of infusing formal education into the world of JCCs. Increasing numbers of members participate in both short-term and long-term adult education courses in Jewish community centers. The development of curriculum and resource materials naturally followed the trend towards more formal educational endeavors in JCCs (Chazan & Poupko, 1989; Chazan, 1990).

While it may seem initially surprising that the move toward enhancing Jewish education in the JCCs moved so rapidly and so wholeheartedly into the more formal end of Jewish education, this probably reflects the earnestness of the planners, the teachers and the participants in pursuing the goal of maximizing the centers' Jewish educational effectiveness. There seems to be a broad-based effort to acquire at least basic Jewish literacy as part of the campaign to transform the JCC into a more substantively Jewish institution.

3. Integration of "Jewish" and "Community Center"

The COMJEE process ignited a search for ways to integrate genuine Jewish content into familiar and novel JCC programs. The success of this pursuit is crucial in terms of the need to create a sense of an accessible, authentic Jewish living experience relevant for center members.

New initiatives include efforts to suffuse JCC camps with Jewish atmosphere and programming. Emphases include Jewish rituals, themes for camp activities, and libraries, in addition to more familiar motifs such as flags, posters, and names of groups, activities, and facilities. JCC camps are also playing an important role in retaining and educating Soviet Jewish youth who immigrate to North America. Some of the inspiration and guidance for these developments may be attributed to the growing numbers of camp program directors and counselors participating in Israel training programs specially designed to enhance the Jewishness of the JCC summer camp.

Early childhood education programs, which are among the largest JCC departments across North America, have also sought ways of augmenting the Jewish dimension of the program, including attempts to involve parents in the project for additional "payoff" at home, the development of special Judaic curricular units, and national training seminars in Israel for early childhood educators. Noteworthy initiatives targeted at other age groups include projects in the area of creative arts (in cooperation with local synagogues). Jewish theatre and exhibits of Jewish art, national and international sports gatherings for Jewish youth, Judaic newsletters, and programs of Jewish content for Soviet immigrants. Fostering the integration of the "Jewish" and "community center" components has caused much attention to be paid to the Jewish ambience of the JCC. Use of Hebrew and the incorporation of Jewish music, art, religious and cultural objects and exhibits are but a few of the areas in which JCCs have invested in enhancing their Jewish ambience.

A personal Israel experience offers rich insights into the Jewish past, present, and future, and the integration of Jewish and general lifestyles. The Israel Seminar Training Programs, for JCC staff and lay leadership, are one of the most potent and successful elements of the Jewish educational campaign. Some 75 programs have brought over 1,000 participants to Israel from more than a quarter of the JCCs in North America, including the JCC Association's National Board, and fourteen key executive directors who spent three months of intense study on a specially-designed seminar. Indeed, the Israel experience has become a standard component of training for future Center executives. Underlying these seminars is an attempt to frame significant contemporary Jewish issues as they express themselves in life in the Jewish state. Because participants are often able to attain a sharper focus on the issue in its Israeli expression, they are simultaneously in a position to reflect on implications for their own personal and professional lives.

In the long term, it would seem that the extent to which JCCs succeed in integrating the "Jewish" and the "community center" components will be the most significant measure of what the maximizing process will ultimately accomplish. The exciting frontier for JCCs is facing the challenge of weaving organic Jewish content and ambiance into the full scope of Jewish community center life.

Nine Principles Underlying The JCCs Approach to Jewish Education

Is there a "JCC concept and method of Jewish education"? The literature of JCC Jewish education is just beginning to be written (Chazan, 1987; Dubin, 1987), but we believe that certain key principles of a JCC philosophy of Jewish education are already clear:

1. *Jewish education is a lifelong process, and is not limited only to the so-called "school" years.*
   The center world is committed to the belief that people continually grow, and hence it regards Jewish education as a never-ending process.

2. *Jewish education does not take place only in the classroom.*
   The center world believes that Jewish education takes places in a multitude of settings—in schools, camps, center buildings, gyms, cafeterias, youth group clubhouses, preschools, and adult education programs—and it proposes to use all corners of its campus to educate.

3. *Every learner is a unique being.*
   The center world is committed to the belief in the inherent worth and dignity of each person, and is committed to treating its constituents accordingly.

4. *There are many forms of Jewish expression today, and there are many routes to Jewish identity.*

   We live in an age of Jewish pluralism and the center is open to all forms of genuine Jewish expression and identity. There are many ways in which Jews reach Jewish expression, and the center attempts to be receptive to a diversity of routes and approaches.

5. *All center workers have a role in doing Jewish education; they are "God's partner" in the act of creation.*

   The center approach to Jewish education regards its entire staff as agents and resources for affecting people Jewishly. It wants to help its staff grow Jewishly so that they will be able to become forces in affecting the Jewishness of their clientele.

6. *The physical plant—the center building—is a means to the larger end of affecting the lives of those we hope to educate.*

   The center building affords wonderful possibilities for creating a Jewish environment and "neighborhood" for the center family. The ultimate purpose of the (physical) structures is the service and enrichment of the human beings who use them, and hence, the structures and their construction are not ends in themselves but means to other ends.

7. *The concern for Jewish education is an overall responsibility of the Jewish community as a whole, shared by all the community agencies—including the Jewish community centers.*

   The commitment to Jewish education is not the mandate of any one agency but is an ongoing and basic responsibility of the Jewish people as a whole.

8. *The social and associational nature of centers is particularly conducive to Jewish growth and learning.*

   Centers are places where Jews spend time together. This enables creative learning in the context of group interaction.

9. *The State of Israel is an indispensable arena for affecting the lives of Jews.*

   The center world believes Israel is a uniquely rich Jewish laboratory and classroom. It is committed to fostering genuine ties with the State of Israel, including promotion of personal experience and study for center leadership, staff and members. The Israel experience is an integral part of Jewish education in the Jewish community center.

Ten years after the Jewish educational revolution began in North American JCCs, the themes which currently prevail include profound commitment to pluralism in Jewish life, and to the importance of the JCCs potential contribution to community-wide Jewish continuity; sensitivity and flexibility regarding the educational potential of different JCC settings and the needs of different center members; creativity and versatility in the development of Jewish educational programming; and the pursuit of substantive Jewish content and a personal Israel experience as pillars of Jewish education in Jewish community centers.

Bibliography

Chazan, B. & Poupko, Y. (1989).*Guide to Jewish Knowledge for the Center Professional.* New York: Jewish Community Centers Association.

Chazan, B. (1990). *Preparation Guide for Israel Seminars.* New York: Jewish Community Centers Association.

Chazan, B. (1987, Spring). A Jewish Educational Philosophy for JCCs. *Journal of Jewish Communal Service.63*(3).

Chazan, B. (1991, Summer). What is Informal Jewish Education? *Journal of Jewish Communal Service.67*(4).

Commission on Maximizing Jewish Educational Effectiveness of Jewish Community Centers (COMJEE).(1982). *Maximizing Jewish Educational Effectiveness of Jewish Community Centers.* New York: Jewish Welfare Board.

Commission on Jewish Education in North America.(1991). *A Time To Act.* Lanham, MD: University of America Press.

Dubin, D. (1990, Fall). Israel and Pluralism:Framing an Ideology for the Jewish Community Center. *Journal of Jewish Communal Service, 67*(1).

Frank, S. (1990, Winter). A New Phenomenon at JCCs: Jewish Education Specialists. *Jewish Welfare Board Circle. 47*(1).

Janowsky, O. (1948). *The Jewish Welfare Board Survey.* NY: Dial Press.

Jewish Welfare Board. (1969). *Jewish Welfare Board Study of 1967-69.* New York: Jewish Welfare Board.

Jewish Welfare Board. (1989a). *A Summary of Recent Progress: Maximizing Jewish Educational Effectiveness of Jewish Community Centers.* New York: Jewish Welfare Board.

Jewish Welfare Board. (1989b). *A Summary of Proceedings: Jewish Welfare Board Consultation of Jewish Community Center Educators.* New York: Jewish Welfare Board.

Kallen, H. (1932). The Dynamics of the Jewish Center. In *Judaism at Bay.* NY.

Kaplan, M. (1935, June). The Jewish Center and Organic Community Organization. In *The Jewish Center.* New York: Jewish Welfare Board.

Kaplan, M. (1957). *Judaism as a Civilization.* New York: Reconstructionist Press.

Reisman, B. (1990). *Informal Jewish Education in North America:* A Report Submitted to the Commission on Jewish Education in North America. Cleveland, Ohio.

Highlights

* The 1982 Report on Maximizing Jewish Educational Effectiveness of Jewish Community Centers lead to a host of practical efforts and programs.
* JCCs have gone through three phases in their history:
    - as settlement house, socializer and language school
    - as a multipurpose suburban venue for recreation, sport and culture
    - as agencies of Jewish life and culture

* New initiatives have been created to reshape JCC activities in terms of:
    -fostering a consciousness of centers' Jewish educational agenda
    -an infusion of Jewish educational content
    -the integration of an enhanced Jewish component into regular JCC activities

The Larger Context

According to the authors, for the first time we are beginning to see JCCs take on a distinctively "Jewish" mission. We seem to be at the beginning of a change in programming and direction. If this is so, we also have the marvelous opportunity of documenting and evaluating this process of change. Indeed, "the extent to which JCCs succeed in integrating the "Jewish" and the "community center" components will be the most significant measure of what the maximizing process will ultimately accomplish".

What We Know About...
Jewish Family Education

Joseph Reimer

Jewish Family Education (JFE) has arisen in recent years as a response to the alienation of the school from the home. Dr. Joseph Reimer, Assistant Professor in the Hornstein Program of Jewish Communal Service at Brandeis University, explores what has become one of the newest buzzwords in the American Jewish Community. What led to the emergence and popularity of this concept? What is unique about it? What does JFE seek to achieve? How can success be measured? These are the questions Dr. Reimer seeks to answer.

I T IS COMMON TO HEAR JEWISH EDUCATORS BEMOAN THE LACK OF PARENTAL SUPPORT FOR THE AGENDA OF the Jewish school. Acknowledging that parents usually take seriously their commitment to bring their children to the school, educators wonder why they do not also commit themselves to what is taught *in* the school.

The alienation of school from home does not serve the educational needs of the children well. A teacher can make a wonderful case for the beauty of Shabbat observance, but if Friday night at home remains unmarked by Shabbat ritual, the child has no real way of connecting with the teacher's words.

Jewish family education (henceforth, JFE) has arisen in recent years as a response to the alienation of the school from the home. Realizing that it is simply ineffective to teach children in isolation from the realities of home life, educators have begun to reach out to the whole family—but especially the parents—to invite them to join in learning together with the children about the joys of Jewish living. Instead of dropping off the children at school, parents have been invited to themselves drop in and learn alongside their children.

JFE, then, takes the family—rather than the individual child—as the client of Jewish education. Most often programs in family education are sponsored by a synagogue for the school or preschool children and their parents. But family includes more than just two married parents and young children. JFE has arisen at a time of increased awareness that Jewish families come in many different forms (Cohen, 1989; Fishman, 1990a). These include single-parent, blended and interfaith families as well as families with grown children, families without children and singles living alone or in joint households. A challenge to Jewish family educators is to welcome "nontraditional" as well as "traditional" families and work with all these populations on the basic agenda: learning to live a richer Jewish life.

JFE is also not limited to the synagogue context. Keller (1990), reviewing a JESNA publication on JFE programs, notes that while synagogues account for the sponsorship of more than one third of the listed programs, bureaus, national organizations, JCCs and Jewish Family Services account together for the sponsorship of almost half the listed programs. The programs are located in settings as diverse as nursery schools, summer camps, museums, universities and even trips to Israel.

JFE came into its own during the 1980s as a popular response to the needs of a changing American Jewish community. To understand this phenomenon in greater depth, we need to answer the following four questions:

1. Where did JFE come from?

2. What is new or unique about its programs?

3. What does it aim to achieve?

4. How do we know when its programs succeed?

The Origins

The 1970s was the decade during which the family surfaced as a focus of great debate in American society. The turmoil of the 60s, the rise of the women's movement, the increase in divorce, the change in the abortion law all contributed to a sense that we as a society no longer share a single vision of the place of family in our society (Berger and Berger, 1983). Some observers thought the family might disappear as the unit of organization; others who disagreed still predicted the family of the future would look very different than the family of the past (Bane, 1978; Keniston, 1977).

The American Jewish community also awoke to a family crisis in its midst. Young Jews were delaying marriage and having fewer children. In seeking marriage partners, they were more attracted to non-Jews, increasing greatly the number of intermarriages. Divorce was rising in incidence almost as fast as in the general American population. The vaunted "Jewish family" seemed to be coming apart at the seams (Cohen, 1983).

There were many different responses within the Jewish community to the perceived crisis in family life—from increasing counseling and outreach services to putting day care on the agenda and setting up Jewish dating services (American Jewish Committee, 1979). But the Jewish educational community did not get involved until the crisis in family life was joined to a crisis in the synagogue supplementary school.

The 1970s saw a dramatic decrease in the number of students attending supplementary schools, offset only partially by a substantial increase in attendance at day schools (Dubb and DellaPergola, 1986). Furthermore, two academic studies were published in the mid 1970s that called into question the effectiveness of supplementary education (Bock, 1977; Himmelfarb, 1977). It seemed that at the moment when the capacity of the average Jewish family to pass Judaism on was being called into question, the school could also no longer be relied upon to fill in the gap. Surely both pillars of Jewish continuity could not be allowed to crumble at once.

This anxiety led in part to an increase in federation and communal investment in the field of Jewish education (Fox, 1989). Among some Jewish educators working in synagogue education there arose a feeling that the best hope for improving the supplementary school lay in involving the family in that education. In their view the supplementary school was sinking primarily from a lack of emotional investment on the part of parents who sent their children (Schoem, 1982). If families could be drawn into their children's education and develop Jewish interests of their own, the whole system would receive a vital motivational boost (Schiff, 1986).

The turn towards family education has coincided with two demographic trends which have proved significant: baby-boomers becoming parents in large numbers and interfaith couples joining synagogues and becoming part of the school's parent body.

As many who in the 1970s delayed marriage and childbirth began having children in the 1980s there arose a new generation of parents and children to join synagogues and seek Jewish education (Goldscheider and Goldscheider, 1989). These parents often have gone through childbirth classes, read the literature on raising children and are very ready to be involved in their children's education. They also, on the whole, have weak Jewish educations that need refreshing if they are to keep up with their children's Jewish learning. Among this generation is an increasing number of parents who are Jews-by-choice or non-Jews who are raising the children as Jews (Fishman, et.al, 1990b; Tobin, 1991). They, in their childhood, did not experience the cycle of Jewish holidays, rituals and family events, and need to learn how to live as Jews if they are to be active in their children's Jewish upbringing. Together these parents' diverse Jewish needs have created a fertile ground for JFE.

Jewish Family Education Defined

What is most clearly new about JFE is that it is "Jewish education for the family." But as that phrase has many different meanings for practitioners, it may be helpful to suggest a set of criteria by which JFE can be defined. These criteria are of my own devising, but are based on the writings of professionals active in the field of JFE.

1. *JFE is explicitly Jewish or Judaic in its content and is to be distinguished from programs for Jews about family life (Wall, 1985).* A synagogue or JCC may sponsor a program on understanding teenagers which is for Jewish families, but would not be considered JFE unless it involved some learning about a traditional and/or modern Jewish understanding of family life.

2. *JFE is for the family as distinct from being for adults and for children (Kelman, 1989).* While JFE programs generally include segments directed to teaching parents apart from

children and children apart from parents (or other adult family members), these segments are part of a larger thrust to address the family as a unit.

As an example, on a family Shabbaton there may be specific moments designated for adult study and children's play. But these activities take place in the context of a larger framework which structures celebrating Shabbat together as a family. That is distinct from a Shabbaton for adults in which children are invited, but not directly involved in the main educational program, or a Shabbaton for children in which some parents come along, but are not directly involved in experiencing the educational program.

3. *JFE is educational and not simply recreational.* There are many family events sponsored by Jewish organizations which are fun and involving, but more recreational than educational. These may include a Chanukah party, Purim carnival, or dinner at a Jewish deli. These are potentially wonderful Jewish experiences, but only become educational when tied in with a larger framework of meaning. When the Purim story is brought to life through the carnival, or dinner at the deli is an opportunity to learn about kashrut or Jewish eating styles, the family event becomes part of a curriculum for JFE

4. *JFE extends over a period of time and is not simply a one-time event.* While a well-planned single event may be a wonderful way to introduce parents to the concept of JFE, the type of learning envisioned requires that families return over time to repeatedly have the experience of being together in Jewishly rich, interactive environment (Appelman, 1985; Bernard, 1991).

The Goals of JFE

If we define programs in JFE as providing families over time with educational experiences with solid Jewish content, then what are goals of the programs? What do their planners hope to achieve in creating these Jewish experiences for families?

In reviewing the literature on JFE, I have found four goals which seem common to the various programs described.

1. *Involving parents in Jewish learning.*

If the alienation of the home from the school is the basic problem that JFE is designed to address, its first goal is involving parents and other family members in the pursuit of Jewish learning. This has taken three forms: parents and children learning together, parents learning the same content as the children but in a parallel, adult-oriented way, and parents pursuing their own plan of learning alongside, but separate from, their children's learning (Lichtig, 1988; Wolfson, 1983).

This overall goal may be seen as having two subgoals: 1) involving parents in caring about and reinforcing the children's learning, and 2) parents becoming more Jewishly knowledgeable in their own right.

2. *Providing quality family time in a Jewish setting.*

   Given how busy everyone is in today's families, it has become important for programs in JFE to provide families with quality time together (Alper, 1987; Bernard, 1991). This goal is especially evident in family camps or retreats, but is also important for attracting families to any program on the weekends. This is not only a pragmatic consideration for marketing purposes, but also a philosophic commitment to help support families in their efforts to cohere together as a unit (Reimer and Kerdeman, 1988). Being involved together in Jewish activity helps the family to focus on itself and allows opportunities for family members to enjoy one another's company on a regular basis.

3. *Building community among families.*

   In the highly mobile corporate world in which many Jews work today, there is a great deal of moving of families from one location to another. Families may join synagogues and JCCs to get to know other Jews, but the facts are that there often is a high degree of social isolation. It is not uncommon for parents to have children in the same class and not to know each other by name (Appelman, 1985).

   While building community among families may not be an intrinsic goal of JFE, it has become a common outcome that ends up reinforcing the other goals of these programs. When families get to know one another and decide to spend time together—especially when that involves a Shabbat or holiday celebration, the learning in the program becomes more real for all the members of the family. It becomes a part of their communal lives (Kaye, 1989).

4. *Bringing Jewish living into the home.*

   What might be seen as the ultimate goal of JFE, and the one hardest to accomplish, is the family's deciding to enhance the quality of Jewish living in their home (Wolfson, 1983). This may involve building a library of Jewish books, records and/or videos, buying Jewish art or subscribing to a Jewish newspaper or magazine. It may also involve introducing or enhancing Shabbat and/or holiday observance. Whatever the initial level of Jewish practice by a family, this goal would represent a deepening of their commitment by some degree.

Difficulties in Accounting for Success

Success or effectiveness in educational practice is often measured by the degree to which the goals or objectives are realized by the program's end. In JFE that would mean assessing the degree to which the goals described above were realized over time by the families participating in these types of programs.

Many difficulties face us in trying to make this type of assessment. To enumerate a few:

1. *There are many programs that are loosely called Jewish family education (Keller, 1990).* By our criteria, some deserve the title more than others. In testing for success, we ought to

begin by looking at programs that involve two or more generations of family members, have a clear Judaic content, call for an elaborated educational methodology and extend over enough time to make a potential difference in the life of the family.

2. *The educator-programmers should have a clear sense of the goals they are working towards.* Often JFE programs are single events that do not lead towards specified goals. It is unlikely that goals can be reached without forethought and direction. Jewish family educators, for example, may wish to involve parents in the synagogue, increase their knowledge of Jewish practice and motivate them to higher levels of home observance. But until the educators specify how the programs they are planning can reasonably be expected to lead to the achievement of these broad goals, they are engaging more in wish-fulfillment than in educational goal setting.

3. *Even when clear goals are embraced, their attainment can be assessed only when the broad goals are articulated in terms of more specific objectives.* What do we mean by increased parental involvement? What concrete actions would we need to be seeing to know that increased involvement was taking place? How can we assess whether these actions are increasing as a result of families participating in these programs?

4. *Someone has to be designated as an evaluator and have the role of carefully observing and monitoring what anticipated (or unanticipated) outcomes are indeed happening.* Ideally the evaluator ought not to be one of the educator-programmers but an outsider so as to establish some distance and objectivity in making these assessments.

Rarely in Jewish education do we set up the conditions to be able to adequately assess whether given programs are successfully reaching their goals. More commonly we get the assessment of the persons responsible for the program who have much at stake in showing how their program is working. In JFE even these kinds of evaluations are rare (Rose, 1988). Thus, from an objective viewpoint we to date know very little about the success of programs in JFE

Future Directions

Given the difficulties involved in assessing programs in JFE and the lack of objective evaluations in this field, we cannot make any definitive statements about its future. We do not know if JFE represents a set of adequate responses to the changing needs of American Jewish families or if it is a first response that will decline as fast as it arose.

But from the many subjective reports on these programs that make up the bulk of the literature on JFE we can draw some tentative conclusions about what future directions this field might take.

1. *JFE is a populist movement with programs springing up in many locations.* As a populist movement it has grown more by inspiration than by direction: educators, rabbis and social workers hear about programs from one another and adapt the basic concepts to their settings. That means JFE has many different meanings and shapes. Yet, as the movement develops a leadership, it will be helpful for those leaders to provide clearer guidelines and

definitions for others to consider.

2. *JFE lacks a curricular base (Keller, 1990).* At present educators are inventing programs as they go along and learning from one another how these programs are run. The educational richness of program offerings and the pursuit of specifiable educational goals could be greatly enhanced if some quality curricular materials were developed, produced, and distributed.

3. *JFE programs are primarily attracting parents and school age children.* We have very few reports as to who these parents are. For the programs to best service this clientele, educators will need to be aware of the makeup of these families in terms of demographic diversity. If some programs are attracting a high percentage of interfaith couples or are failing to attract single parents, the educators may want to plan the educational agenda in ways that address these tendencies.

4. *JFE programs have yet to be designed to appeal to the Jewish family at different stages of the life cycle.* It will be interesting to discover if newly-married or "empty nest" couples would benefit from this type of programming. So too the adult child and the elderly parent may be audiences JFE learns to address.

5. *Introducing evaluation research could be very helpful in providing this new field with valid feedback as to what is working and why.* The field is still in an early stage of trial and error, but until the current experiments are monitored, it will be very hard for educators to learn from mistakes and build confidently on successes.

Bibliography

Alper, J.P. (Ed.). (1987). *Learning Together: A Sourcebook on Jewish Family Education.* Denver: Alternatives in Religious Education.

American Jewish Committee.(1979). *Sustaining the Jewish Family: A Task Force Report on Jewish Family Policy.* New York.

Appelman, H.W. (1985). Jewish Family Life Education in the Synagogue. *Journal of Jewish Communal Service, 62*(2), 166-69.

Bane, M.J.(1978). *Here to Stay:American Families in the 20th Century.* New York: Basic Books.

Berger, B. and Berger, P.L.(1983). *The War over the Family: Capturing the Middle Ground.* Garden City: Anchor Press.

Bernard, S. E.(199). Family Jewishness and Family Education. *Journal of Jewish Communal Service, 67*(4), 290-299.

Bock, G.E.(1977). *Does Jewish Schooling Matter? Jewish Education and Jewish Identity.* New York: American Jewish Committee.

Cohen, S. M.(1983).*American Modernity and Jewish Identity.* New York: Tavistock.

Cohen, S. M. (1989).*Alternative Families in the Jewish Community.* New York: American Jewish Committee.

Dubb, A. and DellaPergola, S.(1986). *First Census of Jewish Schools in the Diaspora 1981/82—1982/83: United States of America.* New York: JESNA and Hebrew University of Jerusalem.

Fishman, S.B.(1990a). *Jewish Households, Jewish Homes: Serving American Jews in the 1990s.* Waltham, MA: Cohen Center for Modern Jewish Studies, Brandeis University.

Fishman, S.B.(1990b). *Intermarriage and American Jews Today: New Findings and Policy Implications.* Waltham, MA: Cohen Center for Modern Jewish Studies, Brandeis University.

Fox, J.(1989). *Federation-Led Community Planning for Jewish Education, Identity and Continuity.* The Commission on Jewish Education in North America, Cleveland.

Goldscheider, C. and Goldscheider, F.(1989). *The Transition to Jewish Adulthood: Education, Marriage and Fertility.* Paper presented at Tenth World Congress of Jewish Studies, Jerusalem.

Himmelfarb, H.S.(April, 1977). The Non-Linear Impact of Schooling:Comparing Different Types and Amounts of Jewish Education. *Sociology of Education, 42*, 114-129.

Kaye, J.S.(1989). *Jewish Family Life Through Jewish Family Education.* Boston: Bureau of Jewish Education of Greater Boston.

Keller, C.F.(June, 1990). *From Creativity to Policy: Charting a Course for Jewish Family Education.* Paper prepared for the Jerusalem Fellows.

Kelman, V.(June, 1989). *Scaffolds vs. Lifesupports: A Theory of Jewish Family Education.* Paper presented at Conference on Research in Jewish Education.

Keniston, K.(1977). *All Our Children: The American Family Under Pressure.* New York: Harcourt Brace Jovanovich.

Lichtig, J.(1988). Parents are Partner. *The Pedagogic Reporter, 39*(3), 4-6.

Reimer, J. and Kerdeman, D.(1988). Family Camp Comes to Ramah. Unpublished paper. Waltham, MA: Brandeis University.

Rose, N.(1988). Do Workshops Work? *The Pedagogic Reporter, 39*(3). 11-12.

Schiff, A.I.(1986). Formula for Jewish Continuity. Milender Lecture in Jewish Communal Leadership, Brandeis University.

Schoem, D.(1982). Explaining Jewish Student Failure and Its Implications. *Anthropology and Education Quarterly, 13*(4), 308-322.

Tobin, G.(1991). Marketing Your Congregation. *The NASA Journal, 43*(1), 4-8.

Wall, S.(1985). *Re-Thinking Jewish Family Education: An Assessment and Some New Dimensions.* Paper prepared for the Jerusalem Fellows.

Wolfson, R.(1983). *Shall You Teach Them Diligently?* Los Angeles: The University of Judaism.

Highlights

* The Jewish Educational community did not get involved in JFE until the crisis in family life was joined to a crisis in the synagogue supplementary school, which coincided with baby-boomers' becoming parents in large numbers and interfaith couples' joining synagogues and becoming part of the school's parent body.
* By definition, Jewish family education is:
    explicitly Jewish or Judaic in its content
    for the family as distinct from being for adults and for children
    educational and not simply recreational
    an ongoing program, not simply a one-time event
* Jewish Family Education programs:
    involve parents in Jewish learning
    provide quality family time in a Jewish setting
    build community among families
    bring Jewish living into the home
* It is difficult to evaluate the success of these programs.

The Larger Context

The concluding part of this article contains suggestions for "future directions". These may hold the key to determining whether Jewish Family Education is a fad or not. Among these suggestions for "future directions" are criteria for evaluation of JFE. Only long-range study over time will determine if, by means of JFE, we have succeeded any better in producing longer-term Jewish identity and knowledge.

What We Know About...
Parent Motivation

Stuart L. Kelman[1]

Why? This is the question that intrigues us as educators and laypeople alike about parents who voluntarily choose to send their child(ren) to our schools. Their motives for certain actions have been the focus of curiosity for many of us. Dr. Kelman, Executive Director of the Agency for Jewish Education in the Greater East Bay, directs our attention to the parents' reasons for enrolling their children in Jewish schools.

PARENTS—NOT CHILDREN—ARE THE FOCUS OF THIS ARTICLE. IT IS THEY WHO MUST CHOOSE, WHILE their child is still young, whether to enroll him/her in some type of formal or nonformal Jewish education. It is they who, when their child is very young, must decide on what may turn out to be a pattern (or no pattern) for lifelong Jewish learning. It is they—not the child, nor the extended family, nor the schools, nor the community—who set the course of learning for their child.

We ask the question about parents for two reasons: out of our own natural curiosity and in order to predict and/or enhance educational success for these children and for our institutions. We who are parents want to know why "other" parents choose as they do—sometimes merely to justify our own behaviors, whether we agree with the reasons or not. This is particularly true in the case of the Jewish day school where parents willingly, and at considerable cost, choose to enroll a child and consciously select one specific type of education.

As a parent, if I know *why* I am enrolling a child in a particular form of Jewish education, I might choose a school which not only shares my concern for academic achievement but also reinforces the values of the home environment. The choice, based on shared values of school and home, might even enhance the likelihood for greater academic success for my child (Himmelfarb, 1974).

There is another group interested in parents and their motivations: the educators. At a minimum level, congruence of goals and values between parents and school may enable educators to design new marketing strategies tailored to the motives of a particular community. Educational planning and success might be enhanced by appropriate formal and nonformal curricular programming, depending on such congruency. Finally, we might be able to understand the hopes, fears, and expectations of parents regarding the choice of precollegiate education for their children (Clerico, 1978).

Motives, Goals and Roles

Motives are "those causes that lead an individual to select some goals rather than others as premises for decisions" (Simon, 1969). Goals may change or be achieved but original motives usually remain constant. While motives and goals are closely linked, we shall see upon closer examination of these concepts that the two groups to whom these concepts refer, parents and educators, may behave differently (i.e., their roles will change) as a result of their understanding of these terms.

Current interest

A search of databases reveals few studies of the motives of parents for enrolling their child in a particular school. More research may be conducted in the near future as a result of renewed interest in the notion of tuition tax credits (vouchers), the increase of home-schooling options, and the creation of year-round schooling. Books about choice are becoming more and more prominent, and not only from the usual "alternative" sources. One, for example, by Susan Weston (1989), *Choosing a School for Your Child,* was published by the U. S. Government and even carries a foreword by the then Secretary of Education, Lauro Cavazos. Recently, an entire issue of *Educational Leadership* (December, 1990/January, 1991) was devoted to the issue of choice. Secular education is in a time of revolt.

The Jewish World: Day Schools

Arguments for and against day school/parochial education now seem to be muted; nevertheless, with the rise of discussion about tuition tax credits in public education, these voices pro and con may once again become a major source of controversy in the Jewish community. Historically, there was vigorous objection by some elements within the Jewish community to day school education. The Reform movement, in particular, favored public education, while the Orthodox have typically endorsed day school education as the primary mode of Jewish education for their children. Today, even the Reform movement has 15 day schools, and more seem to be on the way. Objections which remain seem to be more theoretical than real.

In the Orthodox day schools, the dominant parent motive seems to be the desire to perpetuate Jewish practice and values (Nulman, 1954; Golovensky, 1954). These studies, conducted close to 40 years ago, reflected the values of that community in the 1950s. Newer studies focus on the non-orthodox day schools.

Adams, Frankel and Newbauer (1972) for example, found that parents valued "preservation of Jewish culture" above "quality of general education" when selecting from a list of five possible objectives; while Kapel (1970), found that parents sent their children for primarily secular reasons.

In 1977, I conducted research with parents whose children attended 7 non-Orthodox Jewish day schools in Los Angeles. This was the year which marked the beginning of busing in order to achieve equality of educational opportunity in Los Angeles. It was a year in which it was suspected that the Jews had been a "covert" factor in the occurrence of "white flight." In order to explore more fully parental motives for choosing to enroll their children in Jewish schools, I developed a continuum of possible responses based upon past research. The continuum displayed reasons which reflected, on the one end, a total commitment to 'Jewish' values and Jewish education, and, on the other, concerns for the specifically 'Secular' aspects of education. Responses which suggested an 'Integration of the Judaic and the Secular',[2] i.e., a parental link or balance between the two, were located in the center of the continuum. "We want our child to attend so that he/she can gain an integrated gestalt of the Jewish and the American experience" or "so that he/she can live as a Jew in an American society" were typical of this category.

The majority of parents selected 'secular' reasons as primary motives for sending their child to these schools. Only 9-11% of the parents admitted to doing so in order to "Escape the public school" and/or "because of busing". Parents who responded that the reasons for enrolling their child were due in large measure to either 'Jewish' or 'Integration' motives, tended to alternate their answers depending upon which of two tests was employed. These findings were similar to those of Greeley and Rossi (1966) in their research with parents who send their children to Catholic schools and to those of Kapel (1972) in Jewish schools.

In an additional test to determine the intensity with which parents held their views, it became clear that the Jewish features of the school were a major contributing factor in the choice to send a child to this type of school. Thus, this second measure of parent motives strenghtened the suggestion that parents' goals were not all that different from those of the educators.

As might be expected, when family background factors were cross-tabulated with parent motives, parents who had completed intensive Jewish education programs indicated 'Jewish' motives to a greater degree than did parents with less intensive backgrounds in formal Jewish education.

Schools affiliated with the Reform movement had a concentration of parents who chose 'Secular' motives, while those schools affiliated with the Conservative movement had more parents who sent their children primarily for 'Jewish' reasons. Parents of children in the community schools had motives which lay in between.

Did the goals of the parents match those of the school? Over 80% of the parents unhesitatingly stated that the school had goals. But when asked to specify what the primary goal might be, their responses were less certain. 'Quality of education' and 'Integration of the Jewish and the secular' were the most popular choices, with less than one-fifth of the parents identifying the goal in specifically 'Jewish' terms. By contrast, most principals spoke of 'Integration of the Jewish and the secular' as the primary goal. The concern voiced by many of the professionals that the school might be "taken over" by those whose goals were in "opposition" was apparently unfounded, in that goal compatibility of the two groups was high.

In terms of their roles in the schools, more than half of all the parents surveyed said they had the power to influence educational, financial and overall decisions. Yet almost three-quarters of the parents were remarkably vague when describing the roles they thought they should perform in the school. While the literature views parents in three broad classes as "passive instruments; members who bring attitudes, values or goals; and as decision makers and problem solvers" (March and Simon, 1964), all the principals wanted was "support"—a vague response at best.

The main conclusion was that school personnel should no longer view the parent group as having motives in conflict with the goals of the school. The self-imposed isolation of the parents along with their exclusion by the administrators from curricular involvement ought to be rejected in favor of a school in which parents would be perceived as a primary educative force that would perform roles and tasks which flow from commitment to Jewish education (Kelman, 1984).

For the parents, assuming some of the responsibility for the task of education increases the likelihood of greater pupil academic achievement and mutual reinforcement of shared values since it is known that family differences can account for educational success of a child in school (Himmelfarb, 1975). For the school, sharing the task of education with parents assumes that educational effectiveness will be attained and can be measured in settings other than the classroom. Informal educational locations, the home, and the community become tests of application of classroom effectiveness.

"Getting parents to share...rather than the child" (Fried, 1973)is an approach that can actualize the philosophical ideals of the non-Orthodox Jewish day school, and may become a distinctive feature of such schools. The family, and not simply the child, becomes the educational focus of the institution.

In a later but closely related study, David Kaufman (1986) described the field of Jewish education as a place where "the representatives of Judaism (the teachers) meet the representatives of American-Jewish society (the children), and all too often, do battle." The Jew in contemporary American society faces the classical Diaspora dilemma: how to resolve the competing claims of Judaism and the non-Jewish world. According to Kaufman, 'Integration of the Jewish and the secular' becomes the focal point of curriculum, while at the same time, he claims, the gap, between home and school is widening.

> In the eyes of most American Jews, Judaism is little more than than the sum of occasionally observed customs and an indistinct ethnic attachment. The intellectual, ethical, and spiritual realms of Judaism are outside their experience; instead, their Jewishness is superficial and affiliative in nature. Judaism, as a religious and literary tradition, is seen as irrelevant in relation to their secular lives. My contention is that day school parents fall into this category as well; a conclusion that can only be inferred from the several studies of parental attitudes towards day schools (p.19).

When Kaufman asked parents about the goals of the school, "Transmission of Jewish knowledge" outranked "Providing a quality General education". However, when he asked the same about the goals of the parents, the two responses were reversed, leaving, as he claims, the child in between.

Kaufman proposes, therefore, "real" school-home connections based on a non-hierarchical, havurah-type, deliberation-based model of curriculum implementation with maximum parental involvement. While his recommendations are beyond the scope of this article, his proposals are certainly in line with the view that parents must have maximum involvement in the school.

The Jewish World: Supplementary Schools

Relatively little research has been conducted with parents who choose to enroll their child in the supplementary setting. Only Roberta Louis (1981) has investigated the issue to any significant degree. In her study, most parents said that they chose a particular school because of location. Two other factors, the reputation of the religious school and the particular philosophy of the synagogue, were also important, though they were ranked far below location. In a similar vein, when asked why they chose supplementary education, most parents responded that this was a place where their children could learn about Jewish "culture". It is interesting to note, parenthetically, that the word "religion" or "Hebrew" was not used even though this was a school attached to a synagogue. Of lesser importance to parents, but significant nonetheless, were the other reasons that "afternoon supplementary school can help to integrate the best of the Jewish world with the best of the general world" and that "it prepares him/her for bar/bat mitzvah".

The Secular World

Apart from the public schools, there are two other identifiable types of education: parochial and private or independent. A major study by Margaret Grafton (1980) found four explanations for non-public school choice suggested by the literature: a search for moral/religious values, dissatisfaction with the public schools, parent background characteristics, and a desire for social status. Added to this list in other studies are motives which reflected the disparity between parents' values and teachers' values and concern over government regulation of public schools (Erickson, 1983). However, Grafton concluded that "the proportion of parents choosing nonpublic schools has the potential to increase if either the level of dissatisfaction with public schools increases or if more consumers are provided with an alternative, perhaps in the form of a voucher system. It appears that fewer parents are making the automatic selection of a public school, but are considering many alternatives—including parochial and independent schools—when making their choices."

The Public Sector and Vouchers/Tuition Tax Credits

The issue of vouchers (or, as they are now called, tuition tax credits) in public education is, once again, coming to the fore. Each year, the education journal Phi Delta Kappan conducts a survey of attitudes about education. In 1990 a new dimension was added. Respondents were asked what aspects of a public school would be most influential in decision-making should parental choice be adopted in their community. Teacher quality, student discipline, and the curriculum were judged very important by three-fourths or more of all respondents, but class size and proximity to the student's home were also rated either very or fairly important by large majorities. Naturally, in the public sector, issues of race and ethnicity were called into question, and while these considerations were at the bottom of the list of motives, it "is well to remember a distinction between public opinion and private sentiment drawn by historian John Lukas: public opinion is the formal remarks that folks make to pollsters; private sentiment is the set of beliefs and biases that people are often too embarrassed to disclose. It is possible that racial and ethnic considerations are much more important factors in school choice than people admit to pollsters" (Phi Delta Kappan, 1990).

The public demand for improved quality of education or rather the issue of flight *from* rather than attraction *to* the public schools, may become a more prominent factor in the increasing numbers of parents who choose to enroll their children in any form of alternative education. This increasing flurry of excitement regarding educational choice makes it possible that a new resurgence of interest in day schools, in particular, will occur. Yet, it is this population of parents which should be of concern to those in lay and professional leadership roles at these schools, for these parents and families, in particular, tend to be the least committed to the particularly Jewish values of the school and the least likely to keep their children enrolled through all the grades of the school. While the number of these "white flight" parents may increase, for now at least, the majority of parents who enroll their child in a Jewish day school is clearly a group whose goals and motives are in consonance with those of the institution.

Roles

Do we really want parents to participate? If so, to what degree? The most helpful way to describe parent roles is by creating a continuum stretching from passive to active involvement. On the one end is placed a school where something as simple as a note home would suffice as communication, while on the other is placed a school where parents actually teach in the classroom or where they are educational decision makers (Cervone and O'Leary, 1982). Another way of thinking about parent roles was developed by Sinclair (1980). He lists four kinds of involvement: Parents as Clients (participation for public relations); Parents as Producers (participation for instructional support); Parents as Consumers (participation in community service) and Parents as Governors (participation for accountability and school governance).

In that same volume, Ralph Tyler, in summarizing other articles on improving school-family relationships, suggests three directions for developing productive environments for learning. The first is to conceive of curriculum not as a printed course of study but as environments in which children learn and grow. The second is to examine the assumptions, often unstated, which lead parents and teachers to counterproductive efforts and to substitute for these negative assumptions new ones which can be used to form closer associations between school and home. The third is to follow a proposed design for uniting parents and teachers that would encourage both groups to collaborate in building complementary learning environments.

But the school is not the only arena in which to speak about parent involvement. The home, too, becomes the focus of intervention. While it is not the intention of this chapter to describe the possible programs and theories surrounding the issue of parent involvement in schools, much has been learned from recent research in the public sector.[3]

Conclusion

New data from camps, youth groups, the Orthodox sector, and supplemental schools along with comparative studies will undoubtedly yield more fruitful avenues of information about parents and their motives, goals and roles. Still to be investigated is the relationship between parent motives and attitudes about schooling and Judaism. We might discover a level and depth of parent motivations and commitment which would surprise us. Alternatively, we might uncover a shocking gap between parent motives and attitudes stemming from parental ambivalence or inauthenticity regarding their own Jewish education and/or their own Jewish identity.

Yet, for the time being, to perceive these parents/clients as having values and positions in conflict with those of the school, may be a dangerous oversimplification. Clearly, these parents enroll their children in these particular institutions—not perhaps with the same degree of Jewish intensity that we as educators and policymakers might like to see, but still and all, with a commitment to this form of education. Remember, even in those cases where parents come to a day school through "not-particularly Jewish" reasons, it is possible that, *mitoch lo lishma; ba lishma*—something originating with a not particularly purposeful intent, may change to be of good intent; or, as one person said: "It's like going to the right place for the wrong reasons—and getting more than you hoped for!"

Bibliography

Adams, L., Frankel, J. and Newbauer, N. (1972, Winter). Parental Attitudes toward the Jewish all-day school. *Jewish Education, 41*(4), 26-30.

Cervone, B.T. and O'Leary, K. (1982, November). A Conceptual Framework for Parent Involvement. *Educational Leadership*.

Clerico, D. (1978). *Parents' Rationales for Sending Their Children to a Private Christian School.* Doctoral dissertation proposal. Syracuse University Syracuse, NY.

Erickson, D. A. (1983). *Private Schools in Contemporary Perspective.* Stanford, CA: School of Education, Stanford University.

Fried, I. (June, 1974). Family education—a critical issue in the Hebrew day school. *The Jewish Parent, 26* (4), 8-10, 34.

Gratiot, M. H. (1979). *Why Parents Choose Nonpublic Schools: Comparative Attitudes and Characteristics of Public and Private School Consumers.* Unpublished doctoral dissertation, Stanford University, Palo Alto, CA.

Golovensky, D. (1954). *Ingroup and outgroup attitudes of young people in a Jewish day school compared with an equivalent sample of pupils in public schools.* Unpublished doctoral dissertation, New York University, New York.

Greeley, A.M. and Rossi, P.H. (1966). *The Education of Catholic Americans.* Chicago: Aldine Publishing Co.

Himmelfarb, H. S. (1974). *The impact of religious schooling: The effects of Jewish education upon adult religious involvement.* Unpublished doctoral dissertation, University of Chicago, Chicago.

Himmelfarb, H.S. (1975, September). Jewish education for naught: Educating the culturally Deprived Child. *Analysis.* Institute for Jewish Policy Planning and Research for the Synagogue Council of America (51).

Kapel, D.E. (1972, Summer). Parental Views of a Jewish day school. *Jewish Education. 41,* 28-38.

Kaufman, D. (1986). *Resolving the Conflict Between School and Parent in the Non-Orthodox Jewish Day School.* Unpublished masters thesis, Jewish Theological Seminary, New York.

Kelman, S. L. (1979, Spring). Parent Motivations for Enrolling a Child in a Non-Orthodox Jewish Day School. *Jewish Education, 47*(1), 44-48.

Kelman, S. L. (1984). Why Parents Send Their Children to Non-Orthodox Jewish Day Schools. In Michael Rosenak (Ed.), *Studies in Jewish Education. 2.* Jerusalem: Magnes Press, The Hebrew University.

Lasker, A.A. (Winter, 1976-77). Parents as Partners: Report of a research project. *Impact!, 35,* 1-2.

Louis, R. (1981). *Parental Attitudes Towards Supplementary Schools.* Unpublished masters thesis, Hebrew Union College, Los Angeles.

March, J.G. and Simon, H.A. (1964). *Organizations.* New York: John Wiley and Sons, Inc.

Massing, P. (1974). *The American Jewish day school.* Unpublished manuscript. Los Angeles.

Nulman, L. (1956). *The Parent of the Jewish day school.* Scranton, PA: Parent Study Press.

Phi Delta Kappan. (1990, September), *72*(1).

Reitz, R. (1990). *Parent Involvement in the Schools.* Bloomington, IN: Center on Evaluation, Development and Research, Phi Delta Kappa.

Simon, H.A. (1969). On the concept of organizational goal. In A. Etzioni (Ed.), *A Sociological Reader on Complex Organizations.* New York: Holt, Rinehart and Winston.

Sinclair, R. (Ed.). (1980). *A Two-Way Street:Home-School Cooperation in Curriculum Decision making.* Boston: Institute for Responsive Education.

Weston, S. P. (1989). *Choosing a School for Your Child.* Pueblo, CO: U.S.Government. Consumer Information Center.

Footnotes

[1] I wish to express my appreciation to Elaine Bachrach for her assistance in reviewing this essay.

[2] The word 'integration' is used in this essay to refer to the relationship between the Jewish and the secular usually in the context of curricular or "real life" matters.

[3] See, for example, the recent (1990) publication in the Hot Topics Series produced by the Center on Evaluation, Development, and Research of Phi Delta Kappan, *Parent Involvement in the Schools.* As the editor Raymond J. Reitz states: "Parents are a valuable resource for increasing the quality of our educational system. The responsibility for creating meaningful parent involvement programs rests on school administrators and teachers. However, not all educators have the necessary training or resources to create successful parent-school partnerships. This volume is designed to assist school administrators and teachers who wish to become more involved in designing effective strategies for involving parents in their child's education."

Highlights

* Congruity between motives of the parents and goals of the schools is likely to lead to greater pupil academic achievement.
* In the Orthodox day schools, the dominant parent motive seems to be the desire to perpetuate Jewish practice and values.
* In the non-Orthodox schools, the majority of parents selected "secular " reasons as primary motives for sending their child. Few were doing so in order to "Escape the public school and/or because of busing". Parents who completed intensive Jewish education programs chose "Jewish" reasons to a greater degree than did parents with less intensive backgrounds in formal Jewish education. These findings were similar to those about parents who send their children to Catholic schools.
* The Jewish features of these non-Orthodox schools were a major contributing factor in parent choice.
* These schools should no longer view the parent group as having motives in conflict with the goals of the school. The self-imposed isolation of the parents along with their exclusion by the administrators from curricular involvement ought to be rejected in favor of a school in which parents are perceived as a primary educative force that performs roles and tasks which flow from commitment.
* Getting parents to share in the educational process where the central focus is the family rather than the child may provide a distince feature of the non-Orthodox Jewish day school.
* The Jew in contemporary American society faces the classical diaspora dilemma: how to resolve the competing claims of Judaism and the non-Jewish world. 'Integration' becomes the focal point of curriculum.
* In supplementary schools most parents said that they chose a particular school because of location. Two other factors, the reputation of the religious school and the particular philosophy of the synagogue, were also important though they were ranked far below location.
* We in the Jewish school system have much to learn from the public sector particularly now in the United States.
* Parents can be seen in many lights. How their role is defined in a school will determine greatly their satisfaction and the mutual impact of home and school.

The Larger Context

Our own curiosity leads us to ask: Why? In the case of the present context, parents seem to select institutions in which to enroll their children for any number of reasons—but to a great extent, in conformity with the goals set by those same institutions. The larger question remains: does past research still hold today? Are there new circumstances in all the settings in Jewish education—Orthodox, non-Orthodox, supplementary, camps, youth groups, etc. which might alter the responses we know so far? Are there areas for continued creative links between school and home?

What We Know About...
Communal Planning[1] for Jewish Education

Chaim Lauer

For a while now, Jewish community federations in particular, have engaged in a process called "community planning"—as distinguished from "educational planning". Mr. Lauer, Executive Director of the Board of Jewish Education of Greater Washington, D.C., discusses the results of research he did in his past role as a federation communal planner. The focus of this article is on Jewish education from the communal perspective, defining the goal of community planning as "strengthening the community through informed decisions and actions, thereby assuring communal continuity".

THE VAST MAJORITY OF MATERIAL PUBLISHED BY OR FOR THE JEWISH COMMUNITY ON THE SUBJECT OF planning has not been analytical. It has been primarily hortatory, procedural or descriptive. One generally finds elementary "why and how to" narratives, program and process summaries, or precis of data[2]. The relatively few articles on community planning in Jewish education generally discuss individual program concepts derived from a specific community's planning process. These most often focus on community funding[3], which, though related to planning, is not the same.

Even the paucity of discussion on these subjects can in itself be either the subject or beginning of further inquiry. Is planning as a communal activity so new that there is really little basis for analysis? Is community planning for Jewish education so complex, and perhaps unique, that there is little comprehensive or comparable data to analyze? Is the subject so sensitive, complex or, perhaps, of so little interest that practitioners have avoided it? Does community leadership feel it already understands planning so well that further research is not deemed useful or necessary?

It is the position of this author that communal planning in the Jewish community must be studied as a subject in and of itself and that the impact of communal planning on Jewish education services, institutions and delivery is a specific subset worthy of research. The results of such research would generate, at minimum, a better understanding of the procedures and relationships required for successful community planning, especially for Jewish education. If used correctly, the findings could lead to more successful community planning, improved interagency relationships and eventually better Jewish education services.

Planning

Jewish community or communal planning can be described as the functions, structures, and processes utilized particularly by Jewish federations, to: achieve change; establish new services and priorities; study and evaluate existing programs and services; eliminate those no longer needed; coordinate services; avoid overlapping and duplication; and insure maximum community benefit (Miller, 1987).

Planning is an integral part of the federation system of central campaign, central treasury and coordinated central planning. The goal of community planning is to strengthen the community through informed decisions and actions, thereby assuring communal continuity.

The challenge to successful communal planning is that it is an exceptionally intricate process involving many persons and organizations of diverse and changing views, situations in flux and often inadequate or contradictory information. This is especially true in the area of Jewish education; no other Jewish service area incorporates such emotion as well as so many divergent views, approaches, and providers. Furthermore, the success of any coordinated planning approach is predicated on the assumption that the aggregate knowledge and views of the planning group will serve to balance attitudes and create an organic, informed decision-making unit. With all the divergent views and biases regarding Jewish education, achieving the common ground necessary for successful community planning for Jewish education is clearly a major challenge.

Coordinated, central planning has theoretically been a component of the American Jewish communal structure since the 1880s (Miller, 1986; Bernstein, 1958). Only recently, however, have somewhat successful attempts at proactive, comprehensive community planning been ventured[4]. Despite these recent efforts, most Jewish community planning remains reactive, relatively unsophisticated, and driven by budget realities and campaign needs. Planning efforts, instead of developing community consensus, often generate interagency friction. Furthermore, much of what has been done is conceptually and philosophically derivative of the for-profit sector or imitative of the government and/or welfare sector of the general nonprofit community (Westby, 1985; Sosin, 1985; Sumariwalla, 1982).

I believe that the dissimilarities among these service sectors and between the Jewish and general communities affect how planning is and ought to be performed in the Jewish community, how final decisions are reached and implemented, and whether they achieve their intended goals. I further believe that because of these subtle and unrecognized dissimilarities, particularly the voluntary nature of the American Jewish community structure, central Jewish community planning for Jewish education has been relatively unproductive, even often counterproductive to the goals of Jewish continuity and intense group identification. Because it is impossible in the context of this short article to go into depth on these views, I will suggest two major areas for future discussion and research[5].

A. Community Planning and the Jewish Education Problem

As outlined above, the planning process itself has not been subjected to scrutiny. Among the areas of useful study would be:

1. **Impact.** What is the nature and extent of any impact of central planning on the community as a whole; its capacity and success rate to either achieve a specific long-term goal or work within the services or programs of autonomous agencies; whether and how the process itself affects decisions and community building; what accounts for success or failure in the various steps of the communal planning process.

In effect, these issues begin the review of the nature and efficacy of the Jewish community's planning process—how it works and how it can work better. For example, such a focused review could show whether central planning can and should be always of global or "macro" nature; whether the planning, funding and educational resources of a central body should be targeted solely to the individual service deliverer on a case-by-case needs basis; or whether a flexible process could be developed to meet the communal and institutional challenges that such a review would uncover.

The positive end result of this exercise would be the development of guidelines on when, whether and how a successful communal planning process would work for Jewish education; and how it would relate to the multitude of service deliverers in an area that does not yet constitute a coherent or related system.

2. **Paradigms.** Does the fact that planning and budgeting procedures are derived from business and social welfare paradigms impact on communal decision made for Jewish education?

It could be argued, for example, that the holistic nature of service to a student in an educational setting is different from the departmentalized services to different clients in clinical or group social work settings. This finding could affect funding decisions for schools. Furthermore, such a study could also pinpoint possible impacts of the voluntary nature of the Jewish community on the successful development, implementation and delivery of communal education plans.

3. **Fiscal Realities.** How do community campaign and budget needs drive planning processes and decisions?

This area of research could explore the following hypothesis: How decisions are made ultimately affects the nature of the decision. Campaign and budget are short-range urgencies. Education is a long range issue that can only be evaluated longitudinally. Community planning and campaign requirements as currently perceived and executed may be counter-functional to long-range communal and educational needs.

Research in this area may indicate at least two points regarding the relationship of the immediate needs of campaign and budget processes to the planning process. The relationship may: a. limit funds and time for experimentation with and evaluation of potentially valuable educational programs; and b. lead to giving precedence to what appear to be more immediate needs, disregarding the long-term necessity of Jewish education to communal continuity.

4. **Individuals.** What is the role and effect of the individual leader on a voluntary community planning process (Hosmer, 1982)?

The findings of research in this area could suggest directions for the orientation and training of committee members and professionals on the planning process and its ramifications.

5. **Planning.** Is community planning different from program planning and other internal agency planning activities [example, the difference between educational planning and community planning for Jewish education]; how do they impact on and relate to each other?

Findings in this area would give insight and guidance on potential micromanagement of agency activities and loss of agency prerogatives that can result from community planning processes.

6. **Uniqueness.** Are there any unique aspects in Jewish educational planning or the Jewish educational community that could or should affect community planning procedures or relationships?

It is possible to suggest that the comprehensive and lifelong nature of Jewish education is reflected by the varied nature of the Jewish education providers. There are numerous approaches, not only denominational ones, such as formal and informal, day and synagogue schools, early childhood programs, adult and child programs, and special education. Many of these providers are not community (federation) beneficiaries. Research may demonstrate that this affects how their input, role, responsibilities and product are perceived by the community (federated) planning process.

The results of these inquiries could be used to refine planning procedures and help orient planning committee members. The findings would help community planners focus on the real and relevant differences that exist among components of the Jewish community in regard to goals, terminology and constituencies. This could lead to clearer understandings of mutual needs and goals and to the development of agreed-upon definitions for commonly used planning vocabulary (Frost, 1979).

B. The Nature of the American-Jewish Experience

The American-Jewish experience is historically novel. For the first time in history, religious identification for the Jew is voluntary, not a matter of required corporate affiliation or an imposed external definition. American Jews live in the context of a democratic and individualistically oriented society. The result is that the American-Jewish community is a voluntary community in terms of individual identification, organizational affiliation, and communal leadership.

> **Uniqueness of that experience.** What, if any, ramifications and implications does this situation have on the approach of American Jews to Jewish education and to community planning?

This issue especially deserves in-depth analysis.[6] I believe that the findings would indicate that the voluntary nature of American Judaism has had a major impact on communal planning processes as well as on the goals and target populations of Jewish education and how it is delivered. At minimum, it can be argued that the American-Jewish experience has:

* made Jewish education child oriented, instead of being seen as a lifelong activity;

* equated the goal of Jewish education with generating a vague "Jewish identity"—to feel and not really to know;

* fostered denominationalism and a multiplicity of often competing approaches to providing Jewish education—formal and informal, day and synagogue schools, youth groups, centers, camps, retreats, etc.;

* weakened the family as the primary educational and bonding unit;

* forced on schools, especially those attached to synagogues, the role of providing children with all the Jewish skills, cultural information and bonding sensitivities previously learned and/or reinforced in the family environment; and

* because of upward economic mobility, decreased interest in and respect for traditional Jewish leadership roles of rabbi and teacher, contributing to the educational personnel crisis.

Furthermore, it can also be argued that because of the comfort factor of living in such an accepting environment, the urgency, value and support of Jewish education has been diminished as compared to other more immediate or visible needs. This is why it is hard for many community members to sense the invisible, long-term "theoretical" threat of communal pathology and dissolution that Jewish education combats when everything else seems relatively untroubled for the Jews. The more visible pathologies of individuals and families dealt with by other service agencies are understood by every feeling person as "real and now". This leads caring individuals to direct their tzedakah priorities to other, more immediately satisfying areas and diminishes financial support for schools and other educational institutions and programs.

In-depth analysis as suggested here could demonstrate whether and/or how the American "environmental situation" has affected all the organizational elements of Jewish education: teacher, student, curriculum content, parents, family, community, venues, financial support, planning and fund raising.

The Potential Role of Planning

Regardless of their ultimate results, the areas of research and directions of analysis suggested here could help Jewish community leadership construct more sensitive and successful planning processes for service delivery and educational advocacy, arrive at more informed decisions and develop more constructive, integrated and comprehensive program responses.

Bibliography

Bernstein, P. (1958, Fall). Current and Prospective Trends in Jewish Communal Service. *Journal of Jewish Communal Service, 35*(1), 15-23.

Elazar, D.J. (1976). *Community and Polity: The Organizational Dynamics of American Jewry.* Philadelphia: Jewish Publication Society.

Engel, S.B., Hurwitz, B., Lazarus, B.Z., & Lecker, S.(1977). *Community Planning Manual for Intermediate Size Communities.* New York: Council of Jewish Federations.

Fishman, S.B. (1987, December). *Learning About Learning: Insights on Contemporary Jewish Education from Jewish Population Studies.* Waltham, MA: Brandeis University, Maurice and Marilyn Cohen Center for Modern Jewish Studies, Research Report 2.

Frost, S. (1979, Winter).Come Now and Let Us Reason Together. *Jewish Education, 47*(4), 8-12.

Hosmer, L.T. (1982, Fall). The Importance of Strategic Leadership. *Journal of Business Strategy,* 47-57.

Lauer, H.C. (1984, Winter). Perspective in Jewish Education. *Journal of Jewish Communal Service, 61*(2), 144-149.

McCune, S.D. (1986). *Guide to Strategic Planning for Educators.* Alexandria, VA: Association for Supervision and Curriculum Development.

Miller, C. (1986). *An Introduction to the Jewish Federation.* New York: Council of Jewish Federations.

Miller, C. (1987) *An Introduction to Planning in the Jewish Federation.* New York: Association of Jewish Community Organization Personnel.

Sosin, M. (1985). The Domain of Private Social Welfare: Comparisons between the Public Sector and Voluntary Sector. In G. Tobin (Ed.), *Studies in Social Welfare Policies and Programs, Number 1. Social Planning* (pp. 105-131). Westport, CT: Greenwood Press.

Sumariwalla, R.D. (1982). *Needs Assessment, The State of the Art: A Guide for Planners, Managers, and Funders of Health and Human Care Services.* Alexandria, VA: United Way of America.

Sidorsky, D. (Ed.). (1973). *The Future of the Jewish Community in America.* Philadelphia: Jewish Publication Society.

Trends, Report on Developments in Jewish Education for Community Leadership. (Fall 1989). Jewish Education Service of North America, No. 15.

Westby, O. (1985). Religious Groups and Institutions. In G. Tobin (Ed.), *Studies in Social Welfare Policies and Programs, Number 1. Social Planning* (pp. 47-74). Westport, CT: Greenwood Press.

Wilkinson, G. W. (1986). Strategic Planning in the Voluntary Sector. In J.R. Gardner, Rachlin, & H.W. Sweeny, (Eds.), *Handbook of Strategic Planning.* New York: John Wiley and Sons.

Footnotes

[1]It is necessary to differentiate between community planning for Jewish education and educational planning. In this paper we are focusing on the former, although clearly there is a relationship between the two. Educational planning is a professional activity that includes curriculum and materials development, program planning and personnel deployment. It is undertaken by educators within and for an educational environment. However, educational planning is subject to general community educational policies. These communal policies are established by community leadership with input from interested parties such as institutional leadership, parents and educators. The development of these general policies and finding the requisite resources to support them are major components of community planning and budgeting.

[2]See Council of Jewish Federations Bulletins such as *Community Planning Manual For Intermediate Size Cities.* CJF has published a number of practical bulletins over the years. The increasing sophistication of these bulletins is a fair barometer of the general growth of the Jewish community planning process. Especially useful for background and subtleties is Miller, C. (1987), *An Introduction to Planning in the Jewish Federation,* Association of Jewish Community Organization Personnel; *Forging the Federation and Agency Partnership: Guidelines for Action* (1990). New York: Council of Jewish Federations; Perlman, E. (Fall, 1979), The Jewish Educator in the Jewish Communal Planning Process. *Jewish Education, 47*(3), 44-48; Schiff, A. (Spring/Summer, 1976), Communal Planning and Jewish Education. *Jewish Education. 44*(3-4), 3-13.

[3]See for example articles by Dubin, B. (Winter, 1979) The Role of the Jewish Educator in the Planning Process. *Jewish Education, 47*(4),4-7; Teller, G. (Spring, 1985). Community and Jewish Education. *Jewish Education. 53*(1); Berkey, J. & Meyers, J. (Summer, 1986). The Communal Role in Jewish Education in Communities Without Central Agencies for Jewish Education. *Jewish Education, 54*(2), 23-26; Lauer, H. C.(Winter, 1984). Perspective in Jewish Education. *Journal of Jewish Communal Service,* 61(2), 144-149; and Lauer, H. C. (Summer, 1986); Future Models for Jewish Education. *Jewish Education, 54*(2),15-18.

[4]See: *Long Range Strategic Planning in Jewish Federations: Guidelines* (1988). New York: Council of Jewish Federations; Huberman, S. (Winter, 1984). Evaluation as a Planning and Management Tool. *Journal of Jewish Communal Service. 61*(2); Andron, S. (Winter, 1984) Understanding Jewish Community Needs: The Greater Los Angeles Regional Needs Survey. *Journal of Jewish Communal Service. 61*(2).

[5]Obviously because of space constraints, this essay can only suggest a few of the points to be considered with their implications. The author intends to publish a much extended analysis on community planning in Jewish education in the near future.

[6]For a somewhat more extended discussion of the following points see Lauer, H.C. (Winter 1984), Perspectives in Jewish Education, *Journal of Jewish Communal Service, 61*(2), 144-149; Cohen, J.J. (1964). *Jewish Education in Democratic Society.* NY: The Reconstructionist Press; *Report of the Harvard Committee General Education in a Free Society* (1946). Cambridge: MA; Liebman, C.S. (1973). American Jewry, Identity and Affiliation. In Sidorsky, D. (Ed). *The Future of the Jewish Community in America.* Philadelphia: Jewish Publication Society, 127-152; Elazar, D.J. (1976). *Community and Polity: The Organizational Dynamics of American Jewry* Philadelphia: Jewish Publication Society; Elazar, D.J. (1981). *Kinship and Consent:The Jewish Political Tradition and Its Contemporary Uses.* Philadelphia: Turteldove Publishing; Sklare, M. (1982) *Understanding American Jewry.* New Brunswick: Transaction Books; Woocher, J.S. (1986). *Sacred Survival: The Civil Religion of American Jews.* Bloomington, Indiana: University Press; Prager, D. (June, 1990). A Value-Free Education is the Antithesis of the Jewish View of Education. *Moment,* 14-15. A longer dissertation on a similar point can be found in Samuel, M. (1950). *The Gentleman and the Jew.* New York: Alfred A. Knopf, en passim.

Highlights

* Most Jewish community planning remains reactive, relatively unsophisticated, and driven by budget realities and campaign needs.
* Much of what has been done is derivative of the for-profit sector or imitative of the government and/or welfare sector of the general nonprofit community and thus, unproductive because of the basic dissimilarities of the client populations.
* Central Jewish community planning for Jewish education has been relatively unproductive, if not counterproductive to goals of Jewish continuity and intense identification.

The Larger Context

Mr. Lauer focuses on future possibilities, on the useful areas of study to be found under the twin rubrics of Community Planning and The Unique Nature of the American-Jewish Experience. His extensive suggestions only scratch the surface of the issues for the Jewish community. One point, however, deserves emphasis: the educational setting. Because of the holistic nature of this essential endeavor, it must be intrinsically different from those other services which the community provides.

What We Know About...
Changing Jewish Schools
Or Surf, Don't Pitch![1]

Susan L. Shevitz

A large literature of how institutions change exists in the secular field. Only now are we beginning to do similar kinds of work with Jewish institutions. We know a lot; but implementing change demands not only the knowledge of what works and why. As Dr. Shevitz, Assistant Professor of Jewish Education and Organizational Studies in the Hornstein Program for Jewish Communal Service at Brandeis University suggests, they must be a clear understanding of schools' "behavioral regularities" and their cultural contexts. Some of our conventional wisdom about institutional change is challenged by her penetrating research which focuses on the cultural, symbolic and political aspects of educational change.

ALL EDUCATION INVOLVES CHANGE. TO EDUCATE IS TO DEVELOP A SKILL, ATTITUDE, INSIGHT OR IDENTITY. The irony is that when we seek to change educational institutions we are often stymied. Today there is more incentive for improving Jewish education in North America than ever before. The reasons are rooted in our collective fears and aspirations: How will we survive as a people on this continent with its easy routes to intermarriage and assimilation? How can we ensure that our survival will be spiritually and culturally meaningful? These basic questions concern many communal leaders, not only those from organizations involved with Jewish education. Thus, federations have entered the Jewish education arena with direct and indirect funding of schools and/or programs and by organizing Jewish continuity commissions charged with the responsibility of setting educational priorities for their communities. Family foundations, explicitly committed to improving Jewish education, have emerged. JCCs, camps for children and families, and other informal Jewish educational programs have joined the efforts of the synagogues and schools to inspire and teach. All this is happening within a climate of general concern about public education. Hardly a week goes by without reports of schools' deficiencies accompanied by plans for a promising new

206 What We Know About...

approach. Efforts to improve secular education affect the way we Jews think about our own educational institutions.

If this is a moment, then, of energy and optimism about Jewish education, it is a moment calling also for caution. Very little is known about the process of changing Jewish educational institutions. The vast research on improving secular education, as well as the few studies which have been done on Jewish schools, show that significant, long-term change is often elusive and always hard won. Understanding those factors which impede and those which support positive change —improvement— in educational institutions ought to be the basis from which we work.

This article is a modest attempt to suggest perspectives and guidelines to those who approach Jewish educational institutions and leaders with the hope for improvement. (While I use the language of formal schooling [classes, principals, teachers, school committees, etc.], the analysis is also applicable to other educational settings.) The viewpoint is that of an external group, like a federation, whose mission relates to but is not primarily education. The article addresses change on an institutional and communal level and is not concerned with helping individual educators or students. Focusing on the cultural, symbolic, and political aspects of change, it suggests an orientation towards the process of improving Jewish schooling which emerges from the research on change in Jewish and secular education.[2]

Perspectives on Changing Schools

Were there a way to excavate the dump in which failed school improvement efforts have landed, the remains would reveal a persistent naivete about the nature of schools. When reformers have not recognized how the work of a school —teaching and learning— is accomplished or have misunderstood schools' organizational structures and cultural realities, their initiatives have failed.

Some Characteristics of Schools' Essential Work

Several years ago I had the happy accident of gaining access to Jerusalem's Armenian Quarter. With a church official eager to practice his English I meandered through the sector and was allowed to make a spontaneous visit to the school. Summer vacation had just recently begun and although there were no children in the building, it still bore the evidence of the lessons recently taught. Books were on tables, visuals on the walls, chalkboards adorned with pictures and words. Immediately I was at home; here I needed no interpreter. It was a classroom, shabbier than most I've frequented, but familiar all the same. Desks were arranged in rows; a larger teacher's desk holding the supplies sat on the side. There was a large clock, a map prominently displaying Armenia, pictures of saints and heroes, even a paper airplane stuck on the light fixture. I was surprised by the familiarity the small room, hallways and offices held. While I might rearrange some desks, use different books, exchange Saint Gregory for a poster of Rashi and use Hebrew rather than Armenian script, I could easily set to work here.

Similarities among schools are not accidental. In his 1932 book, *The Sociology of Teaching,* Waller notes that schools have unique cultures. Sarason's classic *The Culture of Schools and the Problem of Change,* (1971/1982) shows schools' "behavioral regularities: characteristics powerful enough to impede and reshape reforms intended to better schools but incompatible with school culture." Even alternative schools of the 1960s and '70s were found to have these behavioral regularities (Swidler, 1979). To work effectively with a school, these behavioral regularities must be understood, especially as they pertain to the school's essential work: teaching and learning.

Lortie (1975) first characterized teaching as a field fraught with "endemic uncertainties." The link between teaching and learning is uncertain and its knowledge base is weak. Lieberman and Miller (1984, pp.2-15) summarize distinctive characteristics of teaching.3 Teaching style is personalized. Teachers bring their distinctive characteristics and develop diverse strategies which advance student learning and maintain good relationships with and among the learners. This style, "forged in the dailiness of work [and] developed by trial and error, becomes one's professional identity and, as such, may be militantly protected and defended (Lieberman and Miller,1984, p.2)."

Teachers' rewards come from students who are the only ones who are regularly with the teacher and see the work. While other professionals receive feedback and recognition from colleagues and supervisors, teachers tend to turn to students for this. Teaching is, in Sarason's words, "a lonely profession." Teachers must learn from their own experiences without shared experiences with peers. Schools have a cellular configuration with teachers largely isolated from each other.4

Teaching has multiple and conflicting goals and, with its weak knowledge base, there "simply is no consensus (as there is in medicine and law) about what is basic to the practice of the profession (Lieberman and Miller, 1984, p.3)." There are powerful daily, weekly, seasonal and yearly rhythms which define the field and formal and informal rules which favor practicality and privacy.

These characteristics suggest that there are limits to rational plans, that resistance to change is inevitable, and that "patience and realism are appropriate guideposts to any interventions in schools (Lieberman and Miller, 1984, p.14-15)."

Schools' Organizational Characteristics

A prevalent but flawed view of schools and school systems emerges from turn-of-the-century theories of management with their beliefs in order, rationality, and a scientific base for organizational structure (Clark and Meloy, 1989; Lieberman and Miller, 1986; Sirotnik, 1989).5 This view assumes that educational institutions and systems are hierarchical and bureaucratic and has yielded many reforms developed in a "top down" fashion (Timar and Kirp, 1988). A project or policy (e.g. a new curriculum, or a different teacher evaluation method, etc.) is developed for the schools, often by outside experts. Practitioners, exposed to some training, are then expected to implement the project or conform to the policy. Advocates for the change are lured into believing that the reforms, moving through the system's chain of command, will achieve intended results! When the results do not materialize or quickly fade, the school or its staff are the easy targets:"if only they would...."

It is the wrong conception of schools and school systems, however, which is at fault. Even a worthy reform will not take root when it relies on the bureaucratic, hierarchical features of schooling. As Timar and Kirp (1988) demonstrate, such reforms rely on two erroneous assumptions: 1) the closer one is to the source of the policy, the greater the influence and authority and 2) clear lines of authority let systems respond to complex problems. Since teaching is a highly personalized and isolated endeavor it cannot be bureaucratically controlled. When it comes to implementation (i.e. enacting the innovation or policy), the people promulgating the change have less power than the teachers who are further down in the organizational chart. Similarly, clear lines of authority actually yield fragmented schools in which personnel cannot easily collaborate (Timar and Kirp, 1988). To approach schools with the assumption that they operate in primarily bureaucratic ways is to mistake the tertiary for the essence.[6] Since much social planning theory is based in a rational view of organizational life and since federations tend to be bureaucratically organized, the warning is especially pertinent when federations enter the Jewish educational scene.

Consider two examples. Central agencies developed codes of practice to regulate educators' activities. These were easily circumvented, however, as situations demanded (Shevitz 1987). In another case a program designed by federations to promote trips to Israel did not have the expected impact on schools because planners assumed that the program, if accepted by the principal, would be embraced by teachers and students. They had mistakenly assumed that by initiating a plan schools would be motivated to change and that the initiative would move systematically through the school (Shevitz 1989).

These examples show the two major problems which occur when reforms rely on the assumption that schools operate in primarily bureaucratic ways. Neither invested in nor comfortable with an innovation, behind the closed classroom or office doors an educator can continue to do whatever she wants (much of the time), regardless of the new reform. It also assumes compliance with rules and regulations; it reduces complex educational problems to straightforward sets of rules which actually do little to change a situation. In other words, we can make it appear as if a situation has changed when in reality it has not (Timar and Kirp, 1988). Even powerful initiatives can be downscaled or blunted as they are adapted by the schools (Huberman and Mills, 1984).

If, then schools are not primarily hierarchical or bureaucratic, what are they?

Schools and school systems are "open systems" (Scott, 1981) which are affected by many things in the environment. Weick (1976) notes that they are "loosely coupled." Different parts of the system can act semiautonomously and are only loosely connected to the other parts:

> ...the [open] system is multicephalous: many heads are present to receive
> information, make decisions, direct performance. Individuals and subgroups
> form and leave coalitions. Coordination and control become problematic....
> Open systems imagery...shifts attention from structure to process (Scott,
> 1981, p.119).

Loose coupling exists if one part of an organization affects another suddenly rather than continuously, indirectly rather than directly, eventually rather than immediately, and negligibly rather than significantly (Weick, 1984, p.380). Consider how lay leaders (or teachers) might try to influence a school committee decision on, for example, attendance standards or how a curriculum coordinator affects the work of a veteran teacher.

Schools' internal and external environments are complex and shifting. Different groups in and out of the school become active when something interests them. They recede as the issue fades only to resurface as occasions demand (Patterson, Purkey and Parker, 1986). Coalitions change as conditions vary!

Schools mediate among many sets of goals and expectations held by these different groups. Not only are there differences between professional and parent groups, but there is considerable variation within them. The effective school, while responsive to these differences, can articulate a vision which is consistently enacted through its policies and programs (Lightfoot, 1983).

Schools as Culture-Bearing Organizations

While schools share many common characteristics, they also vary in significant ways. Like all stable social groups, each *school* also develops and maintains its unique culture. It conveys "socially shared and transmitted knowledge of what is and what ought to be, symbolized in act and artifact (Wilson, 1971, p.90)." This provides a sense of security and meaning to those involved in the school.7

Different aspects of school culture are more or less open to change. Rossman, Corbett and Firestone (1988) argue that schools have both sacred and profane norms. Sacred norms define "what is and ought to be;" they are the "normative anchors which keep the remainder of activity in the proper order (p. 11)." Profane norms are those which reflect the temporary adjustments to what is going on. Altering them does not call into question basic views of how the world is and should be. Changes dealing with the school's sacred values —its core beliefs—[8] are hard to institute and are themselves often modified over time. Differentiating between a school's sacred and profane norms is an essential, though difficult, aspect of a change process.

Sergiovanni (1989) aptly summarizes the complicated reality: schools are managerially loose and culturally tight. Administrative routines can be bureaucratically controlled (e.g.the use of a particular report card form or procedures for requisitioning materials). Yet the things that matter— school's essential work—can not be so easily mandated. Because of their shared and individual characteristics, schools are resistant to change.

Salient Aspects of Jewish Schools

While Jewish schools share many of these behavioral regularities, they possess several traits bearing particular significance for change efforts.

The schools are all voluntary associations. Students are enrolled, committees formed and funds raised and allocated voluntarily. This has vast implications. People come to the enterprise because of their values, commitments and aspirations, although these might inchoate or ambivalent. They choose to align themselves with the endeavor because, on some level, they care about it. This suggests a personal involvement which can be activated. Because they are voluntary organizations, Jewish schools compete for participants, advocates and funding with many other agencies and programs in the general and Jewish community. They need to be vigilant about social, economic, political, educational and ideological factors in the environment which will affect them. These range from the immediate (a revised little league schedule or improvements in a nearby Jewish school, for example) to the remote (events in the Mid-East or regional economic trends).

The schools are also autonomous entities. While they may be affiliated with a denominational movement or regional group which promulgates standards, for example, each school independently decides whether to follow, modify or ignore them. Its program is determined by the involved people. The sense of autonomy is such that data about school enrollments, programs and budgets is guarded by the schools which are not obliged to provide them. Compliance with a policy can be neither legislated nor mandated; those wanting to change a school rely on persuasion.

Although the phrase "system of Jewish education" is often used, there really is no system of Jewish education. There are instead overlapping interest groups and institutions; the picture is a collage rather than a schematic diagram. A synagogue school, for example, may get help from its movement's educational offices, use curricula from a different denomination, turn to its local bureau of Jewish education on some issues and its federation on others. National agencies might be consulted for other reasons. These many institutions do not ordinarily coordinate their activities. There is overlap and competition. Basic information is sometimes, but not necessarily, shared. None can mandate compliance with a policy or involvement in a particular initiative.

There is no professional corps of teachers upon which to rely. While there are some teachers who have professional training, hold credentials, and work reasonably full schedules, most do not. For some, teaching in a Jewish school is a part-time occupation; for others, an avocation. The complicated reality is discussed in a recent paper by Aron (1990). The salient point is that any plan for school improvement must confront the question of the nature of the teacher group in the involved schools.

Jewish schools' constituencies are increasingly diverse9 and the involved subgroups hold different views of the goals and purposes of Jewish education. Curriculum decisions in a day school, for example, are actually the group's expressions of the relationship between western and Jewish worldviews (Bulliavant, 1983; Zeldin,1989).

Demographic studies from communities throughout the country indicate the changing nature of the Jewish family (Council of Jewish Federations, 1991; Fishman, 1987). There is anecdotal evidence that in some schools fully half the students come from intermarried families, to cite only one type of change. As diversity increases, school personnel spend more time mediating among the diverse influences on the school. How any change will affect the school is a complicated question; it is naive to assume that all involved groups will react similarly.

Jewish schools, similar to their secular counterparts, are charged with responsibility for many things and expected to achieve results in many areas. Where once they were responsible for Jewish literacy, they are today expected to acculturate students and to guarantee students' (and sometimes families') Jewish identity (Aron, 1987; Fishman, 1987). Schools rarely have enough time, money or personnel to do all that is expected, even before they are confronted with new initiatives.

In many ways Jewish schools in the decades after the Second World War built the congregations which sponsored them. They have come to symbolize the congregation to its members so that changes to the school affect a broader constituency than the families with enrolled children. As seen in the study of congregational school consolidation, for example, people whose children have long since left the school can be among the most vociferous participants in the debate over the school's future. Changing the school alters the congregation's self-image (Shevitz, 1987).

Issues of organizational culture are potentially troublesome when federations (or other communal agencies) become involved in congregational settings. Congregations and communal agencies hold different notions about Jewish life and organization; they can be seen as separate spheres with overlapping interests. The communal agencies have been conceived as representing the Jewish community's public interests; the synagogues, its private concerns (Shevitz, 1983; 1988). Participants in each sphere have different perspectives: congregational leaders tend to be 'locals' and communal leaders 'cosmopolitans' (Elazar, 1976).10 Communal and congregational institutions can be expected to clash if those involved in school improvement efforts, however unknowingly, rigidly represent different realities and viewpoints.

Action Oriented Guidelines

This discussion of educational research suggests guidelines for efforts to improve Jewish education which focus on cultural, organizational and procedural issues. The list is necessarily selective; other principles could be derived, even based on the same research. They address issues which are likely to be problematic when federations and other external institutions approach Jewish schools.

1. *Understanding the different cultural perspectives of agencies and schools is central to a change process* (Deal, 1987, 1986; Goodlad, 1975; Huberman and Miles, 1986, 1984; Kelleher, 1982; Lieberman and Miller, 1986, 1984; Lightfoot, 1983; Pettigrew, 1979; Sarason, 1971, 1982; Schein, 1985; Sergiovanni, 1989; Shevitz, 1983, 1987, 1988; and Sirotnik, 1989). Until made explicit, the cultural traits of an organization are generally taken for granted. As Schein (1985) and others show, people know that this is "our way," but are not usually conscious of the beliefs which structure their worldview. The challenge to the outsider who would work with the schools is twofold. S/he needs to understand both cultural contexts: that from which and that in which s/he works. It is a sophisticated cross-cultural enterprise; schools and federations have different cultural contexts. Examples from Jewish and secular education repeatedly indicate that programmatic or procedural imperialism yields derailed or discarded innovation.

2. *Changes which rely on bureaucratic or hierarchical compliance do not necessarily improve the teaching and learning process* (Barth, 1989; Cohen and March, 1974, 1986; Cuban, 1989; Kirst, 1989; Lieberman and Miller, 1986, 1984; Rosenholtz, 1987; Rowan, 1990;

Rossman, Corbett and Firestone, 1988; Sarason, 1971, 1982, 1983; Schlecty and Joslin, 1986; Scott, 1981; Sergiovanni, 1989; Shulman, 1989; Sirotnik, Timar and Kirp, 1989; and Weick, 1983, 1976). If the goal of a change process is to improve what matters, the unique occupational and organizational characteristics of schools must be fundamental to the plans. It is deceptive to think in terms of a hierarchy which will encourage or enforce new procedures and policies. Instead concern must be on helping institutions develop their internal capacities for finding solutions to the problems they consider important. This entails collaborative modes of working and providing conditions which support collegiality and experimentation over time.

There is evidence, further, that effective changes need both "top down" and "bottom up" support. Top level leadership needs to create conditions which encourage school improvement efforts; teachers and other "front line" staff need to sustain them.

3. *Successful implementation of an innovation requires specific kinds of support at various stages in the process* (Firestone, 1988; Firestone and Corbett, 1988; Fuhrman, Clune & Elmore, 1988; Huberman and Miles, 1984). At least six functions have been identified: a) Providing and selling a vision of what the intended change is about; b) Obtaining the necessary resources for developing and learning about new procedures or activities (time, staff, lay leadership, instruction, materials, facilities, etc.); c) Providing meaningful public and private recognition for those involved in the change; d) Adapting the standard operating procedures to support the new approach; e) Monitoring the reform effort and using data to refine the process; f) Handling disturbances in and out of the school which detract from the effort. A sensitive blend of administrative support and enforcement is crucial to successful implementation (Huberman and Miles, 1984).[11]

4. *Different types of changes yield different consequences* (Cuban, 1989; Deal and Kennedy, 1982; Deal, 1987; Meyer and Rowan, 1977; Peshkin, 1982; Pettigrew, 1979; Rossman, Corbett & Firestone, 1988). Three cultural change processes are relevant in schools: evolutionary, additive and transformative. (For a full treatment see Wallace, 1970.) Rossman, Corbett & Firestone (1988) apply these concepts to their study of school reform. In evolution, new norms and values are introduced at about the same rate that others fade. The shift in school culture is gradual and seems natural to participants.

Additive change is the most frequent type of change in schools. It more suddenly affects the norms or values of a particular aspect of school culture, often through the introduction of a specific reform. If accepted, it alters the culture's underlying belief system. An example of this is enrolling children from intermarried families. Eventually this will affect many aspects of the Jewish school: curriculum, procedure, and programming. Initiators of additive change do not often consider the many ways the change, if incorporated by the school, will alter it.

Transformative change is when an individual or group purposely sets out to change a culture. This most often occurs when the culture is under severe challenge, usually after a series of crises or when external organization demands that the school change (Rossman, Corbett and Firestone, 1988, p.14).[12]

Deal (1987, pp.13-15) provides examples of creative strategies for revitalizing school culture in ways which support additive and transformative change: recreate the history of the school (e.g. through forums and art); articulate shared values (one school made a commercial for itself); anoint and celebrate heroes (e.g. invite back alumni who have done well); reinvigorate rituals and ceremonies (parents at a public high school gave a banquet for the teachers and distributed ribbons labeled with terms such as guru, mentor, exemplar); and work with the informal network of cultural players who are the direct conduit to the local community. Additive and transformative change takes time, flexibility, creativity and fortitude.

5. *Innovation is difficult and often resisted* (Cohen and March, 1974/86; Deal, 1987; 1986; Lieberman and Miller, 1986; 1984; Peshkin, 1982; Purkey, Patterson and Parker,1986; Sarason, 1983; 1971, 1982; Shevitz, 1987; and Zeldin, 1989). Change upsets people's expectations and world views. Many are potentially affected by a change process, if not directly then by their sense of what the change might mean for their organization and for the Jews! The more symbolically important a change is, the more attention it will attract (Cohen and March, 1974, 1986).

Efforts to consolidate supplementary schools are illustrative (Shevitz, 1987). Even when schools have insufficient students and money to keep going, the possibility of merging with nearby schools evokes many seemingly unrelated concerns. Suddenly a merger plan, which had been proceeding smoothly, is besieged by people expressing concern for everything from discipline standards to neighborhood decline or financial mismanagement. These are the communities' expressions of loss. The school has given meaning to a community; "ours is a synagogue which has always been proud of its school,'" a member might say. Now the community faces the unknown. Faced with the prospect of change, a group might become nostalgic for something it recently opposed. People involved in change processes need to understand that the seemingly tangential issues are expressions of loss and concern; involving the opposition in the change process is an important, though time-consuming, step.

6. *Transition rituals are conceptual and cultural anchors which foster the change process* (Deal, 1986; Lieberman and Miller, 1986; Manthei, 1983; Shevitz, 1987, 1983). Because change upsets people's views of themselves and their groups, conceptual and cultural anchors can guide people through the ambiguity of a change process. Transition ceremonies and rituals are helpful. Deal (1986, p.121) describes the coffin marked "Ma Bell" by a group of AT&T staff members and explains how the ritual helped the group cope with the challenge of divestiture. Ceremonies help teachers and students in newly merged schools express their sense of loss, anxiety and—finally— anticipation (Manthei, 1983). Ceremonies can link the past with the future, thereby helping people accept the change. As

Jews we are no strangers to ritual and ceremony. How to use them during a change of process is a relevant issue.

7. *Enduring change requires ample time and generous support* (Cuban, 1989; Huberman and Miles, 1984; Lieberman and Miller, 1986; Sirotnik, 1989). Much of the school improvement literature asserts that five years is the amount of time it takes for a change to be incorporated into the life of an institution. The process of learning, trying and adapting a project, for example, is arduous. Educators who have collaborated on a project, for example, may back off or experience failure at different points. This is to be expected. During this period the school and the people involved with the change need considerable technical, pedagogic and procedural support. The model of change which suggests that people need the support primarily when they are introduced to the change (through workshops or conferences, for example) has been discredited.

There are three stages in the improvement process: initiation (engagement and awareness), implementation (actually doing and managing the change) and incorporation into the institution. As Lieberman and Miller (1984, p.103), summarizing the research, conclude, movement from stage to stage is not automatic and the "motivations, needs, conflicts and rewards also change as stages change. What may be a reward at one stage may be seen as a punishment at another."

8. *Change efforts need to focus on schools' capacities for self-renewal and growth; the reforms should therefore look different at different sites* (Barth, 1989; Cuban, 1989; Goodlad, 1975; Kirst, 1989; Lieberman and Miller, 1986; 1984; Rosenholtz, 1987; Rowan, 1990; Rossman, Corbett and Firestone, 1988; Sarason, 1971, 1982; Scott, 1981; Sergiovanni, 1989; Shulman, 1989; Sirotnik, 1989). This is a critical departure from the assumption that the "answers"— whether in the form of new policies or programs— are best taught to the schools from outside. Instead, the role of the outside organization is to help create conditions which catalyze and help sustain schools' capacities to define and deal with important issues. Involving educators early in a process of defining the problems and developing solutions is crucial. Norms of collegiality develop slowly and are essential if work within the school is to be sustained.

Conditions, even within and surrounding Jewish schools of similar ideologies, vary markedly. Where one school uses avocational teachers, for example, another in the same community might employ credential-bearing professionals. Family configurations, socioeconomic conditions, history, organizational patterns and educational expectations differ in important ways among schools. The concept of replicibility —especially as a criterion for deciding which initiatives to support— needs reexamination. Teachers' work is highly personalized; schools' contexts and cultures vary. Ways to help schools learn from each others' experiences are needed; a program should *not*, however, be done the same way in different settings! If local problem solving is important to public schools, it is essential in the diverse and voluntary world of Jewish education. As Lieberman and Miller state (1986, p.108), "there are many development efforts; there is no one best way!"

Summary

The different approaches to improving schools are captured by Sergiovanni (1989) in the metaphors he develops in his recent review of school improvement efforts. Some approach schools as if they are *pitching* reforms.

> Schooling is is viewed as a simple process of delivering teaching (the ball) to specific targets (the strike zone). Pitches that miss the zone are declared balls and therefore don't count in the final score. To increase the likelihood that strikes will be thrown, the emphasis is on monitoring and refining the delivery system (p.3).

This metaphor reinforces a belief that teaching and learning are straightforward affairs and that we can isolate specific actions and consequences. It assumes that we can easily see what is happening and whether we are meeting our goals. The problem is, of course, that teaching and learning are far more complex activities. Any initiative brings a host of intended and unintended changes which are hard to detect, harder to measure. Schools, he suggests, are more accurately defined by a *surfing* metaphor:

> The idea is to ride the wave of the pattern until it unfolds, adjusting to the shifting circumstances. The pattern is made up of goals and circumstances that must be handled in a balanced way. Like surfing, schooling is difficult to monitor and improve from a distance; it must be observed and coached up close. Crucial to success in surfing are the successive interrelated decisions the surfer makes as he or she responds to unique and ever-changing situations. Improvement efforts are not designed to program what the surfer does but rather to inform the instincts and decisions he or she makes (p.3).

This article argues for a highly interactive process of improving Jewish schools. Will federations and other central agencies have the interest and devote the time and resources necessary to understand and accept the cultural complexities of Jewish schools? Will they focus on significant issues rather than on those which can be easily monitored or controlled? Will they promote schools' variability and flexibility while providing support for informed experimentation and problem solving? Will they establish dynamic processes for helping schools improve rather than promote set solutions to perceived ills? And will they be willing to support change efforts over time, expecting not a quick fix but rather the slow and arduous school improvement process? These are questions which recent research on educational change pose to those working to improve Jewish schools.

Bibliography

Aron, I. (1990, February). Toward the Professionalization of Jewish Teaching. Paper commissioned by the Commission on Jewish Education in North America.

Aron, I. (1987, June). Instruction and Enculturation in Jewish Education. Paper presented to the Conference on Research in Jewish Education, New York.

Barth, R. (1989). The Principal and the Profession of Teaching. In T. Sergiovanni & J. Moore (Eds.). *Schooling for Tomorrow: Directing Reforms to Issues That Count.* Boston: Allyn and Bacon.

Bullivant, B. (1983). Transmission of Tradition in an Orthodox Day School. *Studies in Jewish Education, Vol. 1.* Jerusalem: Magnes Press.

Clark, D. and Meloy, J. (1989). Renouncing Bureaucracy: A Democratic Structure for Leadership in Schools. In T. Sergiovanni & J. Moore (Eds.). *Schooling for Tomorrow: Directing Reforms to Issues That Count.* Boston: Allyn and Bacon.

Cohen, M. & March, J. (1974, 1986). *Leadership and Ambiguity.* Boston: Harvard Business School Press.

Corbett, H.D. III, Firestone, W. & Rossman, G. Resistance to Planned Change and the Sacred in School Cultures. *Education Administration Quarterly, 23* (4).

Council of Jewish Federation (1991). *1990 National Jewish Population Study.* New York.

Cuban, L. (1989). The District Superintendent and the Restructuring of Schools: A Realistic Appraisal. In T. Sergiovanni & J. Moore (Eds.). *Schooling for Tomorrow: Directing Reforms to Issues That Count.* Boston: Allyn and Bacon.

Deal, T. (1987). The Culture of Schools. In L. Sheive & M. Schoenheit (Eds.). *Leadership: Examining the Elusive.* Alexandria, VA: Association for Supervision and Curriculum Development.

Deal, T. (1986). Educational Change: Revival Tent, Tinkertoys, Jungle or Carnival? In A. Lieberman (Ed.), *Rethinking School Improvement: Research, Craft and Concept.* New York: Teachers College Press.

Deal, T. and Kennedy, A. (1982). *Corporate Culture: The Rites and Rituals of Corporate Life.* Reading, MA: Addison-Wesley.

Elazar, D.(1976).*Community and Polity: The Organizational Dynamics of American Jewry.* Philadelphia: Jewish Publication Society.

Firestone, W. (1988, Summer). Using Reform: Conceptualizing District Initiative. In *Educational Evaluation and Policy Analysis, 11*(2).

Firestone W. & Corbett III, H.D. (1988). Planned Organizational Change. In N. Boyan (Ed.), *Handbook of Research on Educational Administration.* New York: Longman.

Fishman, S. (1987, December). *Learning about Learning: Insights on Contemporary Jewish Education from Jewish Population Studies.* Waltham, MA: Cohen Center for Modern Jewish Studies, Research Report 2.

Fuhrman, S., Clune, W. & Elmore, R. (1988). Research on Education Reform: Lessons on Implementation Policy. *Teachers College Record (90).*

Goodlad, J.(1975). *The Dynamics of Educational Change.* New York: McGraw-Hill.

Goren, A. (1970). *New York Jews and the Quest for Community: The Kehillah Experiment, 1908-1922.* New York: Columbia University Press.

Huberman, A. M. & Miles, M. (1986). Rethinking the Quest for School Improvement. In A. Lieberman (Ed.), *Rethinking School Improvement: Research, Craft and Concept.* New York: Teachers College Press.

Huberman, A. M. & Miles, M. (1984). *Innovation Up Close: How School Improvement Works.* New York: Plenum Press.

Kelleher,P. (1982). A Bad Beginning as a Principal. In B. Jentz and Associates. *Entry.* New York: McGraw-Hill.

Kirst, M. (1989). Who Should Control the Schools? Reassessing Current Policies. In T. Sergiovanni & J. Moore (Eds.). *Schooling for Tomorrow: Directing Reforms to Issues That Count.* Boston: Allyn and Bacon.

Lieberman, A. and Miller, L.(1986). School Improvement: Themes and Variation. In S. Lieberman (Ed.), *Rethinking School Improvement: Research, Craft and Concept.* New York: Teachers College Press.

Lieberman, A. and Miller, L.(1984). *Teachers, Their World and Their Work.* Alexandria, VA: Association for Supervision and Curriculum Development.

Lightfoot, S. L. (1983). *The Good High School: Portraits of Character and Culture.* New York: Basic Books.

Lortie, D. (1975). *Schoolteacher.* Chicago: University of Chicago Press.

Manthei, J. (1983). A Reconsideration of School Consolidation Issues and a Case Study of Two Junior High Schools. Unpublished Analytic Paper, Harvard Graduate School of Education, Cambridge, MA.

Margolis, D. (1984). The Evolution and Uniqueness of the Jewish Educational Structure of Greater Boston. In A. Shapiro & B. Cohen (Eds.), *Studies in Jewish Education and Judaica in Honor of Louis Newman.* New York: Ktav Publishing House.

Meyer, J. and Rowan, B. (1977, September). Institutionalized Organization: Formal Structure as Myth and Ceremony. *American Journal of Sociology, 83.*

Patterson, J., Purkey, S. & Parker, J. (1986). *Productive School Systems for a Nonrational World.* Alexandria, VA: Association for Supervision and Curriculum Development.

Peshkin, A.(1982). *The Imperfect Union: School Consolidation and Community Conflict.* Chicago: University of Chicago Press.

Pettigrew, A. (1979, December). On Studying Organizational Culture. *Administrative Science Quarterly. 24.*

Pilch, J.(Ed.). (1969). *A History of Jewish Education on the United States.* New York: American Association for Jewish Education.

Rosenholtz, S. (1987). Education Reform Strategies: Will They Increase Teacher Commitment? *American Journal of Education. 95.*

Rossman, G., Corbett III, H.D. & Firestone, W. (1988). *Change and Effectiveness in Schools: A Cultural Perspective.* Albany: State University of New York Press.

Rowan, B. (1990). Commitment and Control: Alternative Strategies for the Organizational Design of Schools. In Cazden, C. (Ed.). *Review of Research in Education. No. 16.* AERA.

Sarason, S. (1982). *The Culture of the School and the Problem of Change, (2nd ed.)* Boston: Allyn and Bacon.

Sarason, S. (1983). *Schooling in America: Scapegoat or Salvation?* New York: Free Press.

Schein, E. (1985). *Organizational Culture and Leadership.* San Francisco: Jossey-Bass.

Schlecty, P. and Joslin, A.W. (1986). Image of Schools. In A. Lieberman (Ed.), *Rethinking School Improvement: Research, Craft and Concept.* New York: Teachers College Press.

Scott, W.(1981). *Organizations: Rational, Natural and Open Systems.* Englewood Cliff, NJ: Prentice-Hall.

Sergiovanni, T. (1989). What Really Counts in Improving Schools? In T. Sergiovanni & J. Moore (Eds.). *Schooling for Tomorrow: Directing Reforms to Issues That Count.* Boston: Allyn and Bacon.

Shevitz, S. (1983). The Deterioration of the Profession of Jewish Supplementary School Teaching: An Analysis of the Effect of Communal Myths of Policy and Program. Unpublished qualifying paper, Harvard University, Cambridge, MA.

Shevitz, S. (1987). Supplementary School Consolidation in the Jewish Community. Unpublished doctoral dissertation. Harvard University, Cambridge, MA.

Shevitz, S. (1988). Communal Responses to the Teacher Shortage in the North American Supplementary School. In J. Aviad (Ed.), *Studies in Jewish Education, Volume III.* Jerusalem: Magnes Press.

Shevitz, S. (1989). An Evaluation of the Israel Incentive Savings Programs. Unpublished paper commissioned by Jewish Education Service of North America.

Shulman, L. (1989). Teaching Alone, Learning Together: Needed Agendas for the New Reforms. In T. Sergiovanni & J. Moore (Eds.). *Schooling for Tomorrow: Directing Reforms to Issues That Count.* Boston: Allyn and Bacon.

Sirotnik, K. (1989). The School as the Center of Change. In T. Sergiovanni & J. Moore (Eds.). *Schooling for Tomorrow: Directing Reforms to Issues That Count.* Boston: Allyn and Bacon.

Swidler, A. (1979). *Organization Without Authority.* Cambridge, MA: Harvard University Press.

Timar,T. and Kirp, D. (1988). *Managing Educational Excellence.* New York: The Falmer Press.

Tyack, D. (1974). *The One Best System.* Cambridge, MA: Harvard University Press.

Wallace, A. (1970). *Culture and Personality.* New York: Random House.

Waller, W. (1967). *The Sociology of Teaching.* New York: John Wiley and Sons.

Weick, K. (1976). Educational Organizations as Loosely Coupled Systems. *Administrative Science Quarterly. 21.*

Weick, K. (1983). Management of Organizational Change Among Loosely Coupled Elements. In P. Goodman and Associates. *Change in Organizations.* San Francisco: Jossey-Bass.

Wilson,E. (1971). *Sociology: Rules, Roles and Relationships.* Homewood, IL: Dorsey.

Zeldin, M. (1989). In Yesterday's Shadow: Case Study of the Development of a Jewish Day School. Unpublished paper delivered at the Conference of Research in Jewish Education.

Zeldin, M. (1984). A Framework for Understanding Change in Jewish Education. *Studies in Jewish Education, Vol. 2.* Jerusalem: Magnes Press.

Footnotes

[1] The title is taken from an essay by Sergiovanni (1989) which is discussed at the end of this paper.

[2] The research and literature from secular education are vast. Unfortunately, there have been very few studies which deal with this process specifically from a Jewish setting. I will augment this research by giving examples from Jewish educational settings even if they have not been systematically studied.

[3] This analysis is based, of course, on the work of professional teachers in public school settings. It is likely to be directly applicable to teachers in Jewish day schools. While most of the characteristics would seem to apply to supplementary school teachers, as well, we do not know how avocational or volunteer teachers think about their work. The particular rhythm of the supplementary school, with its more sporadic class schedule, should also be examined.

[4] Many of the reforms of the last decade have attempted to reduce teachers' isolation and create conditions to foster collaboration.

[5] See the histories of educational administration, for example, Tyack. In terms of the Jewish community see Pilch (1969), and Goren (1970). Margolis (1984), Shevitz (1983) and others discuss this in terms of the Boston community. This tendency accounts for some of the contemporary tensions among central agencies, schools, synagogues and federations.

[6]Elements of schools which are bureaucratic and hierarchical relate to its standard operating procedures: how to obtain materials, report attendance, etc. The real business of schools, the teaching and learning, cannot be so tightly regulated; it is part art, part craft and part science and highly variable among teachers both within and among schools.

[7]See Peshkin (1982) for a poignant description of how school consolidation efforts in rural Illinois disrupted communities' self-perceptions.

[8]See Schein (1985) for a detailed discussion of how organizations' core beliefs influence all aspects of their work.

[9]See Patterson, Purkey and Parker (1986), chapter 1, for a full discussion of this in public education. See the 1990 National Jewish Population Study to consider the tremendous diversity within the Jewish community.

[10]Cosmopolitans "regard the community as a total entity and maintain connections and involvements across all of it.... Locals...are persons whose involvements and connections are confined to a small segment of the total community —a neighborhood, a particular social group, or...a particular synagogue, organization or club—and do not extend to the community as a whole, except indirectly (Elazar, 1976, p. 260)."

[11]When friction between those enforcing an innovation (the administrators) and those using it (usually teachers) is unresolved, the innovations do not succeed. (Huberman and Miles, 1984, p. 257)

[12]Some researchers distinguish between first- and second-order change. First-order changes assume that the existing goals and structure are basically adequate and that they can be improved with new policies or procedures. Second-order changes "aim to alter the fundamental way of achieving organizational goals or to introduce new goals... (Cuban, 1989, p. 266)."

Highlights

* schools have "behavioral regularities" which are characteristics powerful enough to impede and reshape reforms intended to better schools but incompatible with school culture. Predictable conditions that arise from these behavioral regularities, which are common to nearly all schools, include:
  - the link between teaching and learning is uncertain
  - teaching styles are personalized
  - rewards come from students
  - teaching is a lonely profession
  - teaching has multiple and conflicting goals
  - there are powerful daily, weekly, seasonal and yearly rhythms
  - formal and informal rules favor practicality and privacy
* A prevalent but flawed view of schools and school systems emerges from turn-of-the-century theories of management with their beliefs in order, rationality, and a scientific base for organizational structure
* Top-down reform does not work because:
  - closeness to the source of the policy does not necessarily yield greater influence and authority

-clear lines of authority do not necessarily let systems respond to complex problems
* Schools and school systems:
    -are open systems and loosely coupled
    -are complex and shifting
    -mediate among many sets of goals and expectations
    -maintain their own unique cultures
    -have different aspects which are more or less open to change
    -are managerially loose and culturally tight
* Jewish schools:
    -are voluntary organizations
    -exist as autonomous entities, such that there is no system of Jewish education nor any professional corps of teachers
    -have constituencies which are increasingly diverse and hold varying views regarding the goals of Jewish education
    -are endowed with the responsibility for many things and expected to achieve results in many areas
* Dr. Shevitz's action-oriented guidelines:
    -understand and work with the school's culture
    -recognize that bureaucratic or hierarchical compliance methods to change teaching/learning process don't work
    -support successful implementation at its various stages in different ways
    -identify type of change process and its consequences
    -expect that change will be difficult and resisted by some
    -provide conceptual and cultural anchors through ceremonies and rituals
    -allot of time and generous support throughout the change process, not just at its start
    -expect reforms to look different at different sites

The Larger Context

These guidelines require us to question our "conventional wisdom" about how Jewish educational organizations work. Top-down models, for example, though efficient in the marketplace and the army, may have a vary limited place in education. Efforts to significantly change Jewish education require adaptive, long-term approaches which are guided by the "behavioral regularities" and cultural contests of our institutions rather than by outsiders' notions of how things are—or ought to be!

What We Know About...
The Role of Lay People

Bernard Reisman

"Lay people" and "professionals" are the terms used to define define the two groups of people who share in providing leadership in the American Jewish community. How the two groups view each other and how they view themselves reflects the changing social context. Their relationship is in a process of change. American Jews in the fourth and fifth generation seem to have survived the "snare of modernity". New leadership pattern(s) need to emerge and/or be created afresh. Dr. Bernard Reisman is Professor of American Jewish Communal Studies and Director of the Hornstein Program in Jewish Communal Service at Brandeis University in Waltham, Massachusetts and has spent the last twenty years involved with this subject.

I. The Changing Social Context

AS WE ENTER THE CONCLUDING DECADE OF THE 20TH CENTURY, THE NORTH AMERICAN JEWISH COMMUNITY appears to be involved in changes of watershed proportions, changes which are likely to result in a significant upgrading of Jewish education services in the community (Reisman, 1989).

Until recently, the prevailing wisdom about the future of the American Jewish community was shaped by the "three-generation theory." According to this theory, Jewish commitment and knowledge diminish progressively from the first generation immigrants, who are most Jewish in their behavior, until the third generation, who become predominantly assimilated into the culture of the majority American society (Silberman, 1985).

This presumed assimilatory thrust was largely confirmed by demographic studies conducted through the 1970s, which showed a diminution of Jewish observances and involvement in synagogue and other Jewish organizations of second and third generation Jews, and an increase in intermarriage.

Leaders of the Jewish community, operating from the perspective of the three-generation theory, have tended to define their leadership role and policies of the American Jewish community as, at best, a holding action with a constituency having a diminishing interest in their Jewishness

(Reisman, 1987). The assumption of the leaders is that it is only through dramatic Jewish programs and issues, e.g., Israel, Holocaust, cults and anti-Semitism, which require no great personal investment, will these marginally motivated Jews be sustained in the Jewish community. In such a perspective Jewish education is not viewed as a priority service.

By the 1980s the American Jewish population had shifted from predominantly a second and third generation to predominantly a third and fourth. The results of the 1990 National Jewish Population Survey are of particular importance because this is the first major national Jewish demographic study which provides information on third and fourth generation American Jews. The most dramatic finding is the increase in the rate of intermarriage, estimated at between 42% and 51%, clearly an indication of assimilation. At the same time the survey provides evidence which suggests a continuing interest in Jewish identity. While the proportion of mixed marriages in which the non-Jewish mate converts is only about one out of six, the majority of the non-converted mixed marrieds choose to rear children as Jews. This is an indication of some appeal of sustaining a Jewish identity. A related finding is seen in the Survey data noting a rise in observance of several important Jewish rituals by third and fourth generation Jews. In a similar vein, there has been a significant increase, in the past decade, of both the numbers of young Jewish families who choose to send their children to day schools and of Jewish college students who choose to take courses in Judaica.

These developments suggest that while third and fourth generation American Jews are highly educated and highly acculturated, they may indeed be experiencing a resurgent interest in their Jewishness. It is not anomalous to infer that despite a greater likeliness to intermarry than their parents' generation, third and fourth generation American Jews continue to want to be Jewish. Perhaps the attraction is the Jewish religious or cultural heritage, the sense of historic rootedness, spirituality, Israel, the sense of community, or some other factor or combination of factors. The dynamics of this appeal need to be better understood and should inform the Jewish educational experience. They key point is the recognition that Jewishness, contrary to the dire prediction of the three generation theory can "survive the snare of modernity." It is a competitive option in a very open and attractive American society. Will leaders of Jewish education recognize and build on that potential?

This then is the paradox of the third and fourth generations of American Jews: a high likelihood of intermarrying, yet a receptivity to continuing to be Jewish. This paradox poses the central challenge for Jewish education as it approaches the end of the century—to teach acculturated American Jews about a Jewish heritage which they sense can provide meaning and direction in their lives. Further, as these Jews learn more about their unique Jewish heritage, as the data indicate, the likelihood of their intermarrying diminishes.

Two other changes have occurred in the course of the maturing of the American Jewish population which have a bearing upon Jewish education. First, few Jews today, aside from the small minority of traditional Jews living in separate enclaves, have direct experience with Jews reared in the Yiddishkeit of the "old country," and who in the past have always served as models for learning Jewish rituals and a Jewish life style. Second, Jews coming of age today have not directly experienced the two primary sources of Jewish identity of their parents and grandparents—the Holocaust and the founding of the modern state of Israel.

In the face of these evidences of a changing Jewish constituency there has been a new response from leaders of the Jewish community, especially leaders of the Jewish federation system, who previously had been indifferent to Jewish education. Today federation leaders are increasingly speaking about Jewish education as the basis for assuring Jewish continuity. This upgraded priority for Jewish education is being translated into increasing allocations from federations for Jewish education (Zibbell, 1987). In addition, a new source of potentially significant financial support for Jewish education is now coming from independent Jewish foundations. In the vanguard is the National Commission on Jewish Education in North America, a collaborative effort of seven major Jewish foundations to fund new projects designed to enhance the effectiveness of Jewish education in America.[1] The impetus of the Commission is being carried forward by the Council for Initiatives in Jewish Education, established in 1991.

Emerging from this review of the changing social context is the central thesis that *if Jewish education is to fulfill the high expectations the community now has for Jewish education, it will require a new leadership pattern*. Up to now leadership has been primarily in the hands of the professional Jewish educator. What is now needed is a more significant role for lay people in sharing leadership with professionals. The involvement of lay people will make it more likely that the Jewish education system will accomplish two important objectives: first, adapt its operating style to be more in tune with the changing needs of Jewish families now rearing children, and second, generate the additional financial resources needed to upgrade the quality of Jewish education services. Morton Mandel articulated the challenge to Jewish education professionals to develop a more collaborative style of work with lay leaders:

> "Significant changes are needed in Jewish education and are made possible by the right partnership between the lay community and the professionals. A simple generalization is that immense power for accomplishing the mission of Jewish education is available if Jewish educators understand the lay community and how to relate to it (Mandel, 1987)."

II. Defining the Lay-Professional Relationship

I distinguish two models of lay-professional relationships, both of which have been developed in nonprofit social welfare organizations. The first I define as: *Professional as Central*.[2] In this model power is afforded to the professional because s/he has a special expertise not available to the lay people; the lay people assume a secondary, subordinate role. The classic example of this model in the general community is the physician as director of the hospital; in the Jewish community the classic example is that of the rabbi in the synagogue. In both cases the lay people defer to the authority of the professional for the key decisions shaping the core functions of the institution; the lay people accept as their role ancillary functions for supporting the institution.

The second leadership model I define as: *Lay-Professional Partnership*. This model is most typically utilized in social work organizations; in the Jewish community it is the model used in Jewish community centers and Jewish federations. In this model the allocation of power and responsibility to lay and professional leaders is more symmetrical, reflecting both the democratic, egalitarian values of social work and the assumption that the agency functions are not so esoteric as to preclude the shared decision making of lay people and professionals.

Given that Jewish education has traditionally been based in the synagogue and that rabbis have been the key professionals in the system, it follows that Jewish schools have followed the "Professional as Central" model. The educational director and his/her teachers define the curriculum and school policies and the lay people, almost always restricted to parents, maintain a quasi-PTA supportive role. Because of changes which have been occurring among today's American Jews—the potential lay leaders—it is now desirable that the Jewish school (and I would argue the synagogue as well) adopt the "Lay-professional partnership" model, with a greater role for lay people in running the school.

In contrast to lay leaders of the first half of the 20th century, lay people today are highly educated and frequently come from the world of corporate management, law and finance (Huberman, 1987). These lay leaders do not generally hold authority figures in awe as did their predecessors.

III. A Rationale for the Lay-Professional Partnership in Jewish Educational Settings Today

These new developments—the combination of a receptive, highly sophisticated constituency and a complex education setting, with larger physical plants and with more specialized professional and support staff—require a different leadership pattern. Such a response is the "Lay-Professional Partnership", which, I believe, is consonant with these new developments, and bodes well for fulfilling the potential for an enhanced Jewish educational experience. The call for such a partnership is supported by the conclusion reached by Gerald Showstack in his recent study of relationships between lay leaders and professionals. "A majority of lay leaders and professionals are in agreement that the primary improvement to be made in relationships between the two groups is the enhancing of the partnership through development of greater mutual respect and appreciation for each other's roles" (Showstack, 1989).

There are eight ways in which the "Lay-Professional Partnership" can be strengthened so as to lead to more effective performance of today's Jewish schools.

1. *Managerial Resources*—The schooling and work experience of today's lay people bring valuable managerial perspectives and skills to complement the educational backgrounds of the professionals in the operation of the school. Decisions emerging from the interaction of people with different backgrounds, and a shared interest in the school, are likely to be sound decisions.

2. *Responsiveness*—A well constituted board, with real authority, is in tune with the expectations of parents for a responsively administered school. Here parents can have confi-

dence that their ideas and concerns will be heard and that their perspectives are fully represented in the process of deciding on the policies and programs of the school.

3. *Financial Resources*—Lay people have the primary responsibility to raise the necessary funds for running the school, both contributing their own money and using their influence to obtain financial support from the Jewish community and from associates.

4. *Helpful Hands*—Lay people make themselves available as volunteers at special school programs and as spokespeople for interpreting the school in the community.

5. *Personal Accountability*—The narrow concentration of power in any human collective poses dangers; an active lay presence, alongside the active professional presence, brings a valuable check and balance function to the school's management. Also, the board hires and evaluates the performance of the school's director.

6. *Legal Accountability*—As a nonprofit organization the ultimate responsibility for the operation of the school legally rests in the hands of its board of directors.

7. *Agents for Change*—The presence of committed lay people in the leadership ranks increases the likelihood of change. Sam Schafler makes the point that most of the innovation in the history of Jewish education in American Jewish education has come from the ranks of volunteer leaders and not professionals (Schafler, 1987).

8. *Preparing Leaders*—As the school's executive director works with his/her volunteer board members in running the Jewish school s/he is also contributing to the training of leaders for the Jewish community.

The essence of the "Lay-Professional Partnership" is that it takes seriously the potential of the lay people and affords them real, not marginal or ceremonial authority and responsibility. Peter Drucker, the eminent theoretician on organizational leadership, points out that what attracts business leaders to volunteer for nonprofit boards is that in their jobs "there isn't much challenge, not enough achievement, and not enough responsibility (Drucker, 1989)." Lay people need to believe that their participation on a board "makes a difference".

IV. Requisites for Achieving an Effective Lay Role in Jewish Education Settings Today

1. *Responsibility*—The classical allocation of responsibility between lay people and professionals in Jewish communal agencies is succinctly described by Bubis and Dauber: "Lay people make policy and professionals implement that policy (Bubis, 1987)." As a general principle this is a sound guideline, but it should be tempered by the understanding that policy and implementation can never be mutually exclusive categories.

   The authors of a recent article in *Harvard Business Review* remind their managerial colleagues that "trustees exist to govern the organization—to monitor quality and to see to it that the organization fulfills its mission. But many trustee broads do not govern. They get bogged down in operating details, matters that are best left to staff, while ignoring the very issues that could determine the enterprise's success or failure (Chait and Taylor, 1989)."

2. *The Key Relationship*—Trust is the second vital ingredient for effective board-staff relations: without it no other guidelines or principles pertain. The basis for a trusting atmosphere between board and staff in any organization is determined by the quality of the relationship between the organization's two top leaders: the chairperson of the board and the executive director.

   The relationship between the board chair and the executive is of critical importance because it serves as a paradigm for relationships between the larger board and staff groups. When this relationship is characterized by mutual respect, open communication and a complementary division of labor, it increases significantly the energy and resources of the board/staff dynamic available to the organization.

3. *Expectations for Board Members*—The expectations for the role of the professional are spelled out in job descriptions and contracts. It would be helpful to have a similar level of specificity about what is expected of volunteer lay people. Indeed, a number of Jewish organizations have begun to use written "job descriptions" for board members. Most people prefer a clear statement of expectations when they take on a responsibility. Among the issues to be defined: the role of the board member, attendance requirements, financial obligations, committee assignments, involvement in leadership development, and "homework" expected (Council of Jewish Federations, 1986).

4. *Structural Policies and Procedures*—Several operating procedures and policies can help assure that the board operates in a way to optimize the skills and resources of its members and to get its work accomplished. These include:
   * a membership which is representative of all elements of the Jewish population to be served in terms of ideology and demographic considerations;
   * the expectation that people who serve on the board of a Jewish school must have demonstrated a commitment to Jewish education and should themselves be Jewishly knowledgeable;
   * the size of the board should be large enough to be representative and to assure a critical mass at meetings, but not so large as to limit active participation of all members (Elkin, 1990);
   * meetings have to be well-planned, conducted efficiently, and achieve results.

5. *Leadership Development*—A leadership training program for lay people should be an integral component of serving on a board of directors. The very presence of such a program interprets to lay people that their job is a serious one. A well designed training program

can both enhance board members' motivation to serve and provide them the knowledge and skills to carry out their stewardship effectively.

6. *Competing for Power*—The nature of the lay-professional relationship is now going through a period of transition because of changing expectations of both board members and professionals. In some few instances problems may arise, generally when either a lay person or a professional is excessively concerned with achieving greater personal power. Peter Hall describes the problem of corporate "fast-trackers" who see their involvement on a non-profit board as a way "to distinguish themselves from their peers in the race up the corporate ladder" (Hall, 1988). Such ambitious board members are not likely to allow a communal professional executive get in their way. On the other side, some professionals become carried away in their own power quest, and aspire to become a dominating C.E.O. Recently there has been a rash of firings or "resignations" of top executives of Jewish communal organizations, which have been reported on in the Jewish press (Lev, 1987; Goldberg, 1988; Richter, 1988). Some writers conclude that lay people have become too powerful; others that professionals have taken on too much power. The truth is that there are examples of both. But the more important development, which seldom is acknowledged, is that there are many more examples of lay people and professionals recognizing that the rules governing their relationship have been changing, and that both are working at making the accommodations to achieve a new partnership. These lay people and professionals realize that in making the partnership work, the Jewish school or communal organization—which they both care about—will ultimately benefit.

Bibliography

Bubis, G. (1987, Spring). The Delicate Balance—Board-Staff Relations. *Journal of Jewish Communal Service*, p.189.

Chait, R.P. & Taylor, B.E. (1989, January/February). Charting the Territory of Nonprofit Boards. *Harvard Business Review*, p. 189.

Council of Jewish Federations. (1986). *The Role of the Federation Board Member: Guidelines for New Board Members*. New York: CJF, 4-12.

Council of Jewish Federations. *Highlights of the CJF 1990 National Jewish Population Survey.* (1991). New York: Council of Jewish Federations.

Drucker, P.E. (1989, July/August). What Business Can Learn from Nonprofits. *Harvard Business Review*, 93.

Elkin, J. (1990). Lay-Professional Relations in the Jewish Day School. In D. Margolis & E.S. Schoenberg (Eds.), *Curriculum, Community and Commitment:Views on the American Jewish Day School-in Memory of Bennett I. Solomon.*

Goldberg, J.J. (1988, February 5). Executive Jitters. *The Jewish Week,* New York.

Hall, P.D. (1988, November 22). To Make Non-Profit Organizations More Effective, End the 'Secret Wars' Between Boards and Staff. *The Chronicle of Philanthropy,* 32.

Huberman, S. (1987, Fall). 'Making' Jewish Leaders. *Journal of Jewish Communal Service*, 32-33.

Lev, Y. (1987, December 25-31). The Crisis at Brandeis Bardin: No Heroes, No Villains. *The Jewish Journal,* Los Angeles.

Lev, Y. (1988, January 1-7). Changes Due in the Nature of Jewish Leadership. *The Jewish Journal,* Los Angeles.

Mandel, M. (1987). To Build A Profession. In J. Reimer (Ed.), *To Build A Profession.* Waltham, MA: Brandeis University, 48.

Reisman, B. (1987). *New Frontiers in Service Delivery:Community and Ideology—The Basis For Jewish Leadership Today.* New York: Council of Jewish Federations.

Reisman, B. (1989, Spring/Summer). A Revolutionary Change in American Jewish Life. *The Forum.* New York: North American Jewish Forum.

Richter, A. (1988, Sept. 2-8). Little Big Men: The Problems of Organizational Leadership. *Jewish World,* Long Island, NY.

Schafler, S. (1987, Winter). Voluntary and Professional Leadership: Partners for More Effective Jewish Education. *Journal of Jewish Communal Service,* 137.

Showstack, G. (1989, Winter). Lay-Professional Relations in Jewish Communal Institutions. *Journal of Jewish Communal Service,* 70.

Silberman, C. (1985). *A Certain People.* NY: Summit Books.

Zibbell, C. (1987). Jewish Education as a Profession: The Current Situation. In J. Reimer (Ed.), *To Build a Profession.* Waltham,MA: Brandeis University, pp. 47-48.

Footnotes

[1]The National Commission on Jewish Education was launched in 1988 by the Mandel Family Foundations. Other foundations include: Charles F. Bronfman Foundation; Crown Foundation; Riklis Family Foundation; Wexner Foundation; Charles H. Revson Foundation; and Blaustein Family.

[2]Two similar models of lay-professional relations emerge in the articles in the January 22, 1988 issue of *Sh'ma.* The subordination of lay people to a strong executive is advocated by Michael Berenbaum, "Effectiveness and Professional Responsibilities," while a partnership model is advocated by Sanford Solender, "We Need Partnership Not Dominance".

Highlights

* The old "three-generation theory" defined the leadership role and policies of the American Jewish community as, at best, a holding action with a constituency having a diminished interest in their Jewishness.
* While third and fourth generation American Jews are highly educated and acculturated, they may be experiencing a resurgent interest in their Jewishness.
* Emerging from this new social context is a new leadership model with more significant roles for lay people who can now share leadership with professionals.
* This new partnership is characterized by lay people:
    bringing new managerial resources
    being more responsive to the constituency
    assuming full fiscal, personal, and legal responsibility
    making themselves available as helping hands
    becoming agents for change
    preparing leaders for the future
* Effective lay leadership needs:
    a clear demarcation or division of labor
    trust
    defined role expectations
    clear structural policies and procedures
    a leadership training program
    recognition that issues of power may cloud functioning

The Larger Context

Starting with the larger context of the American Jewish Community, Dr. Reisman speaks about the role of lay leaders in Jewish education. This new partnership, so eloquently characterized, assumes that Jewish knowledge is at the base of the lay person's desire to become involved. Study may also characterize his/her future involvement. How this new relationship and enhanced knowledge base may affect the lay/professional relationship is yet to be seen. Along with this increase in power and responsibility of the lay leader may come enhanced status and qualifications of the professional as well. This bit of political optimism may well contribute to building stronger institutions.

What We Know About...
The Costs of Jewish Education

J. Alan Winter

Dr. Winter, who is Professor of Sociology at Connecticut College in New London concentrates on the Jewish education of the child. He writes about the policy issues facing communal leaders who address the issues of the costs, affordability, and ultimately, the value that we place upon the "good" which we call "a Jewish education."

THERE CAN BE LITTLE DOUBT THAT JEWISH EDUCATION IS ESSENTIAL IF JEWS, WHETHER INDIVIDUALLY or collectively, are to survive and thrive as such. There also can be little doubt that, as Schiff (1983) and Fishman (1987) report, one of the more common reasons parents give for not providing a Jewish education for their children is that it is "too expensive." Consequently, it is incumbent upon Jewish communal leaders to set and implement policies which help insure that Jewish education is widely regarded as affordable. The aim of this chapter is to identify and discuss key policy issues which Jewish communal leaders face as they decide how to render Jewish education affordable for all who wish their children to have a formal, school-based Jewish education. The focus here is on child-centered education since as a practical matter, "American Jewish education is primarily a child-centered enterprise" (Fishman, 1987). Such a focus does not, of course, gainsay the common rabbinic position that adult education is even more important than that for children, since children may not learn what the indifference and ignorance of adults signifies is unimportant. In any case, the issues to be identified and discussed pertain to the funding of afternoon or Sunday religious schools as well as day schools, the most common settings for child-centered Jewish education according to Fishman's (1987) review of population studies in eighteen major cities in the 1980's. The restrictions of space, unfortunately, preclude addressing the funding of informal educational settings such as day care, camps or teenage social and recreational programs. However, the issues raised by the funding of informal educational settings do overlap with those, dealt with below, involved in the funding of formal, child-centered Jewish education.

Affordability

The affordability of Jewish education for one's children, whether a day school or an after school program (Winter, 1985), can be understood to be dependent upon three factors:

1. the fee or tuition charged for enrolling in the program;

2. the level of discretionary funds, i.e., funds available after providing whatever is necessary to maintain one's desired standard of living; and

3. the rate at which discretionary funds are used to meet the cost of Jewish education rather than some other Jewish or non-Jewish purpose.

The last two factors clearly involve setting priorities and making trade-offs. Consequently, the affordability of Jewish education for one's children is a relative figure, not an absolute amount. It is relative not only to family income, but to how the family unit chooses to use that income for Jewish and other purposes. As I have shown elsewhere (Winter, 1989) the level of Jewish identity is among the factors influencing whether family funds are used for Jewish purposes.

In sum, then, the affordability of Jewish education is determined not just by its cost, but by the *value* of such education to the family in question. Consequently, two general strategies are apparent to enable a Jewish community to render the cost of Jewish education affordable in the eyes of those who do not now believe it is. They are:

1. decrease the tuition or fees charged for those who do not regard it as affordable; and

2. create an atmosphere which will encourage those concerned about the costs to use a higher proportion of their discretionary funds for their children's Jewish education.

Both strategies assume that minimizing the financial consequences of income differences will have a significant impact on enrollment in Jewish education. However, as Cohen notes (1983), "Differences in income relate to differences in class and cultural style." For example, even if the strategies discussed below render the cost of Jewish education affordable to a given family, they or their child may still feel uncomfortable attending school where their very used station wagon pulls up between a new sports car on one side and an even newer convertible on the other or where the hand-me-downs they wear are decidedly less stylish than everybody else's attire. Families uncomfortable with such differences, or others associated with income, may not affiliate with a school program even if it does all it can to make membership financially affordable. That is, more than money may be at the root of reluctance to enroll. Social differences associated with differences in income or differences in family composition associated with income, such as single or divorced parents, may also have to be addressed by programs wishing to extend their membership to those who now think it "too expensive."[1] In addition, as Schiff (1983) observes, some families are too proud and others too peripherally involved to seek financial aid. Consequently, outreach programs may be needed if financial aid is to have the intended effect of increasing enrollment.

Reducing Fees

In any case, the first strategy noted above for rendering Jewish education affordable, that of reducing fees or tuition, may involve additional financial burdens on Jewish organizations already likely to be operating on tight budgets. However, failure to make Jewish education more affordable for more Jews may undermine Jewish survival in America. Thus, reduced costs to the families involved is to be desired. Such reductions may result from one or more of three programs:

1. subsidies or scholarships;
2. a "give-or-get" standard; and
3. reduction in costs.

Subsidies or scholarships are, of course, often underwritten by schools themselves. Of late it is becoming common for local federations to help (Kobernick, 1985). Financial assistance from the local federated campaign might, however, be regarded as controversial in that providing it may be seen by some as diverting funds otherwise destined for Israel. Moreover, even those who agree, in principle, that more federated campaign funds be used to subsidize education can still disagree as to whether to fund both congregationally based after school programs and day schools or only one or the other. Some congregations may, as Pollack (1981) observes, harbor fears that a "loss of exclusive authority over congregational schools...accompanies communal funding." Others may object to communal funding on the grounds that in general, whatever the school, such funds would, directly or indirectly, support sectarian religious activities. Such support would, as Pollack (1981) notes, "be a major departure from established precedent on the American Jewish scene and will have to be dealt with in depth." Nevertheless, it is possible, as Rosenbaum (1984) reports, to devise a formula for federation support which receives widespread support. Some communities may wish to use the National Policy Statement on Communal Support for Jewish Education developed by Jewish Education Services of North America and reviewed by Horn (1987) to devise such formulae. Others may wish to consider some of the innovative funding programs discussed by Horn (1987) such as educational vouchers or teacher subsidization. In any event, as Schiff's (1986) historical overview of the funding sources for Jewish education indicates, federation support has increased to all-time highs in recent years.

However, even if there is agreement that a given fee or tuition be subsidized, whether by a central funding source or by the school or parent organization in question, there are still some rather knotty issues to resolve before a program can be put in place. For example, there is the issue of what constitutes need; i.e., of what a given family can or cannot afford.[2] The basic points to be raised in order to resolve such an issue are outlined in my earlier work on the affordability of living Jewishly (Winter, 1985), namely,

1. determining the cost of the service or affiliation in question;
2. the level of discretionary funds available; and

234 What We Know About...

3. the rate at which discretionary funds are to be made available for the cost in question.

The first is, of course, easily determined by the program in question. It should know what it "normally" charges. However, determination of the second and third points involves some difficult issues.

For example, if subsides are to be income-dependent, the organization must devise some procedures for determining the income of a family seeking subsidy. How to make such determination while balancing due respect for the privacy of the family involved with the organization's need to know the family's (private) income can be very demanding. Of course, an organization can simply take the applicants' word on what their income is. However, such a system is clearly open to question, especially on the part of the full-paying members who may want to be sure "freeloaders" are not among those being subsidized.

In any case, even where the family income is known, the problem of deciding the amount of its funds it should devote to the cost of Jewish education must still be faced. That amount depends, of course, on two factors, one's income and the standard of living one hopes to maintain. Clearly, it is easier to maintain a moderate standard of living with a given income than a higher standard. Thus, those who wish only to maintain a moderate standard of living have more funds available for meeting the cost of education at any given income level than do those who wish to maintain a higher standard of living. For example, a family with an income of $40,000 (in 1990 dollars) can easily maintain a moderate standard of living as defined by a standardized budget devised by the Bureau of Labor Statistics (Winter, 1985). However, such an income would likely not suffice if the family wishes to maintain a higher standard of living. Thus, the same $40,000 leaves one family, that desiring a higher standard of living, little or no money for the cost of Jewish education, and another, wishing only a moderate standard of living, over $3,000 for such costs without reducing any other expenditures. It is likely that any school program would be reluctant to subsidize the dues of a family earning $40,000 which could "afford" their fees or tuition and still maintain a moderate standard of living. Nevertheless, the family may feel strongly that it is entitled to live at a higher standard, as in fact many Jews do, and that it is quite justified in claiming it cannot "afford" the cost of affiliation without some help. In other words, those who decide who is to receive a subsidy must decide what standard of living it is and is not reasonable for them to help potential members support. If it is reasonable to support a higher standard of living, then the income level of those subsidized will be higher than if only a moderate standard of living were supported. Of course, if only those able to live at a lower standard are to be helped, the income levels that will be subsidized will be lower still.

Unfortunately, deciding what standard of living or, for that matter, what income level renders one eligible for support does not answer all the questions facing an organization that undertakes a subsidy or scholarship program. It must also decide at what rate the available discretionary funds are to be used to meet the cost of Jewish education. For example, it must decide if a family which has $5,000 in discretionary funds should be given help to meet $4,000 in day school tuition because it wishes to spend only half of its discretionary funds on tuition and put the remaining $2,500 in a fund for their child's college education or to pay for a needed vacation.

Finally, even after decisions are made as what policies are to be set with regard to the use of discretionary funds to meet the cost of education and other discretionary spending, the Jewish community as a whole still may face the question of how such subsidies affect funds available for other aspects of the cost of living Jewishly. For example, a synagogue may or may not include the cost of day school tuition when deciding who is to permitted join with reduced dues. It is certainly conceivable that a given synagogue will decide not to reduce dues for those who enroll their children in day school on the grounds that doing so is tantamount to subsidizing the day school at the expense of its own religious school.

The provision of either scholarships by the organizations involved or subsidies from some central funding source, then, may create its own difficulties. Thus, a second strategy for reducing costs may be employed, namely, a "give-or-get" policy. That is, those who wish to enroll their children in a given educational program, but who cannot afford to pay its tuition or fees, may instead help it to "get" the funds it needs by assisting in activities designed to help the organization meet its costs. The donation of professional, clerical or other services which help reduce the organization's costs may or may not be counted toward the amount to be "gotten." Time spent on fundraising activities should surely be counted. In any case, some schedule must be devised to establish the dollar value of the time or services that are provided in order to help the organization meet its costs. Unfortunately, many of those least able to "give" money are single parent families which also have the least free time or other resources to help the organization "get" what it needs to reduce costs or raise its income.

Since neither subsidies nor a "give-or-get" program may be feasible, a third program, one which I suspect is rather common, may be employed, namely, reducing the operating costs of the program in question, thereby reducing its need for funds and possibly hard-to-afford tuition or fees. However, since the largest part of any education budget is apt to be the salary and benefits of its professional staff, cost cutting has its own risks. Such professionals, after all, are likely to use their Jewish peers in other professions, or in the same profession, (i.e., public school teachers) as a referent group. Since their Jewish peers, in general, are among the most affluent Americans, and public school teachers, in particular, are apt to be much better paid, the temptation to leave the field of Jewish education would only be increased should the salaries of Jewish educators be held down. Moreover, low salaries for Jewish educators could very well reduce the pool of those willing to enter the field in the first place.

Finally, since cost reduction is difficult and funds from Jewish sources can be inadequate, a program of resource development may be instituted to augment funds. Such a program (See: Blum 1985 and Schiff 1986) may be designed to combine advocacy and lay leadership development to obtain funds from such sources outside the usual ambit of Jewish philanthropy as foundations, corporations and government. Other programs may be designed to augment income through the sale or rental of educational materials such as films or videocassettes (Horn, 1987).

Strengthening Jewish Identity

Each of the three programs for reducing the costs of Jewish education, scholarships, subsidies and cost-cutting, has its own drawbacks. Moreover, each is rather difficult to administer. Little is known, I believe, about the extent and operation of any of these programs. Nevertheless, it is clear that each has its own inherent problems. Thus, the attractiveness of a second major strategy, increasing the proportion of family funds devoted to Jewish education, is obvious. Surely, doing so entails short- and long-term strategies for strengthening Jewish identity, in general, and a commitment to Jewish education, in particular. That is, as Ritterband & Cohen (1979) suggest, "the more the more" theory is a good basis on which to build a strategy to encourage Jews to give support to Jewish organizations. That theory holds that Jews who take one aspect of Jewish life seriously tend to respond in like manner to other aspects including Jewish education. Unfortunately, neither Ritterband & Cohen nor any other social scientist I know of explains just how to build a Jewish identity which will call for educating one's children Jewishly. In other words, not enough is known about how to go about increasing Jewish identity and about how to link a strengthened identity to the realization that one's children must receive a Jewish education and that one must pay for the privilege of fostering their child's Jewish education, i.e., give money to support Jewish educational programs. Nevertheless, the future of Jewish education, and of the Jewish people which depends on it, requires that we learn to convince Jews not only that they can afford to educate their children to be Jews, but that there is great value in doing so.

Bibliography

Blum, D.C. (1985, Winter). Resource Development for Jewish Education. *Jewish Education, 53*(4), 45-49.

Cohen, S. M. (1983). *American Modernity and Jewish Identity*. New York and London: Tavistock.

Fishman, S.B. (1987). Learning About Learning: Thoughts on Contemporary Jewish Education from Jewish Population Studies: *Research Report #2*. Waltham, MA: Cohen Center for Modern Jewish Studies.

Horn, S. (1987, Spring). Communal Funding as a Qualitative Educational Tool. *Jewish Education, 55*(1), 27-35.

Kobernick, G. (1985, Spring). Federations and Jewish Education. *Jewish Education, 53*(1), 3-5.

Pollack, G. (1981, Spring). On Subsidies to Congregational Schools. *Jewish Education, 49*(1), 16-18.

Ritterband, P.and Cohen, S.M. (1979). Will the Well Run Dry? The Future of Jewish Giving in America. *National Jewish Conference Policy Studies, 1979*. mimeo.

Raab, M. (1983, Spring). Make Jewish Day School Education Free. *Jewish Education, 51*(1), 38-40.

Rosenbaum, J. (1984, Spring). Allocation Formulae: A New Solution. *Jewish Education, 52*(1), 16-18; 22.

Schiff, A.I. (1983, Summer). Student Recruitment and Educational Funding. *Jewish Education, 51*(2),12-17.

Schiff, G. (1986, Summer). Funding by Federation and Non-Federation Sources for Jewish Education. *Jewish Education, 54*(2), 31-37.

Winter, J. A. (1985, Spring). An Estimate of the Affordability of Living Jewishly. *Journal of Jewish Communal Service, 61*(3), 247-256.

Winter, J.A. (1989, Winter). Income, Identity and Involvement in the Jewish Community: A Test of an Estimate of the Affordability of Living Jewishly. *Journal of Jewish Communal Service. 66*(2). 149-156

Footnotes

[1]Fishman (1987), for example, finds that divorced or separated parents in Baltimore and separated or divorced parents in MetroWest, NJ (the only studies with the requisite data) are more likely to cite "too expensive" as the reason their children did not receive a Jewish education than are married couples or conventional families, respectively.

[2]Of course, some (e.g., Raab, 1983) contend that the issue of need be mooted by rendering all Jewish education, or at least all day schools, Jewish *public* education; that is, "tuition should not be charged."

Highlights

* Affordability of Jewish education whether after school or day school depends upon:
   1. the fee or tuition charged
   2. the level of a family's discretionary funds
   3. the rate at which discretionary funds are used to meet the cost of Jewish education rather than some other Jewish or non-Jewish purpose
* Two strategies to make Jewish education more affordable:
   1. decrease the tuition or fees charged
   2. create an atmosphere which will encourage use of a higher percentage of discretionary funds for Jewish education
* The affordability of Jewish education is determined not just by its cost but by the *value* of such education to the family in question as well.

The Larger Context

Money is the key to yet another problem in Jewish education. But in this instance, the issue of "perceived value" is a fascinating problem yet to be researched. Where once a Jewish education was considered a minimum base of one's Jewish identity purchased with no questions, now it appears that we have become part of the market economy—where consumerism rules. No longer do we do something just because we are Jews; we now purchase a specific commodity (education) for a specific purpose (furthering a child's Jewish identity) at a specific time in our lives (when our children are young). This book, interestingly, is the product of that very consumer environment. We need to have the facts in order to buy or protect our investment, our identity, our future.

The Curriculum

Teaching Israel
Barry Chazan

Moral Education
Jeffrey Schein

Hebrew Language Instruction
Rivka Dori

Jewish Video and Television
Moshe L. Botwinick

Computers
Leonard A. Matanky

Evaluation
Ron Reynolds

What We Know About...
the Teaching of Israel

Barry Chazan

What are the goals of teaching Israel? What is the subject-matter of teaching? How should we teach Israel? How should Israel be integrated into the cur-riculum? These four questions serve as the overall structure under which Dr. Chazan categorizes what we currently know about the teaching of Israel. This catalogue of options can assist in our efforts to respond to difficult issues for all of us living in North America. Dr. Barry Chazan teaches Jewish education and philosophy of education at the Hebrew University of Jerusalem and is the Jewish educational consultant to the Jewish Community Centers Association of North America.

A Time of Miracle, A Time of Question

WE ARE OF THE GENERATION THAT HAS BEEN ALLOWED TO WITNESS THE REBIRTH OF A JEWISH homeland in Eretz Yisrael. We have the privilege of being alive at one of the cross-roads of Jewish history—the establishment of a modern Jewish State:

> All the generations before me
> donated me, bit by bit, so that I'd be
> erect all at once
> here in Jerusalem
> it obligates me

> (Yehuda Amichai, "All the Generations Before Me")

The creation the state of Israel is an event of profound importance for Jewish people as a whole and for each of us as individuals. Think of the many ways—large and small—in which Israel has impinged on your own life. Do you remember some or all of the following?

* Blue JNF boxes
* 6 days in June 1967
* reading the morning paper to find Israel related articles
* Moshe Dayan, Golda Meir, Nadav Henefield
* Ari Ben Canaan, Eva Marie Saint, Sal Mineo
* Operation Yoni
* getting a tan on Tel Aviv beach
* "Zionism is racism"
* the first Israeli you ever met
* ash trays from Eilat
* Yom Kippur day in 1973
* T-shirts in Hebrew
* Junior year abroad
* Lebanon 82; the Intifada; shooting down the Libyan plane
* the most recent Israeli you met

The existence of Israel has brought with it some grand moments—and also some difficult ones. As the late professor Heschel once suggested, Israel has created some great pride and also much confusion for the Jewish people (Heschel, 1969).

The contradictory emotions of joy and confusion about Israel are very evident in the world of teaching. Israel has given rise to a host of tough issues:

* What are we supposed to teach about?
* What does Israel mean for Jews in the Diaspora?
* Should we tell kids to go live there?
* They are so irreligious, those young Israelis!
* America is our home.
* What does Israel have to do with Judaism?
* Lebanon, Intifada, territories—is that what a Jewish state is about?
* If it's so good, why do so many of them leave?
* There just isn't enough time for another subject.

We have not always been successful in dealing with these issues. In fact, the record of Jewish education in North America, vis-a-vis the teaching of Israel, is uneven (Schiff, Chazan, & Pollack, 1984-85). While there have been lots of textbooks, films, curricula and educational programs about Israel (more than most people realize), there also has been a surprising amount of neglect of the topic (Breakstone, 1986). All in all, after over forty years of having a Jewish state, the treatment of Israel in American Jewish education still leaves much to be desired.

What's the Problem?

Why is the teaching of Israel such a big problem? Why hasn't Jewish education done a better job with it?

First, the meaning of Israel for a Jewish life at the end of the twentieth century is still not clear. *That* Israel is phenomenally important is clear; *what* is the nature of that importance is far less clear (Segal, 1987).

Second, Jewish education in North America is an overloaded system which has so little time to do many things. As important as Israel may be, teaching about it constitutes another headache for an already beleaguered system.

Third, there is little precedent to refer to when approaching the topic of teaching Israel. Both general education and traditional Jewish education are of little help in guiding our efforts since both involve totally different settings and premises about Israel.

Fourth, the subject of Israel is intense and explosive. It's about the "big" issues of Jewish life and existence and consequently it arouses much passion and controversy.

The Goal of this Chapter

My goal in this chapter is to discuss what I believe are the four main questions about teaching Israel that have pre-occupied Jewish teachers and educators over the years and across the continents. I shall not defend one specific set of answers; rather I want to assist you in confronting the questions. Indeed, beware of anyone who comes to give you "the" answers to the questions related to teaching Israel. Teaching Israel is a subject which is better characterized by tough questions than by conclusive answers. Before you can teach Israel in the classroom or decide institutionally on an approach, you have to resolve some complex prior educational and ideological issues.

I have heard the following four questions about teaching Israel over the years from students, teachers , principals, parents, lay leaders, youth workers, camp directors, *shlichim*, and bureau staff.

1. What are the goals of teaching Israel? (The goals question)

2. What is the subject matter in teaching Israel? (The subject matter question)

3. How should we teach Israel? (The pedagogic question)

4. How should Israel be integrated into the curriculum? (The integration question)

1. The Goals Question

"What are the goals of teaching Israel?"

What do Jewish educators really want to know when they ask about the goals of teaching Israel? First, they want to know what is the meaning of Jewish life: "What does Israel have to do with my life as a Jew in the contemporary world at the end of the 20th century?" Second, they want to know what direction or orientation their teaching of Israel should take: "What I am trying to do when I teach Israel in my classroom?"

Five answers

Five kinds of goals that have been prescribed for teaching Israel:

1. cultural transmission
2. religion
3. identity
4. survival
5. aliyah

The cultural transmission approach to teaching Israel says that the goal of teaching Israel is the transmission of basic knowledge about the history, geography, and sociology of Israel. This approach assumes that Jewish education should be concerned about the transmission of Jewish knowledge, that the study of Israel is one of the important dimensions of being a knowledgeable Jew (Schacter and Sharfstein, 1984; Lehman, 1955).

The religious approach to teaching Israel veils this topic within the context of shaping a religious lifestyle. This approach conceives of Israel as a part of Judaism (the religion) and it shifts the emphasis from the transmission of knowledge to the development of a Jewish religious lifestyle and practice (Board of Jewish Education, 1987 {video}).

The identity approach emphasizes the role of shaping the character and personality of young Jews. It shares the religious approach's focus on personality and lifestyle; however, it shifts the emphasis from religious beliefs and behaviors to some general notion of positive Jewish identity or personality (Reisman, 1979).

Teaching Israel for Jewish survival focuses on Israel as a central force in strengthening young people's commitment to the perpetuation of the Jewish people. Its concern is to implant and nourish the commitment of young people to the survival of the state of Israel and to the Jewish people.[1]

Teaching Israel for aliyah is aimed at encouraging—and ultimately causing—people to settle in Israel. This approach assumes that the situation of the Jews in the Diaspora is ultimately doomed and that a complete Jewish life is possible only in Israel. Consequently, advocates of this approach are concerned with preparing young people for life in Israel (World Zionist Organization, 1970).

Which goal is best?

At various times we have all focused on several of these goals in teaching Israel. We certainly want young people to know more about how Israel is connected with Judaism. We should be very concerned that their study of Israel ultimately will affect their lives. We certainly want them to see

Israel within the larger context of the Jewish struggle for survival. There may even be those among us who think that aliyah is something Jews should think about.

There is no need to be concerned about the difficulty of determining the definitive goal of teaching Israel; we often have multiple goals in education and there is no need to think that teaching is defined by more than one goal only. Nevertheless, there are basic differences between some of these five goal orientations, and in the long run, we can't "dance at all these weddings." We don't have to narrowly impose one goal on our system, but your institution will have to choose some general path which probably is characterized by one of these directions.

2. The Subject Matter Question

"What is the subject matter of teaching Israel?"

This question focuses on the content—the themes, the topics, the subjects—that should be dealt with and presented when one teaches Israel. Is it:

> * history?
>
> * religion?
>
> * geography/homeland?
>
> * person identity?
>
> * peoplehood?

Some people have understood the subject matter of teaching Israel to be the history of the land of Israel throughout the ages. This approach utilizes historical methodology and terminology to focus on themes that relate to Israel within the context of general and Jewish history (Rossel, 1985; Lehman, 1955); e.g.:

1. the early history of the land (Biblical, Patriarchal, Judges, Kings, Prophets, Temples, Exile Rabbis)

2. the ongoing relationship of the Jewish people with the land throughout the centuries

3. the emergence of Zionism in the late nineteenth century

4. the struggle for statehood in the early-mid-twentieth century

5. the emergence of the contemporary state.

Others, as we have already seen, regard Israel as one of the basic religious values and practices of Judaism. According to this approach, the subject matter of teaching Israel is the great mitzvah and idea of "Eretz Yisroel".[2] The kinds of topics that this approach would emphasize are:

1. God's promise of Eretz Yisrael to Abraham

2. Israel as a Holy Land

3. mitzvot connected with Israel (e.g. *mitzvat yishuv ha'aretz*)

4. the presence of Israel in Jewish prayer and ritual

5. the ongoing religious link of Judaism with Israel throughout the ages

6. the expression of Jewish religious life in contemporary Israel (synagogues, study, holidays and Shabbat, holy places).

A third notion of subject matter focuses on the contemporary State of Israel as the modern Jewish homeland. It sees the subject matter of teaching Israel as social studies or citizenship about the Jewish State. This approach has been influenced by two subjects which have traditionally been taught in Israeli schools: *"yediat ha'aretz"*—knowledge of the land—and *"ezrachut"*—citizenship.[3] The following themes are emphasized in this notion of subject matter:

1. the Biblical roots of contemporary Israel

2. the historical sites of Israel

3. the major geographical regions of Israel

4. the important contemporary sites of Israel

5. the return of Israel and the ingathering of the exiles

6. the form of government and social structure

7. the main features of the economy

The fourth conception of the subject of teaching Israel focuses on Jewish peoplehood (Fine, 1977; Essrig and Segal, 1977; Rossel, 1985). According to this approach, Israel is part of the larger fabric of Jewish culture or civilization which is really what Jewish education is about. The themes emphasized in this conception are:

1. the roots of the Jewish people in Eretz Yisrael

2. the link of the Jewish people over the ages with Eretz Yisrael

3. the link between Judaism and Israel

4. the importance of Israel to all Jews today

5. the diverse kinds of Jewish lifestyles and customs in contemporary Israel

6. contemporary Israeli culture

7. the Hebrew language

The fifth notion of the subject matter of Israel does not approach it in terms of traditional school subjects; rather it sees Israel within the context of Jewish identity education (London and Chazan, 1990). This approach shifts the focus from "learning about Israel" to utilizing themes, events, people, and places of Israel for stimulating individual Jewish identity. The kinds of themes that this approach is likely to emphasize are:

1. Israel and the wandering of Jews
2. the search for *Mashiach*
3. Who is a Jew?
4. What does Israel mean for You?

What should we choose?

Clearly, one of the great problems of teaching Israel is the fact that there isn't an agreed-upon and well-defined notion of its subject matter.

The historical approach offers a neat and clean conception of subject matter; however, it tends to neglect The State of Israel of today and tomorrow at the expense of the Land of Israel of the past.

Israel as religion promises a comprehensive integration of all the subjects of the school curriculum; however, it requires an ideological world-view which not all modern Jews can accept.

Israel as homeland presents teachers with very clear directives as to what one should teach. However, while most people in the Diaspora love Israel greatly, they probably don't see it as *The* homeland. And while geography is important to learn, not living there and seeing the sites is often difficult.

Israel as identity makes Israel very real and personal for students. However, it doesn't lead to very much knowledge or understanding of the major facts and issues related to contemporary Israel.

The conception of subject matter that seems to have been educationally viable for many schools over the years is Israel as peoplehood. This approach is well-defined enough to give teachers content, sources, and methodologies to use in teaching the subject. It is comprehensive enough to enable teachers to relate the teaching of Israel to other subjects in the curriculum—Bible, history, social studies, music and Hebrew. It encompasses people as well places and history, thereby enabling Israel to speak personally to students. At the same time, the peoplehood approach is not flawless. It demands broad knowledge and creative teaching. It is not a traditional subject and there aren't many precedents for teaching it. Still, it is an approach to teaching Israel which offers exciting options and possibilities.

3. The Pedagogic Question

"How should we teach Israel?"

Several methods have been prescribed for teaching Israel. One set of methods has focused on the use of lectures, textbooks, and informative films to transmit information and concepts about Israel. This approach has utilized methodologies which will enhance a systematic teaching of the "facts and figures" of the State (Davis and Levy, 1972; Schacter and Scharfstein, 1984).

A second methodology has focused on the use of passion, feeling and emotion to arouse and/or deepen consciousness of Israel's importance, plight, and survival. This approach often focuses on charismatic personalities and sensitive topics (e.g. the wars of Israel; the plight of immigrants; the difficult economic conditions; Israel in the aftermath of the Holocaust) to transmit its message.

A third methodology uses techniques aimed at involving the learner in the development of his/her personal relationship with Israel (Reisman, 1979). This approach opts for such techniques as group dynamics, values clarification, and inquiry questions in order to make the learner his/her own teacher.

A fourth approach—the multi-dimensional—attempts to replicate the polyphonic experience of the visit to Israel in which one is affected by sights, smells, and sounds. This approach opts for a well-orchestrated utilization of hummus, Yehoram Goan tapes, Coke bottles in Hebrew, maps, the Bible text, and visiting Israelis to teach about Israel (Melton Centre, n.d.).

A fifth methodology organizes the study of Israel around a select number of conceptual themes or motifs, e.g.:

* power and powerlessness

* the new Zionism

* Israel as a laboratory of Jewish identity

* Jewish pluralism in the twentieth century

* who is a Jew (Elon, 1978)?

A sixth methodology aims at the experiential: i.e., teaching Israel by enabling young people to actually go there. This approach argues that the best way to learn about Israel is to actually experience it. According to advocates of this approach, the great failure of teaching Israel is that we have not taken advantage of the unique opportunity to enable our students to see, feel, smell and live in Israel in-person at some point in their schooling years.

4. The Integration Question

"How should Israel be integrated into the curriculum?"

There have been three approaches to introducing Israel in the curriculum:

1) separate subject

2) integration

3) co-curricular

The "separate subject" approach says that Israel is a topic of such great importance that it deserves a regular slot as a subject of study in Jewish schools (Kuselewitz, 1964). According to this approach, Jewish education is arranged around subjects, and if you are a subject then you at least have a chance of being taught. Consequently, this approach calls for the development of courses of study and educational materials which can be a regular part of the school syllabus.

The "integrated" approach argues that the existing curricula of Jewish schools are already over-burdened in what they have to teach, and there simply is no more room for new subjects. In addition, it claims that Israel is not a subject like other subjects; rather, it is a topic which permeates all of the subjects of the curriculum (Ariav, 1988). Hence, the integrated approach argues that the teaching of Israel should be included in the curriculum as part of Bible, Jewish history, contemporary Jewry, Hebrew, and current events. It proposes presenting Israel in these various subject areas via modular units on relevant topics related to Israel ("One People, Many Faces", "The Israel Connection: Israel—Diaspora Relations", "The Children of Israel?" "Where is Israel?" "Zahal." The Melton Centre Curriculum can be used in diverse settings such as Shabbat retreats, youth groups, camps.

The "co-curricular" approach calls for the introduction of Israel within the ongoing flow of school life, rather than in the formal curriculum per se. While this approach doesn't deny the importance of formal study about Israel, it regards the experiencing of an overall Israeli atmosphere as more important than discrete bits of learning that might be taught over the years. This approach regards Israel as a primal Jewish *experience* which children should meet throughout the school, through assemblies, holiday celebrations, hall decorations, music.

Nu—which is best?

The arguments of each of these approaches are persuasive. The ultimate conclusion is that all are correct, and consequently Israel should be incorporated in the curriculum in a multidimensional fashion.

* There should be systematic study of Israel in the school curriculum. There should be some allotted times in the life of young people's Jewish schooling in which they systematically study about Israel. This can be done through a regular course or through a well-planned and sequential use of a series of instructional modules on Israel.

* Israel should also be presented within other subject areas at relevant moments, e.g.: important sections of Humash, Joshua, the Prophets; the study of Hebrew; the history of the Mishnaic and Talmudic periods, the early twentieth century, the establishment of the state; aspects of Jewish prayer and ritual including prayerbook, weddings, Seder.

* A well-tailored program of co-curricular, experiential Israel activities should be part of the school's approach. The many small and big moments in the calendar year should be utilized to teach Israel.

The bottom line of the issue of introducing Israel in the school is not so much which of the three approaches is used, but rather adoption of the principle of "curricularization." This principle means that what is needed is a systematic approach to teaching Israel which reflects developmental planning of the subject.

Conclusion

Teaching Israel should have been one of the showpieces of American Jewish education, but it isn't. It is a subject that people care about, but they don't know how to deal with it very well. It is a subject which inspires—and confuses at the same time. It is a subject which requires a great initiative by teachers in an age when time is one of the few things teachers have. It is a subject which should be able to change lives but which does so too infrequently.

The irony is that Jewish education says that it cares about teaching Israel and I believe that it does, but it has not taken advantage of the incredible gift and resource which history, fate, providence, whatever, has given it to actually teach the subject: the place itself.

After all is said and done, the best "text" we have for teaching Israel is the experience of actually visiting it. We today have the unparalleled possibility of enabling young people to see, touch, and smell Israel. However, we haven't yet succeeded in making the Israel experience an integral and ongoing part of every child's Jewish educational experience. The bulk of North American Jews have not been to Israel and the Israel experience remains the exception rather than the rule in contemporary Jewish education.

The ultimate task before us is to enable every young Jew of school age to read the "text" with his or her own eyes—to set foot in a modern Jewish society rooted in culture and heritage which is thousands of years old.

This is a unique educational opportunity "that obligates us."

Bibliography

Amichai, Y. (1966). *Selected Poetry*. New York: Harper and Row.

Ariav, T. ((1988). Curriculum Change in the Teaching of Israel. *Pedagogic Reporter, 39*(1), 8-12.

Board of Jewish Education. (1987). *David's City*. {video}. New York.

Breakstone, D. (1986). *The Place of Israel in American Jewish Life*. Unpublished doctoral dissertation. Hebrew University, Jerusalem.

Chazan, B. (1978). Teaching Israel in *The Language of Jewish Education*. Hartford: Hartmore House.

Davis, M. & Levy, I. (1972). *All About Israel*. London: Education Department of the Jewish National Fund.

Dewey, J. (1963). *Experience and Education*. New York: Collier Books.

Elon, A. (1977). *Understanding Israel*. New York: Behrman House.

Essrig, H. & Segal, A. (1977). *Israel Today*. New York: Union of American Hebrew Congregations.

Fine, H. (1978). *Behold The Land*. New York: Union of American Hebrew Congregations.

Hartman, D. (1978). Zionism and the Continuity of Judaism and Israel and the Rebirth of Judaism. In *Joy and Responsibility*. Jerusalem: Ben Zvi Posner.

Hartman, D. (1990). The Challenge of Modern Israel to Traditional Judaism. In *Conflicting Vision: Spiritual Possibilities of Modern Israel*. New York: Schocken Books.

Heschel, A.J. (1969). *Israel: An Echo of Eternity*. New York: Farrar, Strauss and Giroux.

Kaplan, M. (1957). *Judaism as a Civilization*. New York: Thomas Yoseloff.

Kuselewitz, D. (1964). Teaching Israel: A Guide for Jewish Schools. *Pedagogic Reporter, 39*(1). 8-12.

Lehman, E. (1955). *Israel: Idea and Reality.* New York: United Synagogue Commission on Jewish Education.

London, P. and Chazan, B. (1990). *Psychology and Jewish Identity Education.* New York: American Jewish Committee.

Melton Centre. (n.d.). *Israel: A Course of Study.* Jerusalem: Author and World Zionist Organization.

Reisman, B. (1979). *The Jewish Experiential Book: The Quest for Jewish Identity.* New York: Ktav.

Rossel, S. (1985). *Israel: Covenant People, Covenant Land.* New York: Union of American Hebrew Congregations.

Schacter, S. and Scharfstein, S. (1955). *All About Israel.* New York: Ktav.

Scheffler, I. (1988). Philosophical Models of Teaching. In *Reason and Teaching.* Indianapolis: Hackett.

Schiff, A., Chazan, B. & Pollack, G. (1984-85, Winter). The Teaching of Israel. *Jewish Education, 52*(4), 5-14.

Segal, B. (1987). *Returning: The Land of Israel as Focus in Jewish History.* Jerusalem: Department of Education and Culture of the World Zionist Organization.

United Synagogue of America. (1978). *Curriculum for the Afternoon Jewish School.* New York: United Synagogue Commission on Jewish Education.

World Zionist Organization. (1970). *Teaching Yediat Yisrael.* Jerusalem: Department of Education and Culture.

Footnotes

[1] This approach is implicit in the educational and public relations materials produced by the United Jewish Appeal and especially its Young Leadership Programs over the years; e.g., the highly successful slogan "We Are One".

[2] While this approach is usually associated with Orthodox Jewish education, it is also implicit in the Israel curriculum produced in 1978 by the United Synagogue of America as part of its *Curriculum for the Afternoon Jewish School.*

[3] For many years, this approach had been characteristic of materials produced by Israel for use abroad, as well as by Israeli *shelichim* living outside of Israel.

Highlights

* (Goals) Israel can be taught in order to:
      describe the cultural transmission of our people
      develop a religious life style
      shape character and personality of young Jews
      strengthen Jewish survival
      stimulate aliyah
* (Content) Israel can be taught with the focus on:
      history
      religion
      geography/homeland
      personal identity
      peoplehood

* (Methods) Israel can be taught:
  conceptually
  thematically
  experientially
  and each of these can be approached cognitively, affectively or a combination of both
* (Curriculum) Israel can be taught as:
  separate subject
  integrated within another subject(s)
  co-curricular

The Larger Context

Perhaps more than any other subject matter, the teaching of Israel centers on our making of choices. It forces us to confront our own feelings in what has become one of the most complex issues of our time—and one which is constantly changing. This dimension of the issue, change, may be enough to cause us to wonder about how or what to teach—or, indeed, whether to teach the subject at all! Yet, there is no question that a visit to Israel must become a fixed part of every high-school curriculum and become as natural for us as a bar or bat mitzvah. Studies are just now emerging as to the impact of these trips on adolescents and adults. As we continue to learn more about these trips, our approach to the teaching of Israel must remain, as Dr. Chazan indicates, multidimensional.

What We Know About...Moral Education

Jeffrey Schein

How do you create a mentsch? Dr. Jeffrey Schein, Associate Professor of Jewish Education at the Cleveland College of Jewish Studies, explores areas of convergent and discrepant values between the mentschmaking process as seen and as understood in Jewish tradition through the major paradigm of general education. The dialogue, Dr. Schein believes, is richer when Jewish education and the theory of moral education developed by Dr. Larence Kohlberg are in conversation with one another.

A SAYING FROM *PIRKE AVOT* SUGGESTS THAT *DERECH ERETZ*, COMMON DECENCY, PRECEDED THE GIVING OF the Torah. Over the centuries Jewish texts and traditions have served to add depth to the Jewish commitment to "mentschmaking", the fine art of producing moral, decent human beings.

One wonders,then, why interest in moral education as a significant goal of Jewish education seems to have only recently engaged the energies of Jewish educators? Even now, one might argue, the interest is reactive rather than proactive. Jewish education seems to be riding the crest of programmatic and theoretical activity begun in general education over the last 25 years. It is not yet clear whether Jewish education can generate sustained activity in the field of moral education on its own terms.

We begin to understand this apparent inattention better if we first recognize that morality can be viewed as a rather automatic process requiring no special educational effort. We often think we know exactly what morality is. Homely moral aphorisms, universal formulations of the golden rule, and the persistent belief in western civilization of a core "Judaeo-Christian" morality, all tend to shape a perception of morality as something as simple and self-evident as Mom and Apple Pie.

Derech Eretz

Yet, the apparent simplicity of even such a Jewish concept as *derech eretz* (common decency) begins to dissolve under the microscope of careful analysis. The Jewish scholar Max Kaddushin has pointed out that in fact *derech eretz* is a richly nuanced concept. It has four distinct phases. *derech eretz* can, for instance, mean common, human decency. In another context, however, *derech eretz* refers to a sense of natural, balanced instincts that is patterned after the world of nature. It can also mean a core of moral traits that constitute the basis of human civilization (Kaddushin, 1952). Far from being automatic, effective teaching in the realm of Jewish ethics requires a sophistication not often demonstrated by Jewish teachers.

We also begin to come to grips with the place of moral education within a broader framework of educational goals when we admit that we sometimes want conflicting things for our Jewish children. There are built-in dynamic tensions in Jewish life that affect our pursuit of any given goal.

In regard to moral education, for instance, I am reminded of the story of Rabbi Arthur Gilbert, *'alav ha-shalom'*, the first Dean of Students at the Reconstructionist Rabbinical College. Rabbi Gilbert described his own *'brit'* as the product of an intermarriage. The oxymoronic nature of this "intermarriage"—both his parents were Jewish and committed to Jewish survival—is eliminated when we understand what different Jewish values each side of Arthur's family deemed essential. The mother's side of the family stood on one side of the mohel declaring that Arthur should grow up to be a *'gutte yid'*. This projected a life for Arthur full of yearnings for social justice, moral striving, and commitment to a homeland for the Jewish people. The father's side of the family stood on the other side of the *'mohel'* and glared back at the mother's side. They insisted that Arthur should grow up to be a *'frumme yid'*, meaning specifically that he *daven* and put on tefillin daily, study much Torah, and—of course—observe the laws of kashrut and Shabbat. Both sides of the family may have wanted Arthur to become a mentsch but one can hardly imagine them agreeing on what exactly that meant.

Lawrence Kohlberg

The most influential paradigm for moral education these past twenty five years has been that of Lawrence Kohlberg and his colleagues at Harvard University. Kohlberg has claimed that there are universal stages of moral development and that the essential task of education is to help students realize their moral potential by moving on to higher stages of development. The social, psychological, and philosophical bases for Kohlberg's theory have been vigorously debated.

It is important to consider, therefore, an overview of "critical" Jewish opinion about Kohlberg's relevance to Jewish education. First, it seems important, however, to credit Kohlberg with the important contributions even his critics concede. At the heart of the Kohlberg enterprise are twin assumptions that children as well as adults are moral philosophers and that we all actively construct our knowledge of the moral world. These contentions revolutionized the way research is done in moral education.

One captures the flavor of this "constructivist" view of moral outlook if we listen in on a conversation between a father and a son that is part of a story entitled "Aaron and the Wrath of God". The story begins as the father puts his son Aaron to bed and they recite the *'Shema Yisrael'* together. The father describes himself as seized by a "flash of religious zeal" and goes on to talk with Aaron about the paragraphs that follow the *'Shema'*. One of these has to do with reward and punishment. The father had only meant to add a little "Jewish literacy" to Aaron's repertoire. Little did he realize that as a moral philosopher Aaron would keep him up half the night talking about this "business of punishments". Below is a fragment of their conversation:

"What are you going to argue about with God, Aaron?"
"About this business of punishments. I'm going to tell him to stop it."
"Why don't you ask him to stop it. That seems a lot more polite."
"Okay, but if He says no, I am going to argue."
"Aaron?"
"Yes, Daddy."
"Why shouldn't God punish?" I wanted to see what the Lord would be up against.
"Because its not fair. God is too big to be punishing people. People get too afraid of God for that. It's not good. God is too smart for that. He can think of something else to do instead. I'm going to tell him that."
I listened and I knew that God had no chance in this argument. He was clearly outmatched. "You'll let me know what the answer is?" (ben Shlomo, 1988).

According to the Kohlbergian point of view, student questioning, puzzlement and confusion are the seeds of moral growth. Such growth occurs when the structures of moral reasoning are challenged. (In our story Aaron's sense of justice is thrown into disequilibrium by the second paragraph of the *Shema*). As a student discovers inadequacies in the limited reasoning capacity of his/her present stage, he/she becomes ready to move on to the next stage of development.

The challenge must be moderate. Kohlberg and others have theorized that while individuals naturally gravitate towards the next higher stage, the moral reasoning of stages more than one stage higher largely falls on deaf ears. Thus, to imagine a Jewish teacher doing a better job of teaching Jewish ethics by talking more about his or her own ethical commitments would be less to the point (according to the Kohlberg schema) than facilitating a dialogue where students encounter one another's structures of moral reasoning.

Broadly speaking, Kohlberg conceives of three levels of moral reasoning: self-oriented (Stages 1 and 2), conventional (Stages 3 and 4), and principled (Stage 5 and 6). At stages 1 and 2 the person is likely to define what is good as what is instrumental in getting what the person wants and needs. Fear and a "you scratch my back/I'll scratch yours" mentality are the primary motivators here. Individuals at the third and fourth stages of moral development are more likely to think of what is morally good as what is acceptable to family, community, and nation. The primary motivator here is the desire to be a good boy within a family, a good member within a club, or a good citizen of a nation. Finally, at the principled level of moral judgment the frame of reference for morality becomes universal principles of social contract and conscience. A good summary of these and other aspects of the basic Kohlberg paradigm can be found in *Promoting Moral Growth: From Piaget to Kohlberg* by Hersh, Paolitto, and Reimer (1979).

Kohlberg's Critics

Kohlberg's scheme has been criticized by other researchers of moral development. Statisticians have suggested that there is no empirical confirmation for all of his stages. Anthropologists have argued that making principled moral reasoning the crown of moral achievement is to confuse western civilization for universal human culture. Carol Gilligan has written poignantly about the absence of a "female voice" in what she takes to be the male construction of morality offered by Kohlberg. A fine and accessible summary of these critiques can be found in the article by Carolyn Pope Edwards, "Culture and the Construction of Moral Values: A Comparative Ethnography of Moral Encounters in Two Cultural Settings" (in *The Emergence of Morality in Young Children*, edited by Jerome Kagan, University of Chicago Press, 1987).

Jewish Perspectives

Jewish researchers of moral education have echoed some of these criticisms but usually from the vantage point of uniquely Jewish concerns. Barry Chazan (1983), for instance, has suggested that the emphasis on moral autonomy at the heart of Kohlberg's system is very far from the great weight Judaism gives to the needs of the community. Further, the development of a "holy" individual and community is related to but not subsumed by the category of a moral person. Joseph Reimer (1983) and I have both suggested that the gap between moral reasoning and moral judgment noted by secular researchers is particularly problematic from a Jewish point of view (Schein, 1985). Earl Schwartz (1983) has followed Gilligan in raising issues about an "ethic of caring" as well as "justice" that Judaism needs to embrace.

Avraham Feder's *In Search of My Brothers* (1989) is the best attempt in Jewish education to retain Kohlberg's emphasis on moral personality and still address the challenges put by Chazan, Reimer, Schein, and Schwartz. In this work Feder argues for a new stage of development (only alluded to in Kohlberg's work)—Stage 7—where Jewish concerns for peoplehood, ethnicity and Zionism can be synthesized with the concerns of the Kohlberg paradigm.

Two other differentiations between Kohlberg and the concerns of Judaism should be mentioned. Typical dilemmas that are part of Kohlberg's research have to do with extreme conflicts in moral values. The classic Kohlberg dilemma is that of Hans, a young teenager who must decide between obeying the law or stealing a drug that might help his father survive his cancer. Most Kohlbergian dilemmas have this consistently dramatic quality to them.

In contrast, the very nature of Judaism as a way of life often brings our attention to those smaller moments that seem so inglorious from the Kohlberg perspective. Indeed, a set of Jewish folktales attribute the continued existence of the world to the quiet performance of good deeds by the *'lamadvavniks'*, thirty-six righteous individuals who are unobtrusive in their performance of mitzvot.

In addition, one can note a significant difference in method between Judaism and the Kohlberg approach. Cognitive conflict and socratic dialogue are the primary sources of moral growth for Kohlberg. Judaism involves a wider set of cultural resources that includes ritual, prayer, and theology. Jewish ethics seems to be part of a broader process of Jewish acculturation. By way of contrast, Kohlberg's theory goes to great lengths to stake out an independent domain of moral existence beyond the conflicting claims of particular religious traditions.

At the very least, Jewish moral educators ought to feel indebted to Kohlberg for the kind of dialectical insight that has come from comparing and contrasting Jewish and secular approaches to moral education. In the end it might also be that the poetry of the Kohlberg paradigm—its flexible use as a map of development—may be more useful to Jewish educators than its stricter claims to empirical and normative validity.

Bridges between Theory and Practice

At a curricular level, Jerry Friedman (1988) has analyzed three significant programs that have sought to develop the moral component of the school curriculum in an article "New Approaches to Jewish Moral Education." Earl Schwartz (1983) has written a entire volume, *Moral Development: A Practical Guide for Jewish Teachers* that draws on his experience in presenting a range of different kinds of moral dilemmas to children at the Community Day School in Minneapolis.

Schwartz and Friedman both suggest that the quality of moral education in our Jewish schools would be greatly improved if:

a) Jewish teachers were better trained to utilize the sophisticated methodologies required by most moral education programs

b) Jewish principals and/or school committees were clearer about the "curricular niche" of moral education. Unlike such topics as Jewish history and holidays, there often seems to be no clear place to "put" moral education in the schema of a Jewish curriculum.

Several educators have tried to address the issue of the "hidden curriculum" of Jewish schools. I have helped day schools in Los Angeles and in Philadelphia initiate a *Beit Tzedek/Beit Din*, an experiment in Jewish moral democracy involving students in making decisions about justice and fairness from Jewish/moral perspectives. It assumes that since fairness pertains to issues that emerge on the playground and in the classroom. In essence, an attempt can be made to make the social and moral issues that students live between classes an important part of a Jewish school's work in moral education. The implicit message of this program is that we care about the Jewish values students demonstrate as well as the ones they study. *Batei din* now function in a dozen Solomon Schechter schools throughout the country.

Strengthening the Moral Dimension

There are two very promising directions for strengthening the moral education dimension of Jewish schools. The first is formal and is anchored in the belief that the value of the Kohlberg model is its faith that individuals can and will actively construct moral meaning in developmentally appropriate ways. This method suggests that we have a great deal to learn about the way students understand our most fundamental Jewish values. Research into the ways that a child or young adult may understand such concepts as *'kedusha'* (holiness) or *'lashon ha-ra'* (gossip) would be extraordinarily helpful to Jewish teachers in learning how to challenge Jewish students to grow into new insights.

The second thrust of Jewish moral education should be the micro- and macrocosms of Jewish community. It has become rather clear within the Kohlberg tradition of research that the most powerful forms of moral education combine formal pedagogy with "just community" decisions that come out of the life of the school community. Our moral education diet in Jewish schools has achieved no similar equilibrium. Most Jewish students are still likely to view Jewish education as a series of "packaged" moral teachings having little to do with the real world in which they live.

We would do well to visualize Jewish moral education as a series of concentric circles. Our life with students in the classroom, the school, the synagogue community, the Jewish community, and the world community are the ever expanding arenas of Jewish concern for mentschlichkeit. To the extent that we can make the walls in our schools permeable so that students can act on Jewish insights in these broader arenas we will have created a form of Jewish moral education that can make a difference in our Jewish schools. Paradoxically, if we limit our attention to the schools themselves even the most brilliant pedagogy will not achieve our goal.

Bibliography

ben Shlomo, T. (1988). Aaron and the Wrath of God. In J. Schein (Ed.), *Exploring Judaism: A Study and Discussion Guide*. Philadelphia, PA: Reconstructionist Press.

Chazan, B. (1983). Holy Community and Values Education. In *Moral Development Foundations*. Nashville: Abington Press.

Edwards, C.P. (1987). Culture and the Construction of Moral Values: A Comparative Ethnography of Moral Encounters in Two Cultural Settings. In J. Kagan (Ed.), *The Emergence of Morality in Young Children*. Chicago: University of Chicago Press.

Feder, A. (1989) *In Search of My Brothers*. Jerusalem: Maor Publications.

Friedman, J. (1988, Fall). New Approaches to Jewish Moral Education. *Jewish Education, 56*(3).

Hersh, R., Paolitto, D. & Reimer, J. (1979). *Promoting Moral Growth: From Piaget to Kohlberg*. New York: Longman Press.

Kaddushin, M. (1952). *The Rabbinic Mind*. New York: Bloch.

Reimer, J. (1983). Beyond Justice: Moral Development and the Search for Truth—A Contemporary Midrash. In D. Jox (Ed.), *Moral Development Foundations*. Nashville: Abington Press.

Schein, J. (Dec., 1985). Moral Development in Jewish Schools. *Reconstructionist, 50*(5).

Schwartz, E. (1983). *Moral Development: A Practical Guide for Jewish Teachers*. Denver: Alternatives in Religious Education.

Highlights

* Morality is a natural process that springs from the moral philosopher in each of us. The process of moral growth and development can be facilitated by working with the moral philosopher within.
* Kohlberg has posited 6 stages through which one must pass.
* Jewish scholars have tried to correlate Jewish concepts of morality with these stages. The unique concerns of Judaism have necessitated the construction of a seventh stage that deals with issues of theology and peoplehood.
* While programs have been devised using these stages as a structure, sustained evaluation is still lacking.
* Teachers need specialized training and principals need to be clear about moral education's curricular niche.

The Larger Context

Are we now engaged in brand new thinking or is this the product of pouring old concepts into new containers? Perhaps we have the question turned inside out. Perhaps our particularistic forms of Jewish education have something unique to say to the secular world about producing moral individuals. Though evidence from the research literature seems weak, nevertheless those same Jewish values now under scrutiny of a new framework may help us revitalize the quest to produce decent human beings, mentschen.

What We Know About...
Hebrew Language Education

Rivka Dori

Usually, we assume that the basic goal of most of our learning institutions is Hebrew. Not by accident do we call Hebrew Schools "<u>Hebrew</u>" schools. Yet, for all our proclamations, Hebrew language instruction is our least focused part of the curriculum, according to Ms. Dori, Coordinator of Undergraduate Hebrew Program and Instructor of Hebrew Language at Hebrew Union College, Los Angeles, and at the University of Southern California. Educators and laity alike need to confront Hebrew language instruction as a moral obligation and not merely as a methodology. Hard choices have to be made in focusing our Hebrew program. Ms. Dori, one of North America's leading Hebrew educators, shares her experiences as well as the newest thinking about Hebrew acquisition, as she guides us through this instructional maze.

HEBREW LANGUAGE EDUCATION DOESN'T SEEM TO BE AN ACTIVE ISSUE IN JEWISH EDUCATION IN THE United States today. A review of recent Jewish conference programs, Jewish professional school programs, and Jewish education professional publications reveals that few serious attempts are being made to explore important questions regarding Hebrew language education. Questions such as "How do we teach Hebrew?" "Are we effective in our language instruction?" "What is our students' Hebrew language competence at the various levels of schooling?" and so on are raised infrequently and data is absent.

At the same time "Hebrew" seems to be central in our institutions; our students go to "Hebrew" schools to study "Hebrew" and "Hebrew" is a major component of our day schools' Jewish studies curricula.

Why don't Jewish professionals discuss the subject of Hebrew language instruction? There are several reasons for this avoidance, including such real frustrations as the lack of resources, personnel, and motivation. But the main reason seems to be the sense of a lack of congruency we feel in the field of Hebrew education and the fear that these incongruencies will surface if explored. There are conflicts in goals (teaching Hebrew as a communicative language and teaching Hebrew as a ritual instrument aren't the same), approaches (language-centered approaches and learner-centered approaches aren't the same) and curricula (we cannot agree on a Hebrew language curriculum within one educational setting, let alone on a unified curricula for all schools which teach Hebrew).

In raising questions about Hebrew education, these conflicts cannot be ignored: statements regarding goals have to be made clear, preferences for certain approaches have to be stated and defended, curricula have to be detailed, and Hebrew education professionals have to be accountable for their students' achievement and proficiency.

Hebrew Language Education: Then till Now

Prior to the eighteenth century there was no conflict regarding Hebrew language education. Hebrew language was an integral part of Jewish life; it was a major component of Jewish studies, ritual activities, and life cycle events. Hebrew was *"Lashon Hakodesh"*—the holy tongue—not to be used for secular purposes. Most of the communicative functions were performed in other languages. However, in the middle of the nineteenth century, when the Hebrew language also became an academic/scientific subject for Jewish scholars, and later when ideas about Jewish nationalism started to develop, a conflict emerged. Whenever the purpose of Hebrew language education wasn't religious enculturation, the interest in linguistics was prominent. Those who wanted to teach Hebrew as an academic subject and those who wanted to teach Hebrew as a secular communicative language turned to the academic and secular field of language instruction for guidance. From that point on we can trace the influence of linguistic theories on Hebrew language education in liberal Jewish settings.

The pattern which emerged is that whenever there was an agreement within a particular Jewish community on its goals in the teaching of Hebrew and that goal was reached by using an accepted linguistic approach, there seemed to be a period of perceived successful Hebrew education. When the linguistic approach was no longer viable or when the Jewish communal needs changed as a result of historical circumstances and/or ideological changes, there were perceived failures and disappointments.

Three examples:

1. Liberal Jews during the nineteenth century called for a scientific and analytic approach towards Hebrew sacred texts (Plaut, 1963). Some linguistic theories of that period described the study of languages as an intellectual activity which strengthened the brain and sharpened its functions (Freeman, 1986). These two approaches seemed to complement and support each other and most students of Hebrew within that context felt intellectually challenged (Plaut, 1963).

2. Zionists at the beginning of the twentieth century believed that Hebrew should be the communicative language of the Jews in their own land, Israel. Linguistic theories of that time claimed that languages are learned by actually using them. And so, many Jewish

schools with Zionist orientations were successful in producing Hebrew speaking individuals (Haramati, 1977).

3. After the Six Day War in 1967, many Jews who lived outside of Israel were proud of her victory and wanted to identify with her people. One way to do so was to emulate Hebrew speech. The linguistic theory of the time was that languages are sets of habits to be mastered. Aural-Oral (*Shema Ve'daber, Be'Yad Ha'Lashon*) and Audio-Visual (*Habet U'shema*) methods were used to help students master such "habits." Many Hebrew students were able to go to Israel and "perform" their "habits" in learned situations and to connect on a certain level with Israelis in the stores, at the bus stops, in the banks or post offices, and so on (Haramati, 1968; 1977).

These successful episodes did not last, as the needs and attitudes of the Jewish community changed and linguistic theories were altered. Today we witnessing two overwhelming phenomena: Jewish communities are more diverse than ever before, and linguistic theories are changing rapidly. It is difficult to catch up with either of them, and a match between an acceptable linguistic theory and a Jewish communal need has not yet been found.

The Dilemma

Little, if anything, will happen until all who are concerned about and involved with Hebrew Language education are willing to take a stand regarding their Jewish communal needs and goals, and are committed to be more informed about what is available regarding second/foreign language instruction. This can be accomplished by:

1. demanding more knowledge regarding language education from our professionals. This should include historical perspective as well as current linguistic theories.
2. creating open forums to discuss goals.
3. examining Hebrew programs and curricula currently employed in our various educational settings.
4. sharing the findings through professional literature and in conferences.

Hebrew education is highly individualistic today. Individual teachers are defining their own goals and using methods which they know regardless of their effectiveness; individual schools are writing their own curricula and evaluating them themselves at the risk of being biased; and most of the prescribed programs which publishers sell are based not on research, but, rather, on the individual experiences and intuitions of their authors. There are probably many individual "successes" in the field, but few are made public or evaluated systematically. At the same time, there is a lot of activity in the field of linguistics which can have a direct bearing on Hebrew language education. During the last twenty-five years research on language instruction has grown, theories about language acquisition and learning have been developed, and new measurements for evaluation achievement and competence have been constructed.

Currently, language teachers make distinctions between first, second, and foreign language instruction and between "learning" a language (knowing about the language) and "acquiring" a language (being proficient in the language) (Krashen, 1981). We understand better how people read and why their background knowledge is crucial for comprehension (Smith, 1978; 1982; Carrel, Devine and Eskey, 1988).

Hebrew educators must take advantage of the available knowledge of linguistic theory and pedagogy, but not before they are willing to declare their purpose in teaching. But they cannot state their goals if they do not understand the field of language instruction. For example, suppose they view Hebrew as a ritual instrument and their goal is for the students to be proficient in Hebrew prayers. They need to know that because Hebrew prayers are so linguistically condensed and because much previous background knowledge (mostly abstract) is needed for comprehension of the prayers, most children cannot achieve such a goal. Suppose they want their students to be proficient in communicative Hebrew but are short on instruction time and materials which are a must in order to achieve such a goal. Such discrepancies between goals and realities are a source of disappointment.

Personal Experience and Theory

In my own work for more than 25 years, I have been intrigued by the interplay between the goals—or the lack of them— in Hebrew language education and the information available regarding second/foreign language instruction. My intuition was that a. the Hebrew language is an integral part of the Jewish experience; b. the study of Hebrew must be a meaningful experience; and c. the process is more important than the product. Thus, failure is neither possible nor acceptable. After experimenting with most of the methods which have been used during the last twenty five years (Grammar-Translation, *Ivrit Be'Ivrit*, Aural-Oral, Audio-Visual, Comparative Analysis, Confluent, Natural, Communicative., etc.) (Freeman, 1986; Haramati, 1968; 1977; Richards and Rodgers, 1986), I found that there is a greater principle that stands above all others. This principle which was brought in focus by Dr. Stephan Krashen at the beginning of the 1980s, is that the "acquisition" of language can be done only via "comprehensible input." Thus, three important conclusions emerge:

1. While adults can either "learn" (consciously) or "acquire" (subconsciously) a language, children can only "acquire" a language.

2. Acquisition occurs only when there is comprehension of a sufficient amount of meaningful, relevant and interesting input, and when this input is a little bit above the acquirer's linguistic level.

3. Comprehension is dependent on previous background knowledge and new materials must connect to that knowledge in order to confirm it or alter it (Krashen, 1981; 1982; 1985; Goodman, 1975; Smith, 1978; 1982; Anderson and Pearson, 1984).

Consequently, there is no point in teaching Hebrew grammar to our young students. Linguistic information is usually highly abstract in nature and is classified as a "learning" activity and not effective for children. Moreover, there is no point in expecting most of our students to read Hebrew prayers or Torah portions with comprehension. The linguistic complexities of the texts and the lack of background knowledge of this genre make it virtually impossible for most children to comprehend such texts in Hebrew. What follows is that communicative Hebrew must not be exclusive only to Israeli culture. Any current information shared for a particular purpose is communicative in nature.

These conclusions provided me with a whole new conceptual framework regarding Hebrew education which, I believe, should be a starting point in our educational settings regardless of their ideologies.

Three New Programmatic Realities

1.Teaching Hebrew for rituals

Active participation in services and in life cycle events, and celebrating Jewish holidays are very important Jewish activities. Hebrew formulas are central to these activities. The Hebrew formulas are constant utterances which are repeated again and again. There are several levels of participation in these rituals: a. uttering the Hebrew without comprehension; b. uttering the Hebrew and comprehending through the mediation of English (or any other comprehensible language); and c. uttering the Hebrew and comprehending it simultaneously. In all these possibilities the central activity is still the utterance. There is in the utterance something more than just the words or their meanings. It is a statement of belonging as well, and a chance for a spiritual experience. When teaching rituals, the utterances in Hebrew should be central, but students' success shouldn't be measured only by their linguistic comprehension of the utterances. Rather we must measure progress by students' knowledge of when to utter what, by how they utter it, and by their background information regarding the ritual. The development of the students' backgrounds regarding rituals depends on their communal, family, and individual experiences and attitudes. If students come with extensive backgrounds then the development of their linguistic skills will be faster. If their backgrounds are lacking, linguistic skills must be put on hold and the development of backgrounds should be a priority. This might include meaningful ritual experiences, the development of positive attitudes towards rituals, and a cognitive development of related concepts. The Hebrew utterances which are so integral to the experience should be used, but teaching decoding (the match between 'sign' and 'sound') should not be confused with language (transfer of meaning) instruction.

In addition to teaching the rituals, teachers who are also competent in communicative Hebrew can, in the process, incorporate communicative Hebrew as well. They can speak Hebrew to the children when the context is highly comprehensible: commands such as "sit!" "stand!" "read aloud!" "open the Siddur!" can be understood instantly with the help of gestures. Description of who (who is participating?), what (What are we doing?), where (Where are we?) and how (How are we doing?)

can be comprehended if introduced in a meaningful context. These teachers must remember, however, that the two activities are parallel to one another at the beginning stages of Hebrew instruction. Only at very advanced levels of both ritual and communicative competency can we expect to merge these activities.

2. Developing Hebrew Literacy

Literacy in general is highly regarded by all Jews but Hebrew literacy in particular is not prevalent among American Jews today. What seems to prevent many American Jews from entering into the process of developing Hebrew literacy is the general consensus that only texts containing high-level Jewish concepts are worth the effort. Going back to the principle of "comprehensible input", reading such texts is impossible when many of the concepts aren't yet embedded in the readers' minds. Because such texts are loaded linguistically, I suggest that we should consider any text written in Hebrew which is comprehensible to its readers to be an appropriate Hebrew text. When our students develop understanding of the concepts found in classical Jewish texts and when their linguistic competence increases, at that point such texts can be considered for instruction. We must have faith that those who will enter into the process of developing Hebrew literacy will find it satisfying and challenging and will join the Hebrew literacy "club" willingly and with enthusiasm.

3. Experiencing Communicative Hebrew

Researchers are finding that there is a limit to the level of communicative competence which students can achieve in formal language classrooms. At the same time, however, the development of communicative skills is viewed as a gradual progression that can start within the formal settings. Because "comprehensible input" is so central to the acquisition of Hebrew, the teachers in these formal educational settings must create a natural and an evolving environment which elicits genuine communicative activities. Of course only programs which allow sufficient time to process a substantial amount of "comprehensible input" can hope to start the process of Hebrew acquisition. Such programs pose a great challenge for the instructors. There is a vast literature in the academic field of language instruction regarding this challenge and much of it can be useful to us. For example, studies of 'Immersion', the usage of target languages for instruction of subject-matters, show that content-based curriculum is more effective than language-based curriculum (Swain and Lapkin, 1981). Day schools can offer courses such as Physical Education, Music, and Art in Hebrew. In such courses the context is naturally comprehensible. They can also offer "sheltered" content courses which supply comprehensible information via simplified input aided by visuals and edited texts. (Geography and Math are good subjects for sheltered courses.) In addition to content we must provide an opportunity for interpersonal communication as well as for intrapersonal reflection. Our students are concerned about their own identity and ethnic culture and the interplay between these and the larger world in which they live. They need to express their concerns, appreciations, fears, and desires. I found that students who feel that what they talk, read, and write about is meaningful to their lives usually want to continue the experience. We hope that the experiences in formal Hebrew classes will encourage our students to continue to use Hebrew. They can continue to develop their Hebrew communicative skills informally in Jewish summer camps, during visits to Israel, and through the reading of newspapers, magazines, and literature written in Hebrew.

Conclusion

Each of the activities (Hebrew for rituals, Hebrew literacy, and Communicative Hebrew) is equally important and each requires that we cultivate different skills in our students in addition to their linguistic development. Teaching Hebrew for rituals requires mainly the promotion of identification with certain religious ideologies and traditions; teaching Hebrew literacy requires mainly the promotion of Jewish concepts and history; and teaching Hebrew as a communicative language requires mainly the promotion of Israeli/Jewish American culture and its people, self-awareness, and interpersonal communication.

How to achieve our goals is a pedagogical question, but to declare these goals is our moral obligation. Our sense of success is directly connected to our sense of accomplishment, and accomplishment is measured in terms of the goals we set before us.

Bibliography

Aron, I. (1987). *Instruction and Enculturation in Jewish Education.* A paper given at the first Research Conference in Jewish Education, Los Angeles.

Brinton, D., Snow, M.A., & Wesche M.B. (1989). *Content-based Second Language Instruction.* New York: Newbury House Publishers

Brown, J. M. & Adrian, P.S. (1988). *The Listening Approach.* NY: Longman Inc.

Carrell, P., Devine, J., & Eskey, D. (1988). *Interactive Approaches to Second Language Reading.* Boston: Cambridge University Press.

Celce-Murcia, M. (1991, Autumn). Grammar Pedagogy in Second and Foreign Language Teaching. *TESOL Quarterly, 25*(3).

Chamiel, C. (1986). Le'nose Ha'lashon Ha'ivrit Ve'limudah Ba'safa Ha'ivrit. In *Hebetim Bechinuch.* Tel Aviv: Bar-Ilan University.

Fishman, J. (1989). *Language and Ethnicity in Minority Sociolinguistic Perspective.* Philadelphia: Multilingual Matters, Ltd.

Freeman, D. (1986). *Techniques and Principles in Language Teaching.* London: Oxford University Press.

Galyean, B. (1976). *Language From Within.* Santa Barbara: CEDARC.

Gilis, M. (1987). *Min Ha'cheder el Hamachshev.* Tel Aviv: Bar Ilan University.

Grabe, W. (1991, Autumn). Current Developments in Second Language Reading Research. *TESOL Quarterly, 25*(3).

Haramati, S. (1968). *Halachah U'maase Be'horaat Halashon Haivrit.* Jerusalem: World Zionist Organization.

Haramati, S. (1977). *Darchei Horaat Haivrit Batefutzot.* Jerusalem: World Zionist Organization.

Krashen, S.D. (1981). *Second Language Acquisition and Second Language Learning.* New York: Pergamon.

Krashen, S.D. (1982). *Principles and Practice in Second Language Acquisition.* New York: Pergamon.

Krashen, S.D. (1984). *Writing, Research, Theory and Applications.* New York: Pergamon.

Krashen, S.D. (1985). *The Input Hypothesis:Issues and Implications.* New York: Longman.

Krashen, S.D. (1985). *Inquiries and Insights.* San Francisco: Alemany Press.

Krashen, S.D. (May, 1989). *Comprehensible Input and Some Competing Hypotheses.* Paper presented at the Conference on Comprehension-Based Learning and Teaching of Second Languages, University of Ottawa.

Krashen,S.D. and Terrel, T. (1983). *The Natural Approach.* New York: Pergamon.

Krashen S. D. and Biber, D. (1988). On Course:Bilingual Educations Success in California. *California Association of Bilingual Educators.*

Larsen-Freeman, D. (1991, Summer). Second Language Acquisition Research: Staking Out the Territory. *TESOL Quarterly, 25*(2).

Nir, R. (1977). Horaat Ha'lashon Ha'ivrit Ba' tefutsot Le'or Ekronot Ha'balshanut Ha'shimushit. In *Min Hasadna.* (3-4).

Phi Delta Kappan, (1987, February). A Special Issue on Reading, *68*(6).

Regg, P. (1991, Autumn). Whole Language in TESOL. *TESOL Quarterly, 25*(3).

Richards, J. & Rodgers, S.T. (1986). *Approaches and Methods in Language Teaching.* Boston: Cambridge University Press.

Rivers, N.W. & Moshe, N. (1989). *Teaching Hebrew:A Practical Guide.* Tel Aviv: University Publishing Project.

Seliger, W. (1986, October). The Role of Hebrew Language in the Maintenance of Jewish Identity: Some Historical Precedents. *Dor Ledor.*

Shohamy, E. (1984, Fall). The State of the Art of The Hebrew Language Curricula. *Jewish Education, 52*(3).

Smith, F. (1978). *Reading Without Nonsense.* Boston: Cambridge University Press.

Smith, F. (1982). *Understanding Reading.* New York: CBS College Publishing.

Spolsky, B. (Fall, 1986). Teaching Hebrew in the Diaspora: Rationales and Goals. *Jewish Education, 54*(3).

Stevick, E. (1976). *Meaning, Memory and Method.* Rowley, MA: Newbury House Publishers.

Stevick, E. (1980). *A Way and Ways.* Rowley, MA: Newbury House Publishers Inc.

Stevick, E. (1986). *Images and Options in the Language Classroom.* Boston: Cambridge University Press.

Swaffar, A., & Byrnes. (1991). *Reading for Meaning. An Integrated Approach to Language Learning.* New York: Prentice Hall.

Swain, M., & Lapkin, S. (1981). Evaluating Bilingual Education:A Canadian Case Study. *Multilingual Matters, 2.*

Highlights

* Few serious attempts are being made to explore concerns about Hebrew language education.
* Paradoxically, Hebrew is seen as central to our institutions.
* Whenever there has been agreement within a particular Jewish community on its goals in teaching Hebrew and when that goal was reached by using an accepted linguistic approach, there has been a period of perceived successful Hebrew education. When the linguistic approach has been deemed no longer viable or when the Jewish communal needs have changed as a result of historical circumstances and/or ideological changes, there have been perceived failures and disappointments.
* Even within the same community, there have been conflicts regarding Hebrew language instruction/education.
* Modern language theory has found that:
    a. while adults can either "learn" or "acquire" a language, children can only "acquire" a language.
    b. acquisition occurs only when there is comprehension of a sufficient amount of meaningful, relevant, and interesting input, and when this input is a little bit above the acquirer's linguistic level
    c. comprehension is dependent upon previous background knowledge and new materials must connect to that knowledge in order to confirm or alter it.
* Acquisition of language can be done only via "comprehensible input".
* Teaching Hebrew for ritual, developing Hebrew literacy, and experiencing communicative Hebrew are equally valid starting points.

The Larger Context

Based largely on her personal experiences of years in the classroom and study of language acquisition, Ms. Dori has painted an often discouraging picture of Hebrew in the classroom. Our failure to produce a generation of Hebraically literate Jews still gnaws at our conscience. Perhaps the possibility of creating an elite group within the context of offering a Jewish education for all, needs to be considered (or, as some would have it, reconsidered). Our driving myth that Hebrew education is important needs to be placed higher on our agendas, whereas too often it is considered perfunctorily and dismissed.

What We Know About...
Jewish Video and Television

Moshe L. Botwinick

Television has such a powerful impact on the lives of its viewers that it has been called the "hidden curriculum"—to indicate that its influence is at least equal to, if not greater than, that of the written curricula of schools. Dr. Moshe Botwinick, Assistant Professor of Communications at Marymount Manhattan College, has been involved in research efforts centering around Children Television Workshop's Shalom Sesame *and provides a broader focus for video and television in the Jewish world.*

THERE IS LITTLE DOUBT THAT TELEVISION AND ITS TECHNOLOGICAL OFFSPRING, THE VIDEO CASSETTE, have a major impact on the lives of our children. Indeed the 1982 National Institute Mental Health/Surgeon General Report *Television and Behavior* reviewed over 3000 studies in the field and synthesized the results into 30 separate reports that took up several volumes. Since that time there have been literally thousands of additional studies—some trivial, some important, some poorly designed, others well controlled. The vast majority reconfirm the basic finding of the 1982 report: "Almost all the evidence testifies to television's role as a formidable educator whose effects are both pervasive and cumulative. Television can no longer be considered as a casual part of daily life, as an electronic toy. Research findings have long since destroyed the illusion that television is merely innocuous entertainment. While the learning it provides is mainly incidental rather than direct and formal, it is a significant part of the total acculturation process (Pearl, 1982)."

This having been said, the question naturally arises in the context of this paper: what are the implications of television for Jewish education? If we perceive Jewish education as an acculturation process—"an enterprise," as Marshall Sklare (1971) noted, "concerned with formal training in the cultural heritage of the Jewish people," then what, we may ask, is television's role in Jewish education and in this process? While I and others have explored the social and philosophical implications of television and its related construction of social reality, a view that often likens television and its programs to ritualistic practice and a myth-forming dramatization of cultural values (Botwinick, 1984; Goethals, 1981; Postman, 1985), this report will be limited to specific uses and content issues.

What is Jewish Television?

Is there something "out there" called Jewish educational television? How about Jewish television? What could that possibly mean? Is it television with Jewish instructional goals (religious, ritualistic, cultural)? Or do we perhaps means stories about Jews and their history, or perhaps shows with Jewish performers, or Jewish writers? Or perhaps shows with explicit Jewish values? Or maybe any show from which we could ferret out Jewish values. I suspect that the reader would agree that all of these could effectively be used for Jewish education; but how?

Broadly speaking, Jewish television can be placed in one of three categories:

1. **General entertainment programs.** This group would include, but not be limited to, feature length motion pictures, commercial and cable programming, and virtually any other video form that is not curriculum-driven.

2. **Documentaries.** These are tapes and programs depicting slice-of-life reality.

3. **Educational.** These are programs designed with teaching and/or instruction as a major goal.

While it is certainly possible for these three categories to overlap, each has its own implications when used to promote or provide material for the Jewish educator. Distribution and appraisal of these tapes are presently decentralized and often "scatter shot."

The general entertainment category is the easiest to find because it is the most abundant resource, but also the one that may require the greatest insight, attention, and review to use effectively. TV programs and film can be used to explore the nature of values and meaning as they relate to Jewish education-specific curricular goals. A teacher using virtually any program, for example, could attempt to unravel what pattern, types or kinds of values are portrayed in the program and how this relates to Jewish values. Other areas that could be analyzed include responses to such questions as how this specific program depicts the resolution of human problems and difficulties, and what kind of images and characters are portrayed. Work by such social scientists as Neil Postman (1985), Wilbur Schramm (1961), and D. and J. Singer (1981), or children's advocates such as Peggy Charin of Action for Children's Television, explore attempts to use television to transmit values, much of which can be value-adapted by educators and parents.

Documentaries can provide a view of a world that no longer is or a profile of a leader up close and direct. Indeed, it does document a true event, and at its best provides insight and resonates within the viewer. To see *Shoah,* or *Image Before Our Eyes,* or *Number Our Days,* is to relive an incredible experience and see the world or at least part of it anew.

In the third category of educational programming, I place programs developed with a teaching goal in mind. They may be curriculum-driven, or used to illuminate or teach a specific area, such as tradition, holidays, ritual, language, etc. Many a central agency for Jewish education and synagogue bodies have produced programs in this category with varying degrees of success. One program that is very close to my heart, falls easily into this category, and that is *Shalom Sesame.*

A Model: CTW/Shalom Sesame

In my own work I have been most fortunate to be working on one of the few Jewish children's educational projects that has the insights and funds to demand research as a necessary component—the *Shalom Sesame* project, an American coproduction of Israeli Education Television and the Children's Television Workshop. It introduces North American audiences to the land, people, culture, and language of Israel using the familiar *Sesame Street* characters and format. Its early history is reviewed by Lewis Bernstein (1983), its executive producer and leading advocate since its inception.

The series incorporates Hebrew language elements from Israel's *Rechov Sumsum* (their version of *Sesame Street*), many of which have been modified with English-language voice-overs or English print on the screen, as well as specially produced segments which introduce American children to the sights, sounds, and people of Israel. While the primary target for American *Sesame Street* is children 3 –5 years old, the target audience for *Shalom Sesame* consists of children through 9 or 10 years old. Previous research indicates that these older children in particular are both curious about and able to comprehend information about foreign cultures and languages, yet still find many elements of *Sesame Street* appealing, including its humor, its fast pace, and its renewing of "old friends" (Botwinick, 1985).

My work has involved the application of the Children's Television Workshop model in the development of this series. The model is useful for any educational program and has application to other projects, for it carefully weds curricular goals, research, testing, and production. In brief, the steps in the model are:

1. **Curriculum development.** There is strong evidence that television can teach (Salomon, 1979). Deciding what to teach is the task of this first step. Research, seminars, discussions with experts, budget limitations, all contribute to the selection of curricular goals and possible ways of realizing them.

2. **Statements of behavioral objectives.** This is precise goal definition. To know what you expect is essential for follow-up (summative) research.

3. **Measurement of existing competence in existing audience.** Goals specify the educational outcome the show wishes to produce. This step of measuring existing competencies is a necessary and related step in planning, for it determines the existing audience's competence in the program's chosen goal areas.

4. **Development of writer's notebook.** This is the beginning of the creative process of turning curricular goals into practical language and suggesting presentational forms and settings.

5. **Experimental production.** This is the development of pilot material for review and testing. Our pilot was a half-hour show called the *Rechov Sumsum Show*. The data it generated helped enormously in further production. This pilot was used for formative testing both on the appeal and content of the show. Our testing, for example, took place at such var-

ied sites as an urban public school in New York City, a Hebrew supplemental school in New Jersey, a day school in Philadelphia, and a public school in Louisville, Kentucky. Formative testing is the testing that you do while creating the project. The formative testing leads directly to:

6. **Revision and final production.** This is the show that gets distributed—either on tape or broadcast. In our case, at least in the early phases, it was both. In order to find out how successful the show was in reaching our stated objective we moved to:

7. **Summative Evaluation.** This provides data both to measure our success and to prepare for a new round of curricular development.

I should stress that this model is not limited to organizations working on million dollar projects; its systematic approach can be used with minor modification on projects with even the most modest budget. Its power lies in its delineated goals, testing procedures, feedback, and the close ties between research and production.

What the General Television Research Has Taught Us

Children learn by seeing. While this seems to be a truism, it is the basis of the observational learning model. Children can learn certain behaviors, attitudes, and skills from television the same way they can learn social skills from watching parents, peers, and others. Television does provide its viewers with access to a very wide range of observational learning experiences. Because of this, it is widely believed that some attitudes, behaviors, and proclivities can be taught via television. Television has been called a "show and tell machine," yet in reality what is does best is show. "To tell" is to develop a logically reasoned sequence of thought. Television, because of its overpowering use of visual imagery, must relegate discursive "telling" to minor importance. In other words, television is a visual medium, and its power lies in showing. Television can demonstrate a ritual, though it cannot correct nor cultivate a sense of the ritual depicted. Indeed, only another human being can provide the guidance, correction, and feedback that could lead a student to the total experience that Jewish education entails.

The human element is truly the vital factor in determining what a child will get out of television. There is strong evidence that parental intervention can enhance or diminish TV's impact on children (Lesser, 1974; McLeod, 1982). Children, for example, who watched *Sesame Street* with a parent figure present in the room, got more out of the show than others who did not. Intervention does play a powerful role. Because of the amount of time that children spend in front of the television set, on average three and a half hours daily, television has a displacement effect, that is, it displaces more active pursuits such as playing outside with friends, interacting with family, or reading books—three activities that Jewish education values.

So what can parents do? They can limit the amount of time the television is on; guide purposeful programming; provide direct mediation by providing explanatory comments and interpretation; and provide indirect mediation by talking to others about the programs in front of the children.

They can use springboard techniques, alluded to earlier, by demonstrating how the program's information can be applied to and have implications for their life as Jews.

The exploration of the complex interaction between television, Jewish education, and children has hardly begun. This article has only touched the surface of what must be further studied: more specific strategies for viewing, more guidelines for program design, greater analysis of the nature of the viewing experience and the way children respond. The effect of various television techniques on values, attitudes, and behaviors of Jewish children has begun to be demonstrated through programs like *Shalom Sesame*. Indeed, the efforts of dedicated members of the *Shalom Sesame* team, and the foresight of its funders, particularly of Eli Evans of the Charles H. Revson Foundation, have created a critical and educational success, and with sales of close to 80,000 tapes have demonstrated a substantial market exists that could support, wants, and needs this type of material. New terrain is being travelled as it is demonstrated that schools, educators, and parents will purchase and utilize quality programs; and children will enjoy and be motivated to learn from them.

Jewish Television Resources

Besides the obvious, that is, scanning the TV listings and video store shelves, where does one find Jewish television? At this time there is no centralized agency, nor any distribution system to provide this information. And indeed the job of simply listing all available tapes that may be of interest to Jewish educators seems to border on the impossible. If we add to this the task of critiquing and evaluating and suggesting methods of usage, we do enter the realm of the impossible. Nevertheless over the years there have been agencies and bodies who have taken upon themselves the burden and the challenge of compiling such lists, many focusing on a limited area. Among these agencies are the National Center for Jewish Film, the late and lamented Jewish Media Service, catalogues from Agencies for Jewish Education, the Coalition for the Advancement of Jewish Education, the Compilation Project of the Memorial Foundation for Jewish Culture, UAHC, United Synagogue, YIVO Institute for Jewish Research, Harvard Judaica video collection, independent distributors like Alden Films and Ergo Media, and two noteworthy news letters *Jewish TeleVimages* by Professors Pearl and JESNA's comprehensive Media/Meida. Each group has its own limitations, politics, and strengths and could leave the Jewish user feeling overwhelmed. While the contribution of these organizations is essential, their impact is reduced by the diffuse nature of Jewish life in the United States.

An Agenda for the Future

As telecommunications technologies become more widespread, accessible, and decentralized, the Jewish community will have to develop strategies to use a powerful tool, one that with proper planning can yield enormous educational benefits. However, like Pandora's box, it can also be opened to reveal technological goblins beyond our control. To this end I believe that mobilization is needed to explore and develop the following areas:

1. Develop workshops, research papers, and in-service training in the basic concepts and philosophy of the telecommunications media as they apply to Jewish education.

2. Formulate educational goals and objectives that can be achieved through these media.

3. Seek high level policy support, and administrative and management options.

4. Plan curriculum by deciding what can best be done by telecommunications media and integrating that effort into a comprehensive educational framework.

5. Develop techniques to review and evaluate available materials, to aid and develop an efficient system for the dissemination of the information and distribution of the materials themselves.

6. Train Jewish educators as production personnel in the areas of education content and media technology; and train teachers on how to effectively utilize this technology.

7. Develop methods for testing and validating program formats and methodologies by which lessons will be transmitted.

8. Produce ancillary materials such as books, magazines, and workbooks to make the viewing experience interactive and alive.

9. Create procedures for feedback, analysis, and research in all future technological utility.

The agenda is long, the time is short, the reward, however, is worth the effort; for it is, after all, our children's lives, our future, and theirs.

Bibliography

Commission on Jewish Education in North American. *A Time to Act: The Report of the Mandel Commission on Jewish Education in North America.* (1990). Lanham, MD: University Press of America.

Bernstein, L. (1983). Rechov Sumsum: An Israeli Co-Production. *International Research Notes, IV.* New York: Children's Television Workshop.

Botwinick, M. (1984). Jewish Education in a Technological Age, *The Pedagogic Reporter, 35*(1).

Botwinick, M. (1985). *The Rechov Sumsum Show Prototype.* New York: Children's Television Workshop.

Goethals, G. T. (1981). *The TV Ritual.* Boston, MA: Beacon.

Lesser, G.S. (1974). *Children and Television: Lessons from Sesame Street.* New York: Random House.

McLeod, J. M. (1982). Television and Social Relations. In D. Pearl, *TV and Behavior: Ten Years of Scientific Progress. v.2.* Washington, DC: U.S.Government Printing Office.

Palmer, E. (1974). Formative research in the production of television for children. In D.E. Olson. (Ed.), *Media and Symbols.* Chicago, IL: The National Society for the Study of Education.

Pearl, D. (1982). *TV and Behavior: Ten Years of Scientific Progress.* (Vol. II.) Washington, DC: U.S. Government Printing Office.

Postman, N. (1985). *Amusing Ourselves to Death.* New York: Viking.

Salamon, G. (1979). *Interaction of Media, Cognition, and Learning.* San Francisco: Jossey-Bass.

Schramm, W. (1961). *Television and the Lives of Our Children.* Palo Alto, CA: Stanford University Press.

Singer, D.G. & Singer, J. C. (1981). *Getting the Most Out of Television.* Glenview, IL: Scott Foresman & Company.

Sklare, M. (1971). *America's Jews.* New York: Random House.

Highlights

*   The learning that television provides is a significant part of the total acculturation process.
*   Jewish television can be placed in one of three categories:
        general entertainment programs
        documentaries
        educational programs
*   Tested models (such as CTW) now exist for the development of Jewish educational television.
*   Television is a visual medium, and its power lies in showing.
*   Parent intervention can enhance or diminish TV's impact on children.

The Larger Context

If, as Prof. Botwinick indicates, "only another human being can provide the guidance, correction, and feedback that could lead a student to the total experience that Jewish education entails," we as media users need to proceed with extreme caution when using video in our settings. Our tradition relies heavily upon the human give-and-take of logical, sequential reasoning. When "telling" is relegated to a category of "minor importance" we must proceed slowly, questioning whether our educational outcomes are the ones we really intended in the first place.

What We Know About...
Computers in Jewish Education

Leonard A. Matanky

Do computers work in Jewish education? What impact have computers had on student learning? Dr. Leonard A. Matanky, Assistant Superintendent of the Associated Talmud Torahs of Chicago, is also the director of the Morris and Rose Goldman Computer Department for Jewish Studies. He maintains that computers are a uniquely powerful teaching tool that can enhance and enrich the Jewish educational experience. They are not, however, the "wonder drug" that will cure the ills and heal the wounds of Jewish education.

JUST FIFTEEN YEARS HAVE PASSED SINCE THE INTRODUCTION OF THE FIRST MICROCOMPUTER. YET, IN that brief period of time we have witnessed a technological revolution unparalleled in the history of the world. Computers have changed the way we work and play, and have offered opportunities unimagined by previous generations. Today, a preschool child, sitting in front of a simple Apple II computer, has more "computing power" than the entire Allied Armies in World War II.

Schools have not been immune to this revolution. While the typical classroom of today physically resembles a classroom of fifty years ago, computers have afforded students and teachers new opportunities for learning and teaching. Nearly every public elementary and secondary school in America today uses computers for instructional purposes (Office of Technology Assessment [OTA], 1988). While precise data regarding Jewish education is lacking, it is reasonable to assume only slightly lower levels of computer use in Jewish day schools.

Without question, millions of dollars and countless hours have been spent on computers in Jewish schools. Yet, the question remains, "What impact have computers had on student learning?" Or, to put it more succinctly, "Do computers work?"

The State of the Art

Computers have been used in general education for over thirty years and in Jewish education for more than ten years. Until recent years, the predominant use of computers was to enhance learning through drills or tutorials. This use, called CAI (computer assisted instruction) is the oldest educational application of computers and the most researched. In fact, one survey identified over 200 studies of CAI published since 1965 (Kulik, 1987).

In general, CAI offers a number of advantages over traditional classroom methods:

1 The computer interacts individually with the student, providing feedback and correction at an individualized pace;

2. The computer is precise, requiring students to develop precision of thinking and responses (OTA, 1988);

3. The computer increases students' motivation to learn (Becker, 1986a/b);

4. The use of computers actually increases student-to-student interaction (Becker, 1983; Becker, 1984); and

5. The computer releases teachers from the drudgery of repetitive drills, allowing them to work with individual groups of students on higher-order learning (Kulik, 1983).

In view of these advantages it is not surprising that research has found that CAI improves learning and decreases the amount of time needed to learn new information (Kulik, 1983; Becker, 1987; OTA, 1988). In particular, CAI seems to have the greatest impact as a supplement to instruction (Okey, 1985). Many studies also suggest that either the high-achieving or the low-achieving students benefit the most from CAI (Fisher, 1983). Yet, a recent meta-analysis disputes this finding and suggests that all students benefit equally from CAI (Roblyer, 1988).

While the research findings about CAI are favorable, much of the research has been criticized on methodological grounds. For example, one study found that fewer than 40% of all research projects used randomization techniques (Roblyer, 1988). Another study was able to identify only seven research projects since 1984 that used randomized assignment of students (Becker, 1987). Nevertheless, in both cases, the researchers still identified positive results of CAI in those remaining studies that met their rigorous experimental standards.

In the Jewish Classroom

Unfortunately, there is relatively little research about computers in Jewish education, and the studies that exist are primarily surveys (e.g. Jaskoll, 1984; Solow, 1985; Ukeles, 1986). Yet, these surveys and anecdotal information from schools across the country indicate that computers in Jewish schools provide the same advantages as described in the general literature with two notable differences.

The sophistication gap

The first difference is the unique need of Jewish education to narrow the "sophistication gap" between general and Jewish studies (Ukeles, 1986). So long as students are offered modern methods and techniques of education only in their general studies, Judaic studies may be perceived as old-fashioned and limited. Therefore, computer use in Jewish education may serve as a key to changing that perception, thereby increasing the value that students place on those studies.

The software problem

The second difference is the quantity and quality of software available. Recent estimates suggest that nearly 7% of general studies software is of high quality (Neill, 1989). With over 11,000 software programs available since 1985, that translates to approximately 750 "outstanding" programs. In a recent study of Judaic software only 350 software programs since 1977 (!) were identified. Of those, only a third were developed for school use (Matanky, 1987). Obviously there is a dearth of software available for Judaic studies.

This "software problem" has caused Jewish education to rely heavily on mini-authoring software (Matanky, 1989a). Such software allows teachers to input their own information into an existing "drill and practice" or testing program without the need of programming skills. As a result, a single mini-authoring program can be used for multiple academic subjects and levels. Yet, this is not a long-term solution. If good tutorial, simulation and even game Judaic software is not developed the evolution of computer use in Jewish education will be arrested.

The use of computers in education is not limited to CAI. Two growing uses are "tool applications" and telecommunications.

Tool Applications

Tool applications, also known as "productivity tools," are computer programs that take advantage of the computer's ability to manipulate text and numbers faster and more efficiently than by traditional means. This type of software, which represents the fastest growing market segment, includes databases to organize, search and retrieve information, as well as word processing to improve or enhance the writing and editing process. While there has not been as much research into the effectiveness of tool applications as there has been for CAI, there is general agreement and enthusiasm for its educational advantages (Schiffman, 1986).

Databases can be used for two purposes in the classroom. The first use of databases is to teach children how to organize information by gathering data and constructing a database (OTA, 1988). The second approach is to use existing databases for research or to develop decision making skills (McClelland, 1986). For example, databases can be used to: discover commonalities and differences among groups of events or things; analyze relationships; look for trends; arrange information in more useful ways; or test and refine hypotheses (Hunter, 1985).

In 1966, work was begun on a Jewish legal database at the Weizman Institute of Science and Bar-Ilan University. This project, now called the Bar-Ilan Responsa Project, contains over 250 volumes of rabbinic responsa and is available to scholars and rabbis through a telecommunications network (Rosenbaum, 1988). In 1987, a similar project was initiated by a private corporation called Otzar Torah Memuchshav in Bnei Brak, Israel and in 1991 by the Davka Corp. in Chicago. Their efforts have led to a database containing over a hundred volumes of classic legal texts available on either CD-ROM or diskettes.

These projects have had a tremendous impact upon Jewish scholarship and university/yeshiva level studies. However, because the texts are stored in their original Hebrew and contain technical terminology, elementary and secondary classroom level applications are most limited. Their greatest potential for schools is as a resource to teachers. Such a project was initiated in 1988 at the Morris and Rose Goldman Computer Department in Chicago, and has met with success.

Parenthetically, many teachers have found databases to be a great asset for creating individualized tests and worksheets. Using a database, teachers enter questions into the database, coding each question with information regarding its content, difficulty, etc., then print individualized worksheets and tests using these codes. For example, if a teacher would want ten difficult questions from a particular chapter in the Bible, the appropriate codes for difficulty and content could be selected and an individualized test would be printed.

Word Processing

The second major use of tool application software is word processing. In fact, a recent survey of American universities, revealed that the primary use of computers is as "writing machines" (Turner, 1987). The two key advantages to word processing are physical and psychological; the physical ease of revising text, simply pressing a delete key to removed unwanted phrases and the resulting psychological perception that encourages the writer to experiment and enjoy writing (Daiute, 1986).

In elementary schools, word processing has been used successfully from the primary grades to encourage the writing process. Studies have shown that the increased ease of editing compositions that word processing offers, has fostered a more positive attitude towards writing by students (Balajthy, 1987). Of course, placing a child in front of a computer with a word processing program is not sufficient. Keyboarding skills and training in the use of the specific word processing program must precede any serious attempt to incorporate computers into the writing curriculum (Wetzel, 1985).

Hebrew/English word processing software has also begun to have an impact on Jewish schools (Matanky, 1989b). Used both by students, to prepare compositions, and by teachers, to prepare classroom materials, this software offers the same benefits of general word processing programs, in addition to its bilingual capabilities. Many of the programs are "graphically generated" requiring no modification of the computer hardware, yet allow both Hebrew and English to be typed in their appropriate directions, even in mid-sentence. Some even allow vowels and "trop" to be included with the text.

An emerging application of computers in education is the use of telecommunications. Whether it is the use of large databases, "electronic mail" or computer conferencing, telecommunications present great educational potential across a broad spectrum of disciplines (Cohen, 1986; Winer, 1988). Through telecommunication conferences, students of similar ages, but in different communities or even countries, can communicate with each other about events and issues in their respective communities. Such activities allow students to gain an appreciation of other cultures, along with valuable skills in expression and writing (OTA, 1988).

The use of telecommunications for Jewish education is still in its infancy. While major telecommunications services exist for the general public, including CompuServe, Genie, etc., early experiments in Jewish educational telecommunicating have failed to attract a significant audience. Davka Corporation pioneered this field with their short-lived "Golem" service (Rosenbaum, 1988), followed by numerous other efforts, including "Keshernet", the first Jewish electronic bulletin board to link Israel and the United States. In 1988, the Goldman Computer Department in Chicago, introduced a local Jewish educational electronic bulletin board especially for children. Still in operation, this service has received over 7000 callers who have participated in Jewish educational contests, quizzes and conferences.

The most ambitious Jewish telecommunications project is an international Jewish bulletin board for students, teachers, administrators and educational bureaus called GesherNET. This service, just two years old, allows schools and bureaus, especially in the United States and Israel, exciting opportunities to share information and ideas. In 1990, the Jewish Education Services of North America joined with GesherNET and established a inter-bureau "electronic conference," to provide central agencies for Jewish education a method to share ideas and information.

Yet, despite these many exciting applications of computers and their educational potential, the single variable with the greatest impact on success of microcomputers remains the classroom teacher (Adams, 1985; Ukeles, 1986). Even with the best software and hardware, unless the classroom teacher is ready and willing to use computers, the computer will lie dormant in the classroom. In public education, where nearly all elementary and secondary schools have computers, only half of the teachers report that they have used them in instruction (OTA, 1988). Given the dual program of day schools and the supplementary nature of religious schools, it is reasonable to assume even lower levels of computer use in Jewish schools.

So the question exists: How do teachers become "ready and willing" to use computers?

Teacher Willingness

The problem of willingness is the easiest to overcome. The early fears of some educators, that computers would replace the classroom teacher, have been shown to be unsubstantiated and unfounded (Phi Delta Kappa [PDK], 1982). Rather, teachers have a very positive attitude toward classroom computer use, and many would like further training and experience (National Education Association [NEA], 1982; *Instructor*, 1982). The key to this issue is to prove to teachers the efficacy of computers in the classroom (McLaughlin, 1978). Given specific examples of how computers can benefit teachers and students, a teacher will develop a willingness to use computers.

But larger problem remains: How do teachers become "ready" to use computers?

Teacher Readiness

Computer use, as with other educational innovations, requires teachers to change and modify their existing habits (Lipson, 1981; Matanky, 1986). In fact, the changes required, and the training involved in preparing teachers to use computers are more complex than what is required for other technologies (OTA, 1988). For, while the computer allows teachers to work with smaller groups and provide greater opportunities for individualization, it requires a major change in teaching style from the typical classroom, where teachers primarily employ a whole-class lecture-discussion method.

As a result, in-service training of teachers is critical. This fact is even more true for the Judaic studies, where teachers may not be as familiar with new technologies as are their secular counterparts (Ukeles, 1986). Successful in-service training has been found to depend on the following eight variables:

1. Appropriate balance between lecture and guided practice;
2. Detailed curriculum guides and lesson plans;
3. Clear and relevant objectives;
4. Lesson related materials and handouts;
5. In-service lessons linked to classroom needs (efficacy of need);
6. Peer interaction;
7. Practical strategies for teaching heterogeneous classes;
8. Follow-up meetings and support (Stechner, 1987).

Due to the dearth of Judaic software, in-service training of Judaic faculties requires an additional component. Intensive in-service programs must be developed to train teachers to design and develop software, with either authoring programs such as PILOT or "Hypertext," or mini-authoring programs. Such in-service programs require highly motivated teachers, who are open to change, and possess the substantive sequential skills critical to software design (Hoover, 1987). In addition, the intensive in-service programs must also include financial and career incentives to encourage teachers to invest their time and energy in such a large undertaking (Winkler, 1986; OTA, 1988). Finally, the teacher trainer must be an educational expert, able to advise teachers on curricular issues, and not just knowledgeable of the technical aspects of computer software and hardware (Winkler, 1986).

Policy Implications

The success or failure of utilizing computers to enrich Jewish education will depend upon the commitment of Jewish leadership to plan for the following three key factors:

a. Teacher Training;

b. Availability of Equipment; and

c. Software Development.

Teacher Training

Teacher training must be the primary concern of any long-term plan for computer use. Both preservice and in-service, intensive and introductory programs must be created to provide training opportunities commensurate with the abilities and interests of teachers. But whatever form of training is provided, it must include opportunities for practice, follow-up, direct application to the classroom and the development of an "expertise" in a well-defined area of computer utilization.

One successful approach to teacher training has been to identify a select group of highly motivated and talented teachers to serve as the initial target group for training. These teachers participate in a series of intensive seminars that include: software training and evaluation, curriculum integration, and the basics of computer hardware. Once trained, these teachers can serve as peer-supervisors to prepare other teachers for computer use. Through such an approach, schools can create a cadre of veteran educators who can also function as in-school computer consultants.

For Jewish supplementary schools, teacher training must also focus on the problem of the severe lack of flexible time in the school day. In a typical two-hour session, teachers will need to be extremely creative and cautious in the allocation of student time on the computer. Specific plans and suggestions must be presented. In addition, supplementary schools that primarily employ part-time teachers may find that these teachers do not have enough time to dedicate to computer training. For these reasons, supplementary schools may determine that computers may have very limited application in a supplementary school program.

Availability of equipment

In the not-too-distant future, every student and teacher may have a computer at home and one at school to prepare and complete regular assignments. In fact, there are already a few model schools where this situation exists, and there is even an experimental project in a day school where students are given computers to use at home (Goldman, 1990). Yet, for most schools the availability of so many computers is just a dream. Therefore the second key factor for successful computer use in schools is the availability of computers to students and teachers.

The most common configuration of computers in schools is the placement of one, two, or three computers in a classroom. This in-class configuration makes the computers accessible to teachers and thus more likely to be used. Of course this only holds true if the teacher is prepared for computer use. Otherwise, even if the computer is placed directly on the teacher's desk, its most probable use would be as an expensive oversized paperweight!

However, with only a few computers in the classroom, whole-class CAI is not possible. Therefore, teachers have to use various "grouping" techniques where students are divided into small groups, performing different learning activities at the same time. For example, some students would meet with the teacher while some would be doing independent assignments and others would be working on the computer.

Yet, many teachers are unaccustomed to such an approach, and prefer instead "whole-class instruction" in a lecture-discussion style. For these teachers, computer labs are preferable. Unfortunately, using a computer lab creates logistic demands for transferring and scheduling children that discourage many teachers from using them. Beyond the logistical problem, many of our schools lack both the physical space and the budget to create a computer lab.

Therefore, the most viable option for the typical Jewish school is to place computers directly in the classrooms. But, instead of buying all of the computers at once, schools should only buy computers for the teachers who have been trained and are prepared to use computers in their curriculum. In this way, schools can distribute expenses over a period of time, maximize their investment and most importantly, provide an incentive to encourage teachers to prepare themselves for computers in the curriculum.

Teachers also require the availability of computers, both to practice their newly acquired skills and to create classroom materials. While it is reasonable to expect teachers to prepare materials with pen and paper in the evening at home, it is an entirely different matter to ask them to spend late nights in school preparing materials with the school's computers.

Two simple solutions to this problem are available. The first solution is to allow teachers to borrow the school's computers, whether it be overnight or during weekends and vacations. While many schools are hesitant at first to lend such expensive equipment, as long as teachers assume responsibility for the equipment and its care, the overwhelming experience of schools has been very positive.

A second exciting solution is to encourage teachers to purchase their own computers. In Chicago, the Goldman Department established an incentive program called "A Computer for the Teacher" to encourage teachers to attend computer workshops. Following attendance at various computer workshops, teachers received a subsidy of 50% of the purchase price of a computer. Incentive program such as this achieve two goals: 1. Teachers are encouraged and rewarded for attending computer classes; and 2. Teachers obtain computers for home use and therefore become much more likely to use computers for the classroom (Winkler, 1986).

Software development

The most difficult obstacle to the use of computers in Jewish education is the dearth of educational software. Unfortunately, because the market for Jewish educational software is so small and unprofitable, new software is not even being developed at any significant rate. For example, Davka Corporation, the pioneer in the field of computers and Jewish education, has produced only 10 new software programs for school use since 1986.

To overcome this obstacle, schools must adopt a three-pronged approach to software. First, they must identify existing CAI software that is appropriate for their curricula, and use it. Second, they must train teachers to use mini-authoring programs to create teacher-modified software, specific to their classroom needs. Finally, they must take advantage of the many alternative uses of computers in the curriculum, such as the tool applications of Hebrew/English word processing and databases or telecommunications.

Yet, even with this three-pronged approach, there will still be a need for additional software and this is where "hypertext" software can play a role. "Hypertext" is a form of software, available for all major types of computers, that allows "non-programmers" (i.e. teachers) to create with relative ease software that incorporates feedback, testing, branching and many more advanced features. Schools or bureaus will need to train teachers in the basics of software design and "hypertext" technology to allow them to create the new Jewish educational software.

A Final Note

It is painfully obvious that the typical school will not overcome the hurdles of teacher training, equipment acquisition and software development by itself. Partnerships among schools, and partnerships between schools and the private sector must be created to provide a necessary structure for support and direction. Ideally, regional computer centers for Jewish education should be established to enable schools to learn from each other's experiences, exchange ideas and successful projects and even share teacher-developed software. Such has been the successful experience of the Goldman Department and that success can be replicated throughout the country. As has been true throughout Jewish history, alone we are powerless, together we are invincible.

Computers are not a "wonder drug" that will cure the ills and heal the wounds of Jewish education. They cannot transform bad teachers into exemplary educators, nor can they attract the masses of unaffiliated Jews back to our schools. Rather, computers are a uniquely powerful teaching tool that can, given the opportunity, enhance and enrich the Jewish educational experience. Now is the time for action. Whether Jewish education will answer the call is in the hands of our educational and communal leadership.

Bibliography

Balajthy, E., McKeveny, R.; & Lacitignola, (1986-1987, December/January). Microcomputers and the Improvement of Revision Skills. *The Computing Teacher,* 28-31.

Becker, H. J. (1984). *Microcomputers in the Classroom—Dreams and Realities.* Baltimore: Johns Hopkins University, Center for Social Organization of Schools.

Becker, H. J. (1983, April). *Instructional Uses of School Computers: Reports from the 1983 National Survey.* (Issue No. 1). Baltimore: The Johns Hopkins University, Center for Research on Elementary and Middle Schools.

Becker, H.J. (1986, June). *Instructional Uses of School Computers: Reports from the 1985 National Survey.* (Issue No. 1). Center for Research on Elementary and Middle Schools: The Johns Hopkins University.

Becker, H. J. (1986, November). *Instructional Uses of School Computers: Reports from the 1985 National Survey.* (Issue No. 3) Baltimore: The Johns Hopkins University, Center for Research on Elementary and Middle Schools.

Becker, H.J. (1987). *The Impact of Computer Use on Children's Learning: What Research Has Shown and What It Has Not.* (Report No. 18). Baltimore: The Johns Hopkins University, Center for Research on Elementary and Middle Schools.

Billings, K. (1983). *Research on School Computing* in Computers. Curriculum and Instruction. Association for Supervision and Curriculum Development, 12-18

Cohen, M. & Miyake, N. A. (1986). Worldwide Intercultural Network: Exploring Electronic Messaging for Instruction. *Instructional Science, 15,* 257-273.

Daiute, C. (1986, May). Physical and Cognitive Factors in Revising: Insights From Studies With Computers. *Research in Teaching English, 20,* 141-159.

Fisher, G. (1983, November/December). Where CAI is Effective: A Summary of the Research. *Electronic Learning,* 82-84.

Goldman Computer Department. (1990, Fall). Home-School Project. *MicroNews.* Morris and Rose Goldman Computer Department for Jewish Studies of the Associated Talmud Torahs of Chicago, 4(2).

Hunter, B. (1985, May). Problem Solving with Databases. *The Computing Teacher,* 20-27.

Instructor. (1982, May). Computers? You Bet I'm Interested!

Jaskoll, I.L. (1984). Computer Aided Instruction in Jewish Education. *Proceedings of the Fourth Jerusalem Conference on Information Technology* (pp. 414-417). Jerusalem, Israel: Institute of Electrical and Electronics Engineers.

Kulik, J.A. (1983, September). Synthesis of Research on Computer Based Instruction. *Educational Leadership.,* 19-21.

Kulik, J.A., & Kulik, C.C. (1987). Review of recent research literature on computer based instruction. *Contemporary Educational Psychology, 12,* 222-230.

Matanky, L. A. (1986, April). Teacher Developed Courseware for Jewish Education. *Proceedings of the International Conference on Courseware Design and Evaluation* (pp. 309-314). Ramat Gan, Israel: Israel Association for Computers in Education.

Matanky, L.A. (1989a, Spring). The State of Jewish Educational Software. *Ten Da'at.* Torah Education Network, 3(3).

Matanky, L.A. (1989b, Fall). A Guide to Hebrew/English Word Processing. *Ten Da'at.* Torah Education Network, 4(1).

Matanky, L.A. and Friedman, C. (1987). *Catalogue of Electronic Media in Jewish Education: Volume One— Computer Software.* New York:Memorial Foundation for Jewish Culture.

Matanky, L. A. and Hoover, T. (1987, April). Histalmuyot Morim La'avodah B'siyuah Machshev. *Machshevim B'chinuch, 3.* 12-15.

McClelland, J. (1986, Spring). A New Twist on an Old Skill: Retrieving Information With Computers to Enhance Decision-Making Processes. *Computers in the Schools, 3*(1).

McLaughlin, W.W. and Marsh, D.D. (1978). Staff Development and School Change. *Staff Development,* 69-74.

National Education Association. (1982). A Teacher Survey NEA Report: Computers in the Classroom, Washington, D.C.

Neill, S.B. and Neill, G.W. (1989). Only the Best. *Education News Service Special Report.* New York: R.R. Bowker Company.

Office of Technology Assessment of the U.S. Congress. (1988). *Power On! New Tools for Teaching and Learning.* Washthington, DC: U.S. Government Printing Office.

Okey, J.R. (1985, April). *The Effectiveness of Computer Based Education: A Review.* Paper presented at the annual meeting of the National Association for Research in Science Teaching, French Lick Springs, IN. (ERIC Document Reproduction Service ED 257 677).

Phi Delta Kappa. (1982). Practical Application of Research. *Phi Delta Kappa Center for Evaluation, Development and Research.* Bloomington, Indiana, 4(4).

Roblyer, M.D., Castine, W.H., & King, F.J. (1988). Assessing the Impact of Computer Based Instruction: A Review of Recent Research. *Computers in the Schools, 5*(3,4).

Rosenbaum, I.J. (1988). Application of Computers in Jewish Life. *Encyclopedia Judaica 1988 Yearbook.* 112-117.

Schiffman, S. S. (1986, May). Productivity Tools for the Classroom. *The Computing Teacher,* 27-31.

Solow, M. (1985). *An Overview of the Relationship Between Computers and Jewish Education: A Solution in Search of a Problem.* Report to the L.A. Pincus Jewish Education Fund for the Diaspora, Joint Program for Jewish Education. Jerusalem.

Stechner, B.M. & Solorzamo, R.S. (1987). *Characteristics of Effective Computer In-service Programs.* Pasadena, CA.: Educational Testing Service

Taylor, R. (Ed.). (1980). *The Computer in the School: Tutor, Tool, Tutee.* New York: Teachers College Press.

Turner, J.A. (1987, April 29). Microcomputer Found More Available—and More Often Required—at Selective Colleges. *Chronicle of Higher Education, 33,* 14-17.

Ukeles, J.B. (1986). *The New Technology: Strategies for Enhancing Jewish Education.* Report to the Memorial Foundation for Jewish Culture. New York.

Wetzel, K. (1985, June). Keyboarding Skills: Elementary, My Dear Teacher? *The Computing Teacher,* 15-19.

Winer, D. (1988). An Educational Microcomputer Network between Jewish Centers in Israel and the Diaspora. *P. Sapir Regional College of the Negev, Israel.*

Winkler, J.D., Stasz, C. &Shavelson, R. (1986, July). *Administrative Policies for Increasing the Use of Microcomputers in Instruction.* Los Angeles: Rand Corporation.

Yin, R.K. & White, J.L. (1984, March). *Microcomputer Implementation in Schools.* Washington, DC: COSMOS Corporation.

Highlights

* Computers in Jewish schools share the same advantages as described in the general literature with two noticeable differences: the need to narrow the "sophistication gap" and the minimal quality and quantity of software available.
* Learning can be enhanced through drills or tutorials (CAI).

* "Tool applications" (such as databases) have had a tremendous impact upon scholarship. An example of this is the Bar-Ilan Responsa Project containing over 250 volumes of rabbinic responsa available through a telecommunications network
* Word processing is just now being introduced to Jewish schools.
* Telecommunications is just in its infancy.
* The single variable with the greatest impact on success of microcomputers remains the classroom teacher—the key factor in change is in-service training with suitable/appropriate incentives and rewards

The Larger Context

Notwithstanding the necessity to stimulate, motivate, and train teachers to use these machines, and the fact that equipment must be available and new software developed, the evidence is not yet conclusive enough for an adequate answer to Dr. Matanky's original question, "Do computers work?" It seems as if we, like those in secular education, are being pulled by some force into the computer world by sheer dint of power and even magic, while our tradition has taught us to deliberate. On the positive side, the notion of *'shakla vetarya'*, give-and-take in *hevruta*, may indeed be enhanced by going on-line, as it were. Isolation need not be a consequence of technology—it may just be that we are still in the throes of figuring out how to educate via the computer. In a different but related arena, the introduction of computers into supplementary schools presents additional challenges.

What We Know About...Evaluation

Ron Reynolds

A word commonly used by professionals and laity alike is evaluation. Dr. Reynolds, who is Director of School Services at the Bureau of Jewish Education in Greater Los Angeles, takes us on a wonderful review of the literature of evaluation, discussing definitions, goals and the difference between program and teacher evaluations.

WE KNOW THAT EVERYONE EVALUATES. WE CONSTANTLY EVALUATE THE COMMODITIES WE PURCHASE, the persons with whom we associate, the causes to which we either lend or withhold support, and the myriad information which we consume. Whenever we assess the merits of a person, a product or an idea, we are evaluating.

The participants in your school or educational program constantly evaluate. Administrators, teachers, students, parents and lay leaders continually process information, form opinions and make judgments about virtually everything that transpires within the operational boundaries of their school or program.

This type of evaluation, which I will refer to as "informal evaluation," can and does exert its influence. However, its private, informal and subjective nature generally precludes usefulness as a deliberate tool for decision-making, policy development and programmatic improvement.

What is Evaluation?

Evaluators seem to be fond of disagreeing with one another...even regarding the essential nature of evaluation. Some understand evaluation as a formal assessment of the merit or worth of some educational phenomenon (Scriven, 1967; Popham, 1975; Eisner, 1979). Others regard evaluation as a process designed to foster decision-making (Weiss, 1972; Alkin, 1969; Patton, 1978). Yet others view evaluation as an activity designed to ensure the compliance and accountability of organizational subordinates (Dornbusch and Scott, 1975). A number of evaluation researchers have created classification systems which attempt to describe and relate the various approaches to understanding and practicing evaluation (Popham, 1975; Stake, 1976; House, 1980; Guba and Lincoln, 1981).

I believe that there is a common thread to each of these understandings of evaluation. Carol Weiss expressed it cogently: "The basic rationale for evaluation is that it provides information for action" (1972).

Does Evaluation Make a Difference?

Is evaluation useful? Certainly. Are evaluation findings used? More often than not...no. Patton (1978) and Alkin et al., (1979) each conducted studies of evaluation *utilization*. They began by observing that whereas schools and other organizations frequently conducted evaluations, the evaluations typically had little effect upon the programs and/or practices under consideration. Both studies then attempted to identify the factors which contributed to the utilization or non-utilization of evaluation findings. Alkin identified a number of factors which include evaluator credibility, organizational factors, administrator style, information content and reporting, and the evaluator's approach, among others. Patton singles out what he terms "The Personal Factor" as the key to an evaluation's potential to make a difference.

> The personal factor refers to the presence of an identifiable individual or group of people who personally cared about the evaluation and the information it generated. Where such a person or group was present, evaluations were used; where the personal factor was absent, there was a correspondingly marked absence of evaluation impact. The personal factor represents the leadership, interest, enthusiasm, determination, commitment, aggressiveness, and caring of specific, individual people. In terms of power of evaluation...these are the people who are actively seeking information to reduce decision uncertainties so as to increase their ability to predict the outcomes of programmatic activity and enhance their own discretion as decisionmakers. These are the users of evaluation...(1978, p.64)

Who Should Conduct an Evaluation?

What characteristics and qualities does a good evaluator possess? Should evaluations be conducted by professionals or amateurs...by "in-house" staff and/or lay leadership or by some external person(s)? These questions are discussed extensively in the evaluation literature (e.g. Stufflebeam, et al., 1971; Scriven, 1967 and 1975; Worthen,1975; Cronbach et al., 1980). According to these writings, a good evaluator should possess a variety of technical skills, must be good with people, should have a keen grasp of group dynamics and organizational functioning, should be ever-sensitive to political pitfalls and should conduct his/her business in an ethical, practical, trust-engendering manner. At last count, there were three known persons in the Western Hemisphere possessing these such attributes!

Guba and Lincoln (1981) developed the term "stakeholders" to refer to those persons and groups who are likely to be affected by the conduct, findings and utilization of an evaluation. In a school setting, stakeholder groups may include administrators, lay leaders, teachers, parents, students and others. Keeping the "personal factor" in mind, it is a commendable practice to involve, and thus to invest, appropriate members of the various stakeholder groups in the organization and conduct of an evaluation. Such persons are often organized as an "evaluation team" whose work is facilitated by an individual (internal or external to the school/program) possessing some degree of training and experience in the conduct of evaluation.

Goal-based, or Goal-free Evaluation?

Many people, lay and professional alike, understand (program) evaluation as an attempt to determine how well or how poorly a program accomplishes its goals. A number of prominent evaluators, however, caution against an over-reliance upon program goals as yardsticks against which evaluative judgments are to be made. They warn that over-attentiveness to the formal goals of a program can divert the attention of the evaluator away from an assortment of unanticipated outcomes and programmatic "side-effects."

To avoid this problem, Scriven (1972) suggests the use of "goal-free evaluation." In this approach, an evaluation is conducted by a person who possesses no knowledge of the goals of the program being evaluated. In this manner, the evaluator escapes the potential "tunnel vision" produced by focusing exclusively upon a program's stated goals. This type of evaluation is often a useful means of providing a rich, relatively objective *description* of a program or practice. It is sometimes used as an adjunct to other forms of evaluation.

Michael Quinn Patton (1978) provides another sort of caution concerning goals. He writes of an endless game played between evaluators and program staff, the object of which is to produce a neat set of goals which are stated in terms of measurable and/or observable behaviors. The evaluator constantly pushes for greater clarity and specificity. The staff resists, resorting to a variety of ingenious ploys. In the end, both sides are frustrated, and the evaluator will proceed upon his/her personal understanding of the program's goals. Rather than to suggest that evaluators give up on goals, he advises that it is helpful to approach goals clarification at three levels: the overall mission of a program, the goals of specific programmatic units, and the specific objectives which specify client (learner) outcomes.

For a concluding word on the problem of goals, I refer to my own research (Reynolds, 1982) in which I explored various functions performed by goals which are stated in very clear and specific terms, and goals which are stated in very ambiguous, "fuzzy" terms. I found that many Jewish schools stated their (Jewish) educational goals in very general language, such as "The goal of our school is to imbue each child with a deep sense of love and appreciation for the treasures of the Jewish heritage," or "Our goal is to nurture a positive sense of Jewish identity".

There is nothing inherently wrong with goal statements which are stated in such general terms. In fact, "fuzzy" goals can perform several important functions for a school. Vague and/or ambiguous goals appeal to a broader number of potential participants and therefore serve as an effective marketing device. Also, precisely because they are so vague, they succeed in eliciting apparent support from the vast majority of actual participants, and thereby serve as a conflict-management device.

Problems arise, however, when schools fail to spell out what is meant by "positive Jewish identity" and exactly how it is to be "nurtured". Many Jewish schools fail to reach a degree of goal specificity which is helpful, if not necessary for curriculum development, instructional guidance and the conduct of evaluation.

How Should an Evaluation be Conducted?

Most evaluators agree that *there is no one best way to conduct an evaluation.* One reason why this is so derives from the difference between *evaluation* and *research* (Alkin, 1979). The purpose of research is to discover knowledge of a general nature, while evaluation's focus is case-specific. The findings of an evaluation need not be generalizable. If I am a school board chairperson wishing to evaluate a Hebrew language program, I don't care whether the program works in *other* schools, with *other* teachers and *other* students. I want to know whether the program works in *my* school, and what might be done to reap maximum benefit from it. Because each school and program is a unique composite of people, history, politics, and resources, no two evaluations will or should be exactly alike.

Still, most evaluations consist of the following activities:

1. Determining who will conduct the evaluation/organizing relevant decisionmakers and information-users

2. Deciding which questions will be addressed by the evaluation

3. Determining what information must be collected—from whom, in which form, and when—in order to answer the question(s)

4. Deciding how the information to be collected will be organized, analyzed and utilized

5. Organizing the presentation of the evaluation findings

Of these activities, the task of *focusing the evaluation question(s)* may well be the most difficult, as well as the most important. Patton (1978) devotes considerable attention to this problem, providing a checklist of characteristics which characterize good evaluation questions (i.e. focal questions which tend to increase the utilization-potential of an evaluation):

1. It is possible to bring data to bear on the question.

2. There is more than one possible answer to the question, i.e. the answer is not predetermined by the phrasing of the question.

3. The identified decisionmakers *want* information to help answer the question.

4. The identified decisionmakers feel they *need* information to help them answer the question.

5. The identified and organized decisionmakers and information users want to answer the question for themselves, not just for someone else.

6. They care about the answer to the question.

7. The decisionmakers can indicate how they would use the answer to the question; i.e., they can specify the relevance of an answer to the question for future action.

The last consideration deserves additional emphasis. If the members of an evaluation team cannot clearly identify how answering an evaluation question will empower specific actions or policies, the utilization potential of the evaluation will tend to be low. Evaluators should also be clear about the *formative* or *summative* nature of an evaluation (Scriven,1967). Formative evaluation is conducted on programs that are still capable of being modified for the purpose of improving, adapting and fine-tuning program components. Summative evaluation is conducted on completed programs for the purpose of facilitating decisions regarding whether to adopt or retain a program. When decision-makers perform a summative evaluation on programs still in formation, they are likely to draw premature conclusions about such programs' merits.

Knowing who should collect what information from whom, in what form and at which time(s) is a perplexing matter. Knowing just what to do with such information once it has been collected can be even more perplexing. Many a well-intended evaluation has come to an untimely conclusion as the evaluation team sat around a table, staring at a pile of data and wondering what to do with it. In the absence of expert facilitation, Lynn Lyons Morris (1978) provides sound and practical guidelines governing the collection, organization, analysis and presentation of information.

Teacher Evaluation

One of the most meaningful, if non-remunerative, rewards associated with teaching, comes with the knowledge that students have learned, have grown, have been touched by a competent and caring instructor. Yet many teachers report difficulty in knowing just how well they are doing (Lortie, 1975; Ashton, et al., 1983). Such teacher uncertainty often stems from the absence of clear guidelines concerning what is to be taught, as well as the absence of specific criteria upon which teacher performance is to be evaluated. Natriello and Dornbusch (1980-81) found that teachers who report being unaware of the criteria used to evaluate them not only tend to be strongly dissatisfied, but are unable to direct their energies toward improvement. More striking is their finding that receipt of *negative* evaluation is unrelated to teacher satisfaction. A number of studies (e.g. Chapman and Lowther, 1982; Azumi and Madhere, 1983; and Dornbusch and Scott, 1975) demonstrate that regular teacher evaluation based upon shared criteria, are strongly associated with teacher satisfaction.

Given that teacher evaluation is important, what is the best means of doing so? Popham (1975) provides a concise review and critique of the prevailing approaches to this perplexing task. The most frequently-used methods of teacher evaluation are rating scales and systematic observation. These consist of observers entering classrooms armed with lists of (desirable) teacher behaviors. The observers place check marks on the forms which either signify that a particular behavior—such as praising students, or asking questions—took place, or which rate the skill or quality of various teacher behaviors. These are the most popular approaches to teacher evaluation, not because they provide the most valid and reliable picture, but because they take the least time and are the simplest procedures to administer.

The problem with these and other approaches to teacher evaluation, is that there is no one best way to be an effective teacher. Where did the behaviors which appear on the rating scales and systematic observation forms come from? The answer is: they came from research studies which endeavored to identify traits, characteristics and behaviors which were common to teachers identified as highly effective. The difficulty here is that tendency type studies are used to make judgments about the effectiveness of individuals.

McGreal (1983) offers a useful method of teacher evaluation which is sensitive to local context, is improvement-focused and regards goal setting as the major activity of evaluation.

Evaluation in Jewish Education

There is scarcely a literature of evaluation in Jewish education. Pollak (1983) reviewed 52 North American doctoral dissertations written between 1975 and 1982 which focused major attention upon issues relating to Jewish education. Of these, none dealt specifically with evaluation. A number of studies *have* attempted to evaluate the effectiveness of Jewish education in general (Himmelfarb, 1974; Bock,1976), or the effectiveness of a certain *type* of school or program (Schoem,1979; Reynolds,1982; Heilman,1983; New York Board of Jewish Education,1988). Other studies examine general *attitudes* about or perceptions of Jewish education (Kapel,1972; Pollack and Lang,1983; Kelman,1984). These are research studies and offer little in the way of practical assistance to school decision-makers wishing to evaluate particular programs, practices or personnel.

There is a smattering of articles about evaluation to be found in the various English language Jewish education journals, as well as in a limited number of books published during the course of the past two decades. The articles address issues relating to the evaluation of teachers (Hakimian,1982; Solovy and Finesilver, 1985), curriculum (Ackerman, 1980), pupil achievement (Latham,1981; Lowy,1983), staff development programs (Gladstein, 1989), program evaluation and development (Reynolds,1983; Shevitz, 1985), and planned change (Cohen and Lukinsky,1981; Bank,1985). While such articles are well written and interesting, they are not numerous enough to provide a cumulative record of experience or body of knowledge which substantially deepens our understanding or enhances our practice of evaluation in Jewish education.

Evaluation remains a critically underdeveloped and thus underutilized practice in the field of Jewish education. Intensive courses of study focusing upon evaluation theory and practice are conspicuously absent from Jewish teacher and educator training institutions in North America. The handful of Jewish educators who have received formal training in the conduct of evaluation are likely to be products of secular teacher-training programs and graduate schools of education. These institutions generally prepare their students for careers in formal school settings operating in public education systems. Thus, even those possessing formal training are often ill equipped to evaluate much of what we consider basic to our religious educational programs: spiritual development, identification with the Jewish people and Israel, *mentschlichkeit,* etc. As Adrianne Bank, a respected evaluator with many years of experience in the public sector, has cautioned, "Jewish schools and programs cannot be evaluated in the same way as general education schools and programs" (Bank,1988).

The absence of in-depth training in evaluation practices specifically suited to the complexities of Jewish education has produced predictable results. Well-intentioned educators and lay leaders frequently initiate evaluations which often do more harm than good...creating or heightening organizational stress and tension, factionalizing stakeholder groups, and sapping time, effort, and money while all too often providing little information which is of clear and direct use to decision-makers.

Conclusion

What we know about evaluation in Jewish education is that we don't know very much. We don't know much because we don't *do* much. Consequently, we have little experience upon which we can reflect and from which we can learn.

We are thus left in the throes of a *Catch-22.* If we are to solve this conundrum, lay leaders and professionals must resolve to practice evaluation and to reflect upon their practice. Organizations such as JESNA, local central agencies for Jewish Education, Jewish colleges and universities, the Education Departments of the ideological movements, CAJE, and others may then link together those who have used evaluation to try to answer common questions. In this way, experience may be pooled, the beginnings of a knowledge base may be developed, and a good deal of practical wisdom may be accumulated. In the well-known words of Rabbi Tarfon "It is not incumbent upon us to complete the task...neither are we free to desist from it."

Bibliography

Ackerman, W.I. (1980). Toward a History of The Curriculum of the Conservative Congregational School, Part I. *Jewish Education, 48*(1), 19-26.

Ackerman, W.I. (1980).Toward a History of the Curriculum of the Conservative Congregational School, Part II. *Jewish Education, 48*(2), 12-20.

Alkin, M. C.(1969).Evaluation Theory Development. Evaluation Comment. *The Journal of Educational Evaluation.* 2. 2-7.

Alkin, M. C.,Daillak, R. & White, P. (1979). *Using Evaluations.* Beverly Hills, CA: Sage Publications.

Ashton, P. T., Webb, R.B. & Doda,N. (1983). *A Study of Teachers' Sense of Efficacy: Final Report.* Gainesville: University of Florida, Foundations of Education.

Azumi, J. E., & Madhere, S. (1983, April). *Professionalism, Power and Performance: The Relationships between Administrative Control, Teacher Conformity, and Student Achievement.* Paper presented at the Annual Meeting of the American Educational Research Association, Montreal.

Bank, A. (1985, Spring). Evaluation and Accountability in Jewish Education: The Case of the Los Angeles BJE Review. *Jewish Education, 53*(1),20-32.

Bank, A. (1988). Evaluation: Is It Good For Jewish Education? In Aviad, J. (Ed.), *Studies in Jewish Education Vol. 3,* Jerusalem: Magnes Press, 116-133.

Board of Jewish Education of Greater New York. (1988). *Jewish Supplementary Schooling: An Educational System in Need of Change.* New York.

Bock, G. E. (1976). *The Jewish Schooling of American Jews: A Study of Non-Cognitive Effects.* Unpublished doctoral dissertation, Harvard University, Cambridge, MA.

Chapman, D. W. & Lowther, M.A. (1982). Teachers' Satisfaction with Teaching. *Journal of Educational Research, 75*(4), 240-47.

Cohen, B. and Lukinsky, J. (1981, Spring). The Evaluator as a Change Agent. *Jewish Education, 49*(1), 4-9.

Cronbach, L. J., et al. (1980). *Toward Reform of Program Evaluation.* San Francisco: Jossey-Bass.

Dornbusch, S.M. and Scott, W.R. (1975). *Evaluation and the Exercise of Authority.* San Francisco: Jossey-Bass.

Eisner, E.W.(1979). *The Educational Imagination.* New York: Macmillan.

Gladstein, S. (1989, October). Teacher Evaluation: School Values and Staff Development.*Pedagogic Reporter, 40*(2), 32-34.

Guba, E. and Lincoln, Y.S. (1981). *Effective Evaluation.* San Francisco: Jossey-Bass.

Hakimian, L. (1982, October). Teacher Evaluation. *Pedagogic Reporter, 33*(4), 33-34.

Heilman, S. (1983). *Inside the Jewish School: A Study of the Cultural Setting for Jewish Education.* New York: American Jewish Committee.

Himmelfarb, H. (1974).*The Impact of Religious Schooling: The Effects of Jewish Education upon Adult Religious Involvement.* Unpublished doctoral dissertation, University of Chicago.

House, E. R. (1980). *Evaluating With Validity.* Beverly Hills, CA: Sage Publications.

Kapel, D. E. (Spring, 1972). Parental Views of a Jewish Day School. *Jewish Education, 41*(3), 28-38.

Kelman, S. (1984). Why Parents Send Their Children to Non-Orthodox Jewish Day Schools: A Study of Motivations and Goals. In Rosenak, M. (Ed.), *Studies in Jewish Education, Vol. II.* Jerusalem: Magnes Press.

Latham, L. (1981). Telling Tales Out of School: Student Evaluation. In Marcus, A.F. (Ed.), *The Jewish Teachers Handbook, Volume II.* Denver: Alternatives in Religious Education. 129-140.

Lewy, A. (1983). *Basic Jewish Knowledge in Jewish Education: Evaluation of Goals and Contents.* Tel Aviv: The Israel-Diaspora Institute.

Lortie, D.C. (1975) *Schoolteacher: A Sociological Study,* Chicago: University of Chicago Press.

McGreal, T. L. (1983). *Successful Teacher Evaluation.* Alexandria, VA: Association for Supervision and Curriculum Development.

Morris, L.L. (Ed.)(1978). *Program Evaluation Kit.* Beverly Hills, CA: Sage Publications.

Natriello, G. and Dornbusch, S.M. (1980-81). Pitfalls in the Evaluation of Teachers by Principals. *Administrator's Notebook, 29*(6).

Patton, M.Q. (1978). *Utilization-Focused Evaluation.* Beverly Hills, CA: Sage Publications.

Pollack, G. (1983). *Doctoral Dissertations in Jewish Education 1975-1982.* New York: Jewish Education Service of North America Research and Information Bulletin, (53).

Pollack, G. and Lang, G. (1983). *Perceptions of Jewish Education.* New York: Jewish Education Service of North America Research and Information Bulletin, (55).

Popham, W.J. (1975). *Educational Evaluation.* Englewood Cliffs,NJ: Prentice Hall.

Reynolds, R.L. (1983). Program Evaluation. In Marcus, A.F. and Zwerin, R. (Eds.), *The Jewish Principals Handbook.* Denver: Alternatives in Religious Education, pp. 385-402.

Reynolds, R.L. (1982). *Organizational Goals and Effectiveness: The Function of Goal Ambiguity in Jewish Congregational Afternoon Schools.* Unpublished doctoral dissertation, University of California, Los Angeles.

Schoem, D. (1979). *Ethnic Survival in America:An Ethnography of a Jewish Afternoon School.* Unpublished doctoral dissertation, University of California, Berkeley.

Scriven, M. (1967). The Methodology of Evaluation. In R.E.Stake (Ed.), *AERA Monograph Series on Evaluation, No.1.* Chicago: Rand McNally.

Scriven, M. (Dec. 1972). Pros and Cons About Goal-Free Evaluation. *Evaluation Comment: The Journal of Educational Evaluation.* Los Angeles:Center for the Study of Evaluation, UCLA. *3*(4). 1-7.

Scriven, M. (1975). *Evaluation Bias and Its Control.* Occasional paper No. 4. Kalamazoo, MI: Western Michigan University.

Shevitz, S.L. (1985, Sept.). Evaluation: A Tool for Program Development. *Pedagogic Reporter, 36*(3), 10-13.

Solovy, D.K., and Finesilver, M. (1985, Sept.). Evaluation Techniques for the Jewish Classroom. *Pedagogic Reporter, 36*(3), 14-16.

Stake, R. E. (1976). *Evaluating Educational Programmes: The Need and the Response.* Washington, D.C.: OECD Publications Center.

Stufflebeam, D.L. & Madaus, G.F. (Eds.). (1971). *Educational Evaluation and Decisionmaking.* Itasca, IL: Peacock.

Weiss, C.H., (1972). *Evaluating Action Programs.* Boston: Allyn and Bacon, Inc.

Worthen, B.R.(1975). Competencies for Educational Research and Evaluation. *Educational Researcher, 4*(1), 13-16.

Highlights

* The common thread of all definitions for evaluation is that evaluation provides information for action.
* Evaluator credibility, organizational factors, administrator style, information content and reporting, and the evaluator's approach all have been identified as factors influencing the utilization of evaluation reports; but the "personal factor" (an individual or group who personally cares about the project) seems to be the key.
* Stakeholders and a good evaluator are part of a team.
* Both goal-based and goal-free evaluation are possible.

* Many Jewish schools state their goals in very ambiguous, "fuzzy" terms, and because they are so, they succeed in eliciting support from the vast majority of actual participants, and thereby serve as a conflict-management device.
* There is no one best way to conduct an evaluation either for schools or for teachers.
* Jewish schools and programs cannot be evaluated in the same way as general education schools and programs.

The Larger Context

Accountability and evaluation are current buzzwords in the American Jewish community. Yet, what we know about the conduct of evaluation seems primitive given the frequent and adamant usage of these words in our discourse. The fact that there is no "one best way" ought not prevent us from conducting evaluations.

Appendix

Inside the Jewish School
Samuel Heilman

Tzimtzum: A Mystic Model for Contemporary Leadership
Eugene Borowitz

Inside the Jewish School

Samuel Heilman

This report, originally commissioned and published by the American Jewish Committee and reprinted here with permission, has become one of the seminal research pieces on Jewish education. Many of Dr. Heilman's findings illustrate the theme of dissonance between parents, children, and teachers—and yet reflect the community in which we live. Dr. Heilman is Professor of Sociology at Queens College of the City of New York.

THERE IS A STORY ABOUT A LEARNED MAN WHO CAME TO VISIT A REBBE. THE SCHOLAR WAS NO LONGER young—he was close to thirty—but he had never before visited a rebbe. "What have you done all your life?" the master asked him. "I have gone through the whole of the Talmud three times," answered the learned man. "Yes," replied the rebbe and then inquired, "but how much of the Talmud has gone through you?"

Much concern about and research on Jewish education has focused on how successful our schools have been in getting students to go through the Talmud and other Jewish texts. To be sure, the content of Jewish learning is fundamental, since no amount of feeling, however deep or sincere, can take the place of knowledge and Jewish literacy. Moreover, few Jewish educators would argue over what constitutes the basic corpus of information that should be passed on to students. Nevertheless, while we are interested in whether or not our students go through the traditional texts and cover the lesson plans, we are also concerned about the extent to which these texts and all they signify manage to get through *to* them, to penetrate their consciousness and character, their environment and culture.

The Method

Unlike other researchers in the field who have focused on matters of pedagogy, curriculum, administration or educational philosophy, I have, as a social anthropologist and ethnographer, concentrated on the social environment and culture inside the Jewish school. By entering into the school as neither teacher nor administrator nor student nor parent, I have spent my time watching in order to discover what constitutes normalness, to expose the taken-for-granted life as it unfolds within the institution. For it is the normal rather than the exotic that reflects and reveals the inner character of life as experienced by insiders. Throughout, I have concentrated not so much on what is learned but on how it gets through and what impact it has.

This technique, often referred to as "seeing things from the actor's point of view" allows a level of interpretive understanding that is not normally available with other methods of research. It makes it possible to share moods and motivations with those one is studying and renders their behavior less opaque.

Yet, even the most empathic understanding is not enough, for all insiders presumably have that. The professional social scientist brings an additional element of interpretation to the enterprise. He or she can look upon the inhabitants of the Jewish school (both staff and students) as if they were members of a small community, expressing the larger Jewish culture of which they are a part. We thereby discover not only what goes on inside the school, but also gain a sense of that school's connection to Jewish peoplehood. As anthropologist Clifford Geertz (1973) has eloquently put it, "seeing heaven in a grain of sand is not a trick only poets can accomplish". Social scientists, too, can see the larger reality by looking intently and with an informed eye at the particular case.

Doing ethnography, trying to decipher the precise character of human behavior in order to describe it and render it comprehensible, is, however, like trying to read "a manuscript—foreign, faded, full of ellipses, incoherencies, suspicious emendations, and tendentious commentaries, but written not in conventionalized graphs of sound but in transient examples of shaped behavior" (Geertz, 1973, p. 10). One immerses oneself in details not for their own sake but rather because they are symbolic expressions of culture, genuine slices of life from which the informed and careful observer may piece together the narrative line of that manuscript we call human culture.

To reach some understanding about the Jewish school and the culture to which it is bound, I spent a total of approximately 100 hours inside three types of schools: an Orthodox day school and two afternoon schools, one Conservative and the other Reform. I attended classes, loitered in the hallways, went to the neighboring shops to watch the students when they "broke away" from the school, and talked informally with people around me. To be sure, this amount of time was far from sufficient for a comprehensive view of any one of these educational settings; but my own native familiarity as both student or teacher in similar institutions as well as my experience as a social anthropologist, enabled me to reach certain tentative conclusions. I add one disclaimer. Having studied Orthodox, Conservative and Reform Jewish schools, I sought to identify trends common to all three. There are, however, important differences among them, which are beyond the scope of this paper.

Culture Tension and Jewish Learning

A underlying assumption of all education, and especially Jewish education, is that "we are, in sum, incomplete or unfinished animals who complete or finish ourselves through culture—and not through culture in general but through highly particular forms of it" (Geertz, 1973, p.449). The classical educational approach emphasizes completion through knowledge. Knowing is the prerequisite to being and doing. Thus, to train students in skills such as reading and writing, to expose them to history and teach them science is not simply the way to introduce them to western culture and its great tradition. It is to civilize and thereby complete them. Applied to Jewish education this approach suggests that to be a complete Jew one must first learn what it is Jews do and have done. In religious terms, one might say that he who would believe must first know.

In fact there may be an alternative: in order to want to learn about what Jews do and have done, to become complete, as it were, one may first have to feel Jewish, to identify with and be committed to Jewish life, people and culture. He who would know must first believe. As the Book of Proverbs (1:7) puts it: "The fear of the Lord is the beginning of knowledge."

If that is the case, what are the indications for Jewish education? First, an appreciation of the role that Jewish learning can play in one's life may be a necessary *prerequisite* to assimilating the material. The absence of strong attachment and commitment, and a concomitant feeling of *cultural tension,* a sense of distance or alienation from Judaism, Jews or Jewish life, will directly and negatively affect the educational process. Those who do not feel bonded to their Judaism and Jewish peoplehood, and even those who feel only marginally attached will to some extent be unwilling and therefore unable to learn. As Avraham Yehoshua Heshel, the rabbi of Apt, once put it when addressing a crowd that had come to hear his teachings: "Those who are to hear will hear even at a distance; those who are not to hear, will not hear no matter how near they come" (Buber, 1948, p.115).

Second, where there is a confusion about the nature of the Jewish life to which one is tied—as when, for example, the teachers embrace one form of Jewish life and the students another, or if each is unclear as to what is demanded of the other as Jews—the learning process, even if technically successful, will be impaired, and so will Jewish identity. Cultural confusion and dissonance stand in the way of Jewish learning, while cultural competence and harmony abet it.

Flooding Out

These general tendencies can be seen in the details of classroom life. Consider, for example, the phenomenon of "flooding out." First a definition. Commonly, in classrooms as in all encounters, "it is proper involvement that generates proper conduct" (Goffman, 1974, p. 346). "During any spate of activity, participants will ordinarily not only obtain a sense of what is going on but will also (in some degree) become spontaneously engrossed, caught up or enthralled" (Goffman, 1974, p. 345). Thus, for example, during a class in Bible, if the students become involved in and comprehend what is going on, the learning will continue without disruption. Under certain circumstances, however, proper involvement is *not* maintained and a break occurs. People talk out of turn, switch into some activity not at all in line with the lesson plan, break into laughter, radically change the subject and so on. Such a disruption may be called "breaking up," a term often associated with the disengagement that comes by way of laughter, or it may be called "flooding out." When someone has flooded out, "he is momentarily 'out of play'" (Goffman, 1961, p. 55).

Flooding out is contagious because involvement is an interlocking obligation. Whatever causes one individual to break his involvement in an ongoing activity, produces in him behavior which causes others to flood out. "Should one participant fail to maintain prescribed attention, other participants are likely to become alive to this fact," and then they either join in or turn their attention to what the break means and what to do about it (Goffman, 1974, p.346). For example, if someone talks out in class, either others join him in the disrupting talk, or else they shush him. In either case, the whole class is removed from their proper involvement. "So one person's impropriety can create improprieties on the part of others" (Goffman, 1974, p. 346). The one who floods out is thus something of a a revolutionary whose actions threaten the steady flow of proper behavior. But why do people flood out?

In his careful consideration of the phenomenon, Erving Goffman has explained that in social settings, "as the tension level increases, so the likelihood of flooding out increases, until the breaking point is reached and flooding out is inevitable" (Goffman, 1974, p. 57). The source of such tension, while often interpersonal or situational, can also be cultural. When, because of their cultural background, participants cannot "get into" or remain involved in what is going on, they break away or flood out. What follows is "either disorder or a new, more manageable definition of the situation" (Goffman, 1974, p.57).

Three Options of Involvement

There are three options of involvement that culturally tense participants may choose. First there is "high involvement." This occurs when students disattend their sense of unease and can therefore become attached and committed to what is being taught. When the teacher is able to charm his class by his pedagogy or personality, when a significant group of other students become involved and the culturally tense student gets caught up with them, or when the occasion simply has an inherent drama which forces the student to forget himself, this may happen.

The student may also pursue the option of "partial involvement," in which he carries on side involvements (doodling, reading something else, passing a note, and so on) while simultaneously remaining somewhat involved in what is going on in class even though he is not completely absorbed by it. Such students represent a real challenge to the teacher for they are potentially still engageable. However, if the teacher does not involve them, they may ultimately be overcome by a sense of tension, and then break out. The note is passed in a disruptive way, or some other open breach occurs. This leads to the last option: "non-involvement". Here flooding out is the rule, where even a side involvement (a conversation with a friend, a request for a drink of water or permission to leave the room and so on) becomes dominant.

These matters are crucial, for it is not unusual to find a third of class time taken up with matters of structuring and maintaining student involvement. Teachers and students frequently spend much time sparring with one another to see who will succeed in determining the focus of involvement. Will it be the lesson plan, or some other plan of disruption and digression? In every setting, with a variety of students and teachers, I witnessed instances of flooding out. Consider some examples:

Example 1: Prayer

The setting is a Conservative afternoon school. The teacher, personally committed to ritual practice, is training his students in *tefila,* prayer. Each one is supposed to recite a line from the *Ashrei* prayer. But the students come from a world where prayer is rarely if ever part of their lives. To immerse themselves in it, even in the artificial setting of a classroom, does not come easily. Cultural tension arises, and even temporary commitments are difficult.

A student raises his hand, apparently to volunteer to recite or perhaps to make an inquiry about the text. The teacher turns toward her. "Shoshana?" "Can I go to the bathroom?"

The shift in focus is abrupt and wrenching. Other students barely conceal their amusement. The teacher realizes he has been had. Any success he may have enjoyed in weaving an atmosphere of prayer is shredded. What should have been a side involvement at best has been turned into the main act. Soon others request their turn—not to recite the prayer, but to go to the bathroom or get drinks. Finally, the focus of activity becomes so blurred that when the teacher calls on a student, the latter, believing it to be his turn to recite, begins to pray only to be stopped by the teacher.

"No, I thought you wanted to go to the bathroom. It's your turn now."

Example 2: Lamentations

Consider a second example in a similar setting. The instructor is about to begin teaching. He has been spending the opening few minutes of the class in friendly banter, waiting for his students to wander in and settle down. There is a warm atmosphere and the observer can see that these students are happy to be in one another's company. The teacher formally begins the class by announcing that today they will begin *Megillat Eicha,* Lamentations. Discovering that none of his students has ever studied this book before, and that they view it as unconnected to their concerns, he nevertheless asks them to open their texts to page 68, on which the first verse appears.

"Did you say 69?" one student calls out, to the amusement of the others. It is a clear effort to break away from the text and its solemnity with a subtle but unmistakable off-color reference drawing attention away from the lesson plan. It is a barely veiled refusal to become engaged by the activity of study.

The teacher ignored the remark, as if believing that if he did not respond, he would be able to continue to manage the situation. He began to explain the meaning of the opening verse, trying to tap the students' capacity to identify with the devastation and mourning the book recounts. But they would not, perhaps could not, become engaged. To know, one must first believe.

One student raised his hand. The teacher had to make a choice. He could ignore the raised hand, assuming it to be a potential disruption. On the other hand, it might be a genuine inquiry which would move the class into a more engaged learning. The teacher looked up and acknowledged the student. "Are you going to give out snacks in this class like you did in my brother's?"

The teacher gambled and lost. The question broke the flow and the teacher would either have to ignore it, risking additional disruptive inquiries from the others, or else answer it and then try to move back to the text and recreate the mood for which he was aiming.

Example 3: Language

A third case. The setting is a day school during an evening "*mishmar*" (all night) class reviewing Talmud. The teacher tried to explain the topic under discussion: the need to be careful, indeed circumspect, in one's use of language. He offers a talmudic illustration, explaining that the Torah takes great care in its use of language, preferring to use more refined terminology whenever possible. So too, he continues, *b'nai torah* (yeshiva students), must pay heed to the way they speak, using only refined language. Coarse language is something he associates with non-Jews and which by implication he wishes his students to view in the same way. "*Shkotzim*" (the incarnation of evil) use dirty words on the street, on the playing fields, even in the supermarket, he explains. Near me I hear a boy whisper to another, "They're not the only ones."

There are smiles and murmurs from the boys. There is not yet an open break, but the observer can sense the building up of tension. Offering illustrations from contemporary life and from his own experience, the teacher either is unaware of the tension or has chosen to overlook it, hoping perhaps to introduce and ultimately engage his students in a Jewish culture different from the one to which they are accustomed. The boys resist the effort.

To charm his class and involve them in this lesson, he recounts a personal experience. When he was in yehsiva, he tells them, he used to drive a truck during summers. At truck stops, he would meet other truckers—naturally they were all Gentiles, he points out. Their language was foul.

"But when I came to the yeshiva I heard how beautifully the boys addressed the rebbe, never directly but only in the third person. Here I first understood what the Torah means when it teaches us to use nice language." The description of a yeshiva is worlds away from the one in which we sit. The cultural tension explodes and the class floods out.

"What did the truckers say?" a student calls out. "Yeah, tell us what they said," another quickly adds. "Did they talk about Preparation H?" asks a third.

It is a clear effort to get the teacher to flood out or at least to break up the other students. And it works; even the teacher smiles.

Quickly, many of the boys began to outdo one another in placing words in the mouths of the truckers and the teacher. Some others, more intent on returning to the Talmud, cried out for quiet, in an apparent effort to help the teacher regain control. In fact of course, *everyone* flooded out and the teacher spent much of the rest of the time trying to bring everyone back to the original focus on the text and its subject.

These are but three of many examples. The situation is familiar to anyone who has spent time inside the Jewish school. The question is: what does it mean?

Cultural Tension

Reviewing the incidents of flooding out that I witnessed as well as those occasions when it did not occur and everyone remained caught up in the learning at hand, I noticed a pattern emerging that involved cultural tension. When the matters being learned or discussed are difficult to assimilate for social, intellectual or cultural reasons; when other options are unavailable, students are likely to flood out. Moreover, those students who have a sense of marginality, who feel a distance from and ambivalence about matters Jewish are are most likely to initiate or enthusiastically participate in flooding out.

Though it occurred everywhere, flooding out seemed more prevalent among those students who were not clear about why they were in school or what their association with Judaism was, than among those who had an unambiguous sense of Jewish identity and a prevailing commitment to Jewish life. Flooding out thus serves as a kind of signal that something is blocking the Jewish learning from getting through to the students. Recall the examples I have cited. In the first, the teacher has been trying to get the students to pray. But prayer, and specifically *mincha* on which he is concentrating, is not comfortable a part of their lives. They have no attachment to what it implies and can therefore not become involved in it. Going to the bathroom, getting the teacher off the track, involvement in us-versus-him play is far more engaging.

In the second case, the teacher is trying to get his class to comprehend and deal with the matter of mourning over the loss of the Temple and Jerusalem. This is not something they can appreciate. Perhaps in the context of a Tisha B'Av commemoration, with the lights low, candles burning and all the other elements of the environment set into place, they might be able to become involved. But here on a weekday evening, smack in the middle of their lives of civil secularity, the matter of mourning over the Temple is "distant" to them in every sense, and flooding out seems the proper response.

Similarly, the importance of speaking in a refined manner, addressing the teacher in the third person, and avoiding coarse language are hard to accept for modern Orthodox students in a day school. As Orthodox Jews, they already perceive themselves as separated from the outside American Gentile world in many unavoidable ways. As modern Orthodox Jews, they seek to be neither remote from nor untouched by the modern world even as they remain committed to the tradition. One of the ways they have learned to play this dual role is by sounding like the Americans/Gentiles around them, even as they remain bound to Orthodox practices and beliefs. To suggest that they must separate themselves in this way as well raises all the ambivalences inherent in Modern Orthodoxy. Flooding out is a way of avoiding the issue.

In my study of modern Orthodox synagogue life, I argued that the ubiquitous gossip and joking—in fact a kind of ongoing flooding out—that is so much a part of shul life, "blocks out—literally as well as symbolically —the possibility of the speakers' having to come to terms with the deeper antinomies inherent in their modernity and Orthodoxy" (Heilman, 1976, p. 309). The same is occurring here. As their parents do in shul, so the children do in school.

Put another way, one might argue that flooding out signals the presence of cultural dissonance. That is not to say that students are aware of the tension. Commonly, they flood out simply because it "feels right," it gets them out of a tight spot.

Mandatory Behavior

There is another key point here. As insiders will attest, flooding out often seems to be mandatory behavior. Even those students who come to class intending to become involved in the lesson soon discover that there are social pressures which encourage them to join in the flooding out. For example, I observed an occasion in which a student was answering all the questions the teacher asked. Throughout he behaved properly, displaying the ideal level of involvement from the pedagogic point of view, while around him the other students were desperately trying to get the teacher and the class to flood out. Proper answers ran against the grain of the occasion.

"Stop getting so involved," one boy finally called out in desperation. "Would you stop being so smart," said another. Embarrassed, the "good" student became silent. It was an extraordinarily graphic illustration of a process which is usually much more subtle. The lesson was not lost on the other students.

In these instances of group pressure there is tacit agreement among the participants to limit their engagement, because all more or less share the same cultural dilemma. Only when there are varying cultural groups in a class do such pressures fail. Thus, for example, in classes where some of the students come from more Jewishly observant homes than others, where a variety of communities are served in the same setting, cleavage occur in levels of classroom involvement—with teachers sometimes playing only to the engaged.

Interestingly, in those day schools and yeshivas where the Jewish curriculum is most emphasized, attitudes toward secular studies reflect a similar pattern of disruption. Thus traditionalist yeshiva boys are more likely to flood out during a lesson in social studies than during a Talmud class (Bullivant, 1975, pp. 388-9).

Indeed, teachers have found ways of coming to terms with the flooding out, perhaps reflecting their own difficulties in becoming engaged too deeply in subjects that their students cannot embrace. The teachers' response is seen in their willingness to move with the flow, to allow digressions as long as the subjects of these digressions do not lead to disruptions and seem in some way associated with Jewish learning. Moreover, those unwilling or unable to "go with the flow," but who remain wedded to their lesson plans even when they do not engage their students, may sometimes maintain decorum, but usually lose all but those students already committed to the material. Hence, the class which started out as a recitation of *mincha* devolved into a march to the bathroom and water fountain. Yet the teacher continued the liturgical recitation while keeping an eye on who went out and who came in. Students were lost in boredom, seeking ways to leave their seats or get the teacher to flood out. The class reviewing Lamentations evolved into a discussion about tenets of Conservative Judaism. Other classes in other schools got on other tracks in the same way. Digressions were the teachers' way of impeding flooding out. A continuous flow of changing activities requiring only the shortest commitments were the best way to get and keep students engaged.

Indeed in one afternoon school, the principal exhibited this very attitude. After he explained that he would have liked all his students to have more intensive Jewish educations and to come from Jewishly committed homes, he concluded that this, alas, was not possible. So his goals had changed: "I am happy if I can get my kids to the point where they are happy to come to school here." A similar attitude was echoed by a day school principal who explained: "The school is *haymish* and we want it to be *haymish* and the kids feel at home here".

The Jewish School as Jewish Home

The principals' stated aims should not be viewed negatively. While from a pessimistic perspective they constitute an admission of pedagogic failure, they may also be considered in more positive terms. What does it mean, after all, that the students "are happy to come to school?"

It is worth recalling that for many contemporary Jewish children, the Hebrew school represents the only environment which celebrates Judaism as a civilization and where they are completely surrounded by other Jews. This is more true for those attending afternoon schools, but it is to a degree true in day schools as well. That is what often tinges the Hebrew school or religious side of the curriculum with an aura of intimacy that some day school students refer to as "*haymish*" or homey. While pursuing the secular curriculum, they are in a more formal environment, surrounded by ideas and echoes of the non-Jewish world. This is true even in day schools since few if any of them integrate the Jewish and secular curricula; compartmentalization is rather the rule.

Thus, the Jewish school and classroom become the last ghetto, an extension of and often a replacement for the Jewish home, a standing contrast to the public school, the secular curriculum. In some ways, Hebrew school is the Jewish cultural analogue of an after-school extra-curricular club. Thus, for example, in preparing the grade point average for college admissions, one of the day schools observed does not average in grades for *chumash* (Bible) and *navi* (Prophets), in spite of the fact that such courses are taught in college and students often seek transfer credits for them. This suggests that two separate worlds are involved in the teaching, and that the world of Jewish studies is, so to speak, off the record. This may make students feel more relaxed and more at home in the Jewish studies environment.

To paraphrase Y. L. Gordon, who urged Jews to "be a man in the street and a Jew in the home," most of the students attending today's Jewish schools are "Men in the streets and Jews in Hebrew school". Indeed, for some parents, particularly those who are marginally concerned with the content of Hebrew school, the major reason for sending their children to the schools (beyond the matter of bar or bat mitzva preparation) is to insure that they maintain contacts with other Jews, that they experience Jewish community.

By and large this goal has been reached. In every setting I observed, even those students who were clearly alienated or at least distant from the content of the curriculum displayed a closeness to their fellow students. Not only during class, when the display of camaraderie might be interpreted as a vehicle for flooding out, but also during breaks and before and after school, the students demonstrated closeness and communion in many ways. They exchanged news about their lives. They shared food with one another and at times with their teachers. They often came to and from school together. Indeed, at times the most important part of coming to school seems to be opportunity to enjoy one another's company, in spite of their commonly experienced feelings of unease with the curriculum, and this explains the otherwise curious fact that students claim to "like Hebrew school" even though they may have little or no interest in what is learned there (Simmel, 1950, pp. 40-57).

Comfort

The homey quality of the Jewish school not only characterizes relationships among students and their peers, but is also found between students and staff. This comes out in a number of ways. First, even when there is boisterousness and "misbehaving" in class, there is a notable absence of overt hostility. Teachers may get irritated and students may feel aggrieved, but both sides manage to overcome these feelings much as everyday conflicts fail to leave lasting trauma on a stable family. There appears to be a tacit agreement that, in spite of all tensions, the basic unity of the group remains intact. No teacher, however harassed, ever evinced the kind of anxiety and fear that public school teachers often experience. To be sure, this may be a product of the middle-class nature of the environment. It may, however, also have a Jewish source, which may be called the "kehilla imperative." This communal bond is of great value for it leaves students with warm feelings for their fellow Jews. And we all know how sorely that has been missed at various times in Jewish history.

If there were nothing also positive emerging from the Jewish school experience than a residual feeling of comfort when one is with other Jews, that might be sufficient reason to perpetuate the institution. It is quite conceivable, moreover, that youngsters who feel at home in the Jewish school will as adults feel more bonded to the Jewish people than their peers who have missed that school experience with its Jewish relationship. And might these sorts of Jews not be the ones best suited to survive in an American Judaism that, on the one hand, retains some vague notions about the value and importance of Jewish life, while on the other is uncomfortable with much of its substance and ambivalent about its demands?

This homey quality of the school has consequences for learning. When students feel at home in the school, their acquisition of knowledge becomes an expression of this feeling, Thus, for example, in the day school it is common to find students independently reciting prayers or reviewing texts because this is a way of displaying their belongingness to the place. And even in the afternoon schools students would refer to matters Jewish (Bible stories, dietary laws, prayer and so on) which they would be unlikely to talk about anywhere else, simply because these students were at home in the school. To be sure, this will only happen if the school injects Jewish content into the homey environment, making clear that the feeling of closeness requires familiarity with Jewish lore.

Surprisingly, flooding out, while signalling cognitive tensions, can sometimes lead to feelings of intimacy because it creates a sudden atmosphere of informality. When the teacher allows himself to get caught up in the flooding out, he can share in the feeling of closeness. Therefore, teachers will sometimes not only join in, but also encourage flooding out.

For example, in one fifth grade I observed, the class was reviewing grammar, going over their workbooks. This was rote learning; the material was excruciatingly boring, and neither teacher nor students seemed engaged by what they were doing. Still, the class was decorous and seemed to get along well with the teacher. He made jokes occasionally, some related to the exercises in the workbook, and some about relationships he had with the children or about sports. In a sense these bracketed remarks, moments when everyone flooded out, were among the most animated periods of the class. It was as if the group truly came to life only when they digressed from—indeed, abandoned—their formal class. They were intimate and warm toward one another, close friends who were, alas, caught up in a task they were not excited about but structurally committed to doing. They did it, therefore, out of a sense of loyalty to the teacher and the formal definition of the situation—but all were happy whenever they could break into something more animating.

On another occasion, after a particularly intense period of learning, a teacher in one afternoon school pre-empted all student efforts at flooding out by organizing a musical chairs game. The exercise itself, virtually an organized pandemonium, had nothing to do with formal learning except that the commands in the game were all given in Hebrew. Yet, if the students did not learn these Hebrew phrases, they surely had a good time playing, and clearly displayed feelings of closeness to one another and to the teacher at the end of the hour.

School as Community

There are other ways in which the Jewish school plays the role of Jewish community. One, already mentioned above, is that cultural attitudes towards Gentiles are easily expressed. The attitudes I heard served to distinguish Jews from Gentiles and celebrate Jewish superiority. Sometimes these contrasts are subtle, as when a Bible teacher associated all the grumbling and discontent among the Israelites with the *"eruv rav"*, the so-called mixed rabble, non-members of the covenant who during the exodus from Egypt joined the Jews. And sometimes the message is far more obvious. I have already noted how the teacher in the day school contrasted refined Jewish behavior with alleged Gentile coarseness. It is interesting to recall how common this practice and its reverse among non-Jews has been throughout history. These contrasts were made on numerous occasions.

Calling students by their Hebrew rather than their English names also stresses Jewish-Gentile differences. It is as if the school and teacher are saying that in the Jewish environment you are someone different, the possessor of a separate identity by which no Gentile knows you and by which no Gentile could be known. Students who fail to respond to their Hebrew names or who do not know them are sometimes locked in subtle but unmistakable struggles with the teacher, and by implication, with their Jewish identities. Thus, one is far more likely to see students called by their given English names in those schools which make only partial Jewish demands on students' involvement or where a sense of Jewish marginality reigns supreme.

Cultural Discovery

Attending a Jewish school is not only an opportunity to share in the experience of Jewish communion. It may also be an experience of cultural discovery and sentimental education during which the child learns what it means to be a Jew—and not simply a Jew in general, but a particular kind of Jew. The latter is the case because schools are often agencies of one or another ideological movement. As the students recite and reiterate their lessons, review and react to what their teachers tell them, speak in Hebrew, perceive the world in Jewish terms, students *and* teachers—at least within the boundaries of their classes—can form and discover their relationship to both their ethnic Jewishness and their religious Judaism.

In afternoon schools the process has largely become an oral tradition. Students simply are not sufficiently competent in Hebrew to read and comprehend texts in the original, so they must depend on translations and the teachers' explications. Informal conversation, questions and answers, and discussion are the primary media of learning. This means that their contact with the sources of Judaism are at best secondary. In the day school, students have a greater facility in Hebrew and can therefore study original texts. Consequently, their study resonates greater authenticity. But even here, culturally bound interpretation of the texts—what, for example, is metaphor and what reality—is an important component of the learning.

Listening to themselves and other students bring the tradition to life—in however limited a way—gives students what for some are their only direct encounters, not just with the texts, but with the substance of Judaism. For many students the Hebrew school and what they learn there disambiguates the fuzzy ideas of what it means to be Jewish.

Sometimes these cultural discoveries occur outside of class. For example, during informal conversations which took place between teachers and students in the break between classes in one afternoon school, I recorded the following 29 Jewish terms which made their way into talk: *minyan* (quorum), *kaddish* (memorial prayer), *shul* (synagogue), *kol boynick* (jack-of-all-trades), *aliya* (call to the Torah reading), *yahrzeit* (anniversary of bereavement), *omud* (synagogue podium), *pasken shaylos* (to adjudicate religio-legal questions), *tsaddik* (righteous man), *meshullach* (charity emmisary), *nedava* (donation pledge), *pilpul* (casuistic argument), *mitzva* (Jewish observance), *minhag* (custom), *shulchan oruch* (a codex of Jewish law), *sefer* (holy book), *shiva* (Jewish seven day mourning period), *shloshim* (Jewish thirty day mourning period), *kichel* (a type of cake), *shalosh seudot* (the three Sabbath meals), *aufruf* (the bridegroom's call to the Torah on the Sabbath before his wedding), *simcha* (joyous occasion), *bris* (circumcision), *tefilin* (phylacteries), *chupe* (wedding canopy). Some of these terms the students knew; others were at first foreign to them and were therefore defined matter-of-factly in the flow of conversation. Their insertion into the informal banter in the halls turned this activity into an occasion for literally speaking in Jewish terms. To speak in these terms, moreover, is to see the world from a Jewish perspective, to evoke, discover and explore Jewish cultural reality.

Example 1: Passover and morality

To see how Judaism is disambiguated and acquired *in class* it is worth reviewing, however, briefly, a strip of classroom activity in which such cultural activity occurs. Consider the following: The class in an afternoon school is reviewing the story of the exodus from Egypt. The students are reading from a translation because they are not versed in biblical Hebrew. They are limited, therefore, to talking about general concepts. One student reads the text aloud, as others follow along. The teacher, as a sort of surrogate for the traditional commentators which are inaccessible in their original, periodically offers glosses to accompany the text. There are references to midrash and Talmud, Rashi commentaries are retold by the teacher, and a variety of other Jewish texts and traditions are cited. Throughout, the teacher structures the learning by asking questions that will elicit from the students the desired, doctrinaire responses. As a result, the students repeat fundamental elements of Jewish tradition, and sometimes tenets of a sectarian form of Judaism: what we Conservative, Reform, or Orthodox Jews believe. It is an indirect but not unsuccessful form of learning.

This approach also allows students to display their "knowledge." Once committed to the action by their displays, they seem more willing to expand that knowledge. But the questions must be carefully framed lest they generate flooding out. And the teacher must be ready to move in the direction of student interest too, which runs the risk of disruption and digression

In the midst of a discussion of the exodus a girl speaks up, recalling her experience with hand-baked matza. Interrupting the teacher's review of the biblical narrative, she asks the reason for such matza. The teacher turns the disruption into a part of the ongoing lesson, explaining that this is called *matza shmura* (specially-guarded Matza). The question and subsequent digression are just as appropriate as the Bible is for the upcoming Passover holy days. The ability to go off on tangents so naturally communicates openness and a relaxed air about the learning. The students are discovering the extent to which digression is build into their Jewish learning experience. At the same time, however, they are learning something substantive about the Jewish tradition. Moreover, one observes here how conversation between students and teachers in the Jewish school takes place against the background of a world that is silently but unmistakably taken for granted. This is precisely the sort of teaching Franz Rosenzweig idealized when he argued that one who desires to tap the spontaneous interests of his students "cannot be a teacher according to a plan; he must be much more and much less, master and at the same time a pupil." And, he concluded, in the encounter between teacher and student, "the discussion should become a conversation…[that] brings people to each other on the basis of what they all have in common—the consciousness, no matter how rudimentary, no matter how obscured or concealed, of being a Jewish human being" (Rosenzweig, 1965, pp. 69-70).

"What's the difference between *matza shmura* and the matza we eat?" the teacher asks, simply continuing the line of conversation begun by her students. "The other has to cook in the sun," the girl shoots back. "No, but technically it should be," the teacher replies. "Can we try that? Take a piece of bread and put it in the sun," a boy asks.

"We can make matza here," the teacher responds, altering the boy's request or perhaps refining it. "What we would be making would be something more like *shmura matza.*"

The teacher is treading carefully here, avoiding the flooding out and the consequent alienation from the activity of learning that is possible. Her control of the situation requires self-confidence and competence in harnessing student interest, rare qualities in teachers. But she is successful, and the students get caught up in the line of discussion that the teacher is able to dominate. They learn about the details of *matza shmura.*

Some of the students seem confused and murmur explanations among themselves. The teacher inserts herself into the discussion almost immediately and goes with the flow. When one girl says that this matza tastes "like cardboard," the teacher quickly agrees. No uncontrolled breaks in the action will occur here. As long as all digressive breaks can be assimilated into the learning, the teacher remains in charge and the class does not break up. An examination of the details of her method is in order. The teacher is plumbing the depths of the exodus story.

"What is Pharaoh like? He keeps saying 'I'll be good, I'll be good' and he's bad. And you have to believe he means he's going to be good. Why does he keep being bad?" the teacher asks, elaborating her question by animating Pharaoh. She tried to make him sound like a contemporary character as she speaks his words in tones and phrases the students would presumably comprehend and even identify with. This is how an ancient tale is made applicable to a contemporary youth. It is an expression of the timelessness of bible stories that they can be thus 'translated'.

"Because when he sees that it works out so well…." one boy begins to say but is interrupted by another who explains: "He continues because there's nothing he can do about it." The students are vying with one another, trying to come up with an answer. They are obviously getting caught up in the lesson. It touches them.

"Well, what is Pharaoh lacking?" the teacher asks. "Oh! responsibility," one boy suggests, as if this long and special word which resonates established moral lessons of childhood will satisfy his teacher. He has clearly identified the situation as an opportunity for a repetition of the classic moral lessons. Some of the students giggle at this—flooding out because they cannot allow themselves to take this all too seriously or because they believe this boy has obviously missed his cue.

Other students continue in the face of the teacher's silence, her non-ratification of his answer. To them, Pharaoh is missing: "Truth". "Brains". "Loyalty? Something like that."

But the teacher is searching for something else. "What keeps you from doing the same thing wrong twice when your mother says not to?" she asks. Again she tries to bring the ancient text into terms the students can understand and through which they can be touched.

"Because my mother smacks me," a boy breaks in, amidst the chuckling of the others. The teacher, moving with the student and thereby trying to avoid his flooding out, responds immediately to his idea, "Okay. God is smacking him and he keeps doing it. What is he missing? He's an evil person and he keeps doing the same evil thing. What is he missing, what feeling? What is he missing?"

"Oh," the boy calls out. He's been captured by the topic and has caught the teacher's drift. He continues: "Conscience". "Conscience," the teacher repeats softly for emphasis. This was what she was looking for. With it she has humanized the character of Pharaoh and perhaps set the stage for the students' empathetic comprehension of the story.

"Yeah, Pharaoh was like Pinocchio," one of the students suggested. he wanted to show he understood, but through the banality of his example could still display a degree of distance from the proceedings. He at least was not ready to be wholly caught up in this discussion. Yet even this somewhat alienated youngster has obviously been stimulated enough to be engaged, albeit in a limited way. It is eloquent testimony to the teacher's masterful performance.

A question from another student, however, is even more impressive for it leads to a further exploration of the underlying theological questions with which the lesson is undeniably concerned. He asks about free choice and destiny, something that has concerned and puzzled commentators for generations. "Why didn't they give him a conscience?"

Asking this question as if it were personal and original of course gives it an urgency far above what it would gain had the teacher expressed it as part of a formal review of some commentary. Moreover, these kinds of students—largely illiterate in Jewish matters—could not even follow such a commentary if it were open before them. Only if the teacher stimulates them to ask these classical questions from out of their own consciousness will they have any meaning to them.

"Because Pharaoh, like all people," the teacher replies, "has free choice as a human being to either be good or bad. Nobody's going to make you be good or bad." The switch from "Pharaoh" to "you" is a subtle one but it cannot help but bring the two characters—the one in the story and the one hearing it—together. The teacher was in a sense being asked to speak in behalf of the Jewish tradition.

"People are responsible for the choices they make. They were given the choice to do right or wrong, and Pharaoh was one of those people who chose to do wrong again and again and again."

The class was silent, apparently satisfied with this response from the teacher.

"I have one last question," the teacher added. "When people read the (story of the) ten plagues at the seder, why do we spill the wine?" She subtly takes for granted a certain degree of cultural competence on her students' part: that they are familiar with and carry out (she says "We spill") this practice. "Is that a symbol of something?" she continues.

"Is that the blood that was given, something like that?" a boy answers. It is a chance to repeat lessons learned, to recite Jewish traditions. "Whose blood?" the teacher asks. "The Egyptians!" "Right. Why are we commemorating the loss of their blood?" "'Cause they're human?" "Right. What happens when they came out of Egypt? What's the first, when they cross the sea, what's the first thing Moses does?" she now asks.

After a few wrong answers, the students finally recall the *Az Yashir,* the song of thanksgiving that Moses offered. The teacher continues:

"Now, what's God's response to *Az Yashir?*" "He liked it; he thinks the Jews are nice," a boy answers, drawing what to him seems to be a logical conclusion and one that the teacher does not agree with but is not prepared to reject completely. "What else?" What's wrong with Moses singing a song of praise to God after 20,000 Egyptians have drowned in an (sic) ocean?"

"Oh, you told us about that. He doesn't like when they're happy cause he killed them, that they're happy that his creatures died."

"Same thing." she now responds, "with the wine. We want to show we agree; we're not completely happy that human beings died."

Suddenly, in the midst of this rather free-wheeling discussion, one boy asked the teacher to tell the story of the time that Moses struck the rock. It was clearly a narrative he and all of the others knew but which he believed deserved retelling in the present context. His request, reaffirmed by some of the other students, called for a cultural performance, an opportunity to reflect, communicate and perpetuate an inherited conception of Jewish tradition. Retelling old stories, already known, as if they were new and fresh is after all the blood and tissue of ritual Jewish learning.

The teacher agreed and retold the story, inserting commentary into the narrative, and bringing the encounter between God and Moses vividly to life. The students listened attentively and at last asked why Moses was punished at all. The teacher, turning the question back to them, elicited at last a response she considered adequate when one boy explained Moses "was losing his trust in God". This turned the conversation toward a consideration of the responsibilities placed upon the righteous man. Hearing the consequences of righteousness, one boy asserted, "then I'd rather not be a righteous man".

"You take a risk," the teacher admitted. Here were moral lessons quietly but undeniably inserted into the digressive flow of a routine class. The classroom is the place where Judaism is discovered and explored, and cultural performance takes place in that *everyone gets to see where everyone else is coming from Jewishly.* To be sure, sometimes such learning is accomplished serendipitously. Sometimes it is segmented and incomplete. but, it can still occur, even if to a far more limited degree than it perhaps once did.

I have reviewed this class at some length for I believe it exemplifies relatively successful Jewish learning. In the day school, the discussion might be more detailed and nuanced. it might refer more often to original texts and commentaries while drawing more deeply from Jewish tradition. The questions and answers might vary in content. But in all cases the basic method of digression and discussion, of a teacher sensitive and responsive to students' interests, is what makes for learning.

Example 2: Conservative philosophy

To be sure, the variety of Jewish perspectives in the classroom do not always lead to a fruitful encounter. As I earlier suggested, when the Jewish world which the teacher takes for granted is not the same one that the students inhabit, the conversation can sometimes undermine Judaism rather than inform and strengthen it. When neither side understands the nature of the Jewish world that the other accepts learning is endangered.

A simple illustration will help. The setting is a Conservative afternoon school. The teacher has just announced to his students: "I'm prepared to discuss any topic if it's presented to me before class or even during class…if you find it in the *Mishneh Torah* (Maimonides, *Code of Jewish Law*)." This is a fairly loose mandate, but it was accepted in the free-wheeling discussions that this class often had about matters of Jewish law. Following some general remarks about definitions of the word "kosher," the teacher was interrupted by one of the students. The speaker, a boy who comes from a mixed marriage (his mother is Vietnamese), asked a question. It began a digression which lasted through the rest of the class hour.

He referred to an article which another teacher in the school had read to the class earlier, one which discussed some principles of Conservative Judaism.

"I learned that the Conservative movement is based on that you take the laws and you weigh them and say what is necessary, what is applicable to today's society, and then you decide that this is what we as Conservative Jews are going to do."

He had hardly finished when the teacher paced to the other side of the room, leaned against the wall and looking furious, replied: "You know me. You know me for two years, maybe longer, okay. And you know my background; you know I'm from the Orthodox world." The teacher continued: "When I hear this, I have very serious questions."

The class was silent; they listened attentively.

"For me, I believe that the Torah is divinely written. *Vezot hatorah asher...*" (This is the Torah which God commanded ...). He let the students complete the verse, which several of them knew. Here was a clear cultural performance, a chance for the students to hear themselves verbally reaffirm and at least partially associate themselves with the traditional belief in divine revelation.

"In other words," the teacher went on, "Moses wrote every letter, as dictated to him by God."

The students remained silent once again; they had, after all, just recited words that according to their teacher asserted this truth, words they were familiar with and which on occasion they recited as part of the liturgy.

Now came an oblique reference to the text they were nominally studying: "And the Rambam (Maimonides) will say when we learn about what is a prophet—we will find that Moses is the father of prophets." The teacher was using this class to insert into his students' consciousnesses a whole variety of little tidbits of information about Judaism and Jewish tradition. But, and it is a big but, the Jewish world which he inhabited and the one they did were not the same one. The conversation took place against two different backgrounds which were not necessarily compatible—that is what made the encounter troubling for the class. When, for example, at one point the teacher remarked that in Conservative Judaism "people pick and choose what they want from religion," he meant it as a criticism. His students responded, "That's right," and clearly understood such a characterization of their brand of Judaism as one of its positive qualities, its flexibility and capacity to meet the particular needs of their lives. Neither side, however, seemed able to perceive the viewpoint of the other. Thus, a number of students left the hour shaking their heads in frustration about their inability to resolve this issue. Afterwards the teacher explained to me: "They just don't understand it at all." In both cases, the frustration expressed was not generated by bad interpersonal relationships between students and teachers; these seemed good by and large. Rather, the frustration was rooted in the cultural contradictions of their situation.

When the teacher concluded his lesson with a kind of Orthodox creedal question and asked "Who, who today in this generation, in the last generation," and now with his voice rising to a crescendo, "in any generation—including the generations of Moses—could stand up and abrogate something that is written in the Torah?" he was at last confronted by a chorus of "no's" from the students who tried, in the words of one, to explain "A Conservative Jew isn't saying that."

Yet as the class went on it was clear that the students were not altogether certain what was demanded of them as Conservative Jews nor was the teacher clear about the nature of the Jewish commitment they were prepared to accept. Each side tried to communicate its attachment to Judaism, but the Judaism to which each felt attached was not the same.

Example 3: The *eruv*

Something similar occured in another class I observed where the teacher, an Orthodox Jew, and his students, marginally Conservative in background and outlook, discussed an *eruv,* the boundary within which certain activities otherwise prohibited may be carried on during the Sabbath. A student had asked *why* an *eruv* was necessary; the teacher responded by explaining *how* an *eruv* works halakhically (according to Judaic law). Neither seemed able to conceive the cultural perspective of the other.

In this case, the cultural backgrounds and Jewish orientations of students and teacher are not different but at odds with one another. Can the Orthodox teacher serve as vehicle for the Reform or Conservative Jewish student's discovery of his and his parents' brand of Judaism? Can a non-Orthodox teacher stimulate Orthodox practice and foster a traditionalist worldview? Yes, but only if the teacher is able to suspend his own conceptions of the world and become sensitive to those of the communities he serves.

Often, though, out of the sincerest of intentions, teachers and students serve unknowingly as agent-provocateurs, trying to undermine one another's cultural assumptions. Thus in one class I observed the students who were non-Orthodox tried to convince their Orthodox teacher of the ludicrousness of a "Shabbat elevator" while he tried to persuade them of the benefits of living within the "four cubits of the *halacha* (law)." And in another, teachers, acting in accord with their day school's policy, instructed their students to pray, but did not do so themselves, thereby communicating at best an indifference to prayer.

The Educator as Part of the Religious Community

These examples and the many others like them illustrate that the teacher cannot always disambiguate the substance of Judaism for his students. It requires more than technical training; it takes cultural competence. "Religion requires a religious community," sociologists Peter Berger and Thomas Luckmann (1967, p.147) argue: "And to live in a religious world requires affiliation with that community." To this one could add that religious education requires that the educator be part of the religious community into which he or she is presumably leading students. When this is not the case, when the Jewish world the teacher and student inhabit are not the same one, and neither can make the leap toward the other, learning is replaced by frustration and cultural continuity by disruption.

This is not only a problem in afternoon schools where the teachers are often Orthodox and the students something else; it can happen in the day school as well. The teachers responsible for secular studies, and sometimes even the principals responsible for that side of the curriculum, are all too often culturally segregated from the Jewish studies side. Or, just as the afternoon schools are forced to draw their teachers from the liberal wing of Orthodoxy, so analogously the day schools sometimes find their teachers drawn from more traditionalist elements.

While the groups nominally subscribe to the same 'Great Jewish tradition', they often overlook, at their own risk, the 'little tradition', the cultural nuances and differences among them and this weakens their schools. It is clear, therefore, that insofar as each wing of American Judaism feels committed to its own interpretations of Judaism, it must accordingly produce its own culturally competent and pedagogically trained teachers. Without a cadre of teachers who share the value systems, worldview, and ethos of the communities they serve, cultural dissonance will continue to be built into even the best classrooms.

In addition, this suggests that students and staff should share community life (and the associated ethos and cosmology) outside of the class as well as in it. In this way the teacher will persuasively play his role as cultural agent, guide into Jewish life. If that community, however, is one which at best is ambivalent about matters Jewish and at worst is indifferent or even hostile to them, then both teacher and students need to share a world which is insulated from the host community. This is precisely what successful Jewish summer camps or yeshivas accomplish by locating themselves far from the homes of their students in environments which force the school to become a cultural island. That is what many prep schools and colleges with their isolated campuses have always done.

Jewish Identity

Critics of Jewish education often argue that the Jewish school does not work. It works. It is a model *of* the Jewish community it serves, a mirror image of what goes on in the Jewish world around the school. And, the Jewish school is a model for Jewish community life, a blueprint, or more precisely a template, that produces Jews who are suited to inhabit and sustain the community. As psychoanalyst Allen Wheelis (1989) has explained: "Every culture creates the characters best fitted to survive in that culture." The Jews are no exception. Thus, each of the schools I observed turns out students who will feel at home in the community, and will in turn give life to that community. The Orthodox day school produces students who can inhabit and sustain the same sort of dualistic and compartmentalized culture their parents lived in, often experiencing the same conflicts and cultural dissonances that their parents do. Similarly, the Conservative and Reform school students display the same confusions about Jewish life that their parents do: on the one hand retaining some vague notion about the value and importance of Jewish education, while on the other expressing discomfort with much of its substance and ambivalent about its demands.

Those critics who argue that Jewish schooling does not succeed really mean, therefore, that it succeeds too well; what they are actually lamenting is that the Jewish community, instead of being altered by the education it provides, perpetuates itself along with all its attendant problems. But how can we expect a school which is not a cultural island to create anything radically different from what exists in the surrounding milieu? To be sure, the school can provide knowledge in place of ignorance, if it has devoted students, a competent staff and a community committed to Jewish education (elements often lamentably missing). But in great measure the Jewish school's aims are not limited to inculcation.

Indeed, one might accurately describe the school's essential goals as enculturation and socialization. While we Jews have always believed that the study of Torah was an invaluable intellectual exercise, we also understood that such regular review would help us keep spiritually in touch with the tradition, allow us to replay the past in the present, and serve to communicate as well as perpetuate the inherited conceptions that define Jewish culture.

Example: Conservative Judaism

To demonstrate how a school may reflect and reinforce the nature of Judaism and Jewish identity which the students and teachers bring to it, I offer an extended and telling illustration.

The teacher, a Conservative rabbinical student, obviously committed to traditional values and norms, was exploring with his students the question of what they believed Conservative Judaism demanded of them. In response to his opening inquiry about the nature of their Jewish identity, all the students characterized themselves as Conservative. He then proceeded to ask them a series of questions about beliefs and practices, to which they would call out answers. Often one or two students spoke for the entire class. If there was agreement, the rest would signal their concurrence with nods, murmurs or silence. In cases of disagreement, two or three students would voice the varieties of opinion for all.

One boy volunteered a definition of himself as a Conservative Jew. "Well, I celebrate most of the holidays and ..." He ran out of things to say. There was apparently nothing more that he could immediately call to mind.

"What makes you different from an Orthodox or a Reform?" the teacher asked.

"Well, I'm not Reform because I go to Hebrew school and I do celebrate the holidays and stuff."

"But so do Reform Jews," one of the other students pointed out, to which the first seemed to have no answer. The distinctions were obviously fuzzy.

The teacher tried to focus their attention. "How many of you can safely say that you can give me a good definition at least of Conservative Judaism?"

A girl tried. "Somebody who is not as strict as Orthodox. Because they go to the Temple on holidays but they—but they don't have to, like, not ride on Shabbat."

"Well, it's just in-between Reform and Orthodox," another suggested.

"Is there anyone who disagrees firmly with that?" the teacher asked. No one did. "So everyone would agree here that Conservative practice is in between Orthodox and Reform? What would you do if I said that that's not true."

"I'd say you lied," one student responded.

"But then all Jews would be the same," another girl broke in. She continued. "There wouldn't be Orthodox, Conservative and Reform. So how would Conservative Jews know if they should be kosher or they shouldn't be kosher?"

The teacher ignored the questions and instead began to list behaviors and beliefs and asked the students whether or not they believe these to be part of the formal definition of Conservative Judaism. He asked them about keeping kosher in the home. Most seemed to agree it was important; a few did not.

"How about observing kashrut when eating out?" he continued. Some said "yes" while the majority called out "no." Still others responded, "Half the time" only to met with a chorus of "no, not at all".

"Being a member of a Conservative synagogue?" Everyone agreed that was crucial to the definition.

"Speaking Hebrew?"

"Well, speaking it but not understanding it," one student said. For most if not all of the others this was a particularly apt way of putting it. "I know how to read it," added one girl (whose earlier performance left some doubts on this score), "but I don't understand it." This was a particularly telling admission to be made in "Hebrew School".

The teacher continued listing such matters as contributing to Jewish charities, observing the Sabbath, lighting Sabbath candles, saying *kiddush* (blessing over wine) and attending Shabbat services, spending time in Israel, making aliya, participating in high holy day services, having a Passover seder, praying every day, and helping the poor or the aged. Throughout, the students gave responses that reflected all of the ambivalences and attitudes of Conservative Jewry. They were for giving charity, having Passover seders and participating in high holy day services; split on the importance of Sabbath observance and kashrut, confused about how important Israel should be in their lives but convinced that they were not expected to move there.

"Remember," the teacher added, "I'm not asking you what you do, just what you think is important for Conservative Judaism." To him there was clearly a useful distinction to be made here, but for the students, as indeed for their parents, the difference between ideology and behavior was minimal. It might not even have been conceivable.

The teacher now asked the students whether or not they believed that maintaining regular Jewish study throughout the rest of their lives was part of the Judaism they practiced. At first the immediate response was a uniform "no".

"Listen to this one: dating only Jewish people," the teacher continued. Here there was some division, with a vocal majority agreeing but a minority saying that it was all right as long as there was no marriage involved.

"What about marrying non-Jewish people?" "No," one boy answered on behalf of the rest, and then another added: "That's very important." No one explained why this prohibition was to be maintained but all had clearly received the message that it was. This stimulated conversation among the students during which some asked others if they would abide by this structure. They all—at least here and now—agreed that they would.

"Do you believe that Conservative Jews should believe that the Torah is the word of God?" the teacher continued. When quite a few said "yes", the teacher remarked, somewhat incredulously, "You believe a Conservative Jew should?" Now the students seemed less sure. A subtle message about the theology of Conservative Judaism, as understood by this teacher, had been passed on to them.

He continued. "Conservative Judaism on the books, what it is ideologically—what it is in written form, so to speak—what it's supposed to be is a lot different from what it is. Now, those of you who raised their hands and said they're Conservative Jews—are all your parents members of a Conservative synagogue?"

As one, the students answered: "yes."

"Then you have a perfect right to say you're a Conservative Jew. But when I tell you—it'll take maybe twenty seconds to tell you what Conservative Judaism demands of people who call themselves Conservative Jews, you'll find that there's a big gap between what it's supposed to be and what it is."

"All right, so what is it?" one of the boys asked. There was silence now, perfect and utter silence for the first time all class.

"According to Conservative Judaism, Conservative Jews are supposed to observe all *halacha* which means they must observe all Jewish law. So you're not allowed to go shopping on Shabbes, according to Jewish law."

There were rumblings of conversation among the students, while the teacher continued. "According to Conservative Judaism you have to abide by all these laws: you have to pray three times a day; you have to go to services—."

"Forget that," one girl said.

"No way," added another.

"So Reform must really be reform, reform, reform," said a boy.

"Now," the teacher continued, "someone tell me what the difference is between that and Orthodoxy."

One girl answered immediately: "Because Orthodox is a lot worse. Orthodox probably says if you don't do it…" The teacher completed the line: "lightning".

The students were not quite prepared for this sort of explanation and moved instead to a description of Orthodoxy that was anchored in specific practices.

"Orthodox have to wear a yarmulke everywhere you go if you're a boy," a girl explained.

"Conservative Judaism doesn't say you have to, but when you're eating, saying any *bracha* (blessing)—most of the day you should have one on," the teacher explained. He continued: "Have you ever seen those *tsitsiyot, arba kanfot*?" (fringes on garments).

"Like Tevya wore?" asked one of the boys, making references to the closest he may have ever come to an image of a traditional Jew.

"Yeah," the teacher answered. The students had seen these. "Well, Conservative Jews have to wear those."

"Oh no!" a boy called out.

"Do you wear them?" asked another, without getting an answer from the teacher.

"Only on Shabbat?" asked a girl, referring to the one day that in her calendar seemed to have been set aside for religious life.

"Every day," answered the teacher.

"Now what's the difference between Conservative and Reform?" he asked.

One boy was ready with an answer. "Reform is more assimilated than Conservative. They don't follow all the rules. You know they're the ones with the Chanukah Bush and all that."

"On the books," the teacher continued, "what is a Reform Jew supposed to do?" There was no ready answer, so the teacher gave one.

"According to Reform Judaism, you must follow all of the moral rules of the Torah," the teacher explained.

"Because you believe in them?" one of the girls asked.

The teacher did not really address this question but went on to suggest that Reform Judaism does require one to carry out the laws between man and man but not between man and God. This meant, for example, that adultery was prohibited but driving on Shabbat was not. From this the teacher concluded: "The Conservative Jews says, 'We have to be concerned about what God cares about;' and the Reform Jew says, 'We have to be concerned about what we do with other men.'"

The students were not quite sure what to make of this. Quite a few had already turned their attention away and were involved in conversations among themselves. They had already begun to flood out. The teacher concluded: "Chaverim, (friends) what I want to leave you with, although not everyone meets up to what Conservative Judaism is supposed to be, that doesn't mean we're not Conservative Jews."

As one listens to this exchange between teacher and students one cannot help but be struck by the extent to which the students reflect the Jewish community from which they come. The teacher has not simply been polling his students about Conservative Judaism, he has also provided them with an opportunity to recite their understanding of these basic tenets. In the process, all the classic values, behaviors and attitudes have been passed on and are reflected and reaffirmed in this classroom encounter. The session is a model of and for Conservative Judaism. It presents and sustains a particular form of Jewish identity. And it appears to work.

To Conclude

The example cited is not unique. In all the settings I observed, the participants found ways of communicating culture and forming Jewish identity. Sometimes there were problems of cultural dissonance created by the varying backgrounds of the participants. But then flooding out often occurred, making it clear that there was a problem. A teacher sensitive to the meaning of such disruptions and willing and able to try again could turn things around. He could digress along with his students, reach out to them, as long as he remained aware of who they were and from whence they came. That is, as long as the teacher was culturally and pedagogically competent and had basic interpersonal skills, he could succeed. To be sure, teachers like that are not easy to find, and once found even harder to keep, considering the meager rewards they receive from the community.

Policy Implications

Commonly, in anthropology, working hypotheses and explanations of behavior are most successful for translating the meaning of human behavior *in situ*. Longer explanations run the risk of drifting into theoretical fantasies because cultural theory—for which anthropology aims—is not strictly speaking predictive. Since, however, the mandate of my research called for some policy recommendations which have emerged as a result of my work and because every field researcher inevitably places his observations and interpretation of action into some overall conceptual framework from which certain conclusions may be refined, I shall close this paper with such comments.

1. Preparation

Certain conclusions seem obvious. I began by arguing that a sense of attachment to being a Jew may precede learning, and that the process of Jewish education may be understood as a form of cultural expression and completion. Therefore, some form of cultural preparation may be necessary before sending children to Hebrew school. This may take the form of enrolling parents and children in Jewish cultural enrichment programs before the beginning of formal instruction so that the entire family comes to feel a more intensive Jewish identity and involvement. Jewish family summer camps, institutes or family preschool programs are some possible vehicles for this.

2. A Shared Jewish Culture

I pointed out that sometimes confusion or ambivalence about cultural matters results in flooding out, breaking away from the substance of learning. I have shown that there are, nevertheless, occasions when successful learning does occur. For such success, I have suggested that teachers and students must share a single Jewish culture, or at least be able to comprehend and even empathize with the ones from which each other come, and teachers should be willing and able to move with the flow of their students' interests. This requires minimally that teachers must be informed about the Jewish world from which their students come. Maximally, this requires a sharing of culture and community. As noted earlier, the most effective way to accomplish this would be to create separate self-contained school communities.

3. Vocation

Simply stated, for the teachers and students to share a controlled learning environment where there is cultural continuity between the world inside of class and the one outside of it, they must have their own input. Before this can happen, though, teachers will have to become endowed with a sense of vocation, the sort that *roshei yeshivot* (heads of yeshivot), camp directors, and prep school dons have. That requires better pay, facilities that can be used to house staff and students, deeper commitments all around, and a fundamental rethinking on the part of American Jews about the sincerity of their interest in Jewish education. If this sounds grandiose, it is. But the stakes, after all, are high.

No one imagines that this will be easy, especially given the modest compensation that teaching in general and Jewish teaching in particular now offers. Salaries and benefits are abysmal, prestige is essentially nonexistent; and a sense of vocation has for all intents and purposes disappeared. As a number of recent studies have documented, only a minority of teachers in Jewish education plan to stay in the profession. In a particularly striking finding George Lebovitz (1981) in a survey of day school teachers, discovered that less than half them planned to be in the same profession five years from now, nearly all those planning to leave were under forty, and 30% of the teachers under forty planned to leave at the first opportunity .

4. School/Home

The problem that teachers and students come from different cultural milieux is compounded by the fact that parents are often only marginally aware of what happens inside the school. This is not to say that they do not receive the information that schools send home via their children or in the mails. But they do not often have an opportunity to share the experience of the school with their children.

One might object, perhaps, that no public school allows the parents to share its experiences with their children. This is true but irrelevant when one realizes that the purpose of the Jewish school, as I have suggested, is to act as a model of and model for Jewish cultural life. And, as I have also noted, for many students in afternoon schools, the institutions represents the only totally Jewish environment in which they regularly participate. What goes on there becomes the embodiment of their Jewishness. Simply stated, "To be a Jew," as one young girl in one of the schools I observed put it, "is to become one who goes to Hebrew school."

If being Jewish is so tied up with the school experience, then it behooves the parents to share that experience. There was a time when Jewish education in the school was an extension of the home and the Jewish community. Now it has largely become a replacement for them. Parents must now join the children in school in order to share in the Jewish experience. As long as Jewish schools are housed within local communities, parents must become part of what goes on inside the classroom. In one Conservative school I observed, just this sort of program had been established, and it succeeded beyond expectations. Not only did many parents attend once a week with their children, but the same children who at other times might not be engaged by the classroom activities become far more involved in learning when their parents learned along with them. To be sure, there must be some generating sense of commitment to get them into the school in the first place, but once they are both there, that commitment can develop and deepen. Students and parents acquire during such joint sessions a capacity for what Bateson (pp.285-6) has called "deutero-learning," learning how to learn. And that is a significant skill for a people who values *"Torah lishma"* (Torah for its own sake) and believes that *"talmud Torah keneged koolam"* (the value of studying Torah outweighs all).

5. Motivation

Another significant problem is that of motivation. In both types of afternoon schools, and, to an extent, in the day school, countervailing curricula confront both students and teachers. On the one hand there is the secular curriculum, with its academic demands and career objectives. On the other is the Jewish curriculum, connected to all intents and purposes with another world. In all the schools I observed there was seldom if ever a continuity between the two. Rather, each implicitly interrupted the domain of the other, and students were forced to choose between them. In the afternoon schools there is a tacit affirmation that the secular curriculum dominates. Hebrew school, as noted earlier, is an after-hours involvement, often competing and sometimes identified with extracurricular activities in the public schools. Commonly, students miss Hebrew school in order to attend some activity at public school. With the exception of missing public school on holy days, the reverse never occurred. On one occasion in one school, two thirds of the class was missing because they were rehearsing a play at the public school. The teacher did not challenge the legitimacy of that excuse for their absence; she simply accepted it as a fact of life. Another time, when the vacations of the Hebrew and public schools did not match, it was taken for granted by students and tacitly accepted by teachers that the students would skip Hebrew school during the public school recess. In a third instance it was understood that students would absent themselves from their Jewish studies in order to prepare for Regents Examinations.

6. Dissonance

The dissonance is undeniable even in the day schools, which value an effort to demonstrate the dominance of Jewish studies by putting them first in the day or scheduling the day to make the students see that each curriculum demands equal time and effort. On rare occasions there is a dialectical interplay between the two curricula, and hence the two traditions. In most cases, however, there is simply compartmentalization. The student moves first to the Jewish tradition, then to the secular one, back again and so on. Recall the fact that *chumash* (Pentateuch) and *navi* (prophets) grades are not averaged into the student's official transcript. As the adept day school students learn to compartmentalize their Jewish and secular concerns in school, so they repeat this skill in later life.

But if the temporal differences are clear, the value orientations which distinguish the two curricula are even more important. The secular curriculum emphasizes achievement and perhaps, in some secondary way, character training. The accumulation of skills and knowledge is paramount, leading to some specified goal, variously articulated as "high school," "college" or "career." For students who aspire to this goal, work is largely teacher-dominated, for the teachers have the information the students seek to master. This is of no small consequence to Jews for, as Rosen and D'Andrade (pp. 58-84) have shown, they stress achievement.

The Jewish curriculum, while ostensibly also aiming for specific achievements and skills, primarily emphasizes Jewish identification and the development of a Jewish consciousness. Thus, while secular studies provide skills and specific knowledge, Jewish studies provide students with a sense of peoplehood, something that might best be described as "*Yiddishkeit*". The presence of other Jewish students and the social world constructed in the classroom may therefore be as or more important than the teaching. Recall that especially in the case of afternoon schools. the students' time there may be the only one in their entire day when they are surrounded completely and solely by Jews. The school becomes the symbolic Jewish home, *the* Jewish community for all intents and purposes. In this situation, moreover, the teacher must be a facilitator and catalyst, role model and co-participant to a greater degree than a teacher of secular subjects. Perhaps only a genuine community insider can achieve this.

7. Evaluation

These special goals of the Jewish curriculum also make success harder to measure. The secular teacher has succeeded when the student has mastered certain skills: reading, mathematics, geography and so on. The Jewish teacher may succeed in getting his students to learn some Hebrew, comprehend some sacred text, or acquaint themselves with points of Jewish law. But even so, he has not necessarily fulfilled his mandate which, in the final analysis, is to make Jews out of his students. Conversely, even if the Jewish school teacher does not succeed in making his students fluent in Hebrew or enabling them to make their way independently through a Jewish text, he may still succeed in eliciting a warmth towards and attachment to their Judaism and ethnic identity.

Accordingly, the secular achievements can more easily be evaluated—graded if you will—than the Jewish ones. Yet strangely, the same grading system is used for the Jewish curriculum as for the secular one—and this even when Jewish studies grades are not part of the official grade point average. Lacking the same basis in reality, however, these grades are largely meaningless, and students look upon them with a jaundiced eye. They realize that time in Hebrew school is not like time anywhere else. "Another world to live in—whether we expect ever to pass wholly over into it or not— is what we mean by having a religion," philosopher George Santayana once suggested.

If the Jewish school is in fact a religious school, an institution forming and confirming religious identification, then it ought to stress its difference from rather than its sameness with the secular curriculum. In practice this might mean a different system of evaluations, a different format of teaching (stressing, for example, the intimacy of religious community rather than the formality of the classroom, a different language and so on). Too often our Jewish schools try to mirror secular institutions. They need and can forge their own identity from the bes medresh and cheder (European-style Jewish schools) rather than the public school. "Religion for the Jews," as Herman Wouk has put it, "is intimate and colloquial, or it is nothing."

Conclusion

Since we agree that the goal of Jewish education is worth the effort, what is to be done? I am convinced that to know, one must first believe; that feeling and being actively Jewish may be a prerequisite to becoming more so; that the number of volumes of the Talmud we have gone through may be less important than how many of them we have let get through to us. Nearly half a century ago, the great Jewish student and educator, Franz Rosenzweig (1965), in an essay arguing for a renaissance of Jewish learning, wrote something eerily similar: "Books are not now the prime need of the day...what we need more than ever, or at least as much as ever, are human beings—Jewish human beings..." (p. 53). If we form communities in which being Jewish is a positive and active element of life, then we shall produce Jewish human beings, and our schools will ineluctably reflect that success. If we fail, our schools will mirror that failure.

Bibliography

Bateson, G. (1958). *Naven* (2nd Edition). Stanford: Stanford University Press.

Berger, P & Luckmann, T. (1967). *The Social Construction of Reality.* Garden City: Doubleday.

Buber, M. (1948). *Tales of the Hasidim: The Later Masters.* New York: Schocken.

Bullivant, B.M. (1975). *Competing Values and Traditions in an Orthodox Day School: A Study of Enculturation and Dissonance.* Unpublished doctoral dissertation, Monash University.

Geertz, C. (1973). *The Interpretation of Cultures.* New York: Basic Books.

Goffman, E. (1961). *Encounters.* Indianapolis: Bobbs-Merrill.

Goffman, E. (1974). *Frame Analysis.* Cambridge, MA: Harvard University Press.

Heilman, S.C. (1976). *Synagogue Life: A Study in Symbolic Interaction.* Chicago: University of Chicago Press.

Lebovitz, G. (1981). *Satisfaction and Dissatisfaction Among Judaic Studies Teachers in Midwestern Jewish Day Schools.* Unpublished doctoral dissertation, University of Cincinnati, Cincinnati, OH.

Rosen, B.C. & D'Andrade, R.G. The Psychosocial Origins of Achievement Motivation. In B. C. Rosen, H. R. Crockett, & C. Z. Nunn (Eds.), *Achievement in American Society.* Cambridge, MA: Schenkman.

Rosenzweig, F. (1965). *On Jewish Learning* (N. Glatzer & W. Wolf Trans.). New York: Schocken.

Simmel, G. (1950). *The Sociology of Georg Simmel* (K. Wolff Trans.). New York: Free Press.

Wheelis, A. (1958). *The Quest for Identity.* New York: Norton.

Tzimtzum:
A Mystic Model for
Contemporary Leadership[1]

Eugene Borowitz

In this article, which appeared in 1974 and is reprinted with permission, Dr. Eugene Borowitz, Professor of Education and Jewish Religious Thought at the Hebrew Union College in New York, discusses a Lurianic model of leadership. While this article is not in the same format as the others in this volume, it is nevertheless, a fitting close to these essays since all of us as readers find ourselves repeatedly in this position. I have chosen to include it here exactly as it appeared in the original, with full understanding that in 1974, few of us were sensitive as yet to issues of gender.

I F SEX WAS ANOTHER GENERATION'S "DIRTY LITTLE SECRET," AS D. H. LAWRENCE TERMED IT, SURELY ours is power. Now that we can admit we bear this primal lust, we see it operating everywhere, often more decisively than money, class, conditioning, genetics or the other usual determinants of behavior. The "purest" relationships reveal a political structure. In sex and not only between parents and children, in education and not only in political dealing, in religion, art, literature and culture and not only in business strategy, most decisions are made on the basis of power. So our hope of accomplishment in most fields rests largely on how power is organized there or what can be done to change that arrangement.

Perhaps we should not have been shocked to discover the extent to which power determines most human affairs. It is more than a century now since Nietzsche proclaimed man's will to power as his dominant characteristic. Yet what has moved many in our generation to despair is neither the ubiquity not the decisiveness of power but rather the recognition that almost everywhere we see power in action we see it abused. Ethically we may be far more relativistic and contextual than our fathers were. But even if we have given up ethical absolutes and moral rules, many of us still cling to the notion that each of us is a person, not merely an animal, and that, a la Buber, we ought to be treated by others as persons and not as things. Hence we retain a strong ethical sense, though it often pits us against the forms which once claimed to make the dignity of persons explicit but today only operate to demean it; e.g., children should be seen and not heard. In an imperfect world, we could probably tolerate the fact that most relationships are inevitably hierarchical, particularly when more than a few people are involved for more than a few months. So we would not mind some people having power if they used it much of the time to enable us and others to be persons; that is, to be true to the selves we know we ought to be. But they don't. Again and again, people—parents, lovers, teachers, politicians, chairmen, bosses, nurses, bureaucrats, scoutmasters, friends, therapists, children, hosts—force us to be something other than what we know we are. We despair because the abuse of power seems endemic.

Our constant experience is that we have not been consulted, or have not been listened to, or have not really had a voice in matters which deeply affect our lives. In short, we exist in the continuing consciousness of being the objects of someone else's power rather than being persons in our own right though we are involved with people of greater status than ours.

Modern times brought democracy into human relationships. This change may properly be called a revolution for, despite the varying forms in which it was effectuated, it gave those of little power some significant power. By contrast, the best previous generations had been able to do to humanize man's will to power was to appeal to his better nature, to beg the mighty to act with mercy. Thus, in the Bible's classic formulation, the test of the Covenant community's faithfulness to its gracious Partner-God is its treatment of the widow, the orphan and the stranger, the figures who epitomize social powerlessness. Much remains to be said for inculcating compassion in the possessors of power; that is, all of us. Yet the sad truth is that despite their occasional acts of charity, truly benevolent tyrants are rare. Rather than rely on a sovereign's good will we prefer to share his power. So today almost every social arrangement we know is under pressure to transform itself in the direction of more effective democracy.

I

The problems involved in moralizing the use of power are so great that any contribution to their mitigation should be welcome. While I believe that our best hope in this direction lies in giving ever greater power to the people, it also seems clear to me that we are nowhere near the stage where we can have leaderless associations. I therefore want to make a suggestion which might help ethicize the leader's role and which does so by going a step further on the road which turned the benevolent tyrant into the responsive chairman-executive. I believe we can find a fresh model for contemporary leadership in the mystic speculations about God of Isaac Luria (1534-1572) of Safed in the Holy Land. The reasons for utilizing Luria's extraordinary teaching will, I trust, become clear below. Here a word is needed about the methodological validity of transposing images of transcendent being into a purely human dimension. I hereby follow Ludwig Feuerbach's insight that statements about God are, in fact, projections of our sense of what it is to be a person. Hence to Feuerbach, concepts of God are essentially concepts of man and those about the way God relates to his creatures are implicitly theses about the way people ought to relate to each other. Feuerbach, of course, thought that theological assertions were assertions only about humankind. I think that aspect of Feuerbach's thinking is wrong, but surely it is not the only case in intellectual history of a useful idea being turned into an all-embracing absolute by its enraptured creator. Hence I propose to bracket the question of what God-talk says about God while still utilizing a Feuerbachian analysis to determine what Luria's visions of God say about us.

Luria's doctrine centers about two themes rarely treated so directly in traditional Jewish literature yet of intense concern to us today: God as creator and man as co-creator. Though creation grandly opens the book of Genesis, it and all the later texts are extraordinarily reticent, for ancient documents, of what was involved in God's creating. This anti-mythological bent became law, for the Mishnah (compiled about 200 of the common era) decrees that one may not publicly teach *Maaseh Bereshit*, The Work of Creation. So we can find only hints of this esoteric doctrine until, centuries later, mystic writings begin to record some of the possibilities, reaching a spectacular climax in Luria's rather detailed description of the process.

What appeals to our generation in the focus on God as creator is that His power is used to bring others into being. By contrast, the normal Biblical/liturgical terms for Him, Lord and King, speak of his status and power. This sense of God's power is modified by images which envision Him as using it lovingly, e.g., God as Father, Husband or Lover. Yet remembering the realities of Near Eastern life and the continuing tradition of male dominance in Jewish life, even these symbols speak strongly of sovereignty and obedience.

Luria's teaching about God is appealing because it makes man, quite literally, His cocreator. His teaching involves so complete a shift to human activism that scholars can even speak of God becoming passive in the process.

The Lurianic doctrine is most conveniently discussed around three major terms: *tzimtzum*, *shevirah*, and *tikkun*. Since there are three stages in the Work of Creation it will be best to explain the theory as a whole first and then draw its implications for leadership. (In the description which follows, I work largely from the analyses of Gershom Scholem, the pioneering master of the modern study of Jewish mysticism).

Creation is commonly thought of in spatial terms and is envisioned as a movement of externalization: what was God's will now is turned, by an application of his power, into a reality "outside" him. Think for a moment of Michelangelo's Sistine Chapel depiction of the creation of man. The mighty God stretches forth the full length of his arm to one fingertip and thus brings man into being. For us humans, creation is normally an act in extension of ourselves, of producing something "there" that was previously only within us.

Something of this picture is to be seen in the biblical texts despite their apparent efforts to avoid the gross anthropomorphism of Near Eastern creation stories. Thus, in the first version, Genesis 1, God utters words in order to let the light be and, if some modern translators are correct ("When God began to create the heaven and the earth—the earth being unformed and void..."), there already was material external to him to shape. The story in Genesis 2 simply begins with the dry ground and then, with explicit externality, has God mold man out of the dust of the earth before putting the breath of life into him. Creation as externalization is fully explicit in the neo-Platonic teaching (from the first century of the common era on) and thus in the Jewish mystic tradition which often borrowed from it (from the early Middle Ages on). Here creation is generally spoken of as emanation, the gentle but efficacious spilling over of the plenteous being of God. The usual image is of a fountain which, out of its fullness, pours water over its basin, thus creating new pools. God has such plenitude of reality that some of it emerges in a lesser form, which, in turn, makes possible an emergence in even lesser form, and so on, down a series of variously interpreted gradations, until our world exists. The neo Platonists and mystics thought in this way to ease the problem of the infinite God creating finite beings. To us it seems reasonably clear that the very first movement from infinity to finitude—no matter how extensive the finite is thought to be—is as difficult to understand as the Universal God creating ants or pebbles. In any case, the doctrine of emanation, though it links all creatures to God by an unbroken progression of being, is a clear expression of our usual sense that creation is a species of externalization.

II

Luria felt otherwise. I cannot say to what extent his radical shift of creation images was due to the memories and continuing effects of the mass expulsion of the Jewish community of Spain in 1492. The fact is, Isaac Luria alone created a radically new mystic theory of creation. It will be simplest then to limit ourselves to his intellectual trail and we may best prepare ourselves for his ideas by confronting a logical issue with regard to creation. If God is everywhere, how can there by any place outside Him for Him to create in? Michelangelo, for example, had to limit God to one majestic sized human figure if he was to leave room to paint an Adam. But God is not a man and we are taught that He fills all space. If that way of speaking about God is unsatisfactory because spatiality is a poor metaphor for God, consider the question in ontological form; if God is fundamental being, fully realized, how can there be secondary being, that is, being only partly realized? Or, if God is all-in-all, how can the partial or the transitory, which must depend upon Him for their being, ever come to exist?

One response might be to deny the reality of creation much as Hindu thought has done (and as, from the Divine perspective, the later Jewish mystic, Shneour Zalman of Lyady, 1747-1813, would do). Luria is too much under the influence of classic Jewish creation theory for that. Instead he boldly suggests that creation begins with an act of contraction, *tzimtzum*. God does not initiate the existence of other things by extending himself. There would be no place for them then to be, no area of non-being or partial being in which they might exist. Hence to create, He must first withdraw into Himself. God must, so to speak, make Himself less than He is so that other things can come into being. So great, says Luria, is God's will to create; so great is His love for creation.

It is not without interest that Luria has utterly reversed the older meaning of the term *tzimtzum*. In the rabbinic usage from which he almost certainly took the term, the verb form means "to concentrate" but in an externalizing way. The reference there is to God being especially present between the cherubim atop the Ark of the Covenant in the Holy of Holies. And the comment is made that the God of all universes "concentrates" Himself particularly at that point in space. For Luria, *tzimtzum* is the exact opposite. God concentrates Himself not out there, at a point in the world, but within Himself. By this act He leaves a void in which His creatures can come into being.

Tzimtzum, then, is not itself creation but the necessary prelude to it. Now the externalizing act can occur, but with certain ultimately troublesome consequences derived from its taking place in a realm from which God has withdrawn. Of course, He could not have removed Himself completely for without something of Him being present nothing at all could exist. Luria says He leaves behind, in the creation—space, a residue of His reality, something like the oil or wine, he nicely notes, that is always still there after we think we have emptied the jug.

The positive externalizing movement of creation begins with God sending forth a beam of light into the void He has left. From this light, in various extraordinary stages, the creation we know eventually took form. For Luria, then, creating is a twofold process, a contraction which leads to an expansion. More, it is a continuing double movement, for God continues the work of Creation each day, continuously, and hence all existence as we know it pulsates to the divine regression and egression. Here Luria's sense of time and opportunity moves in a mystic realm no fine-tuned atomic instrument can ever hope to clock.

Perhaps we should already be prepared by the doctrine of *tzimtzum* for the next major stage in creating but most people find it not only dramatic but somewhat disturbing. Luria teaches that the creative act speedily results in a cosmic catastrophe, that creation begins with a calamity. Luria describes it in metaphors which today could easily be taken from our experiments to harness thermo-nuclear energy, specifically to find "containers" for the enormous heat of the plasma gases involved in the fusion process. As the divine beam of created light comes into the void, it goes through various transformations. Ultimately it produces certain "vessels" which are to come to full existence when they are filled with the creating light. But now, as God's great power fills some of the lesser vessels, it proves too mighty for them and they are shattered, the *shevirah* mentioned above. The result is an imperfect creation, one in which things are not as they ought to be or were intended by God to be, a cosmos which from almost its very beginning is alienated from itself, a created order where evil abounds instead of good.

Luria, however, is not a pessimist. Once again his sense of the dialectic implicit in all things reasserts itself and he turns the doctrine of a flawed creation into the basis of man's having cosmic significance. To begin with, the *shevirah* does not mean that the creation collapses into nothingness. It cannot, for God's energy was poured into it. True, what we see around us today is largely the "shells" or "husks" of what should have been, without their proper kernels of God's energizing light. But by their very existence we know that something of God's power is in them. Thus Luria speaks of the divine sparks which are to be found everywhere in creation. If all these sparks were lifted up from the husks and restored to their proper place in God's spiritual order for creation, then all things would become what they were intended to be. Creation can be restored and *tikkun* means restoration, the reintegration of the organic wholeness of creation, the reestablishment of the world in the full graciousness of God's primal intent.

What astonishes us here is Luria's bold insistence that *tikkun* is primarily humanity's work, not God's. In everything one faces, in every situation one finds oneself in, one should realize that there is a fallen spark of God's light waiting to be returned to its designated spiritual place. Hence, as people do the good moment by moment and give their acts of goodness a proper, inner, mystic intention—more specifically, as the Jew practices Jewish law and manifests Jewish virtues with full concentration of the soul on the task of uplifting the Divine sparks—the shattered creation is brought into repair. The ailing cosmos is healed. The Messiah is brought near. People do that, each person by each act. And if enough people did that enough of the time, Luria teaches, God would send the Messiah. Or, to put it with more appropriate divine passivity, if people, by their acts, restored the creation to what God had hoped it would be, then all the benefits of his gracious goodness would be available to them. Such a messianic estimate of human initiative is unique—so much so that some scholars have argued that Luria's ideas, transmitted by Christian Cabbalists and transformed by late Renaissance and early rationalize humanism, were influential in producing the heady confidence in humankind of the 18th century enlightenment. But I do not think we need carry Luria's ideas any further.

III

The excitement of the Lurianic teaching arises from its radical shift in the application and hence the structure of cosmic power. Traditional creation theories focus on God and the effectuation of His will. God is understood in a transitive mode. In such an approach, the creatures are, so so speak, only the objects of God's activity. So, by Feuerbachian inversion, leadership comes to mean using power to achieve one's ends. The greatest leaders, then, are the people who mobilize massive energies to accomplish vast projects. And since, until recently, social power has been political-military, most of the great figures of world history were warriors or warrior-kings. Though today we might add executives or administrators to the list of those eligible for adulation, our ideal leader remains the achiever, the person who imposes designs upon reality.

The Lurianic God moves in radically other ways. He is understood in a reflexive mode. From the very beginning, thinking of Him involves consideration of his creatures; how can their independent existence be assured? Where will they find sufficient emptiness of being to make their limited reality significant? With this in mind, the exercise of God's power is drastically redirected. It must first be applied to itself, to the extent of constricting its all-encompassing quality. Only when God withdraws can He create—if His creatures are to have full dignity.

This readily translates into contemporary human terms. We seek a leadership construed not primarily in terms of the accomplishment of plans but equally in terms of its humanizing effect on the people being led. Our ethics demand a leader who uses power to enable people to be persons while they work together. Such a leader, as against the stereotype of the cruel general or ruthless exec-utive is not essentially goal oriented, but recognizes that people are always as important as, if not more important, than the current undertaking.

The extension and the withdrawal visions of creation retain something in common. Even tyrants know that people can be pushed only so far and the biblical God, who by his unlimited power could have been the greatest of tyrants, nonetheless creates a man independent enough to resist him. On the other hand, in the Lurianic theory, though the creatures are given initial consideration, the creation is not oriented to their satisfaction but by the divine will. Yet though these creation visions overlap, they assign quite different status to those of lesser power and so must be considered alter-native models for exercising leadership. Think of the sort of leadership we all have known in groups of small to moderate size, the family, the classroom, the church or synagogue. (One could easily expand the list). These institutions have goals to accomplish. Yet in being part of them, it has made all the difference in the world to us whether we felt our parents or teachers or clergy were using us to accomplish their purposes or helping us grow as we labored for our common ends. I suggest that the ability to practice *tzimtzum* can sharply distinguish accomplishment-directed from person-fos-tering leadership.

Leaders, by their power, have a greater field of presence than most people do. When they move into a room they seem to fill the space around them. We say they radiate power. Hence the greater the people we meet the more reduced we feel—though as in fascist or fantasy adulation we may hope that by utterly identifying ourselves with our hero, we can gain the fullest sort of existence. So in the presence of the mighty we are silent and respectful, we await their directions and are fearful of their judgments. Who we are is defined by what they think of us. Like God the preeminent have true existence and we, their creatures, exist only in part. In such a system the activists strive for the day when they will be God and others will have to serve them. Professors, who suffered through the indignities of the old Ph.D. apprenticeship system and have finally made it to full rank and tenure, today face students who increasingly demand to be treated as persons; that is, as partners whose independent reality is respected in the relationship. But the professors, having finally become Number One in the academic hierarchy, want to realize the benefits of that status, not the least as a compensation for the pain in achieving it. They want to rule as they were ruled—and that is only one of the many varieties of refusing to make room for others so neatly summarized in the term "ego trip".

The Lurianic model of leadership has, as its first step, contraction. The leader withholds presence and power to that the followers may have some place in which to be. Take the case of a parent who has the power to insist upon a given decision and a good deal of experience upon which to base his judgment. In such an instance, the urge to compel is almost irresistible. Yet if it is a matter the parent feels the child can handle—better, if making this decision and taking responsibility for it will help the child grow as a person—then the mature parent withdraws and makes it possible for the child to choose and thus come more fully into his own. *Tzimtzum* here means not only not telling the child what to do but not manipulating the decision by hinting or "sharing experience" or "only" giving some advice. Leaving room for the other means just that, including allowing the child sometimes to make a foolish choice. Not ever to be permitted to choose the wrong thing means not truly to be free. Parents, like all other leaders, should seek to emulate God's maturity. He gives His children their freedom even though they may use it against Him because He knows His dignity cannot be satisfied in the long run with anything less than a relationship in which we come to Him freely rather than in servility.

Tzimtzum operates in a similar way in the leadership of teachers and clergy. Normally both are so busy doing things for us that they leave us little opportunity to do things on our own and thus find some personal independence. Both talk too much—so much so, that when they stop talking for a moment and ask for questions or honest comments, we don't believe them. We know if we stay quiet for a moment they will start talking again. We realize that their professional roles have been built around creation by extension of the self, so they will have to prove to us by a rigorous practice of *tzimtzum* that they really want us to be persons in our own right.

One common misinterpretation of this approach is to think it calls for a swing from dominance to abandonment, a sort of petulant declaration that if one's lessers do not want one's guidance then they should get no help at all and suffer the consequences of being on their own. There are many parents who vacillate between enforcing a harsh law and granting complete license. In school or church situations, withdrawal to give others freedom easily becomes a rationalization for indolence, the refusal to plan, or provide resources, or make proper demands upon the community. Luria's God does not indulge in *tzimtzum* to sulk or feel sorry for Himself. He bears no resemblance to Aristotle's self-centered God who was not only pure thought, thinking, but did His thinking about the purest of things, Himself. *Tzimtzum* is rather the first of a two-part rhythm, for it is always followed by sending the creative beam of light into the just-vacated void. The withdrawal is for the sake of later using one's power properly. Contraction without a following expansion, regression without subsequent egression does not produce creation. But once room has been made for an other, even simple applications of power can prove effective. How often it has been the seemingly casual word, the side comment, the quizzical look we got which, coming from someone we knew respected us, powerfully affected us. So in the classroom, though the teacher's summary of the data or interpretation of the material is regularly needed, it is also the good question, the challenge of stimulating options, the pause which is receptive that is the most effective means of educating. Indeed, perhaps the greatest effect one can have on someone seeking to become a person is to provide him with a model. Here the exercise of power is, directly speaking, all on oneself and only indirectly on the other. Yet in creating persons, the effectiveness of a good example, particularly as contrasted to laying down rules or verbalizing ideals, is immeasurable.

Leadership in the Lurianic style is particularly difficult, then, because it requires a continuing alternation of the application of our power. Now we hold back; now we act. To do either in the right way, is difficult enough. To develop a sense when to stop one and do the other and then reverse that in due turn, is to involve one in endless inner conflict. An example will make this clearer. In a seminar, though the teacher may have spent a lifetime on a topic, the teacher elects to sit silently so as to give the student an opportunity to speak. If the teacher does not keep still, allowing, say, slight errors of fact or misinterpretations to pass by uncontested, but regularly interrupts, the student's presentation, and his self, are as good as destroyed. At the same time, incompetence can be tolerated only so far. If the student is well on the way to ruining an important topic for the class or making such major misstatements that all which follows will be false, the teacher must interrupt. Danger lurks equally in action and inaction. Premature or too frequent intervention is as fateful as missing danger signs or giving insufficient aid. And with all this, we cannot help but realize that our judgment to intervene may only be a power-grab while our decision to stay silent may really mean we are unwilling to take the responsibility for interrupting.

The seminar situation illustrates well the complexities of functioning as a Lurianic leader. No wonder then that the call for a modern style of leadership throws many people into great anxiety. Their masters did not use their power this way and no one now can give them a rule as to when and how they ought to step back or step in. So failures in trying to exert the new leadership abound and examples of successful leadership are rare even in face-to-face associations, much less the giant organizations of which our society is so largely composed.

IV

Some implications for leadership of the ideas of *shevirah* and *tikkun* also deserve mention, though they are perhaps at greater distance from Luria's teaching than the ones mentioned above. Those who lead by *tzimtzum* must quickly reconcile themselves to the fact that leaving room for others to act is likely to mean their own purposes will be accomplished only in blemished form. The student will, in terms of the content presented or material covered, not lead the seminar as well as the teacher could. The children who write their own college application biographies or seek out summer jobs themselves are not likely to do as expert a job as the parent. The congregants who read or create a service will probably not reach the level of expression nor educe the religious traditions in a way the clergy might have. *Shevirah*, imperfect creation, is the logical consequence of leadership by *tzimtzum*. Hence, if our eyes are only on what has been accomplished in our plans and we cannot see what has happened in the creation of persons, we are likely to be deeply disturbed. The next step is to take over ourselves. It is, indeed, often easier to get things done by doing them oneself rather than allowing others to do so, particularly in their way. But to seize power from others is to deprive them of the possibility of significant action and thus of dignity. We must learn to trust them if they are to be given a chance to be persons and that means learning to "put up" with their bumbling ways. Of God we say that He "bears" with us. Without His forgiveness for our sins, we would not be able to continue as real shapers of history. The graciousness implicit in *tzimtzum* is not only the grant of space in which we might have being but the will to forgive the faults we may commit once we have that independent being. Anyone who would lead by *tzimtzum*, then, must know that *shevirah* is likely if not inevitable. Thus, Lurianic leadership depends not only on an exquisite sense of interpersonal rhythm but a capacity to forgive and go on working with those whose need for independence is a major cause of the frustration of our plans.

The strength to persist in so frustrating a role can come from recognizing that the leaders' *tzimtzum* and the resulting *shevirah* are the occasion for the followers' work of *tikkun*, restoration and completion. The group's objectives may not have been accomplished now but the leader may be confident that the effort will go on. Its continuation no longer depends upon the presence of the present leader. By the act of *tzimtzum*, confirmed in bearing with the *shevirah*, the leader has taught the disciples to work out of their own initiative and not by coercion from above. The painful process has created a new generation to carry on the work. And it, in turn, following the leader's model, will create another generation of workers, ad infinitum, until the goal has been accomplished. This is as much messianism as we are entitled to in human endeavors. So the parents who see their children able to make their own decisions maturely, though they choose a peculiar lifestyle; so the teachers who see their students become competent scholars, though they reach conclusions at variance from what they were taught; so the clergy who develop laymen committed to living religiously, come what may, though they transform the traditions they received; such leaders by *tzimtzum* know they have done as much as men can do to save a troublesome and treacherous world. Their hope, then, arises from seeing the present and the future as two parts of a whole. They are patient during the *shevirah* and endure the self-denial of their *tzimtzum* to create an indomitable commitment to *tikkun*. Leadership with so long a view is not muscular enough for Michelangelo's God, or his heroes, Moses and David. The great Florentine was a Renaissance man and believed power means lordship, not person-making. We can still learn much from Michelangelo's sense of grandeur but we must move beyond it to implement our new sense of humanity.

Did Isaac Luria himself see, far beyond Feuerbach, that his vision of a withdrawing creator could be a model for personal leadership? We cannot quite tell. In some respects he seems to have been unassertive beyond the customary humility of the pious. Thus, we are told that he usually allowed one of his disciples to walk ahead of him—an act firmly prohibited in the etiquette of respect for a master—because the student considered it a special honor. He is also reported never to have bargained over the price asked for any object he needed for religious purposes nor questioned his wife's requests with regard to household or personal expenses. So too, he emphasized to his followers that they were all parts of one organism and therefore needed to care and pray for each other. And he was quite uncommunicative about his deepest mystical doctrines, not only refusing to write anything down but apparently instructing his most trusted adepts only by hints and allusions.

But we dare not press this interpretation further. In most respects Luria seems to have exercised authority in the typical kingly fashion of one who is recognized as wearing the crown of the Torah. He organized his disciples into a group called The Lion's Whelps (a pun made on the initials of this title, Rabbi Isaac, gave him the title The Lion) and he set high admission standards which were stringently enforced. He then divided them into two categories, apparently according to how much mystic knowledge he felt he could share with them. The extent of his dominance of the group may perhaps be gauged from the fact that he refused Joseph Karo, the greatest authority on Jewish law of that time, permission to be part of the inner circle. Another intriguing fact gives us some indication that Luria's leadership had limited effectiveness. He arranged to have all his followers live together in a sort of commune, but within a few months there was considerable difficulty among them. The texts say, typically enough, that the wives began to quarrel among themselves and this caused the disturbances among the adepts. Yet, if this seems to compromise Luria's stature somewhat, we should also keep in mind that his career as a mystic teacher in Safed comprised just three years, after which he died. In that short time he changed the course of Jewish mysticism and did so, apparently, by imbuing his disciples with so deep a commitment to his doctrine that they, and their followers in turn, spread it throughout the Jewish world. More, they brought it into the thought and lifestyle of much of Jewry, the first time that mysticism, which had always been an elitist interest, became part of mass Jewish living. So if we cannot know whether Luria led by *tzimtzum* we can nonetheless say that his leadership had an extraordinary effect in his day and his teaching retains a powerful message for our time.

Footnote

[1]Reprinted, by permission of the publisher, from *Religious Education, 69*(6), November-December, 1974.

BIOGRAPHIES

Walter I. Ackerman is Shane Family Professor of Education of Ben Gurion University of the Negev, Beer Sheva, Israel. A graduate of Boston Hebrew Teachers College, Harvard College and the Harvard Graduate School of Education, Dr. Ackerman served as Vice President for Academic Affairs of the University of Judaism in Los Angeles prior to settling in Israel. He has published widely on Jewish education in the United States and education in Israel and holds honorary degrees from the Hebrew College in Boston and the Jewish Theological Seminary in New York.

H. A. Alexander serves as Dean of Academic Affairs and Associate Professor of Philosophy and Education at the University of Judaism in Los Angeles and is Lecturer in Education at the University of California in Los Angeles. He holds a Ph.D. from Stanford University and has Rabbinic Ordination from the Jewish Theological Seminary in New York. A prolific writer, Dr. Alexander has published numerous articles for both popular and professional audiences and presented numerous workshops throughout North America.

Isa Aron is Associate Professor of Education at the Hebrew Union College–Jewish Institute of Religion in Los Angeles. Prior to her current appointment, she served as Coordinator of Museum Education for the Skirball Museum at that institution. Dr. Aron has published extensively in the fields of philosophy and sociology of education and currently is investigating issues related to Jewish teaching. She is the recipient of numerous research grants relating to the shortage of teachers in Jewish supplementary schools.

Eugene Borowitz is the Sigmund L. Falk Distinguished Professor of Education and Jewish Religious Thought at the New York School of the Hebrew Union College–Jewish Institute of Religion. In his thirteen books and numerous articles he has exhibited an intellectual boldness and creativity which have made him widely recognized as one of Liberal Judaism's leading theologians. In the Jewish community, Rabbi Borowitz is best known as the editor of *Sh'ma, a Journal of Jewish Responsibility,* a magazine of Jewish social concern which he founded in 1970. Prior to assuming his academic position, Rabbi Borowitz was the National Director of Education for Reform Judaism at the Union of American Hebrew Congregations.

Moshe L. Botwinick has been Assistant Professor of Communications at Marymount Manhattan College for the past six years. He did his graduate work at the Annenberg School of Communication of the University of Pennsylvania, and post-graduate work at New York University's School of Education. Professor Botwinick has been Associate Producer and Director of Research for Children Television Workshop's Shalom Sesame since its inception. He is also Vice-President of Design and Research for Comet International, Inc., a multiservice communications corporation, and has received grants from the NSF and NEH. His work in Jewish education has been a major focus in much of his research and productions.

Barry Chazan teaches Jewish education and philosophy of education at the Hebrew University of Jerusalem. He is also Jewish Educational Consultant to the Jewish Community Centers Association of North America. His writings include books and articles in the areas of religious, moral and ethnic education. His special interest over the years is the subject of the teaching of Israel and he has written, taught and developed curricula and instructional units in this area.

Steven M. Cohen is Professor of Sociology at Queens College. He has written widely on American Jewish identity, intermarriage, family and on American Jews' attitudes toward Israel. Professor Cohen is the coauthor of two recently published books: *Two Worlds of Judaism: The Israeli and American Experiences* and *Cosmopolitans and Parochials:Modern Orthodox Jews in America*. The results of his frequent national surveys of American Jews have been widely cited in the mass media. He has been a Visiting Professor at Brandeis University, The Hebrew University, Yale University and the Jewish Theological Seminary.

Arnold Dashefsky is Professor of Sociology and Director of the Center for Judaic Studies and Contemporary Jewish Life at the University of Connecticut in Storrs. In addition to publishing many articles, he is the author and editor of *Ethnic Identification Among American Jews, Ethnic Identity in Society* and *Contemporary Jewry, Volumes 7 and 8*. Having served as consultant to various local and national organizations, he is the president of the Association for the Social Scientific Study of Jewry.

Rivka Dori is the Coordinator of the undergraduate Hebrew Language program, at the Hebrew Union College, Los Angeles, and Instructor of Hebrew Language there and at the University of Southern California (since 1972). Beginning with her studies at Levinsky in Tel Aviv, she has, throughout her career, been a student of language acquisition both in the Hebrew and general field.

Sharon Feiman-Nemser is a Professor of Teacher Education at Michigan State University and a senior researcher with the National Center for Research on Teacher Learning. For the past twenty years, Dr. Feiman-Nemser has been actively involved in the study and practice of teacher education. She teaches preservice students, works in classrooms with experienced teachers, and studies teacher learning. Dr. Feiman-Nemser has written extensively about teacher centers, learning to teach, the curriculum of teacher education, and the induction of beginning teachers. An avocational teacher at Kehillat Israel in East Lansing, she has consulted with various institutions engaged in Jewish teacher education in Israel and in North America.

Ruth Pinkenson Feldman is the Early Childhood Consultant at the Auerbach Central Agency for Jewish Education in Philadelphia and serves on the faculty of Gratz College. Her doctorate is from Temple University and she has studied at Harvard University, Bank Street College of Education and Tufts University. She is president of Resources for Parents at Work.

Misha Galperin was born and raised in Odessa on the Black Sea coast of the Ukraine. Dr. Galperin came to the United States in 1976, attended Yeshiva University and received a Ph.D in Clinical Psychology from New York University. He is currently developing programs for Soviet emigres at the New York Association for New Americans and at the Federation Employment and Guidance Service in New York.

Roberta L. Goodman received a M.A. in Jewish Education from Hebrew Union College and a M.S. in Education from the University of Southern California, and did graduate work with Dr. James Fowler in the area of faith development at Emory University. She is completing her doctoral studies at Columbia University Teachers College in Adult Education. Ms. Goodman has worked in congregational education for over ten years in addition to writing curricula and articles based on faith development theory. She presently resides in Madison, Wisconsin.

Patricia Cipora Harte serves as Director of the New York Association for New Americans' Acculturation Department. She is responsible for creating programs that introduce newly arrived Jewish emigres to American and Jewish culture. Ms. Harte has a master's degree in Social Work from Yeshiva University's Wurzweiler School of Social Work and has held administrative posts with the Melton Research Center, the Coalition for the Advancement of Jewish Education, and Hadassah.

Samuel Heilman earned his Ph.D. from the University of Chicago. He is Professor of Sociology at Queens College of the City of New York and author of *Synagogue Life* and *The People of the Book*. He is the author of numerous articles on the sociology of American Jewry.

Leora W. Isaacs is the Director of Research for the Jewish Education Services of North America (JESNA). Prior to this, Dr. Isaacs was Research Specialist at the Jewish Communal Affairs Department and William Petshek National Jewish Family Center, American Jewish Committee. Her avocational activities include serving as a faculty member of the Hebrew High School and coordinator of family programs at Temple Sholom in Bridgewater, NJ.

Richard Juran is the Director of Educational Programs for the Jewish Community Centers Association, Israel office. Formerly the central *shaliach* for community affairs at the American Zionist Youth Foundation, Mr. Juran holds an M.A. degree from the Hebrew University. He has been actively engaged in youth work with Young Judaea and with the Institute for Youth Leaders from Abroad and serves as a faculty associate for the Jerusalem Fellows Program.

Betsy Katz is Director of the Department of Reform Education for the Board of Jewish Education in Metropolitan Chicago. She is the North American Project Director for the Florence Melton Adult Mini-School. She is a member of the Board of Directors of the Coalition for the Advancement of Jewish Education (CAJE) of which she was chairperson from 1986 to 1990 and serves on the Board of Rosenwald Day School, Chicago. Dr. Katz has published on varied subjects in Jewish education and has taught and spoken extensively in North America and Israel.

Stuart L. Kelman is currently the Executive Director of the Agency for Jewish Education of the Greater East Bay in Northern California. Prior to holding this position, he was Assistant Professor of Education at the Hebrew Union College-Jewish Institute of Religion in Los Angeles. Rabbi Kelman was ordained by the Jewish Theological Seminary and holds a Ph.D. from the University of Southern California in Sociology of Education. Formerly, he served as the national Chairperson of the Coalition for the Advancement of Jewish Education (CAJE), and chaired two of its conferences.

Chaim Lauer has been the Executive Director of the Board of Jewish Education of Greater Washington since July, 1988. For the prior eleven years he was associated with that city's United Jewish Appeal Federation as its Director of Budget and Planning and later as its Assistant Executive Vice President. He staffed both the demographic study of Jewish Washington and a special Task Force on Jewish Education. A native of Miami Beach, he attended Yeshiva University, received his master's at Cornell and was a doctoral candidate at the College of William and Mary.

Leonard A. Matanky is Assistant Superintendent, Associated Talmud Torahs of Chicago and Director, Morris and Rose Goldman Computer Department for Jewish Studies. He holds a Ph.D. from New York University and rabbinic ordination from Hebrew Theological College. Dr. Matanky has written numerous articles on the subject of computers and was awarded the Kohl International Teaching Award in 1990.

Rela Geffen Monson is Professor of Sociology and Dean of Academic Affairs at Gratz College in Philadelphia. She received her M.A. at Columbia University and her Ph.D. at the University of Florida. She is the past president of the Association for the Social Scientific Study of Jewry and vice president of the Association for Jewish Studies. Dr. Monson's research interests lie in the fields of sociology of religion and the sociology of the family. A prolific writer and speaker, she participates in a variety of communal service and professional associations.

Joseph Reimer is an Assistant Professor in the Hornstein Program of Jewish Communal Service at Brandeis University. He is the first author of *Promoting Moral Growth: From Piaget to Kohlberg* (Waveland Press), a contributor to *Lawrence Kohlberg's Approach to Moral Education* (Columbia University Press) and editor of *To Build A Profession: Careers in Jewish Education* (Brandeis University). He has served as a staff member for the Commission on Jewish Education for North America, which recently published his monograph "The Synagogue as Context for Jewish Education."

Bernard Reisman is Professor of American Jewish Communal Studies and Director, Hornstein Program in Jewish Communal Service at Brandeis University where he has been for the past twenty years. He has also taught at the Hebrew University, at Loyola University and at the University of Illinois in Chicago. He has served as a consultant to educational and communal organizations in Argentina, Australia and Europe.

Ron Reynolds is Director of School Services at the Bureau of Jewish Education of Greater Los Angeles. He earned his Ph.D. in Comparative and International Education at the University of California at Los Angeles and has spoken widely and published articles on educational evaluation, planned change and organizational studies. Dr. Reynolds has served as a member of the board of directors of the Coalition for the Advancement of Jewish Education (CAJE) and was instrumental in planning that organization's landmark conference in Israel in 1988. He has worked in numerous formal and nonformal educational settings and has taught students spanning the primary grades to graduate school.

Ian Russ is the Saul E. White Visiting Professor in the department of psychology at the University of Judaism in Los Angeles. He is licensed as a family and child therapist and has a private practice in Encino, having received a doctorate from the Wright Institute in Los Angeles. Currently, he is a mental health consultant to the Stephen S. Wise and the Adat Ari El Day Schools. Dr. Russ is also a past president of the Association of Child Development Specialists.

Jeffrey Schein is Associate Professor of Jewish Education at the Cleveland College of Jewish Studies and National Education Director for the Federation of Reconstructionist Congregations and Havurot. Prior to this, he was a consultant in Jewish family education for the Central Agency for Jewish Education of Greater Philadelphia while directing the Temin Center for Jewish Education at the Reconstructionist Rabbinical College. Coauthor of *Creative Jewish Education*, he is a graduate of the Reconstructionist Rabbinical College and holds a doctorate in Curriculum Theory and Development from Temple University.

Alvin I. Schiff, Executive Vice President Emeritus of the Board of Jewish Education of Greater New York is a distinguished professor of education at Yeshiva University, and serves as chairman of the American Advisory Council, Joint Authority for Jewish Zionist Education (World Zionist Organization/Jewish Agency for Israel). A prolific researcher and author of over 100 articles and several books, Dr. Schiff is editor of *Jewish Education* and continues to serve on numerous boards and advisory councils. He has received many honors, including the Rothberg Prize from the Hebrew University in Jerusalem.

Susan L. Shevitz is an Assistant Professor at Brandeis University's Hornstein Program in Jewish Communal Service where she teaches courses in Organizational Behavior and Jewish Education. She received her Ed.D. from Harvard University in Administration, Planning, and Social Policy and is interested in the nonrational aspects of organizational life. She conducts evaluations of educational programs and admits to being fascinated and sometimes frustrated by efforts to change Jewish institutions.

David Schoem is Assistant Dean for Undergraduate Education at the University of Michigan where he teaches courses in Sociology of the American Jewish Community and on Ethnic Identity and Intergroup Relations. He is author of *Ethnic Survival in America: An Ethnography of a Jewish*

Afternoon School and editor of *Inside Separate Worlds: Life Stories of Young Blacks, Jews, and Latinos.*

Gary A. Tobin is the Director of the Maurice and Marilyn Cohen Center for Modern Jewish Studies at Brandeis University in Waltham, Massachusetts. He earned his Ph.D. in City and Regional Planning from the University of California at Berkeley and has published extensively in the areas of antisemitism, planning and social policy, and philanthropy in the Jewish community. Dr. Tobin has directed demographic studies in cities throughout the United States and has served as a planning consultant to the Council of Jewish Federations, the United Jewish Appeal, and Federations, Jewish Community Centers, synagogues and other Jewish organizations.

J. Alan Winter is Professor of Sociology at the Connecticut College and has been a Visiting Professor at the University of Connecticut and the Hebrew University. His Ph.D. is from the University of Michigan and he has taught at Temple University, Rutgers and the University of Michigan. A well-known author, Dr. Winter has been president of his temple, the local federation and the Jewish Family Service, and has served as consultant to Council on Jewish Federations.